DENOTATIONAL SEMANTICS

DENOTATIONAL SEMANTICS
A Methodology for Language Development

David A. Schmidt
Kansas State University

wcb
Wm. C. Brown Publishers
Dubuque, Iowa

Library of Congress Catalog Card Number: 86–7943

ISBN 0–697–06849–8

Printed in the United States of America by Wm. C. Brown Publishers
2460 Kerper Boulevard, Dubuque, IA 52001

10 9 8 7 6 5 4 3 2

Contents

Chapter 6
DOMAIN THEORY II: RECURSIVELY DEFINED FUNCTIONS ______ 103

Chapter 7
LANGUAGES WITH CONTEXTS ______ 137

Chapter 8
ABSTRACTION, CORRESPONDENCE, AND QUALIFICATION ______ 174

Preface

Denotational semantics is a methodology for giving mathematical meaning to programming languages and systems. It was developed by Christopher Strachey's Programming Research Group at Oxford University in the 1960s. The method combines mathematical rigor, due to the work of Dana Scott, with notational elegance, due to Strachey. Originally used as an analysis tool, denotational semantics has grown in use as a tool for language design and implementation.

This book was written to make denotational semantics accessible to a wider audience and to update existing texts in the area. I have presented the topic from an engineering viewpoint, emphasizing the descriptional and implementational aspects. The relevant mathematics is also included, for it gives rigor and validity to the method and provides a foundation for further research.

The book is intended as a tutorial for computing professionals and as a text for university courses at the upper undergraduate or beginning graduate level. The reader should be acquainted with discrete structures and one or more general purpose programming languages. Experience with an applicative-style language such as LISP, ML, or Scheme is also helpful.

CONTENTS OF THE BOOK

The Introduction and Chapters 1 through 7 form the core of the book. The Introduction provides motivation and a brief survey of semantics specification methods. Chapter 1 introduces BNF, abstract syntax, and structural induction. Chapter 2 lists those concepts of set theory that are relevant to semantic domain theory. Chapter 3 covers semantic domains, the value sets used in denotational semantics. The fundamental domains and their related operations are presented. Chapter 4 introduces basic denotational semantics. Chapter 5 covers the semantics of computer storage and assignment as found in conventional imperative languages. Nontraditional methods of store evaluation are also considered. Chapter 6 presents least fixed point semantics, which is used for determining the meaning of iterative and recursive definitions. The related semantic domain theory is expanded to include complete partial orderings; "predomains" (complete partial orderings less "bottom" elements) are used. Chapter 7 covers block structure and data structures.

Chapters 8 through 12 present advanced topics. Tennent's analysis of procedural abstraction and general binding mechanisms is used as a focal point for Chapter 8. Chapter 9 analyzes forms of imperative control and branching. Chapter 10 surveys techniques for converting a denotational definition into a computer implementation. Chapter 11 contains an overview of Scott's inverse limit construction for building recursively defined domains. Chapter 12 closes the book with an introduction to methods for understanding nondeterminism and concurrency.

Throughout the book I have consistently abused the noun "access," treating it as a verb. Also, "iff" abbreviates the phrase "if and only if."

ORGANIZATION OF A COURSE

The book contains more material than what can be comfortably covered in one term. A course plan should include the core chapters; any remaining time can be used for Chapters 8 through 12, which are independent of one another and can be read in any order. The core can be handled as follows:

- Present the Introduction first. You may wish to give a one-lecture preview of Chapter 4. A preview motivates the students to carefully study the material in the background Chapters 1 through 3.
- Cover all of Chapters 1 and 2, as they are short and introduce crucial concepts.
- Use Chapter 3 as a "reference manual." You may wish to start at the summary Section 3.5 and outline the structures of semantic domains. Next, present examples of semantic algebras from the body of the chapter.
- Cover all of Chapter 4 and at least Sections 5.1 and 5.4 from Chapter 5. If time allows, cover all of Chapter 5.
- Summarize Chapter 6 in one or two lectures for an undergraduate course. This summary can be taken from Section 6.1. A graduate course should cover all of the chapter.
- Cover as much of Chapter 7 as possible.

REFERENCES AND EXERCISES

Following each chapter is a short list of references that suggests further reading. Each reference identifies the author and the year of publication. Letters *a*, *b*, *c*, and so on, are used if the author has multiple references for a year. The references are compiled in the bibliography in the back of the book. I have tried to make the bibliography current and complete, but this appears to be an impossible task, and I apologize to those researchers whose efforts I have unintentionally omitted.

Exercises are provided for each chapter. The order of a chapter's exercises parallels the order of presentation of the topics in the chapter. The exercises are not graded according to difficulty; an hour's effort on a problem will allow the reader to make that judgment and will also aid development of intuitions about the significant problems in the area.

ACKNOWLEDGEMENTS

Many people deserve thanks for their assistance, encouragement, and advice. In particular, I thank Neil Jones for teaching me denotational semantics; Peter Mosses for answering my questions; Robin Milner for allowing me to undertake this project while under his employ; Paul Chisholm for encouraging me to write this book and for reading the initial draft; Allen Stoughton for many stimulating discussions; Colin Stirling for being an agreeable office mate; and my parents, family, and friends in Kansas, for almost everything else.

John Sulzycki of Allyn and Bacon deserves special thanks for his interest in the project, and Laura Cleveland, Sue Freese, and Jane Schulman made the book's production run smoothly. The reviewers Jim Harp, Larry Reeker, Edmond Schonberg, and Mitchell Wand contributed numerous useful suggestions. (I apologize for the flaws that remain in spite of their efforts.) Those instructors and their students who used preliminary drafts as texts deserve thanks; they are Jim Harp, Austin Melton, Colin Stirling, David Wise, and their students at the universities of Lowell, Kansas State, Edinburgh, and Indiana, respectively. My students at Edinburgh, Iowa State, and Kansas State also contributed useful suggestions and corrections.

Finally, the text would not have been written had I not been fortunate enough to spend several years in Denmark and Scotland. I thank the people at Aarhus University, Edinburgh University, Heriot-Watt University, and The Fiddler's Arms for providing stimulating and congenial environments.

I would be pleased to receive comments and corrections from the readers of this book.

DENOTATIONAL SEMANTICS

Introduction

Any notation for giving instructions is a programming language. Arithmetic notation is a programming language; so is Pascal. The input data format for an applications program is also a programming language. The person who uses an applications program thinks of its input commands as a language, just like the program's implementor thought of Pascal when he used it to implement the applications program. The person who wrote the Pascal compiler had a similar view about the language used for coding the compiler. This series of languages and viewpoints terminates at the physical machine, where code is converted into action.

A programming language has three main characteristics:

1. *Syntax*: the appearance and structure of its sentences.
2. *Semantics*: the assignment of meanings to the sentences. Mathematicians use meanings like numbers and functions, programmers favor machine actions, musicians prefer audible tones, and so on.
3. *Pragmatics*: the usability of the language. This includes the possible areas of application of the language, its ease of implementation and use, and the language's success in fulfilling its stated goals.

Syntax, semantics, and pragmatics are features of every computer program. Let's consider an applications program once again. It is a *processor* for its input language, and it has two main parts. The first part, the input checker module (the *parser*), reads the input and verifies that it has the proper syntax. The second part, the evaluation module, evaluates the input to its corresponding output, and in doing so, defines the input's semantics. How the system is implemented and used are pragmatics issues.

These characteristics also apply to a general purpose language like Pascal. An interpreter for Pascal also has a parser and an evaluation module. A pragmatics issue is that the interpretation of programs is slow, so we might prefer a compiler instead. A Pascal compiler transforms its input program into a fast-running, equivalent version in machine language.

The compiler presents some deeper semantic questions. In the case of the interpreter, the semantics of a Pascal program is defined entirely by the interpreter. But a compiler does not define the meaning— it *preserves* the meaning of the Pascal program in the machine language program that it constructs. The semantics of Pascal is an issue independent of any particular compiler or computer. The point is driven home when we implement Pascal compilers on two different machines. The two different compilers preserve the same semantics of Pascal. Rigorous definitions of the syntax and semantics of Pascal are required to verify that a compiler is correctly implemented.

The area of syntax specification has been thoroughly studied, and Backus-Naur form (BNF) is widely used for defining syntax. One of reasons the area is so well developed is that a close correspondence exists between a language's BNF definition and its parser: the definition dictates how to build the parser. Indeed, a parser generator system maps a BNF definition to a guaranteed correct parser. In addition, a BNF definition provides valuable documentation that can be used by a programmer with minimal training.

Semantics definition methods are also valuable to implementors and programmers, for they provide:

1. A precise standard for a computer implementation. The standard guarantees that the language is implemented exactly the same on all machines.
2. Useful user documentation. A trained programmer can read a formal semantics definition and use it as a reference to answer subtle questions about the language.
3. A tool for design and analysis. Typically, systems are implemented before their designers study pragmatics. This is because few tools exist for testing and analyzing a language. Just as syntax definitions can be modified and made error-free so that fast parsers result, semantic definitions can be written and tuned to suggest efficient, elegant implementations.
4. Input to a compiler generator. A compiler generator maps a semantics definition to a guaranteed correct implementation for the language. The generator reduces systems development to systems specification and frees the programmer from the most mundane and error prone aspects of implementation.

Unfortunately, the semantics area is not as well developed as the syntax area. This is for two reasons. First, semantic features are much more difficult to define and describe. (In fact, BNF's utility is enhanced because those syntactic aspects that it *cannot* describe are pushed into the semantics area! The dividing line between the two areas is not fixed.) Second, a standard method for writing semantics is still evolving. One of the aims of this book is to advocate one promising method.

METHODS FOR SEMANTICS SPECIFICATION

Programmers naturally take the meaning of a program to be the actions that a machine takes upon it. The first versions of programming language semantics used machines and their actions as their foundation.

The *operational semantics* method uses an interpreter to define a language. The meaning of a program in the language is the evaluation history that the interpreter produces when it interprets the program. The evaluation history is a sequence of internal interpreter configurations.

One of the disadvantages of an operational definition is that a language can be understood only in terms of interpreter configurations. No machine-independent definition exists, and a user wanting information about a specific language feature might as well invent a program using the feature and run it on a real machine. Another problem is the interpreter itself: it is represented as an algorithm. If the algorithm is simple and written in an elegant notation, the interpreter can give insight into the language. Unfortunately, interpreters for nontrivial languages are large and complex, and the notation used to write them is often as complex as the language being defined. Operational definitions are still worthy of study because one need only implement the interpreter to implement the language.

The *denotational semantics* method maps a program directly to its meaning, called its *denotation*. The denotation is usually a mathematical value, such as a number or a function. No interpreters are used; a *valuation function* maps a program directly to its meaning.

A denotational definition is more abstract than an operational definition, for it does not specify computation steps. Its high-level, modular structure makes it especially useful to language designers and users, for the individual parts of a language can be studied without having to examine the entire definition. On the other hand, the implementor of a language is left with more work. The numbers and functions must be represented as objects in a physical machine, and the valuation function must be implemented as the processor. This is an ongoing area of study.

With the *axiomatic semantics* method, the meaning of a program is not explicitly given at all. Instead, *properties* about language constructs are defined. These properties are expressed with axioms and inference rules from symbolic logic. A property about a program is deduced by using the axioms and rules to construct a formal proof of the property. The character of an axiomatic definition is determined by the kind of properties that can be proved. For example, a very simple system may only allow proofs that one program is equal to another, whatever meanings they might have. More complex systems allow proofs about a program's input and output properties.

Axiomatic definitions are more abstract than denotational and operational ones, and the properties proved about a program may not be enough to completely determine the program's meaning. The format is best used to provide preliminary specifications for a language or to give documentation about properties that are of interest to the users of the language.

Each of the three methods of formal semantics definition has a different area of application, and together the three provide a set of tools for language development. Given the task of designing a new programming system, its designers might first supply a list of properties that they wish the system to have. Since a user interacts with the system via an input language, an axiomatic definition is constructed first, defining the input language and how it achieves the desired properties. Next, a denotational semantics is defined to give the meaning of the language. A formal proof is constructed to show that the semantics contains the properties that the axiomatic definition specifies. (The denotational definition is a *model* of the axiomatic system.) Finally, the denotational definition is implemented using an operational definition. These *complementary semantic definitions* of a language support systematic design, development, and implementation.

This book emphasizes the denotational approach. Of the three semantics description methods, denotational semantics is the best format for precisely defining the meaning of a programming language. Possible implementation strategies can be derived from the definition as well. In addition, the study of denotational semantics provides a good foundation for understanding many of the current research areas in semantics and languages. A good number of existing languages, such as ALGOL60, Pascal, and LISP, have been given denotational semantics. The method has also been used to help design and implement languages such as Ada, CHILL, and Lucid.

SUGGESTED READINGS

Surveys of formal semantics: Lucas 1982; Marcotty, Ledgaard, & Bochman 1976; Pagan 1981

Operational semantics: Ollengren 1974; Wegner 1972a, 1972b

Denotational semantics: Gordon 1979; Milne & Strachey 1976; Stoy 1977; Tennent 1976

Axiomatic semantics: Apt 1981; Hoare 1969; Hoare & Wirth 1973

Complementary semantics definitions: deBakker 1980; Donohue 1976; Hoare & Lauer 1974

Languages with denotational semantics definitions: SNOBOL: Tennent 1973
LISP: Gordon 1973, 1975, 1978; Muchnick & Pleban 1982
ALGOL60: Henhapl & Jones 1982; Mosses 1974
Pascal: Andrews & Henhapl 1982; Tennent 1977a

Ada: Bjorner & Oest 1980; Donzeau-Gouge 1980; Kini, Martin, & Stoughton 1982
Lucid: Ashcroft & Wadge 1982
CHILL: Branquart, Louis, & Wodon 1982
Scheme: Muchnick & Pleban 1982

Chapter 1

Syntax

A programming language consists of syntax, semantics, and pragmatics. We formalize syntax first, because only syntactically correct programs have semantics. A syntax definition of a language lists the symbols for building words, the word structure, the structure of well formed phrases, and the sentence structure. Here are two examples:

1. *Arithmetic*: The symbols include the digits from 0 to 9, the arithmetic operators +, −, ×, and /, and parentheses. The numerals built from the digits and the operators are the words. The phrases are the usual arithmetic expressions, and the sentences are just the phrases.
2. *A Pascal-like programming language*: The symbols are the letters, digits, operators, brackets, and the like, and the words are the identifiers, numerals, and operators. There are several kinds of phrases: identifiers and numerals can be combined with operators to form expressions, and expressions can be combined with identifiers and other operators to form statements such as assignments, conditionals, and declarations. Statements are combined to form programs, the "sentences" of Pascal.

These examples point out that languages have internal structure. A notation known as *Backus-Naur form* (BNF) is used to precisely specify this structure.

A BNF definition consists of a set of equations. The left-hand side of an equation is called a *nonterminal* and gives the name of a structural type in the language. The right-hand side lists the forms which belong to the structural type. These forms are built from symbols (called *terminal symbols*) and other nonterminals. The best introduction is through an example.

Consider a description of arithmetic. It includes two equations that define the structural types of *digit* and *operator:*

```
<digit> ::= 0 | 1 | 2 | 3 | 4 | 5 | 6 | 7 | 8 | 9
<operator> ::= + | − | × | /
```

Each equation defines a group of objects with common structure. To be a digit, an object must be a 0 or a 1 or a 2 or a 3 . . . or a 9. The name to the left of the equals sign (::=) is the nonterminal name <digit>, the name of the structural type. Symbols such as 0, 1, and + are terminal symbols. Read the vertical bar (|) as "or."

Another equation defines the numerals, the words of the language:

<numeral> ::= <digit> | <digit> <numeral>

The name <digit> comes in handy, for we can succinctly state that an object with numeral structure must either have digit structure or . . . or what? The second option says that a numeral may have the structure of a digit grouped (concatenated) with something that has a known numeral structure. This clever use of recursion permits us to define a structural type that has an infinite number of members.

The final rule is:

<expression> ::= <numeral> | (<expression>)
| <expression> <operator> <expression>

An expression can have one of three possible forms: it can be a numeral, or an expression enclosed in parentheses, or two expressions grouped around an operator.

The BNF definition of arithmetic consists of these four equations. The definition gives a complete and precise description of the syntax. An arithmetic expression such as $(4 + 24) - 1$ is drawn as a *derivation tree*, so that the structure is apparent. Figure 1.1 shows the derivation tree for the expression just mentioned.

We won't cover further the details of BNF; this information can be found in many other texts. But there is one more notion that merits discussion. Consider the derivation trees in Figures 1.2 and 1.3 for the expression $4 \times 2 + 1$. Both are acceptable derivation trees. It is puzzling that one expression should possess *two* trees. A BNF definition that allows this phenomenon is called *ambiguous*. Since there are two allowable structures for $4 \times 2 + 1$, which one is proper? The choice is important, for real life compilers (and semantic definitions) assign meanings based on the structure. In this example, the two trees suggest a choice between multiplying four by two and then adding one versus adding two and one and then multiplying by four.

Ambiguous BNF definitions can often be rewritten into an unambiguous form, but the price paid is that the revised definitions contain extra, artificial levels of structure. An unambiguous definition of arithmetic reads:

<expression> ::= <expression> <lowop> <term> | <term>
<term> ::= <term> <highop> <factor> | <factor>
<factor> ::= <numeral> | (<expression>)
<lowop> ::= + | −
<highop> ::= × | /

Figure 1.1

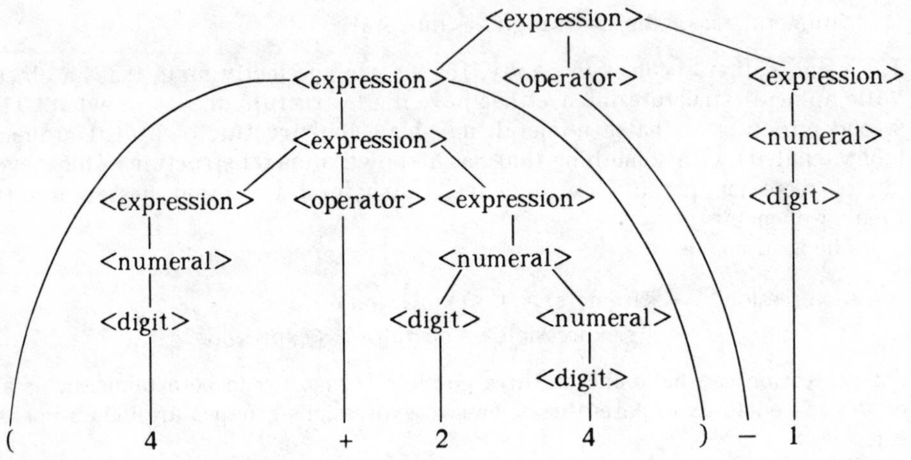

Figure 1.2

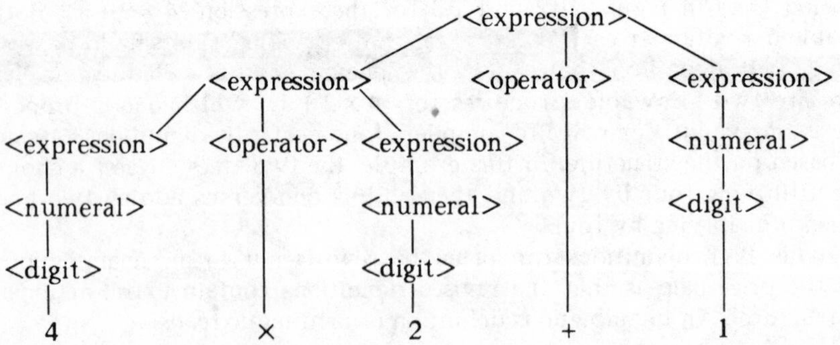

Figure 1.3

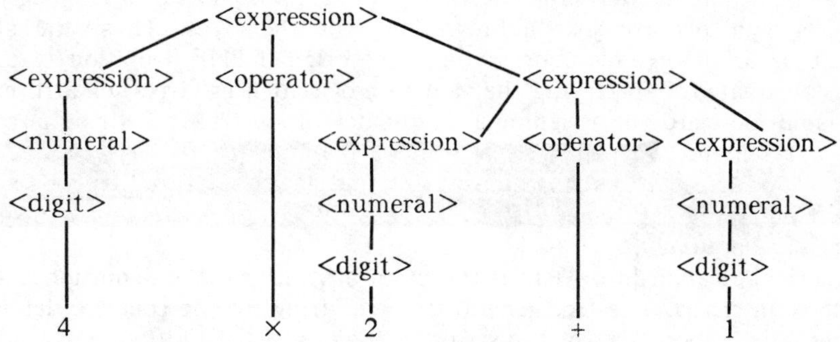

(The rules for <numeral> and <digit> remain the same.) This definition solves the ambiguity problem, and now there is only one derivation tree for $4 \times 2 + 1$, given in Figure 1.4. The tree is more complex than the one in Figure 1.2 (or 1.3) and the intuitive structure of the expression is obscured. Compiler writers

Figure 1.4

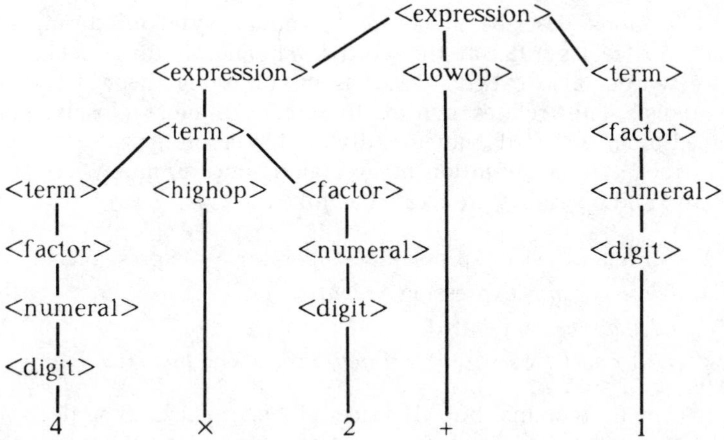

further extend BNF definitions so that fast parsers result. Must we use these modified, complex BNF definitions when we study semantics? The answer is no.

We claim that the derivation trees are the *real* sentences of a language, and strings of symbols are just abbreviations for the trees. Thus, the string $4 \times 2 + 1$ is an ambiguous abbreviation. The original BNF definition of arithmetic is adequate for specifying the structure of sentences (trees) of arithmetic, but it is not designed for assigning a unique derivation tree to a string purporting to be a sentence. In real life, we use *two* BNF definitions: one to determine the derivation tree that a string abbreviates, and one to analyze the tree's structure and determine its semantics. Call these the *concrete* and *abstract syntax definitions*, respectively.

A formal relationship exists between an abstract syntax definition and its concrete counterpart. The tree generated for a string by the concrete definition identifies a derivation tree for the string in the abstract definition. For example, the concrete derivation tree for $4 \times 2 + 1$ in Figure 1.4 identifies the tree in Figure 1.2 because the branching structures of the trees match.

Concrete syntax definitions will no longer be used in this text. They handle parsing problems, which do not concern us. We will always work with derivation trees, not strings. Do remember that the concrete syntax definition is derived from the abstract one and that the abstract syntax definition is the true definition of language structure.

1.1 ABSTRACT SYNTAX DEFINITIONS

Abstract syntax definitions describe structure. Terminal symbols disappear entirely if we study abstract syntax at the word level. The building blocks of abstract syntax are words (also called *tokens*, as in compiling theory) rather than terminal symbols. This relates syntax to semantics more closely, for meanings are assigned to entire words, not to individual symbols.

Here is the abstract syntax definition of arithmetic once again, where the numerals, parentheses, and operators are treated as tokens:

<expression> ::= <numeral> | <expression> <operator> <expression>
| *left-paren* <expression> *right-paren*
<operator> ::= *plus* | *minus* | *mult* | *div*
<numeral> ::= *zero* | *one* | *two* | · · · | *ninety-nine* | *one-hundred* | · · ·

The structure of arithmetic remains, but all traces of text vanish. The derivation trees have the same structure as before, but the tree's leaves are tokens instead of symbols.

Set theory gives us an even more abstract view of abstract syntax. Say that each nonterminal in a BNF definition names the set of those phrases that have the structure specified by the nonterminal's BNF rule. But the rule can be discarded: we introduce syntax builder operations, one for each form on the right-hand side of the rule.

Figure 1.5 shows the set theoretic formulation of the syntax of arithmetic.

The language consists of three sets of values: expressions, arithmetic operators, and numerals. The members of the *Numeral* set are exactly those values built by the "operations" (in this case, they are really constants) *zero, one, two,* and so on. No other values are members of the *Numeral* set. Similarly, the *Operator* set contains just the four values denoted by the constants *plus, minus, mult,* and *div*. Members of the *Expression* set are built with the three operations *make-numeral-into-expression, make-compound-expression,* and *make-bracketed-expression.* Consider *make-numeral-into-expression*; it converts a value from the *Numeral* set into a value in the *Expression* set. The operation reflects the idea that any known numeral can be used as an expression. Similarly, *make-*

Figure 1.5

Sets:

Expression
Op
Numeral

Operations:

make-numeral-into-expression: *Numeral* → *Expression*
make-compound-expression: *Expression* × *Op* × *Expression* → *Expression*
make-bracketed-expression: *Expression* → *Expression*

plus: *Op*
minus: *Op*
mult: *Op*
div: *Op*

zero: *Numeral*
one: *Numeral*
two: *Numeral*
. . .
ninety-nine: *Numeral*
one-hundred: *Numeral*
. . .

---

compound-expression combines two known members of the *Expression* set with a member of the *Operation* set to build a member of the *Expression* set. Note that *make-bracketed-expression* does not need parenthesis tokens to complete its mapping; the parentheses were just "window dressing." As an example, the expression 4 + 12 is represented by *make-compound-expression (make-numeral-into-expression(four), plus, make-numeral-into-expression(twelve))*.

When we work with the set theoretic formulation of abstract syntax, we forget about words and derivation trees and work in the world of sets and operations. The set theoretic approach reinforces our view that syntax is not tied to symbols; it is a matter of structure. We use the term *syntax domain* for a collection of values with common syntactic structure. Arithmetic has three syntax domains.

In this book, we use a more readable version of set-theoretic abstract syntax due to Strachey. We specify a language's syntax by listing its syntax domains and its BNF rules. Figure 1.6 shows the syntax of a block-structured programming language in the new format.

As an example from Figure 1.6, the phrase B∈Block indicates that Block is a syntax domain and that B is the nonterminal that represents an arbitrary member of the domain. The structure of blocks is given by the BNF rule

Figure 1.6

Abstract syntax:

P∈ Program
B∈ Block
D∈ Declaration
C∈ Command
E∈ Expression
O∈ Operator
I ∈ Identifier
N∈ Numeral

P ::= B.
B ::= D;C
D ::= **var** I | **procedure** I; C | D_1; D_2
C ::= I:=E | **if** E **then** C | **while** E **do** C | C_1;C_2 | **begin** B **end**
E ::= I | N | E_1 O E_2 | (E)
O ::= + | − | * | **div**

B::= D;C which says that any block must consist of a declaration (represented by D) and a command (represented by C). The ; token isn't really necessary, but we keep it to make the rule readable.

The structures of programs, declarations, commands, expressions, and operators are similarly specified. (Note that the Expression syntax domain is the set of arithmetic expressions that we have been studying.) No BNF rules exist for Identifier or Numeral, because these are collections of tokens. Figures 1.7 and 1.8 give the syntax definitions for an interactive file editor and a list processing language. (The **cr** token in Figure 1.7 represents the carriage return symbol.)

Figure 1.7

Abstract syntax:

P∈ Program-session
S∈ Command-sequence
C∈ Command
R∈ Record
I ∈ Identifier

P ::= S **cr**
S ::= C **cr** S | **quit**
C ::= **newfile** | **open** I | **moveup** | **moveback** |
  insert R | **delete** | **close**

Figure 1.8

Abstract syntax:

P∈ Program
E∈ Expression
L∈ List
A∈ Atom

P ::= E,P | **end**
E ::= A | L | **head** E | **tail** E | **let** $A = E_1$ **in** E_2
L ::= (A L) | ()

A good syntax definition lends a lot of help toward understanding the semantics of a language. Your experience with block-structured languages helps you recognize some familiar constructs in Figure 1.6. Of course, no semantic questions are answered by the syntax definition alone. If you are familiar with ALGOL60 and LISP, you may have noted a number of constructs in Figures 1.6 and 1.8 that have a variety of possible semantics.

1.2 MATHEMATICAL AND STRUCTURAL INDUCTION

Often we must show that all the members of a syntax domain have some property in common. The proof technique used on syntax domains is called *structural induction.* Before studying the general principle of structural induction, we first consider a specific case of it in the guise of *mathematical induction.* Mathematical induction is a proof strategy for showing that all the members of $\mathbb{N}$, the natural numbers, possess a property P. The strategy goes:

1. Show that 0 has P, that is, show that $P(0)$ holds.
2. Assuming that an arbitrary member $i \in \mathbb{N}$ has P, show that $i+1$ has it as well; that is, show that $P(i)$ implies $P(i+1)$.

If steps 1 and 2 are proved for a property P, then it follows that the property holds for all the numbers. (Why? Any number $k \in \mathbb{N}$ is exactly $(\cdots((0+1)+1)+\cdots+1)$, the 1 added k times. You take it from there.) Here is an application of mathematical induction:

1.1 Proposition:

For any $n \in \mathbb{N}$, there exist exactly $n!$ permutations of n objects.

Proof: We use mathematical induction to do the proof.

Basis: for 0 objects, there exists the "empty" permutation; since 0! equals 1, this case holds.

Induction: for $n \in \mathbb{N}$ assume that there exist $n!$ permutations of n objects. Now add a new object j to the n objects. For each permutation $k_{i1}, k_{i2}, \cdots, k_{in}$ of the existing objects, $n+1$ permutations result: they are $j, k_{i1}, k_{i2}, \cdots, k_{in}$; $k_{i1}, j, k_{i2}, \cdots, k_{in}$; $k_{i1}, k_{i2}, j, \cdots, k_{in}$; $k_{i1}, k_{i2}, \cdots, j, k_{in}$; and $k_{i1}, k_{i2}, \cdots, k_{in}, j$. Since there are $n!$ permutations of n objects, a total of $(n+1)*n! = (n+1)!$ permutations exist for $n+1$ objects.

This completes the proof. □

The mathematical induction principle is simple because the natural numbers have a simple structure: a number is either 0 or a number incremented by 1. This structure can be formalized as a BNF rule:

N ::= 0 | N+1

Any natural number is just a derivation tree. The mathematical induction principle is a proof strategy for showing that all the trees built by the rule for N possess a property P. Step 1 says to show that the tree of depth zero, the leaf 0, has P. Step 2 says to use the fact that a tree t has property P to prove that the tree $t+1$ has P.

The mathematical induction principle can be generalized to work upon any syntax domain defined by a BNF rule. The generalized proof strategy is structural induction. Treating the members of a syntax domain D as trees, we show that all trees in D have property P inductively:

1. Show that all trees of depth zero have P.
2. Assume that for an arbitrary depth $m \geqslant 0$ all trees of depth m or less have P, and show that a tree of depth $m+1$ must have P as well.

This strategy is easily adapted to operate directly upon the BNF rule that generates the trees.

1.2 Definition:

The structural induction principle: for the syntax domain D and its BNF rule:

$d ::= Option_1 \mid Option_2 \mid \cdots \mid Option_n$

all members of D have a property P if the following holds for each $Option_i$, *for* $1 \leqslant i \leqslant n$: *if every occurrence of d in* $Option_i$ *has P, then* $Option_i$ *has P.*

The assumption "every occurrence of d in $Option_i$ has P" is called the *inductive hypothesis*. The method appears circular because it is necessary to assume that trees in D have P to prove that the D-tree built using $Option_i$ has P, but the tree being built must have a depth greater than the subtrees used to build it, so steps 1 and 2 apply.

1.3 Theorem:

The structural induction principle is valid.

Proof: Given a proposition P, assume that the claim "if every occurrence of d in $Option_i$ has P, then $Option_i$ has P" has been proved for each of the options in the BNF rule for D. But say that some tree t in D doesn't have property P. Then a contradiction results: pick the D-typed subtree in t of the least depth that does not have P. (There must always be one; it can be t if necessary. If there are two or more subtrees that are "smallest," choose any one of them.) Call the chosen subtree u. Subtree u must have been built using some $Option_k$, and all of its proper D-typed subtrees have P. But the claim "if every occurrence of d in $Option_k$ has P, then $Option_k$ has P" holds. Therefore, u must have property P— a contradiction. □

Here are two examples of proofs by structural induction.

1.4 Example:

For the domain E: Expression and its BNF rule:

E ::= **zero** | E_1*E_2 | (E)

show that all members of Expression have the same number of left parentheses as the number of right parentheses.

Proof: Consider each of the three options in the rule:

1. **zero**: this is trivial, as there are zero occurrences of both left and right parentheses.
2. E_1*E_2: by the inductive hypothesis, E_1 has, say, m left parentheses and m right parentheses, and similarly E_2 has n left parentheses and n right parentheses. Then E_1*E_2 has $m+n$ left parentheses and $m+n$ right parentheses.
3. (E): by the inductive hypothesis, E has m left parentheses and m right parentheses. Clearly, (E) has $m+1$ left parentheses and $m+1$ right parentheses. □

The structural induction principle generalizes to operate over a number of domains simultaneously. We can prove properties of two or more domains that are defined in terms of one another.

1.5 Example:

For BNF rules:

S ::= *E*

E ::= +S | **

show that all S-values have an even number of occurrences of the * token.

Proof: This result must be proved by a simultaneous induction on the rules for S and E, since they are mutually recursively defined. We prove the stronger claim that "all members of S *and* E have an even number of occurrences of *." For rule S, consider its only option: by the inductive hypothesis, the E tree has an even number of *, say, m of t' em. Then the *E* tree has $m+2$ of them, which is an even value. For ule E, the first option builds a tree that has an even number of *, because by the inductive hypothesis, the S tree has an even number, and no new ones are added. The second option has exactly two occurrences, which is an even number. □

SUGGESTED READINGS

Backus-Naur form: Aho & Ullman 1977; Barrett & Couch 1979; Cleaveland & Uzgalis 1977; Hopcroft & Ullman 1979; Naur et al. 1963
Abstract syntax: Barrett & Couch 1979; Goguen, Thatcher, Wagner, & Wright 1977; Gordon 1979; Henderson 1980; McCarthy 1963; Strachey 1966, 1968, 1973
Mathematical and structural induction: Bauer & Wossner 1982; Burstall 1969; Manna 1974; Manna & Waldinger 1985; Wand 1980

EXERCISES

1. a. Convert the specification of Figure 1.6 into the classic BNF format shown at the beginning of the chapter. Omit the rules for <Identifier> and <Numeral>. If the grammar is ambiguous, point out which BNF rules cause the problem, construct derivation trees that demonstrate the ambiguity, and revise the BNF definition into a nonambiguous form that defines the same language as the original.
   b. Repeat part a for the definitions in Figures 1.7 and 1.8.

2. Describe an algorithm that takes an abstract syntax definition (like the one in Figure 1.6) as input and generates as output a stream containing the legal sentences in the language defined by the definition. Why isn't ambiguity a problem?

3. Using the definition in Figure 1.5, write the abstract syntax forms of these expressions:

   a. 12
   b. (4 + 14) * 3
   c. ((7 / 0))

   Repeat a–c for the definition in Figure 1.6; that is, draw the derivation trees.

4. Convert the language definition in Figure 1.6 into a definition in the format of Figure 1.5. What advantages does each format have over the other? Which of the two would be easier for a computer to handle?

5. Alter the BNF rule for the Command domain in Figure 1.6 to read:

   C ::= S | S;C
   S ::= I:=E | **if** E **then** C | **while** E **do** C | **begin** B **end**

Draw derivation trees for the old and new definitions of Command. What advantages does one form have over the other?

6. Using Strachey-style abstract syntax (like that in Figures 1.6 through 1.8), define the abstract syntax of the input language to a program that maintains a data base for a grocery store's inventory. An input program consists of a series of commands, one per line; the commands should specify actions for:

   a. Accessing an item in the inventory (perhaps by catalog number) to obtain statistics such as quantity, wholesale and selling prices, and so on.
   b. Updating statistical information about an item in the inventory
   c. Creating a new item in the inventory;
   d. Removing an item from the inventory;
   e. Generating reports concerning the items on hand and their statistics.

7. a. Prove that any sentence defined by the BNF rule in Example 1.4 has more occurrences of zero than occurrences of *.
   b. Attempt to prove that any sentence defined by the BNF rule in Example 1.4 has more occurrences of zero than of (. Where does the proof break down? Give a counterexample.

8. Prove that any program in the language in Figure 1.6 has the same number of **begin** tokens as the number of **end** tokens.

9. Formalize and prove the validity of simultaneous structural induction.

10. The principle of *transfinite induction* on the natural numbers is defined as follows: for a property P on $\mathbb{N}$, if for arbitrary $n \geqslant 0$, ((for all $m < n$, $P(m)$ holds) implies $P(n)$ holds), then for all $n \geqslant 0$, $P(n)$ holds.

    a. Prove that the principle of transfinite induction is valid.
    b. Find a property that is provable by transfinite induction and not by mathematical induction.

11. Both mathematical and transfinite induction can be generalized. A relation $\lessdot \subseteq D \times D$ is a *well-founded ordering* iff there exist no infinitely descending sequences in D, that is, no sequences of the form $d_n \gtrdot d_{n-1} \gtrdot d_{n-2} \gtrdot \cdots$, where $\gtrdot = \lessdot^{-1}$.

    a. The general form of mathematical induction operates over a pair $(D, \lessdot)$, where all the members of D form one sequence $d_0 \lessdot d_1 \lessdot d_2 \lessdot \cdots \lessdot d_i \lessdot \cdots$. (Thus $\lessdot$ is a well-founded ordering.)

       i. State the principle of generalized mathematical induction and prove that the principle is sound.
       ii. What is $\lessdot$ for $D = \mathbb{N}$?

iii. Give an example of another set with a well-founded ordering to which generalized mathematical induction can apply.

b. The general form of transfinite induction operates over a pair $(D, <)$, where $<$ is a well founded ordering.

i. State the principle of general transfinite induction and prove it valid.
ii. Show that there exists a well-founded ordering on the words in a dictionary and give an example of a proof using them and general transfinite induction.
iii. Show that the principle of structural induction is justified by the principle of general transfinite induction.

Chapter 2

Sets, Functions, and Domains

Functions are fundamental to denotational semantics. This chapter introduces functions through set theory, which provides a precise yet intuitive formulation. In addition, the concepts of set theory form a foundation for the theory of *semantic domains*, the value spaces used for giving meaning to languages. We examine the basic principles of sets, functions, and domains in turn.

2.1 SETS

A *set* is a collection; it can contain numbers, persons, other sets, or (almost) anything one wishes. Most of the examples in this book use numbers and sets of numbers as the members of sets. Like any concept, a set needs a representation so that it can be written down. Braces are used to enclose the members of a set. Thus, $\{ 1, 4, 7 \}$ represents the set containing the numbers 1, 4, and 7. These are also sets:

$\{ 1, \{ 1, 4, 7 \}, 4 \}$
$\{ red, yellow, grey \}$
$\{ \}$

The last example is the *empty set*, the set with no members, also written as $\emptyset$.

When a set has a large number of members, it is more convenient to specify the conditions for membership than to write all the members. A set S can be defined by $S = \{ x \mid P(x) \}$, which says that an object a belongs to S iff (if and only if) a has property P, that is, $P(a)$ holds true. For example, let P be the property "is an even integer." Then $\{ x \mid x \text{ } is\ an\ even\ integer \}$ defines the set of even integers, an infinite set. Note that $\emptyset$ can be defined as the set $\{ x \mid x \neq x \}$. Two sets R and S are equivalent, written $R = S$, if they have the same members. For example, $\{ 1, 4, 7 \} = \{ 4, 7, 1 \}$.

These sets are often used in mathematics and computing:

1. *Natural numbers*: $\mathbb{N} = \{ 0, 1, 2, \cdots \}$
2. *Integers*: $\mathbb{Z} = \{ \cdots, -2, -1, 0, 1, 2, \cdots \}$
3. *Rational numbers*: $\mathbb{Q} = \{ x \mid \textit{for } p \in \mathbb{Z} \text{ and } q \in \mathbb{Z}, q \neq 0, x = p/q \}$
4. *Real numbers*: $\mathbb{R} = \{ x \mid x$ *is a point on the line*
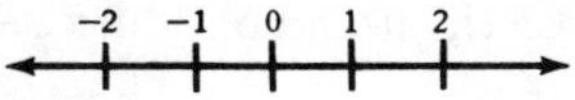

$\}$
5. *Characters*: $\mathbb{C} = \{ x \mid x \text{ is a character} \}$
6. *Truth values (Booleans)*: $\mathbb{B} = \{ \textit{true}, \textit{false} \}$

The concept of membership is central to set theory. We write $x \in S$ to assert that x is a member of set S. The membership test provides an alternate way of looking at sets. In the above examples, the internal structure of sets was revealed by "looking inside the braces" to see all the members inside. An external view treats a set S as a closed, mysterious object to which we can only ask questions about membership. For example, "does $1 \in S$ hold?," "does $4 \in S$ hold?," and so on. The internal structure of a set isn't even important, as long as membership questions can be answered. To tie these two views together, set theory supports the *extensionality principle*: a set R is equivalent to a set S iff they answer the same on all tests concerning membership:

$$R = S \text{ if and only if, for all } x,\ x \in R \text{ holds iff } x \in S \text{ holds}$$

Here are some examples using membership:

$1 \in \{ 1, 4, 7 \}$ holds
$\{1\} \in \{ 1, 4, 7 \}$ does not hold
$\{1\} \in \{ \{1\}, 4, 7 \}$ holds

The extensionality principle implies the following equivalences:

$\{ 1, 4, 7 \} = \{ 4, 1, 7 \}$
$\{ 1, 4, 7 \} = \{ 4, 1, 7, 4 \}$

A set R is a *subset* of a set S if every member of R belongs to S:

$$R \subseteq S \text{ if and only if, for all } x,\ x \in R \text{ implies } x \in S$$

For example,

$\{1\} \subseteq \{ 1, 4, 7 \}$
$\{ 1, 4, 7 \} \subseteq \{ 1, 4, 7 \}$
$\{ \} \subseteq \{ 1, 4, 7 \}$

all hold true but $\{1\} \not\subseteq \{ \{1\}, 4, 7 \}$.

2.1.1 Constructions on Sets

The simplest way to build a new set from two existing ones is to *union* them together; we write $R \cup S$ to denote the set that contains the members of R and S and no more. We can define set union in terms of membership:

for all x, $x \in R \cup S$ if and only if $x \in R$ or $x \in S$

Here are some examples:

$\{1,2\} \cup \{1,4,7\} = \{1,2,4,7\}$
$\{\} \cup \{1,2\} = \{1,2\}$
$\{\{\}\} \cup \{1,2\} = \{\{\},1,2\}$

The union operation is commutative and associative; that is, $R \cup S = S \cup R$ and $(R \cup S) \cup T = R \cup (S \cup T)$. The concept of union can be extended to join an arbitrary number of sets. If $R_0, R_1, R_2, \cdots$ is an infinite sequence of sets, $\bigcup_{i=0}^{\infty} R_i$ stands for their union. For example, $\mathbb{Z} = \bigcup_{i=0}^{\infty} \{-i, \cdots, -1, 0, 1, \cdots, i\}$ shows how the infinite union construction can build an infinite set from a group of finite ones.

Similarly, the *intersection* of sets R and S, $R \cap S$, is the set that contains only members common to both R and S:

for all x, $x \in R \cap S$ if and only if $x \in R$ and $x \in S$

Intersection is also commutative and associative.

An important concept that can be defined in terms of sets (though it is not done here) is the *ordered pair*. For two objects x and y, their pairing is written (x,y). Ordered pairs are useful because of the indexing operations *fst* and *snd*, defined such that:

$fst(x,y) = x$
$snd(x,y) = y$

Two ordered pairs P and Q are equivalent iff $fst\ P = fst\ Q$ and $snd\ P = snd\ Q$. Pairing is useful for defining another set construction, the product construction. For sets R and S, their *product* $R \times S$ is the set of all pairs built from R and S:

$R \times S = \{ (x,y) \mid x \in R \text{ and } y \in S \}$

Both pairing and products can be generalized from their binary formats to n-tuples and n-products.

A form of union construction on sets that keeps the members of the respective sets R and S separate is called *disjoint union* (or sometimes, *sum*):

$R + S = \{ (zero, x) \mid x \in R \} \cup \{ (one, y) \mid y \in S \}$

Ordered pairs are used to "tag" the members of R and S so that it is possible to examine a member and determine its origin.

We find it useful to define operations for assembling and disassembling members of $R+S$. For assembly, we propose in$R$ and in$S$, which behave as follows:

$$\text{for } x \in R, \quad \text{in}R(x) = (zero, x)$$
$$\text{for } y \in S, \quad \text{in}S(y) = (one, y)$$

To remove the tag from an element $m \in R+S$, we could simply say $snd(m)$, but will instead resort to a better structured operation called *cases*. For any $m \in R+S$, the value of:

```
cases m of
    isR(x) → ··· x ···
    [] isS(y) → ··· y ···
end
```

is "$\cdots x \cdots$" when $m = (zero, x)$ and is "$\cdots y \cdots$" when $m = (one, y)$. The *cases* operation makes good use of the tag on the sum element; it checks the tag before removing it and using the value. Do not be confused by the is$R$ and is$S$ phrases. They are not new operations. You should read the phrase is$R(x) \rightarrow \cdots x \cdots$ as saying, "if m is an element whose tag component is R and whose value component is x, then the answer is $\cdots x \cdots$." As an example, for:

```
f(m) = cases m of
           isℕ(n) → n+1
           [] is𝔹(b) → 0
           end
```

$f(\text{in}\mathbb{N}(2)) = f(zero, 2) = 2 + 1 = 3$, but $f(\text{in}\mathbb{B}(true)) = f(one, true) = 0$.

Like a product, the sum construction can be generalized from its binary format to n-sums.

Finally, the set of all subsets of a set R is called its *powerset*:

$$\mathbb{P}(R) = \{\, x \mid x \subseteq R \,\}$$

$\{\,\} \in \mathbb{P}(R)$ and $R \in \mathbb{P}(R)$ both hold.

2.2 FUNCTIONS

Functions are rather slippery objects to catch and examine. A function cannot be taken apart and its internals examined. It is like a "black box" that accepts an object as its input and then transforms it in some way to produce another object as its output. We must use the "external approach" mentioned above to understand functions. Sets are ideal for formalizing the method. For two sets R and S, f is a *function* from R to S, written $f: R \rightarrow S$, if, to each member of R, f associates exactly one member of S. The expression $R \rightarrow S$ is called the *arity* or *functionality* of f. R is the *domain* of f; S is the *codomain* of f. If $x \in R$ holds, and the element paired to x by f is y, we write $f(x) = y$. As a simple example, if $R = \{1, 4, 7\}$, $S = \{2, 4, 6\}$, and f maps R to S as follows:

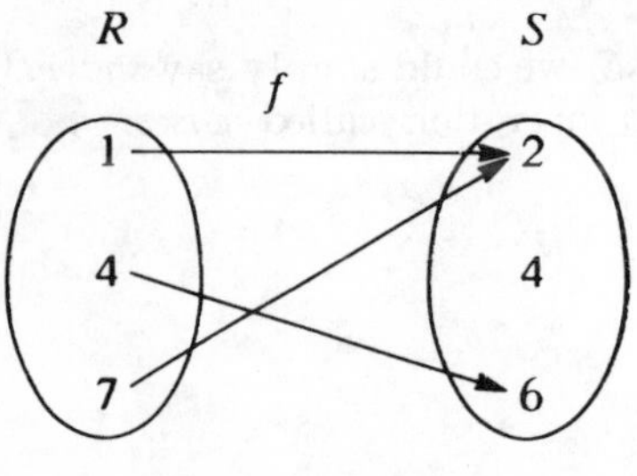

then f is a function. Presenting an argument a to f is called *application* and is written $f(a)$. We don't know *how* f transforms 1 to 2, or 4 to 6, or 7 to 2, but we accept that somehow it does; the results are what matter. The viewpoint is similar to that taken by a naive user of a computer program: unaware of the workings of a computer and its software, the user treats the program as a function, as he is only concerned with its input-output properties. An extensionality principle also applies to functions. For functions $f: R \rightarrow S$ and $g: R \rightarrow S$, f is equal to g, written $f = g$, iff for all $x \in R$, $f(x) = g(x)$.

Functions can be combined using the composition operation. For $f: R \rightarrow S$ and $g: S \rightarrow T$, $g \circ f$ is the function with domain R and codomain T such that for all $x: R$, $g \circ f(x) = g(f(x))$. Composition of functions is associative: for f and g as given above and $h: T \rightarrow U$, $h \circ (g \circ f) = (h \circ g) \circ f$.

Functions can be classified by their mappings. Some classifications are:

1. *one-one*: $f: R \rightarrow S$ is a *one-one* (1-1) function iff for all $x \in R$ and $y \in R$, $f(x) = f(y)$ implies $x = y$.
2. *onto*: $f: R \rightarrow S$ is an *onto* function iff $S = \{ y \mid$ *there exists some* $x \in R$ *such that* $f(x) = y \}$.
3. *identity*: $f: R \rightarrow R$ is the *identity* function for R iff for all $x \in R$, $f(x) = x$.
4. *inverse*: for some $f: R \rightarrow S$, if f is one-one and onto, then the function $g: S \rightarrow R$, defined as $g(y) = x$ iff $f(x) = y$ is called the *inverse function of* f. Function g is denoted by f^{-1}.

Functions are used to define many interesting relationships between sets. The most important relationship is called an *isomorphism*: two sets R and S are *isomorphic* if there exist a pair of functions $f: R \rightarrow S$ and $g: S \rightarrow R$ such that $g \circ f$ is the identity function for R and $f \circ g$ is the identity function for S. The maps f and g are called *isomorphisms*. A function is an isomorphism if and only if it is one-one and onto. Further, the inverse f^{-1} of isomorphism f is also an isomorphism, as $f^{-1} \circ f$ and $f \circ f^{-1}$ are both identities. Here are some examples:

1. $R = \{1, 4, 7\}$ is isomorphic to $S = \{2, 4, 6\}$; take $f : R \to S$ to be $f(1)=2$, $f(4)=6$, $f(7)=4$; and $g : S \to R$ to be $g(2)=1$, $g(4)=7$, $g(6)=4$.
2. For sets A and B, $A \times B$ is isomorphic to $B \times A$; take $f : A \times B \to B \times A$ to be $f(a,b) = (b,a)$.
3. $\mathbb{N}$ is isomorphic to $\mathbb{Z}$; take $f : \mathbb{N} \to \mathbb{Z}$ to be:

$$f(x) = \begin{cases} x/2 & \textit{if } x \textit{ is even} \\ -((x+1)/2) & \textit{if } x \textit{ is odd} \end{cases}$$

You are invited to calculate the inverse functions in examples 2 and 3.

2.2.1 Representing Functions as Sets

We can describe a function via a set. We collect the input-output pairings of the function into a set called its *graph*. For function $f : R \to S$, the set:

$$graph(f) = \{ (x, f(x)) \mid x \in R \}$$

is the graph of f. Here are some examples:

1. $f : R \to S$ in example 1 above:
   $graph(f) = \{ (1,2), (4,6), (7,4) \}$
2. the successor function on $\mathbb{Z}$:
   $graph(succ) = \{ \cdots, (-2,-1), (-1,0), (0,1), (1,2), \cdots \}$
3. $f : \mathbb{N} \to \mathbb{Z}$ in example 3 above:
   $graph(f) = \{ (0,0), (1,-1), (2,1), (3,-2), (4,2), \cdots \}$

In every case, we list the domain and codomain of the function to avoid confusion about which function a graph represents. For example, $f : \mathbb{N} \to \mathbb{N}$ such that $f(x)=x$ has the same graph as $g : \mathbb{N} \to \mathbb{Z}$ such that $g(x)=x$, but they are different functions.

We can understand function application and composition in terms of graphs. For application, $f(a)=b$ iff (a,b) is in $graph(f)$. Let there be a function *apply* such that $f(a) = apply(graph(f), a)$. Composition is modelled just as easily; for graphs $f : R \to S$ and $g : S \to T$:

$$graph(g \circ f) = \{ (x,z) \mid x \in R \textit{ and there exists a } y \in S \textit{ such that } (x,y) \in graph(f) \textit{ and } (y,z) \in graph(g) \}$$

Functions can have arbitrarily complex domains and codomains. For example, if R and S are sets, so is $R \times S$, and it is reasonable to make $R \times S$ the domain or codomain of a function. If it is the domain, we say that the function "needs two arguments"; if it is the codomain, we say that it "returns a pair of values." Here are some examples of functions with compound domains or codomains:

1. $add : (\mathbb{N} \times \mathbb{N}) \rightarrow \mathbb{N}$
   $graph(add) = \{ ((0,0), 0), ((1,0), 1), ((0,1), 1), ((1,1), 2), ((2,1), 3), \cdots \}$
2. $duplicate : R \rightarrow (R \times R)$, where $R = \{ 1, 4, 7 \}$
   $graph(duplicate) = \{ (1, (1,1)), (4,(4,4)), (7, (7,7)) \}$
3. $which\text{-}part : (\mathbb{B}+\mathbb{N}) \rightarrow S$, where $S = \{ isbool, isnum \}$
   $graph(which\text{-}part) = \{ ((zero, true), isbool), ((zero, false), isbool), ((one, 0), isnum), ((one,1), isnum), ((one, 2), isnum), \cdots ,((one, n), isnum), \cdots \}$
4. $make\text{-}singleton : \mathbb{N} \rightarrow \mathbb{P}(\mathbb{N})$
   $graph(make\text{-}singleton) = \{ (0, \{0\}), (1, \{1\}), \cdots ,(n, \{n\}), \cdots \}$
5. $nothing : \mathbb{B} \cap \mathbb{N} \rightarrow \mathbb{B}$
   $graph(nothing) = \{ \}$

The graphs make it clear how the functions behave when they are applied to arguments. For example, $apply(graph(which\text{-}part), (one, 2)) = isnum$. We see in example 4 that a function can return a set as a value (or, for that matter, use one as an argument). Since a function can be represented by its graph, which is a set, we will allow functions to accept other functions as arguments and produce functions as answers. Let the *set of functions from R to S* be a set whose members are the graphs of all functions whose domain is R and codomain is S. Call this set $R \rightarrow S$. Thus the expression $f : R \rightarrow S$ also states that f's graph is a member of the set $R \rightarrow S$. A function that uses functions as arguments or results is called a *higher-order function.* The graphs of higher-order functions become complex very quickly, but it is important to remember that they do exist and everything is legal under the set theory laws. Here are some examples:

6. $split\text{-}add : \mathbb{N} \rightarrow (\mathbb{N} \rightarrow \mathbb{N})$. Function *split-add* is the addition function "split up" so that it can accept its two arguments one at a time. It is defined as $split\text{-}add(x) = g$, where $g : \mathbb{N} \rightarrow \mathbb{N}$ is $g(y) = add(x,y)$. The graph gives a lot of insight:

$$graph(split\text{-}add) = \{ (0, \{ (0,0), (1,1), (2,2), \cdots \}), (1, \{ (0,1), (1,2), (2,3), \cdots \}), (2, \{ (0,2), (1,3), (2,4), \cdots \}), \cdots \}$$

   Each argument from $\mathbb{N}$ is paired with a graph that denotes a function from $\mathbb{N}$ to $\mathbb{N}$. Compare the graph of *split-add* to that of *add*; there is a close relationship between functions of the form $(R \times S) \rightarrow T$ to those of the form $R \rightarrow (S \rightarrow T)$. The functions of the first form can be placed in one-one onto correspondence with the ones of the second form— the sets $(R \times S) \rightarrow T$ and $R \rightarrow (S \rightarrow T)$ are isomorphic.
7. $first\text{-}value : (\mathbb{N} \rightarrow \mathbb{N}) \rightarrow \mathbb{N}$. The function looks at the value its argument produces when applied to a zero; $first\text{-}value(f) = f(0)$, and:

$$\begin{aligned} graph\,(\mathit{first\text{-}value}) = \{ & \cdots, (\{(0,1),(1,1),(2,1),(3,6),\cdots\}, 1), \\ & \cdots, (\{(0,49),(1,64),(2,81),(3,100),\cdots\}, 49), \\ & \cdots \} \end{aligned}$$

Writing the graph for the function is a tedious (and endless) task, so we show only two example argument, answer pairs.

8. *make-succ* : $(\mathbb{N} \to \mathbb{N}) \to (\mathbb{N} \to \mathbb{N})$. Function *make-succ* builds a new function from its argument by adding one to all the argument function's answers: $\mathit{make\text{-}succ}(f) = g$, where $g : \mathbb{N} \to \mathbb{N}$ and $g(x) = f(x)+1$.

$$\begin{aligned} graph\,(\mathit{make\text{-}succ}) = \{ & \cdots, \\ & (\{(0,1),(1,1),(2,1),(3,6),\cdots\}, \\ & \quad \{(0,2),(1,2),(2,2),(3,7),\cdots\}), \\ & \cdots, \\ & (\{(0,49),(1,64),(2,81),(3,100),\cdots\}, \\ & \quad \{(0,50),(1,65),(2,82),(3,101),\cdots\}) \\ & \cdots \} \end{aligned}$$

9. *apply* : $((\mathbb{N} \to \mathbb{N}) \times \mathbb{N}) \to \mathbb{N}$. Recall that $apply(f,x) = f(x)$, so its graph is:

$$\begin{aligned} graph\,(apply) = \{ & \cdots, ((\{(0,1),(1,1),(2,1),(3,6),\cdots\}, 0), 1), \\ & ((\{(0,1),(1,1),(2,1),(3,6),\cdots\}, 1), 1), \\ & ((\{(0,1),(1,1),(2,1),(3,6),\cdots\}, 2), 1), \\ & ((\{(0,1),(1,1),(2,1),(3,6),\cdots\}, 3), 6), \\ & \cdots, \\ & ((\{(0,49),(1,64),(2,81),(3,100),\cdots\}, 0), 49), \\ & ((\{(0,49),(1,64),(2,81),(3,100),\cdots\}, 1), 64), \\ & \cdots \} \end{aligned}$$

The graph of *apply* is little help; things are getting too complex. But it is important to understand why the pairs are built as they are. Each pair in *graph* (*apply*) contains an argument and an answer, where the argument is itself a set, number pair.

2.2.2 Representing Functions as Equations

The graph representation of a function provides insight into its structure but is inconvenient to use in practice. In this text we use the traditional equational format for specifying a function. Here are the equational specifications for the functions described in examples 1-5 of Section 2.2.1:

1. $add : (\mathbb{N} \times \mathbb{N}) \to \mathbb{N}$
   $add(m,n) = m + n$
2. $duplicate : R \to (R \times R)$
   $duplicate(r) = (r, r)$
3. $whichpart : (\mathbb{B} + \mathbb{N}) \to S$
   $which\text{-}part(m) =$ cases m of
   is$\mathbb{B}(b) \to isbool$
   [] is$\mathbb{N}(n) \to isnum$
   end
4. $make\text{-}singleton : \mathbb{N} \to \mathbb{P}(\mathbb{N})$
   $make\text{-}singleton(n) = \{n\}$
5. $nothing : \mathbb{B} \cap \mathbb{N} \to \mathbb{B}$ has no equational definition since its domain is empty

The equational format is so obvious and easy to use that we tend to take it for granted. Nonetheless, it is important to remember that an equation $f(x) = \alpha$, for $f : A \to B$, *represents* a function. The actual function is determined by a form of evaluation that uses substitution and simplification. To use f's equational definition to map a specific $a_0 \in A$ to $f(a_0) \in B$, first, *substitute* a_0 for all occurrences of x in α. The substitution is represented as $[\,a_0/x\,]\alpha$. Second, *simplify* $[\,a_0/x\,]\alpha$ to its underlying value.

Here is the process in action: to determine the the value of $add(2,3)$, we first substitute 2 for m and 3 for n in the expression on the right-hand side of add's equation, giving $add(2,3) = [3/n][2/m]m+n = 2+3$. Second, we simplify the expression 2+3 using our knowledge of the primitive operation + to obtain $2+3 = 5$. The substitution/simplification process produces a value that is consistent with the function's graph.

Often we choose to represent a function $f(x) = \alpha$ as $f = \lambda x.\, \alpha$; that is, we move the argument identifier to the right of the equals sign. The λ and . bracket the argument identifier. The choice of λ and . follows from tradition, and the format is called *lambda notation*. Lambda notation makes it easier to define functions such as $split\text{-}add : \mathbb{N} \to (\mathbb{N} \to \mathbb{N})$ as $split\text{-}add(x) = \lambda y.\, x+y$ or even as $split\text{-}add = \lambda x.\lambda y.\, x+y$. Also, a function can be defined without giving it a name: $\lambda(x,y).\, x+y$ is the add function yet again. Functions written in the lambda notation behave in the same way as the ones we have used thus far. For example, $(\lambda(x,y).\, x+y)(2,3) = [3/y][2/x]x+y = 2+3 = 5$. Section 3.2.3 in the next chapter discusses lambda notation at greater length.

As a final addition to our tools for representing functions, we will make use of a function updating expression. For a function $f : A \to B$, we let $[\,a_0 \mapsto b_0\,]f$ be the function that acts just like f except that it maps the specific value $a_0 \in A$ to $b_0 \in B$. That is:

$([\,a_0 \mapsto b_0\,]f)(a_0) = b_0$
$([\,a_0 \mapsto b_0\,]f)(a) = f(a)$ for all other $a \in A$ such that $a \neq a_0$

2.3 SEMANTIC DOMAINS

The sets that are used as value spaces in programming language semantics are called *semantic domains.* A semantic domain may have a different structure than a set, but sets will serve nicely for most of the situations encountered in this text. In practice, not all of the sets and set building operations are needed for building domains. We will make use of *primitive domains* such as $\mathbb{N}$, $\mathbb{Z}$, $\mathbb{B}$, . . ., and the following four kinds of *compound domains*, which are built from existing domains A and B:

1. Product domains $A \times B$
2. Sum domains $A + B$
3. Function domains $A \rightarrow B$
4. Lifted domains $A_\perp$, where $A_\perp = A \cup \{\perp\}$

The first three constructions were studied in the previous sections. The fourth, $A_\perp$, adds a special value $\perp$ (read "bottom") that denotes *nontermination* or "no value at all." Since we are interested in modelling computing-related situations, the possibility exists that a function f applied to an argument $a \in A$ may yield no answer at all— $f(a)$ may stand for a nonterminating computation. In this situation, we say that f has functionality $A \rightarrow B_\perp$ and $f(a) = \perp$. The use of the codomain $B_\perp$ instead of B stands as a kind of warning: in the process of computing a B-value, nontermination could occur.

Including $\perp$ as a value is an alternative to using a theory of *partial functions.* (A *partial function* is a function that may not have a value associated with each argument in its domain.) A function f that is undefined at argument a has the property $f(a) = \perp$. In addition to dealing with undefinedness as a real value, we can also use $\perp$ to clearly state what happens when a function receives a nonterminating value as an argument. For $f : A_\perp \rightarrow B_\perp$, we write $f = \underline{\lambda} x.\, \alpha$ to denote the mapping:

$$f(\perp) = \perp$$
$$f(a) = [\, a / x \,]\alpha \quad \text{for } a \in A$$

The underlined lambda forces f to be a *strict* function, that is, one that cannot recover from a nonterminating situation. As an example, for $f : \mathbb{N}_\perp \rightarrow \mathbb{N}_\perp$, defined as $f = \underline{\lambda} n.0$, $f(\perp)$ is $\perp$, but for $g : \mathbb{N}_\perp \rightarrow \mathbb{N}_\perp$, defined as $g = \lambda n.0$, $g(\perp)$ is 0. Section 3.2.4 in the next chapter elaborates on nontermination and strictness.

2.3.1 Semantic Algebras

Now that the tools for building domains and functions have been specified, we introduce a format for presenting semantic domains. The format is called a *semantic algebra*, for, like the algebras studied in universal algebra, it is the grouping of a set with the fundamental operations on that set. We choose the algebra format because it:

1. Clearly states the structure of a domain and how its elements are used by the functions.
2. Encourages the development of standard algebra "modules" or "kits" that can be used in a variety of semantic definitions.
3. Makes it easier to analyze a semantic definition concept by concept.
4. Makes it straightforward to alter a semantic definition by replacing one semantic algebra with another.

Many examples of semantic algebras are presented in Chapter 3, so we provide only one here. We use pairs of integers to simulate the rational numbers. Operations for creating, adding, and multiplying rational numbers are specified. The example also introduces a function that we will use often: the expression $e_1 \rightarrow e_2 \, [] \, e_3$ is the *choice function*, which has as its value e_2 if $e_1 = true$ and e_3 if $e_1 = false$.

2.1 Example: *Simulating the rational numbers*

Domain $Rat = (\mathbb{Z} \times \mathbb{Z})_\perp$
Operations

$makerat : \mathbb{Z} \rightarrow (\mathbb{Z} \rightarrow Rat)$
$makerat = \lambda p.\lambda q.\, (q{=}0) \rightarrow \perp \, [] \, (p,q)$

$addrat : Rat \rightarrow (Rat \rightarrow Rat)$
$addrat = \underline{\lambda}(p_1,q_1).\underline{\lambda}(p_2,q_2).\, ((p_1{*}q_2){+}(p_2{*}q_1),\, q_1{*}q_2)$

$multrat : Rat \rightarrow (Rat \rightarrow Rat)$
$multrat = \underline{\lambda}(p_1,q_1).\underline{\lambda}(p_2,q_2).\, (p_1{*}p_2,\, q_1{*}q_2)$

Operation *makerat* groups the integers p and q into a rational p/q, represented by (p,q). If the denominator q is 0, then the rational is undefined. Since the possibility of an undefined rational exists, the *addrat* operation checks both of its arguments for definedness before performing the addition of the two fractions. *Multrat* operates similarly.

The following chapter explains, in careful detail, the notion of a domain, its associated construction and destruction operations, and its presentation in semantic algebra format. If you are a newcomer to the area of denotational semantics, you may wish to skip Chapter 3 and use it as a reference. If you decide to follow this approach, glance at Section 3.5 of the chapter, which is a summary of the semantic operations and abbreviations that are used in the text.

SUGGESTED READINGS

Naive set theory: Halmos 1960; Manna & Waldinger 1985
Axiomatic set theory: Devlin 1969; Enderton 1977; Lemmon 1969

EXERCISES

1. List (some of) the members of each of these sets:
   a. $\mathbb{N} \cap \mathbb{Z}$
   b. $\mathbb{Z} - \mathbb{N}$
   c. $\mathbb{B} \times (\mathbb{C} + \mathbb{B})$
   d. $\mathbb{N} - (\mathbb{N} \cup \mathbb{Z})$

2. Give the value of each of these expressions:
   a. $fst(4+2, 7)$
   b. $snd(7, 7+fst(3-1, 0))$
   c. cases in$\mathbb{N}(3+1)$ of is$\mathbb{B}(t) \rightarrow 0$ ▯ is$\mathbb{N}(n) \rightarrow n+2$ end
   d. $\{\,true\,\} \cup (\mathbb{P}(\mathbb{B}) - \{\,\{true\}\,\})$

3. Using the extensionality principle, prove that set union and intersection are commutative and associative operations.

4. In "pure" set theory, an ordered pair $P = (x,y)$ is modelled by the set $P' = \{\,\{\,x\,\},\{\,x,y\,\}\,\}$.
   a. Using the operations union, intersection, and set subtraction, define operations fst' and snd' such that $fst'(P') = x$ and $snd'(P') = y$.
   b. Show that for any other set Q' such that $fst'(Q') = x$ and $snd'(Q') = y$ that $P' = Q'$.

5. Give examples of the following functions if they exist. If they do not, explain why:
   a. a one-one function from $\mathbb{B}$ to $\mathbb{N}$; from $\mathbb{N}$ to $\mathbb{B}$.
   b. a one-one function from $\mathbb{N} \times \mathbb{N}$ to $\mathbb{R}$; from $\mathbb{R}$ to $\mathbb{N} \times \mathbb{N}$.
   c. an onto function from $\mathbb{N}$ to $\mathbb{B}$; from $\mathbb{B}$ to $\mathbb{N}$.
   d. an onto function from $\mathbb{N}$ to $\mathbb{Q}$; from $\mathbb{Q}$ to $\mathbb{N}$.

6. For sets R and S, show that:
   a. $R \times S \neq S \times R$ can hold, but $R \times S$ is always isomorphic to $S \times R$.
   b. $R + S \neq R \cup S$ always holds, but $R + S$ can be isomorphic to $R \cup S$.

7. Prove that the composition of two one-one functions is one-one; that the composition of two onto functions is onto; that the composition of two isomorphisms is an isomorphism. Show also that the composition of a one-one function with an onto function (and vice versa) might not be either one-one or onto.

8. Using the definition of *split-add* in Section 2.2.1, determine the graphs of:

   a. *split-add*(3)
   b. *split-add*(*split-add*(2)(1))

9. Determine the graphs of:

   a. *split-sub* : $\mathbb{Z} \to \mathbb{Z} \to \mathbb{Z}$ such that *split-sub*$(x) = g$, where $g : \mathbb{Z} \to \mathbb{Z}$ is $g(y) = x - y$
   b. *split-sub* : $\mathbb{N} \to \mathbb{N} \to \mathbb{Z}$, where the function is defined in part a.

10. The previous two exercises suggest that there is an underlying concept for "splitting" a function. For a set D, we define *curryD*: $((D \times D) \to D) \to (D \to (D \to D))$ to be *curryD*$(f) = g$, where $g(x) = h$, where $h(y) = f(x,y)$. Write out (part of) the graph for *curry*$\mathbb{B}$: $((\mathbb{B} \times \mathbb{B}) \to \mathbb{B}) \to (\mathbb{B} \to (\mathbb{B} \to \mathbb{B}))$.

11. For $\mathbb{B} = \{$ *true*, *false* $\}$ and $\mathbb{N} = \{ 0, 1, 2, \cdots \}$, what are the functionalities of the functions represented by these graphs?

    a. { (*true*, 0), (*false*, 1) }
    b. { ((*true*, 0), (*true*, *true*)), ((*true*, 1), (*true*, *false*)), ((*true*, 2), (*true*, *false*)), · · · ,((*false*, 0), (*false*, *true*)), ((*false*, 1), (*false*, *false*)), ((*false*, 2), (*false*, *false*)), · · · }
    c. { ({ (*true*, *true*), (*false*, *true*) }, *true*), ({ (*true*, *true*), (*false*, *false*) }, *false*), · · · , ({ (*true*, *false*), (*false*, *true*) }, *true*), · · · }

12. Use the definitions in Section 2.2.2 to simplify each of the following expressions:

    a. *make-singleton*(*add*(3,2)) ∪ { 4 }
    b. *add*(*snd*(*duplicate*(4)), 1)
    c. *which-part*(in$\mathbb{N}$(*add*(2,0)))
    d. ([3↦{ 4 }]*make-singleton*)(2)
    e. ([3↦{ 4 }]*make-singleton*)(3)

13. For the equational definition *fac*$(n) = (n{=}0) \to 1$ [] n**fac*$(n-1)$, show that the following properties hold (hint: use mathematical induction):

    a. For all $n \in \mathbb{N}$, *fac*(n) has a unique value, that is, *fac* is a function.
    b. For all $n \in \mathbb{N}$, *fac*$(n+2) > n$.

14. List the elements in these domains:

    a. $(\mathbb{B} \times \mathbb{B})_\perp$
    b. $\mathbb{B}_\perp \times \mathbb{B}_\perp$
    c. $(\mathbb{B} \times \mathbb{B}) + \mathbb{B}$
    d. $(\mathbb{B} + \mathbb{B})_\perp$
    e. $\mathbb{B}_\perp + \mathbb{B}_\perp$
    f. $\mathbb{B} \rightarrow \mathbb{B}_\perp$
    g. $(\mathbb{B} \rightarrow \mathbb{B})_\perp$

15. Simplify these expressions using the algebra in Example 2.1:

    a. *addrat* (*makerat* (3) (2)) (*makerat* (1) (3))
    b. *addrat* (*makerat* (2) (0)) (*multrat* (*makerat* (3) (2)) (*makerat* (1) (3)))
    c. ($\lambda r.$ *one*) (*makerat* (1) (0))
    d. ($\underline{\lambda} r.$ *one*) (*makerat* (1) (0))
    e. ($\lambda(r, s).$ *addrat*(r) (s)) ((*makerat* (2) (1)), (*makerat* (3) (2)))
    f. ($\lambda(r, s). r$) ((*makerat* (2) (1)), (*makerat* (1) (0)))

16. The sets introduced in Section 2.1 belong to *naive set theory*, which is called such because it is possible to construct set definitions that are nonsensical.

    a. Show that the definition $\{ x \mid x \notin x \}$ is a nonsensical definition; that is, no set exists that satisfies the definition.
    b. Justify why the domain constructions in Section 2.3 always define sensical sets.

Chapter 3

Domain Theory I: Semantic Algebras

Before we can study the semantics of programming languages, we must establish a suitable collection of meanings for programs. We employ a framework called *domain theory:* the study of "structured sets" and their operations. A programmer might view domain theory as "data structures for semantics." Nonetheless, domain theory is a formal branch of (computing-related) mathematics and can be studied on its own.

The fundamental concept in domain theory is a *semantic domain*, a set of elements grouped together because they share some common property or use. The set of natural numbers is a useful semantic domain; its elements are structurally similar and share common use in arithmetic. Other examples are the Greek alphabet and the diatonic (musical) scale. Domains may be nothing more than sets, but there are situations in which other structures such as lattices or topologies are used instead. We can use domains without worrying too much about the underlying mathematics. Sets make good domains, and you may safely assume that the structures defined in this chapter are nothing more than the sets discussed in Chapter 2. Chapter 6 presents reasons why domains other than sets might be necessary.

Accompanying a domain is a set of *operations*. The operations are functions that need arguments from the domain to produce answers. Operations are defined in two parts. First, the operation's domain and codomain are given by an expression called the operation's *functionality*. For an operation f, its functionality $f: D_1 \times D_2 \times \cdots \times D_n \rightarrow A$ says that f needs an argument from domain D_1 and one from D_2, . . ., and one from D_n to produce an answer in domain A. Second, a description of the operation's mapping is specified. The description is usually an equational definition, but a set graph, table, or diagram may also be used.

A domain plus its operations constitutes a *semantic algebra*. Many examples of semantic algebras are found in the following sections.

3.1 PRIMITIVE DOMAINS

A *primitive domain* is a set that is fundamental to the application being studied. Its elements are atomic and they are used as answers or "semantic outputs." For example, the real numbers are a primitive domain for a mathematician, as are the notes in the key of C for a musician, as are the words of a dictionary for a copyeditor, and so on. Here is the most commonly used primitive domain:

3.1 Example: *The natural numbers*

Domain $Nat = \mathbb{N}$
Operations
$zero : Nat$
$one : Nat$
$two : Nat$
...
$plus : Nat \times Nat \rightarrow Nat$
$minus : Nat \times Nat \rightarrow Nat$
$times : Nat \times Nat \rightarrow Nat$

The operations *zero*, *one*, *two*, ... are *constants*. Each of the members of *Nat* is named by a constant. We list the constants for completeness' sake and to make the point that a constant is sometimes treated as an operation that takes zero arguments to produce a value. The other operations are natural number addition, subtraction, and multiplication, respectively. The *plus* and *times* operations are the usual functions, and you should have no trouble constructing the graphs of these operations. Natural number subtraction must be clarified: if the second argument is larger than the first, the result is the constant *zero*; otherwise a normal subtraction occurs.

Using the algebra, we can construct expressions that represent members of *Nat*. Here is an example: $plus(times(three, two), minus(one, zero))$. After consulting the definitions of the operations, we determine that the expression represents that member of *Nat* that has the name *seven*. The easiest way to determine this fact, though, is by simplification:

$$plus(times(three, two)), minus(one, zero))$$
$$= plus(times(three, two)), one)$$
$$= plus(six, one)$$
$$= seven$$

Each step of the simplification sequence preserved the underlying meaning of the expression. The simplification stopped at the constant *seven* (rather than continuing to, say, *times*(*one*, *seven*)), because we seek the simplest representation of the value. The simplification process makes the underlying meaning of an expression easier to comprehend.

From here on, we will use the arithmetic operations in infix format rather than prefix format; that is, we will write *six plus one* rather than *plus*(*six*, *one*).

To complete the definition of natural number arithmetic, let us add the operation $div : Nat \times Nat \rightarrow Nat$ to the algebra. The operation represents natural number (nonfractional) division; for example, *seven div three* is *two*. But the operation presents a technical problem: what is the answer when a number is divided by *zero*? A computer implementation of *div* might well consider this an error situation and produce an error value as the answer. We model this situation by adding an extra element to *Nat*. For any $n \in \mathbb{N}$, *n div zero* has the value *error*. All the other operations upon the domain must be extended to handle *error* arguments, since the new value is a member of *Nat*. The obvious extensions to *plus*, *minus*, *times*, and *div* make them produce an answer of *error* if either of their arguments is *error*. Note that the *error* element is not always included in a primitive domain, and we will always make it clear when it is.

The truth values algebra is also widely used, as shown in Example 3.2.

3.2 Example: *The truth values*

Domain $Tr = \mathbb{B}$

Operations

$true : Tr$

$false : Tr$

$not : Tr \rightarrow Tr$

$or : Tr \times Tr \rightarrow Tr$

$(\_\rightarrow\_ [\!]\ \_) : Tr \times D \times D \rightarrow D$, for a previously defined domain D

The truth values algebra has two constants— *true* and *false*. Operation *not* is logical negation, and *or* is logical disjunction. The last operation is the choice function. It uses elements from another domain in its definition. For values $m, n \in D$, it is defined as:

$$(true \rightarrow m\ [\!]\ n) = m$$
$$(false \rightarrow m\ [\!]\ n) = n$$

Read the expression $(\ x \rightarrow y\ [\!]\ z\ )$ as saying "if x then y else z."

Here are some expressions using numbers and truth values:

1. $((not(false))\ or\ false$

   $= true\ or\ false$

   $= true$

2. $(true\ or\ false) \rightarrow (seven\ div\ three)\ \square\ zero$
   $= true \rightarrow (seven\ div\ three)\ \square\ zero$
   $= seven\ div\ three = two$

3. $not(not\ true) \rightarrow false\ \square\ false\ or\ true$
   $= not(not\ true) \rightarrow false\ \square\ true$
   $= not\ false \rightarrow false\ \square\ true$
   $= true \rightarrow false\ \square\ true$
   $= false$

The utility of the choice function increases if relational operations are added to the *Nat* algebra. Here are some useful ones:

equals : $Nat \times Nat \rightarrow Tr$
lessthan : $Nat \times Nat \rightarrow Tr$
greaterthan : $Nat \times Nat \rightarrow Tr$

All have their usual definitions. As an example, the expression *not(four equals (one plus three))* $\rightarrow$ *(one greaterthan zero)* $\square$ *((five times two) lessthan zero)* simplifies to the constant *false*.

3.3 Example: *Character strings*

Domain *String* = the character strings formed from the elements of $\mathbb{C}$ (including an "error" string)
Operations
A, B, C, . . . , Z: *String*
empty : *String*
error : *String*
concat : $String \times String \rightarrow String$
length : $String \rightarrow Nat$
substr : $String \times Nat \times Nat \rightarrow String$

Text processing systems use this domain. Single characters are represented by constants. The constant *empty* represents the string with no characters. Words are built using *concat*, which concatenates two strings to build a new one. We will be lazy and write a string built with *concat* in double quotes, e.g., "ABC" abbreviates A *concat* (B *concat* C). Operation *length* takes a string as an argument and returns its length; *substr* is a substring extraction operator: given a string s and two numbers n_1 and n_2, $substr(s, n_1, n_2)$ extracts that part of s that begins at character position number n_1 and is n_2 characters long. (The leading character is at position *zero*.) Some combinations of (s, n_1, n_2) suggest impossible tasks. For example, what is the value represented by *substr ("ABC", one, four)* or *substr ("ABC", six, two)*? Use *error* as the answer for such combinations. If *concat* receives an *error* argument, its result is *error;* the length of the *error* string is *zero;* and any attempt to use *substr* on an *error* string also leads to *error.*

3.4 Example: *The one element domain*

Domain *Unit*, the domain containing only one element
Operations
  $() : Unit$

This degenerate algebra is useful for theoretical reasons; we will also make use of it as an alternative form of error value. The domain contains exactly one element, (). *Unit* is used whenever an operation needs a dummy argument. Here is an example: let $f: Unit \rightarrow Nat$ be $f(x) = one$; thus, $f(()) = one$. We will discard some of the extra symbols and just write $f: Unit \rightarrow Nat$ as $f() = one$; thus, $f() = one$.

3.5 Example: *Computer store locations*

Domain *Location*, the address space in a computer store
Operations
  first-locn : *Location*
  next-locn : *Location* → *Location*
  equal-locn : *Location* × *Location* → *Tr*
  lessthan-locn : *Location* × *Location* → *Tr*

The domain of computer store addresses is fundamental to the semantics of programming languages. The members of *Location* are often treated as numbers, but they are just as likely to be electrical impulses. The constant *first-locn* gives the "lowest address" in the store, and the other locations are accessed in order via the *next-locn* operation. (Think of *next-locn*(l) as $l+1$.) The other two operations compare locations for equality and lessthan.

This algebra would be inadequate for defining the semantics of an assembly language, for an assembly language allows random access of the locations in a store and treats locations as numbers. Nonetheless, the algebra works well for programming languages whose storage is allocated in static or stack-like fashion.

3.2 COMPOUND DOMAINS

Just as programming languages provide data structure builders for constructing new data objects from existing ones, domain theory possesses a number of domain building constructions for creating new domains from existing ones.

Each domain builder carries with it a set of operation builders for assembling and disassembling elements of the compound domain. We cover in detail the four domain constructions listed in Section 2.3 of Chapter 2.

3.2.1 Product

The *product* construction takes two or more component domains and builds a domain of tuples from the components. The case of binary products is considered first.

The product domain builder $\times$ builds the domain $A \times B$, a collection whose members are ordered pairs of the form (a, b), for $a \in A$ and $b \in B$. The operation builders for the product domain include the two disassembly operations:

$fst: A \times B \rightarrow A$
which takes an argument (a,b) in $A \times B$ and produces its first component $a \in A$, that is, $fst(a,b) = a$

$snd : A \times B \rightarrow B$
which takes an argument (a,b) in $A \times B$ and produces its second component $b \in B$, that is, $snd\,(a,b) = b$

The assembly operation is the ordered pair builder:

if a is an element of A, and b is an element of B, then (a, b) is an element of $A \times B$

The product domain raises a question about the functionalities of operations. Does an operation such as $or : Tr \times Tr \rightarrow Tr$ receive two elements from Tr as arguments or a pair argument from $Tr \times Tr$? In domain theory, as in set theory, the two views coincide: the two elements form one pair.

The product construction can be generalized to work with any collection of domains $A_1, A_2, \cdots, A_n$, for any $n>0$. We write $(x_1, x_2, \cdots, x_n)$ to represent an element of $A_1 \times A_2 \times \cdots \times A_n$. The subscripting operations *fst* and *snd* generalize to a family of n operations: for each i from 1 to n, $\downarrow i$ denotes the operation such that $(a_1, a_2, \cdots, a_n)\downarrow i = a_i$. Theoretically, it is possible to construct products from an infinite number of component domains, but infinite products raise some technical problems which are considered in exercise 16 in Chapter 6.

Example 3.6 shows a semantic algebra built with the product construction.

3.6 Example: *Payroll information: a person's name, payrate, and hours worked*

Domain *Payroll-record*= *String* $\times$ *Rat* $\times$ *Rat*
(Note: *Rat* is the domain defined in Example 2.1 in Chapter 2)

Operations

new-employee : *String* → *Payroll-record*
new-employee(*name*)= (*name*, *minimum-wage*, 0),
where *minimum-wage* ∈ *Rat* is some fixed value from *Rat*
and 0 is the *Rat* value (*makerat* (0) (1))

update-payrate : *Rat* × *Payroll-record* → *Payroll-record*
update-payrate (*pay*, *employee*)= (*employee* ↓1, *pay* , *employee* ↓3)

update-hours : *Rat* × *Payroll-record* → *Payroll-record*
update-hours (*hours*, *employee*)= (*employee* ↓1, *employee* ↓2, *hours* *addrat* *employee* ↓3)

compute-pay : *Payroll-record* → *Rat*
compute-pay (*employee*)= (*employee* ↓2) *multrat* (*employee* ↓3)

This semantic algebra is useful for the semantics of a payroll program. The components of the domain represent an employee's name, hourly wage, and the cumulative hours worked for the week. Here is an expression built with the algebra's operations:

compute-pay(*update-hours*(35, *new-employee*("*J.Doe*")))
= *compute-pay*(*update-hours*(35, ("*J.Doe*", *minimum-wage*, 0)))
= *compute-pay*(("*J.Doe*", *minimum-wage*, 0)↓1, ("*J.Doe*", *minimum-wage*, 0)↓2,
35 *addrat* ("*J.Doe*", *minimum-wage*, 0)↓3)
= *compute-pay*("*J.Doe*", *minimum-wage*, 35 *addrat* 0)
= *minimum-wage* *multrat* 35

3.2.2 Disjoint Union

The construction for unioning two or more domains into one domain is *disjoint union* (or *sum*).

For domains *A* and *B*, the disjoint union builder + builds the domain *A* + *B* , a collection whose members are the elements of *A* and the elements of *B* , labeled to mark their origins. The classic representation of this labeling is the ordered pair (*zero*, *a*) for an *a*∈*A* and (*one*, *b*) for a *b*∈*B*. .

The associated operation builders include two assembly operations:

in*A*: *A* → *A* + *B*
which takes an *a*∈*A* and labels it as originating from *A*; that is, in*A*(*a*) = (*zero*, *a*), using the pair representation described above.

in$B$: $B \rightarrow A + B$

which takes a $b \in B$ and labels it as originating from B, that is, in$B(b) = (one, b)$.

The "type tags" that the assembly operations place onto their arguments are put to good use by the disassembly operation, the *cases* operation, which combines an operation on A with one on B to produce a disassembly operation on the sum domain. If d is a value from $A + B$ and $f(x)=e_1$ and $g(y)=e_2$ are the definitions of $f: A \rightarrow C$ and $g: B \rightarrow C$, then:

(cases d of is$A(x) \rightarrow e_1$ [] is$B(y) \rightarrow e_2$ end)

represents a value in C. The following properties hold:

(cases in$A(a)$ of is$A(x) \rightarrow e_1$ [] is$B(y) \rightarrow e_2$ end) $= [a/x]e_1 = f(a)$

and

(cases in$B(b)$ of is$A(x) \rightarrow e_1$ [] is$B(y) \rightarrow e_2$ end) $= [b/y]e_2 = g(b)$

The *cases* operation checks the tag of its argument, removes it, and gives the argument to the proper operation.

Sums of an arbitrary number of domains can be built. We write $A_1 + A_2 + \cdots + A_n$ to stand for the disjoint union of domains $A_1, A_2, \cdots, A_n$. The operation builders generalize in the obvious way.

As a first example, we alter the *Payroll-record* domain of Example 3.6 to handle workers who work either the day shift or the night shift. Since the night shift is less desirable, employees who work at night receive a bonus in pay. These concepts are represented with a disjoint union construction in combination with a product construction.

3.7 Example: *Revised payroll information*

Domain *Payroll-rec* $= String \times (Day + Night) \times Rat$

where $Day = Rat$ and $Night = Rat$

(The names *Day* and *Night* are aliases for two occurrences of *Rat*. We use *dwage* $\in$ *Day* and *nwage* $\in$ *Night* in the operations that follow.)

Operations

newemp : *String* $\rightarrow$ *Payroll-rec*

newemp (*name*)= (*name* , in*Day*(*minimum-wage*), 0)

move-to-dayshift : *Payroll-rec* $\rightarrow$ *Payroll-rec*

move-to-dayshift(*employee*)=(*employee* $\downarrow$1,

(cases (*employee* $\downarrow$2) of is*Day*(*dwage*)$\rightarrow$ in*Day*(*dwage*)

[] is*Night*(*nwage*)$\rightarrow$ in*Day*(*nwage*) end),

employee $\downarrow$3)

move-to-nightshift : *Payroll-rec* → *Payroll-rec*
move-to-nightshift(*employee*)= (*employee* ↓1,
(cases (*employee* ↓2) of is*Day*(*dwage*)→ in*Night*(*dwage*)
[] is*Night*(*nwage*)→ in*Night*(*nwage*) end),
employee ↓3)

. . .

compute-pay : *Payroll-rec* → *Rat*
compute-pay(*employee*)= (cases (*employee* ↓2) of
is*Day*(*dwage*)→ *dwage* *multrat* (*employee* ↓3)
[] is*Night*(*nwage*)→ (*nwage*
multrat 1.5) *multrat* (*employee* ↓3)
end)

A person's wage is labeled as being either a day wage or a night wage. A new employee is started on the day shift, signified by the use of in*Day* in the operation *newemp*. The operations *move-to-dayshift* and *move-to-nightshift* adjust the label on an employee's wage. Operation *compute-pay* computes a time-and-a-half bonus for a night shift employee. Here is an example: if *jdoe* is the expression *newemp*("*J.Doe*") = ("*J.Doe*", in*Day*(*minimum-wage*), **0**), and *jdoe-thirty* is *update-hours*(**30**, *jdoe*), then:

compute-pay(*jdoe-thirty*)
= (cases *jdoe-thirty*↓2 of
is*Day*(*wage*)→ *wage* *multrat* (*jdoe-thirty*↓3)
[] is*Night*(*wage*)→ (*wage* *multrat* **1.5**) *multrat* (*jdoe-thirty*↓3)
end)
= (*cases* in*Day*(*minimum-wage*) of
is*Day*(*wage*)→ *wage* *multrat* **30**
[] is*Night*(*wage*)→ *wage* *multrat* **1.5** *multrat* **30**
end)
= *minimum-wage* *multrat* **30**

The tag on the component in*Day*(*minimum-wage*) of *jdoe-thirty*'s record helps select the proper pay calculation.

The primitive domain *Tr* can be nicely modelled using the *Unit* domain and the disjoint union construction.

3.8 Example: *The truth values as a disjoint union*

Domain *Tr* = *TT* + *FF*
where *TT* = *Unit* and *FF* = *Unit*

Operations

$true : Tr$
$true = \text{in}TT()$

$false : Tr$
$false = \text{in}FF()$

$not : Tr \rightarrow Tr$
$not(t) = \text{cases } t \text{ of is}TT() \rightarrow \text{in}FF() \ [] \ \text{is}FF() \rightarrow \text{in}TT() \text{ end}$

$or : Tr \times Tr \rightarrow Tr$
$or\,(t, u) = \text{cases } t \text{ of}$
$\quad \text{is}TT() \rightarrow \text{in}TT()$
$\quad [] \ \text{is}FF() \rightarrow (\text{cases } u \text{ of is}TT() \rightarrow \text{in}TT() \ [] \ \text{is}FF() \rightarrow \text{in}FF() \text{ end})$
$\quad \text{end}$

The dummy argument () isn't actually used in the operations— the tag attached to it is the important information. For this reason, no identifier names are used in the clauses of the *cases* statements; () is used there as well. We can also define the choice function:

$$(t \rightarrow e_1 \ [] \ e_2) = (\text{cases } t \text{ of is}TT() \rightarrow e_1 \ [] \ \text{is}FF() \rightarrow e_2 \text{ end})$$

As a third example, for a domain D with an *error* element, the collection of finite lists of elements from D can be defined as a disjoint union. The domain

$$D^* = Unit + D + (D \times D) + (D \times (D \times D)) + \cdots$$

captures the idea: *Unit* represents those lists of length zero (namely the empty list), D contains those lists containing one element, $D \times D$ contains those lists of two elements, and so on.

3.9 Example: *Finite lists*

Domain D^*

Operations

$nil : D^*$
$nil = \text{in}Unit()$

$cons : D \times D^* \rightarrow D^*$
$cons\,(d, l) = \text{cases } l \text{ of}$
$\quad \text{is}Unit() \rightarrow \text{in}D(d)$
$\quad [] \ \text{is}D(y) \rightarrow \text{in}D{\times}D(d,y)$
$\quad [] \ \text{is}D{\times}D(y) \rightarrow \text{in}D{\times}(D{\times}D)(d,y)$
$\quad [] \ \cdots \text{ end}$

$hd : D^* \to D$
$hd\ (l) =$ cases l of
isUnit()→$error$
[] isD(y)→y
[] isD×D(y)→$fst(y)$
[] isD×(D×D)(y)→$fst(y)$
[] · · · end

$tl : D^* \to D^*$
$tl\ (l) =$ cases l of
isUnit()→ inUnit()
isD(y)→ inUnit()
[] isD×D(y)→ inD(snd(y))
[] isD×(D×D)(y)→ inD×D(snd(y))
[] · · · end)

$null : D^* \to Tr$
$null\ (l) =$ cases l of
isUnit()→$true$
[] isD(y)→$false$
[] isD×D(y)→$false$
[] · · · end

Even though this domain has an infinite number of components and the *cases* expressions have an infinite number of choices, the domain and codomain operations are still mathematically well defined. To implement the algebra on a machine, representations for the domain elements and operations must be found. Since each domain element is a tagged tuple of finite length, a list can be represented as a tuple. The tuple representations lead to simple implementations of the operations. The implementations are left as an exercise.

3.2.3 Function Space

The next domain construction is the one most removed from computer data structures, yet it is fundamental to all semantic definitions. It is the *function space builder*, which collects the functions from a domain A to a codomain B.

For domains A and B, the function space builder → creates the domain $A \to B$, a collection of functions from domain A to codomain B. The associated disassembly operation is just function application:

$\_(\_) : (A \to B) \times A \to B$
which takes an $f \in A \to B$ and an $a \in A$ and produces $f(a) \in B$

An important property of function domains is the principle of *extensionality:* for any f and g in $A \rightarrow B$, if for all $a \in A$, $f(a) = g(a)$, then $f = g$. Functions are understood in terms of their argument-answer behavior, and an extensional function domain never contains two distinct elements representing the same function.

The assembly principle for functions is:

> if e is an expression containing occurrences of an identifier x, such that whenever a value $a \in A$ replaces the occurrences of x in e, the value $[a/x]e \in B$ results, then $(\lambda x.e)$ is an element in $A \rightarrow B$.

The form $(\lambda x.e)$ is called an *abstraction.* We often give names to abstractions, say $f = (\lambda x.e)$, or $f(x) = e$, where f is some name *not* used in e. For example, the function $plustwo(n) = n\ plus\ two$ is a member of $Nat \rightarrow Nat$ because $n\ plus\ two$ is an expression that has a unique value in Nat when n is replaced by an element of Nat. All of the operations built in Examples 3.6 through 3.9 are justified by the assembly principle.

We will usually abbreviate a nested abstraction $(\lambda x.(\lambda y.\, e))$ to $(\lambda x.\lambda y.\, e)$.

The binding of argument to binding identifier works the expected way with abstractions: $(\lambda n.\, n\ plus\ two)one = [one/n]n\ plus\ two = one\ plus\ two$. Here are other examples:

1. $(\lambda m.\, (\lambda n.\, n\ times\ n)(m\ plus\ two))(one)$
   $= (\lambda n.\, n\ times\ n)(one\ plus\ two)$
   $= (one\ plus\ two)\ times\ (one\ plus\ two)$
   $= three\ times\ (one\ plus\ two) = three\ times\ three = nine$

2. $(\lambda m.\, \lambda n.\, (m\ plus\ m)\ times\ n)(one)(three)$
   $= (\lambda n.\, (one\ plus\ one)\ times\ n)(three)$
   $= (\lambda n.\, two\ times\ n)(three)$
   $= two\ times\ three = six$

3. $(\lambda m.\, (\lambda n.\, n\ plus\ n)(m)) = (\lambda m.\, m\ plus\ m)$

4. $(\lambda p.\lambda q.\, p\ plus\ q)(r\ plus\ one) = (\lambda q.\, (r\ plus\ one)\ plus\ q)$

Here is a bit of terminology: an identifier x is *bound* if it appears in an expression e in $(\lambda x.e)$. An identifier is *free* if it is not bound. In example 4, the occurrences of p and q are bound (to λp and λq, respectively), but r is free. In an expression such as $(\lambda x.\lambda x.\, x)$, the occurrence of x is bound to the innermost occurrence of λx, hence $(\lambda x.\lambda x.\, x)(zero)(one) = ([zero/x](\lambda x.\, x))(one) = (\lambda x.\, x)(one) = one$.

Care must be taken when simplifying nested abstractions; free identifiers in substituted arguments may clash with inner binding identifiers. For example, the proper simplification of $(\lambda x.\, (\lambda y.\lambda x.\, y)x)$ is $(\lambda x.\, (\lambda x'.\, x))$ and *not* $(\lambda x.(\lambda x.\, x))$. The problem lies in the re-use of x in two different abstractions.

The solution is to rename the occurrences of identifiers x in $(\lambda x.M)$ if x clashes with a free occurrence of x in the argument that must be substituted into M. For safety's sake, avoid re-using binding identifiers.

Finally, we mention again the abbreviation introduced in Section 2.2.2 of Chapter 2 for function creation:

$[n \mapsto v]r$ abbreviates $(\lambda m.\, m \textit{ equals } n \rightarrow v \,[]\, r(m))$

That is, $([n \mapsto v]r)(n) = v$, and $([n \mapsto v]r)(m) = r(m)$ when $m \neq n$.

Let's look at some algebras. Example 3.10 is simple but significant, for it illustrates operations that will appear again and again.

3.10 Example: *Dynamic arrays*

Domain $Array = Nat \rightarrow A$

where A is a domain with an *error* element

Operations

$newarray : Array$

$newarray = \lambda n.\, error$

$access : Nat \times Array \rightarrow A$

$access\,(n, r) = r(n)$

$update : Nat \times A \times Array \rightarrow Array$

$update\,(n, v, r) = [n \mapsto v]r$

A *dynamic array* is an array whose bounds are not restricted, so elements may be inserted into any position of the array. The array uses natural number indexes to access its contents, which are values from A. An empty array is represented by the constant *newarray*. It is a function and it maps all of its index arguments to *error*. The *access* operation indexes its array argument r at position n. Operation *update* creates a new array that behaves just like r when indexed at any position but n. When indexed at position n, the new array produces the value v. Here is the proof:

1. for any $m_0, n_0 \in Nat$ such that $m_0 \neq n_0$,

   $access\,(m_0, update\,(n_0, v, r))$

   $= (update\,(n_0, v, r))(m_0)$ by definition of *access*

   $= ([n_0 \mapsto v]r)(m_0)$ by definition of *update*

   $= (\lambda m.\, m \textit{ equals } n_0 \rightarrow v \,[]\, r(m))(m_0)$ by definition of function updating

   $= m_0 \textit{ equals } n_0 \rightarrow v \,[]\, r(m_0)$ by function application

   $= \textit{false} \rightarrow v \,[]\, r(m_0)$

   $= r(m_0)$

2. $access\,(n_0, update\,(n_0, v, r))$
   $= (update\,(n_0, v, r))(n_0)$
   $= ([n_0 \mapsto v]r)(n_0)$
   $= (\lambda m.\, m \text{ } equals \text{ } n_0 \to v \,[\!]\, r(m))(n_0)$
   $= n_0 \text{ } equals \text{ } n_0 \to v \,[\!]\, r(n_0)$
   $= true \to v \,[\!]\, r(n_0)$
   $= v$

The insight that an array is a function from its index set to its contents set provides interesting new views of many computer data structures.

3.11 Example: *Dynamic array with curried operations*

Domain $Array = Nat \to A$
Operations

$newarray : Array$
$newarray = \lambda n.\, error$

$access : Nat \to Array \to A$
$access = \lambda n.\lambda r.\, r(n)$

$update : Nat \to A \to Array \to Array$
$update = \lambda n.\lambda v.\lambda r.\, [n \mapsto v]r$

This is just Example 3.10 rewritten so that its operations accept their arguments in *curried form*, that is, one argument at a time. The operation $access : Nat \to Array \to A$ has a functionality that is more precisely stated as $access : Nat \to (Array \to A\,)$; that is, the default precedence on the arrow is to the right. We can read *access*'s functionality as saying that *access* takes a *Nat* argument and then takes an *Array* argument to produce an *A*-value. But $access(k)$, for some number k, is itself a well-defined operation of functionality $Array \to A$. When applied to an argument r, operation $access(k)$ looks into position k within r to produce the answer $(access(k))(r)$, which is $r(k)$. The heavily parenthesized expression is hard to read, so we usually write $access(k)(r)$ or $(access\ k\ r)$ instead, assuming that the default precedence of function application is to the left.

Similar conventions apply to *update*. Note that $update : Nat \to A \to Array \to Array$ is an operation that needs a number, a value, and an array to build a new array; $(update\ n')$: $A \to Array \to Array$ is an operation that builds an array updated at index n'; $(update\ n'\ v')$: $Array \to Array$ is an operation that updates an array at position n' with value v'; $(update\ n'\ v'\ r') \in Array$ is an array that behaves just like array r' except at position n', where it has stored the value v'. Curried operations like *access* and *update* are useful for situations where the data values for the operations might be supplied one at a time rather than as a group.

3.2.4 Lifted Domains and Strictness

In Section 2.3 of Chapter 2 the element $\perp$ (read "bottom") was introduced. Its purpose was to represent undefinedness or nontermination. The addition of $\perp$ to a domain can itself be formalized as a domain-building operation.

For domain A, the *lifting* domain builder $(\ )_\perp$ creates the domain $A_\perp$, a collection of the members of A plus an additional distinguished element $\perp$. The elements of A in $A_\perp$ are called *proper elements;* $\perp$ is the *improper element.*

The disassembly operation builder converts an operation on A to one on $A_\perp$; for $(\lambda x.e): A \rightarrow B_\perp$:

$(\underline{\lambda} x.e): A_\perp \rightarrow B_\perp$ is defined as
$(\underline{\lambda} x.e)\perp = \perp$
$(\underline{\lambda} x.e)a = [a/x]e \quad \text{for } a \neq \perp$

An operation that maps a $\perp$ argument to a $\perp$ answer is called *strict*. Operations that map $\perp$ to a proper element are called *nonstrict*. Let's do an example.

$(\underline{\lambda} m.\, zero)((\underline{\lambda} n.\, one)\perp)$
$= (\underline{\lambda} m.\, zero)\perp$, by strictness
$= \perp$

On the other hand, $(\lambda p.\, zero): Nat_\perp \rightarrow Nat_\perp$ is nonstrict, and:

$(\lambda p.\, zero)((\underline{\lambda} n.\, one)\perp)$
$= [(\underline{\lambda} n.\, one)\perp /p]zero$, by the definition of application
$= zero$

In the first example, we must determine whether the argument to $(\underline{\lambda} m.zero)$ is proper or improper before binding it to m. We make the determination by simplifying the argument. If it simplifies to a proper value, we bind it to m; if it simplifies to $\perp$, we take the result of the application to be $\perp$. This style of "argument first" simplification is known as a call-by-value evaluation. It is the safe way of simplifying strict abstractions and their arguments. In the second example, the argument $((\underline{\lambda} n.one)\perp)$ need not be simplified before binding it to p.

We use the following abbreviation:

$(\text{let } x = e_1 \text{ in } e_2)$ for $(\underline{\lambda} x.\, e_2)e_1$

Call this a *let* expression. It makes strict applications more readable because its "argument first" appearance matches the "argument first" simplification strategy that must be used. For example:

1. let $m = (\underline{\lambda} x.\ zero)\bot$ in m *plus one*
   $=$ let $m = zero$ in m *plus one*
   $=$ *zero plus one* $=$ *one*

2. let $m =$ *one plus two* in let $n = (\underline{\lambda} p.\ m)\bot$ in m *plus* n
   $=$ let $m = three$ in let $n = (\underline{\lambda} p.\ m)\bot$ in m *plus* n
   $=$ let $n = (\underline{\lambda} p.\ three)\bot$ in *three plus* n
   $=$ let $n = \bot$ in *three plus* n
   $= \bot$

Here is an example using the lifting construction; it uses the algebra of Example 3.11:

3.12 Example: *Unsafe arrays of unsafe values*

Domain *Unsafe*$= Array_\bot$,
  where $Array = Nat \rightarrow Tr'$ is from Example 3.11
    (A in Example 3.11 becomes Tr')
  and $Tr' = (\mathbb{B} \cup \{error\})_\bot$

Operations

new-unsafe: *Unsafe*
  new-unsafe $=$ *newarray*

access-unsafe: $Nat_\bot \rightarrow Unsafe \rightarrow Tr'$
  access-unsafe $= \underline{\lambda} n.\underline{\lambda} r.\ (access\ \ n\ \ r\ )$

update-unsafe: $Nat_\bot \rightarrow Tr' \rightarrow Unsafe \rightarrow Unsafe$
  update-unsafe $= \underline{\lambda} n.\lambda t.\underline{\lambda} r.\ (update\ \ n\ \ t\ \ r\ )$

The algebra models arrays that contain truth values that may be improper. The constant *new-unsafe* builds a proper array that maps all of its arguments to the *error* value. An array access becomes a tricky business, for either the index or the array argument may be improper. Operation *access-unsafe* must check the definedness of its arguments n and r before it passes them on to *access*, which performs the actual indexing. The operation *update-unsafe* is similarly paranoid, but an improper truth value may be stored into an array. Here is an evaluation of an expression (let $not' = \underline{\lambda} t.\ not(t)$):

let *start-array* $=$ *new-unsafe*
in *update-unsafe*(*one plus two*)($not'(\bot)$)(*start-array*)

$=$ let *start-array* $=$ *newarray*
  in *update-unsafe*(*one plus two*)($not'(\bot)$)(*start-array*)

$= \text{let } \textit{start-array} = (\lambda n.\, \textit{error})$
$\quad \text{in } \textit{update-unsafe}(\textit{one plus two})(\textit{not}'(\bot))(\textit{start-array})$
$= \textit{update-unsafe}(\textit{one plus two})(\textit{not}'(\bot))(\lambda n.\, \textit{error})$
$= \textit{update-unsafe}(\textit{three})(\textit{not}'(\bot))(\lambda n.\, \textit{error})$
$= \textit{update}\,(\textit{three})(\textit{not}'(\bot))(\lambda n.\, \textit{error})$
$= [\textit{three} \mapsto \textit{not}'(\bot)\,]\,(\lambda n.\, \textit{error})$
$= [\textit{three} \mapsto \bot\,]\,(\lambda n.\, \textit{error})$

You should study each step of this simplification sequence and determine where call-by-name and call-by-value simplifications were used.

3.3 RECURSIVE FUNCTION DEFINITIONS

If you read the description of the assembly principle for functions carefully, you will note that the definition $f(x_1, \cdots, x_n) = e$ does *not* permit f itself to appear in e. There is good reason: a recursive definition may not uniquely define a function. Here is an example:

$$q(x) = x \textit{ equals zero} \rightarrow \textit{one} \;[]\; q(x \textit{ plus one})$$

This specification apparently defines a function in $\mathbb{N} \rightarrow \mathbb{N}_\bot$. The following functions all satisfy q's definition in the sense that they have exactly the behavior required by the equation:

$$f_1(x) = \begin{cases} \textit{one} & \text{if } x = \textit{zero} \\ \bot & \text{otherwise} \end{cases}$$

$$f_2(x) = \begin{cases} \textit{one} & \text{if } x = \textit{zero} \\ \textit{two} & \text{otherwise} \end{cases}$$

$$f_3(x) = \textit{one}$$

and there are infinitely many others. Routine substitution verifies that f_3 is a meaning of q:

for any $n \in \textit{Nat}$, $n \textit{ equals zero} \rightarrow \textit{one} \;[]\; f_3(n \textit{ plus one})$
$= n \textit{ equals zero} \rightarrow \textit{one} \;[]\; \textit{one}$ by the definition of f_3
$= \textit{one}$ by the definition of the choice function
$= f_3(n)$

Similar derivations also show that f_1 and f_2 are meanings of q. So which of these functions does q really stand for, if any? Unfortunately, the tools as currently developed are not sophisticated enough to answer this question. The problem will be dealt with in Chapter 6, because recursive function definitions are essential for defining the semantics of iterative and recursive constructs.

Perhaps when you were reading the above paragraph, you felt that much ado was made about nothing. After all, the specification of q could be typed into a computer, and surely the computer would compute function f_1. However, the computer gives an *operational semantics* to the specification, treating it as a program, and the function expressions in this chapter are mathematical values, not programs. It is clearly important that we use only those function expressions that stand for unique values. For this reason, recursive function specifications are suspect.

On the positive side, it is possible to show that functions defined recursively over abstract syntax arguments *do* denote unique functions. Structural induction comes to the rescue. We examine this specific subcase because denotational definitions utilize functions that are recursively defined over abstract syntax.

The following construction is somewhat technical and artificial, but it is sufficient for achieving the goal. Let a language L be defined by BNF equations:

$$\begin{aligned} &\mathrm{B}_1 ::= Option_{11} \mid Option_{12} \mid \cdots \mid Option_{1m} \\ &\mathrm{B}_2 ::= Option_{21} \mid Option_{22} \mid \cdots \mid Option_{2m} \\ &\cdots \\ &\mathrm{B}_n ::= Option_{n1} \mid Option_{n2} \mid \cdots \mid Option_{nm} \end{aligned}$$

and let $\mathbf{B}_i$ be a function symbol of type $\mathrm{B}_i \rightarrow D_i$ for all $1 \leqslant i \leqslant n$. For an $Option_{ij}$, let $\mathrm{S}_{ij1}, \mathrm{S}_{ij2}, \cdots, \mathrm{S}_{ijk}$ be the nonterminal symbols used in $Option_{ij}$, and let $\mathbf{B}_{ijl}$ represent the $\mathbf{B}_l$ appropriate for each S_{ijl} (for example, if $\mathrm{S}_{ijl} = \mathrm{B}_p$, then $\mathbf{B}_{ijl} = \mathbf{B}_p$).

3.13 Theorem:

If, for each B_i *in L's definition and each* $Option_{ij}$ *of* B_i*'s rule, there exists an equation of form:*

$$\mathbf{B}_i(Option_{ij}) = f_{ij}(\mathbf{B}_{ij1}(\mathrm{S}_{ij1}), \mathbf{B}_{ij2}(\mathrm{S}_{ij2}), \cdots, \mathbf{B}_{ijk}(\mathrm{S}_{ijk}))$$

where f_{ij} *is a function of functionality* $D_{ij1} \times D_{ij2} \times \cdots \times D_{ijk} \rightarrow D_i$, *then the set of equations uniquely defines a family of functions* $\mathbf{B}_i : \mathrm{B}_i \rightarrow D_i$ *for* $1 \leqslant i \leqslant n$.

Proof: The proof is by a simultaneous structural induction on the rules of L. We show that each $\mathbf{B}_i(Option_{ij})$ is uniquely defined for a syntax tree of form $Option_{ij}$. Let $\mathbf{B}_i(Option_{ij})$ be defined as above. By the inductive hypothesis, for $1 \leqslant l \leqslant k$, each $\mathbf{B}_{ijl}(\mathrm{S}_{ijl})$ is uniquely defined. Since f_{ij} is a function, its application to the $\mathbf{B}_{ijl}(\mathrm{S}_{ijl})$'s yields a unique answer, so $\mathbf{B}_i(Option_{ij})$ is uniquely defined. The equations for all the $Option_{ij}$'s of rule B_i taken together define a unique function $\mathbf{B}_i : \mathrm{B}_i \rightarrow D_i$. □

3.4 RECURSIVE DOMAIN DEFINITIONS

We have used an equation format for naming semantic domains. For example, $Payroll\text{-}record = String \times Rat \times Rat$ associates the name *Payroll-record* with a product domain. In later chapters, we will see that certain programming language features require domains whose structure is defined in terms of themselves. For example, $Alist = Unit + (A \times Alist)$ defines a domain of linear lists of A-elements. Like the recursively defined operations mentioned in the previous section, a domain may not be uniquely defined by a recursive definition.

What's more, equations such as $F = F \rightarrow Nat$, specifying the collection of functions that accept themselves as arguments to produce numeric answers, apparently have no solution at all! (It is not difficult to show that the cardinality of the collection of all functions from F to Nat is larger than F's cardinality.) Chapter 11 provides a method for developing solutions to recursive domain definitions.

3.5 SUMMARY

Here is a summary of the domain constructions and their operations that were covered in this chapter.

1. *Domain construction*: primitive domain, e.g., natural numbers, truth values

   Operation builders: the operations and constants that are presented in the semantic algebra. For example, the choice function is presented with the *Tr* algebra; it is $(e_1 \rightarrow e_2 [\!]\, e_3) \in A$, for $e_1 \in \mathbb{B}$, $e_2, e_3 \in A$.

   Simplification properties: as dictated by the definition of the operations, e.g., *not*(*true*) simplifies to *false* because the pair (*true*, *false*) is found in the graph of the operation *not*. The simplification properties of the choice function are:
   $true \rightarrow e_2 [\!]\, e_3 = e_2$
   $false \rightarrow e_2 [\!]\, e_3 = e_3$

2. Domain construction: product space $A \times B$

   Operation builders:
   $fst : A \times B \rightarrow A$
   $snd : A \times B \rightarrow B$
   $(a, b) \in A \times B$ for $a \in A$ and $b \in B$
   $\downarrow i : A_1 \times A_2 \times \cdots \times A_i \times \cdots \times A_n \rightarrow A_i$, for $1 \leqslant i \leqslant n$

Simplification properties:
$fst(a, b) = a$
$snd(a, b) = b$
$(a_1, a_2, \cdots, a_i, \cdots, a_n)\downarrow i = a_i$, for $1 \leqslant i \leqslant n$

3. Domain construction: disjoint union (sum) space $A + B$

Operation builders:
$\text{in}A : A \to A + B$
$\text{in}B : B \to A + B$
$(\text{cases } d \text{ of is}A(x) \to e_1 \,\square\, \text{is}B(y) \to e_2 \text{ end}) \in C$
for $d \in A+B$, $(\lambda x.e_1): A \to C$, and $(\lambda y.e_2): B \to C$

Simplification properties:
$(\text{cases in}A(a) \text{ of is}A(x) \to e_1 \,\square\, \text{is}B(y) \to e_2 \text{ end}) = [a/x]e_1$
$(\text{cases in}B(b) \text{ of is}A(x) \to e_1 \,\square\, \text{is}B(y) \to e_2 \text{ end}) = [b/y]e_2$

3a. Domain construction: list space A^*

Operation builders:
$nil : A^*$
$cons : A \times A^* \to A^*$
$hd : A^* \to A$
$tl : A^* \to A^*$
$null : A^* \to Tr$

Simplification properties:
$hd(a \; cons \; l) = a$
$tl(a \; cons \; l) = l$
$null(nil) = true$
$null(a \; cons \; l) = false$

4. Domain construction: function space $A \to B$

Operation builders:
$(\lambda x.e) \in A \to B$ such that for all $a \in A$, $[a/x]e$ has a unique value in B.
$g(a) \in B$, for $g : A \to B$ and $a \in A$

$(g\ a)$ abbreviates $g(a)$
$[\,x \mapsto v\,]g$ abbreviates $(\lambda x'.\, x' \; equals \; x \to v \,\square\, g(x'))$
$[a/x]e$ denotes the substitution of expression a for all free occurrences of identifier x in expression e

Simplification properties:
$g(a) = [a/x]e$, where g is defined equationally as $g(x) = e$
$(\lambda x.\, e)a = [a/x]e$
$([\, x \mapsto v\,]g\,)x = v$
$([\, x \mapsto v\,]g\,)y = g(y)$, where $y \neq x$

5. Domain construction: lifted space $A_\perp$

Operation builder:
$(\underline{\lambda} x.\, e) : A_\perp \to B_\perp$, for $(\lambda x.\, e) : A \to B_\perp$

(let $x = e_1$ in e_2) abbreviates $(\underline{\lambda} x.\, e_2)e_1$
(Note: the above expression occasionally abbreviates $(\lambda x.e_2)e_1$ when $e_1 \in A$ and A is an *unlifted* domain; that is, A has no $\perp$ element.)

Simplification properties:
$(\underline{\lambda} x.\, e_2)e_1 = [e_1/x]e_2$, when e_1 is a proper member of $A_\perp$, i.e., $e_1 \neq \perp$
$(\underline{\lambda} x.\, e)\perp = \perp$
(let $x = e_1$ in e_2) $= [e_1/x]e_2$, when e_1 is a proper member of $A_\perp$
(let $x = \perp$ in e) $= \perp$

SUGGESTED READINGS

Semantic domains: Gordon 1979; Scott 1976, 1982; Stoy 1977; Strachey 1973; Tennent 1981
Semantic algebras: Bauer & Wossner 1982; Burstall & Goguen 1977, 1981; Cohn 1981; Gratzer 1979; Mosses 1979a, 1983, 1984

EXERCISES

1. Given the algebras of natural numbers and truth values, simplify the following expressions. Show all the steps in your simplification.

   a. ((*six equals* (*two plus one*)) $\to$ *one* [] (*three minus one*)) *plus two*
   b. (*two equals* (*true* $\to$ *one* [] *two*)) *and true*
   c. *not*(*false*) $\to$ *not*(*true*) [] *not*(*true*)

2. Define primitive semantic algebras for each of the following:

   a. The musical notes playable on a piano.
   b. The U.S. (or your favorite) monetary system.
   c. The "colors of the rainbow."

3. Using the operations defined in Section 3.5, simplify the following (note that we use identifiers $m,n \in Nat$, $t \in Tr$, $p \in Tr \times Tr$, $r \in Tr+Nat$, and $x,y \in Nat_\bot$):

   a. $fst((\lambda m.zero)two, (\lambda n.n))$
   b. $(\lambda p.(snd\ p, fst\ p))(true, (two\ equals\ one))$
   c. $((\lambda r.$ cases r of
      is$Tr(t) \rightarrow (\lambda m'.\ zero)$
      $[]$ is$Nat(n) \rightarrow (\lambda m.\ n)$
      end)(in$Nat(two)$))(one)
   d. cases $(false \rightarrow$ in$Nat(one)\ []$ in$Tr(false))$ of
      is$Tr(t) \rightarrow true\ or\ t$
      $[]$ is$Nat(n) \rightarrow false$ end
   e. $(\lambda x.\lambda y.y(x))(one)(\lambda n.\ n\ plus\ two)$
   f. $((\underline{\lambda n}.[\ zero \mapsto n](\lambda m.\ zero))(two))\ zero$
   g. $(\lambda x.\ (\lambda m.\ m\ equals\ zero \rightarrow x\ []\ one)(two))(\bot)$
   h. $(\underline{\lambda m}.\ one)(true \rightarrow \bot\ []\ zero)$
   i. $(\lambda(x, y).\ (y, x))(\bot, (\underline{\lambda n}.\ one)\bot)$
   j. let $m = \bot$ in $zero$
   k. let $m = one\ plus\ two$ in let $n = m\ plus\ one$ in $(\lambda m.\ n)$
   l. let $m = (\lambda x.\ x)zero$ in let $n = (m\ equals\ zero \rightarrow one\ []\ \bot)$ in $m\ plus\ n$
   m. let $m = one$ in let $m = m\ plus\ two$ in m

4. Let $Tr = \{\ tt, ff\ \}$. List all the elements in these domains:

   a. $Unit + ((Tr \times Tr)_\bot)$
   b. $(Unit + (Tr \times Tr))_\bot$
   c. $(Unit_\bot + (Tr_\bot \times Tr_\bot))$
   d. $(Unit + Tr) \times Tr$
   e. $Unit \rightarrow Tr_\bot$
   f. $(Unit \rightarrow Tr)_\bot$

5. a. Complete the definition of the algebra in Example 3.7 by defining these operations:

      i. *update-payrate* : *Rat* × *Payroll-rec* → *Payroll-rec*
      ii. *update-hours* : *Rat* × *Payroll-rec* → *Payroll-rec*

   b. Use the completed algebra to define a payroll record stating that

      i. "Jane Doe" has been assigned a payroll record.
      ii. She is moved to the night shift.
      iii. She works 38 hours that week.

iv. Her payrate goes to 9.00.

Next, write an expression denoting Jane Doe's pay for the week.

c. What other operations should this algebra possess to make it more useful for defining the semantics of a payroll system?

6. Using the algebra of Example 3.9, simplify these list-valued expressions:

a. $(hd(one\ cons\ nil)\ cons\ nil)$
b. $(\lambda l.\,(null\ l) \rightarrow (zero\ cons\ nil)\ [\!]\ (one\ cons\ nil))(tl(one\ cons\ nil))$
c. $((one\ cons\ (two\ cons\ nil))\ cons\ nil)$
d. $(\lambda l.\,tl\ l)(tl(zero\ cons\ nil))$

7. Design an algebra called *Set-of-A* (where A is any primitive domain) with operations:

$empty\text{-}set : Set\text{-}of\text{-}A$
$make\text{-}singleton : A \rightarrow Set\text{-}of\text{-}A$
$member\text{-}of : A \times Set\text{-}of\text{-}A \rightarrow Tr$
$union : Set\text{-}of\text{-}A \times Set\text{-}of\text{-}A \rightarrow Set\text{-}of\text{-}A$

The operations are to satisfy the expected set theoretic properties, e.g., for all $a \in A$, $member\text{-}of(a, make\text{-}singleton(a)) = true$. (Hint: use the domain $A \rightarrow Tr$ in the definition.)

8. Modify the dynamic array algebra of Example 3.11 so that arrays carry with them upper and lower bounds. The operations are altered so that:

a. $newarray : Nat \times Nat \rightarrow Array$ establishes an empty array with lower and upper bounds set to the values of the two arguments.
b. *access* and *update* both compare their index argument against the lower and upper bounds of their array argument. (Hint: use $Array = (Nat \rightarrow A) \times Nat \times Nat$.)

9. Use the algebra of payroll records in Example 3.6 and the array of Example 3.11 to derive an algebra describing data bases of payroll records. A data base indexes employees by identity numbers. Operations must include ones for:

a. Adding a new employee to a data base.
b. Updating an employee's statistics.
c. Producing a list of employee paychecks for all the employees of a data base.

10. Specify algebras that would be useful for defining the semantics of the grocery store inventory system that is mentioned in Exercise 6 of Chapter 1.

11. a. Describe the graphs of the following operations:

    i. $(\_ \rightarrow a \,\square\, b) : \mathbb{B} \rightarrow D$, for $a, b \in D$

    ii. $fst : A \times B \rightarrow A$ and $snd : A \times B \rightarrow B$

    iii. $\text{in}A : A \rightarrow A + B$, $\text{in}B : B \rightarrow A + B$, and $(\text{cases}\ \_\ \text{of is}A(a) \rightarrow f(a)\ \square\ \text{is}B(b) \rightarrow g(b)\ \text{end}) : A + B \rightarrow C$, for $f: A \rightarrow C$ and $g : B \rightarrow C$

    iv. $(\lambda x. E) : A \rightarrow B$, for expression E such that for all $a \in A$, $[a/x]E$ is a unique value in B

    v. $(\underline{\lambda} x. E) : A_\perp \rightarrow B_\perp$, for $(\lambda x. E) : A \rightarrow B_\perp$

    b. Using the definitions in part a, prove that the simplification rules in Section 3.5 are *sound*; that is, for each equality $L = R$, prove that the set-theoretic value of L equals the set-theoretic value of R. (Note: most of the proofs will be trivial, but they are still well worth doing, for they justify all of the derivations in the rest of the book!)

Prove it Exists, prove it is unique

12. The assembly and disassembly operations of compound domains were chosen because they possess certain *universal properties* (the term is taken from *category theory*; see Herrlich and Strecker 1973). Prove the following universal properties:

    a. For arbitrary functions $g_1: C \rightarrow A$ and $g_2: C \rightarrow B$, there exists a unique function $f: C \rightarrow A \times B$ such that $fst \circ f = g_1$ and $snd \circ f = g_2$.

    b. For arbitrary functions $g_1: A \rightarrow C$ and $g_2: B \rightarrow C$, there exists a unique function $f: A + B \rightarrow C$ such that $f \circ \text{in}A = g_1$ and $f \circ \text{in}B = g_2$.

    c. For arbitrary function $g: A \times B \rightarrow C$, there exists a unique function $f: A \rightarrow B \rightarrow C$ such that $(f(a))(b) = g(a, b)$.

    d. For arbitrary function $g: A \rightarrow B_\perp$, there exists a unique function $f: A_\perp \rightarrow B_\perp$ such that $f(\perp) = \perp$ and $f(a) = g(a)$, for $a \in A$.

13. The function notation defined in this chapter is a descendant of a symbol manipulation system known as the *lambda calculus*. The abstract syntax of lambda expressions is defined as:

    $$\text{E} ::= (\text{E}_1\ \text{E}_2) \mid (\lambda\text{I.E}) \mid \text{I}$$

    Lambda expressions are simplified using the β-rule:

    $$((\lambda\text{I.E}_1)\text{E}_2) \Rightarrow [\,\text{E}_2/\text{I}\,]\text{E}_1$$

    which says that an occurrence of $((\lambda\text{I.E}_1)\text{E}_2)$ in a lambda expression can be rewritten to $[\,\text{E}_2/\text{I}\,]\text{E}_1$ in the expression. All bound identifiers in E_1 are renamed so as not to clash with the free identifiers in E_2. We write $M \Rightarrow^* N$ if M rewrites to N due to zero or more applications of the β-rule.

    a. Using the β-rule, simplify the following expressions to a final (*normal*) form, if one exists. If one does not exist, explain why.

i. $((\lambda x.\,(x\,y))(\lambda z.\,z)$
ii. $((\lambda x.\,((\lambda y.\,(x\,y))x))(\lambda z.\,w))$
iii. $((((\lambda f.\,(\lambda g.\,(\lambda x.\,((f\,x)(g\,x)))))(\lambda m.(\lambda n.\,(n\,m))))(\lambda n.\,z))p)$
iv. $((\lambda x.(x\,x))\,(\lambda x.\,(x\,x)))$
v. $((\lambda f.\,((\lambda g.\,((f\,f)\,g))(\lambda h.\,(k\,h))))(\lambda x.\,(\lambda y.y)))$
vi. $(\lambda g.\,((\lambda f.\,((\lambda x.(f\,(x\,x)))\,(\lambda x.\,(f\,(x\,x)))))\,g))$

b. In addition to the β-rule, the lambda calculus includes the following two rules:

$$\alpha\text{-}rule: \quad (\lambda x.E) \Rightarrow (\lambda y.\,[y/x]E)$$
$$\eta\text{-}rule: \quad (\lambda x.\,(E\,x)) \Rightarrow E \text{ where } x \text{ does not occur free in } E$$

Redo the simplifications of i-vi in a, making use of the η-rule whenever possible. What value do you see in the α-rule?

c. A famous result regarding the lambda calculus is that it can be used to simulate computation on truth values and numbers.

i. Let **true** be the name of the lambda expression $(\lambda x.\lambda y.\,x)$ and let **false** be the name of the lambda expression $(\lambda x.\lambda y.\,y)$. Show that $((\mathbf{true}\,E_1)\,E_2) \Rightarrow^* E_1$ and $((\mathbf{false}\,E_1)\,E_2) \Rightarrow^* E_2$. Define lambda expressions **not**, **and**, and **or** that behave like their Boolean operation counterparts, e.g., $(\mathbf{not\ true}) \Rightarrow^* \mathbf{false}$, $((\mathbf{or\ false})\mathbf{true}) \Rightarrow^* \mathbf{true}$, and so on.

ii. Let **0** be the name of the lambda expression $(\lambda x.\lambda y.y)$, **1** be the name of the expression $(\lambda x.\lambda y.(x\,y))$, **2** be the name of the expression $(\lambda x.\lambda y.(x(x\,y)))$, **3** be the name of the expression $(\lambda x.\lambda y.(x(x(x\,y))))$, and so on. Prove that the lambda expression **succ** defined as $(\lambda z.\lambda x.\lambda y.(x\,((z\,x)\,y)))$ rewrites a number to its successor, that is, $(\mathbf{succ\ n}) \Rightarrow^* \mathbf{n{+}1}$. There also exists a lambda expression **pred** such that $(\mathbf{pred\ 0}) \Rightarrow^* \mathbf{0}$ and $(\mathbf{pred\ n{+}1}) \Rightarrow^* \mathbf{n}$ (but we won't give it here, as it is somewhat ungainly).

d. Recursively defined functions can also be simulated in the lambda calculus. First, let **Y** be the name of the expression $(\lambda f.\,((\lambda x.\,(f\,(x\,x)))\,(\lambda x.\,(f\,(x\,x)))))$.

i. Show that for any expression E, there exists an expression W such that $(\mathbf{Y}\,E) \Rightarrow^* (W\,W)$, and that $(W\,W) \Rightarrow^* (E\,(W\,W))$. Hence, $(\mathbf{Y}\,E) \Rightarrow^* E(E(E(\cdots E(W\,W)\cdots)))$.

ii. Using the lambda expressions that you defined in the previous parts of this exercise, define a recursive lambda expression **add** that performs addition on the numbers defined in part ii of b, that is, $((\mathbf{add\ m})\,\mathbf{n}) \Rightarrow^* \mathbf{m{+}n}$. (Hint: first define an expression **IF** such that $(((\mathbf{IF\ 0})\,E_1)\,E_2) \Rightarrow^* E_1$ and $(((\mathbf{IF\ n{+}1})\,E_1)\,E_2) \Rightarrow^* E_2$.) Say that your definition of **add** has the form $\mathbf{add} = \lambda x.\lambda y.\ \cdots \mathbf{add} \cdots$. Let **ADD** be the lambda expression $(\mathbf{Y}\,(\lambda h.\lambda x.\lambda y.\ \cdots h \cdots))$. Show that $((\mathbf{ADD\ m})\,\mathbf{n}) \Rightarrow^* \mathbf{m{+}n}$.

14. a. Give examples of recursive definitions of the form $n = \cdots n \cdots$ that have no solution; have multiple solutions; have exactly one solution.
    b. State requirements under which a recursively defined function $f: Nat \to A$ has a unique solution. Use mathematical induction to prove your claim. Next, generalize your answer for recursively defined functions $g: A^* \to B$. How do your requirements resemble the requirements used to prove Theorem 3.13?

15. Show that each of the following recursively defined sets has a solution.

    a. $Nlist = Unit + (\mathbb{N} \times Nlist)$
    b. $N = Unit + N$
    c. $A = A$
    d. $Blist = \mathbb{B} \times Blist$.

    Do any of them have a unique solution?

Chapter 4

Basic Structure of Denotational Definitions

This chapter presents the format for denotational definitions. We use the abstract syntax and semantic algebra formats to define the appearance and the meaning of a language. The two are connected by a function called the *valuation function*. After giving an informal presentation of an application of the valuation function, we present the denotational semantics of two simple languages.

4.1 THE VALUATION FUNCTION

The valuation function maps a language's abstract syntax structures to meanings drawn from semantic domains. The domain of a valuation function is the set of derivation trees of a language. The valuation function is defined structurally. It determines the meaning of a derivation tree by determining the meanings of its subtrees and combining them into a meaning for the entire tree.

Some illustrations will make this point better than just words. A sentence in the language of binary numerals is depicted in Diagram 4.1.

(4.1)

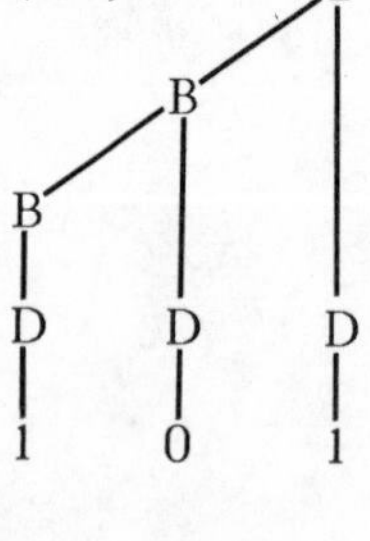

(4.2)

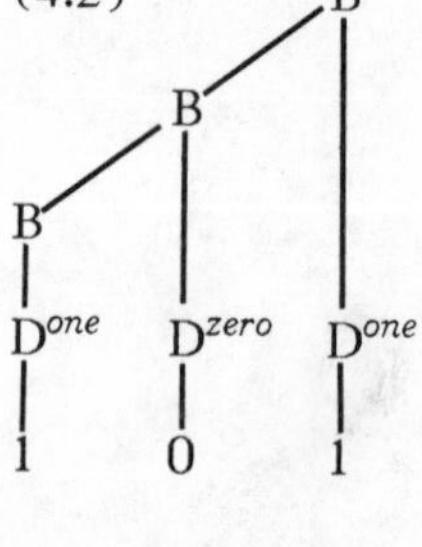

The tree's internal nodes represent nonterminals in the language's abstract syntax definition:

B∈ Binary-numeral
D∈ Binary-digit
B ::= BD | D
D ::= 0 | 1

For this example, we take the somewhat artificial view that the individual binary digits are the "words" of a binary numeral "sentence."

The valuation function assigns a meaning to the tree by assigning meanings to its subtrees. We will actually use two valuation functions: **D**, which maps binary digits to their meanings, and **B**, which maps binary numerals to their meanings. The distinct valuation functions make the semantic definition easier to formulate and read.

Let's determine the meaning of the tree in Diagram 4.1 in a "bottom-up" fashion. First, the meaning of the digit subtree:

```
D
|
0
```

is the number *zero*. We might state this as:

```
D( D ) = zero
   |
   0
```

That is, the **D** valuation function maps the tree to its meaning, *zero*. Similarly, the meanings of the other binary digits in the tree are *one*; that is:

```
D ( D ) = one
    |
    1
```

We will find it convenient to represent these two-dimensional equations in one-dimensional form, and we write:

$\mathbf{D}[\![0]\!] = \textit{zero}$
$\mathbf{D}[\![1]\!] = \textit{one}$

The double brackets surrounding the subtrees are used to clearly separate the syntax pieces from the semantic notation. The linearized form omits the D nonterminal. This isn't a problem, as the **D** valuation function maps only binary digits to meanings— D's presence is implied by **D**'s.

To help us note our progress in determining the meaning of the tree, Diagram 4.2 shows the meanings placed next to the nonterminal nodes. Now that we know the meanings of the binary digit subtrees, we next determine the meanings of the binary numeral trees. Looking at the leftmost B-tree, we see it has the form:

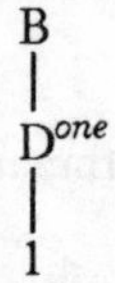

The meaning of this tree is just the meaning of its D-subtree, that is, *one*. In general, for any unary binary numeral subtree:

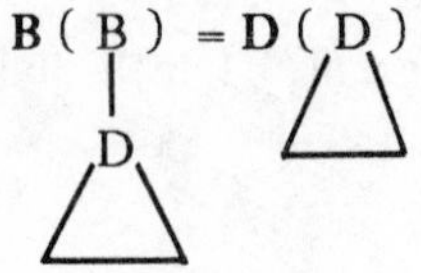

that is, **B**[[D]] = **D**[[D]]. Diagram 4.3 displays the new information.

(4.3)

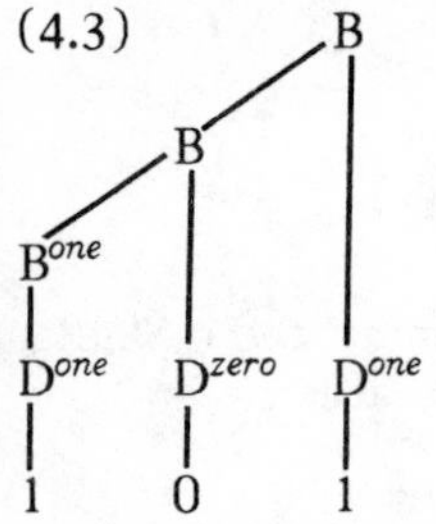

(4.4)

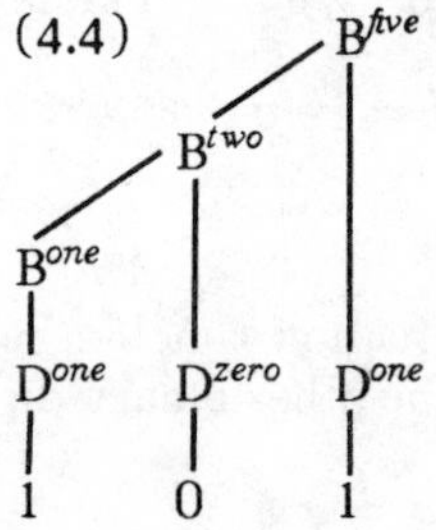

The other form of the binary numeral tree is:

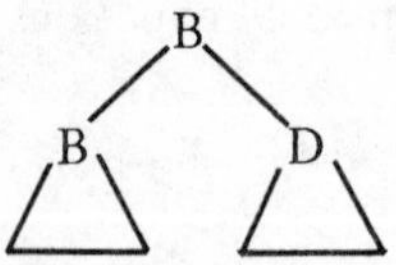

The principle of binary arithmetic dictates that the meaning of this tree must be the meaning of the left subtree doubled and added to the meaning of the right subtree. We write this as **B**[[BD]] = (**B**[[B]] *times two*) *plus* **D**[[D]]. Using this definition we complete the calculation of the meaning of the tree. The result, *five*, is shown in Diagram 4.4.

Since we have defined the mappings of the valuation functions on all of the options listed in the BNF rules for binary numerals, the valuation functions are completely defined.

We can also determine the meaning of the tree in Diagram 4.1 in a "top-down" fashion. The valuation functions are applied to the tree in Diagrams 4.5 through 4.8 and again show that its meaning is *five*.

(4.5)

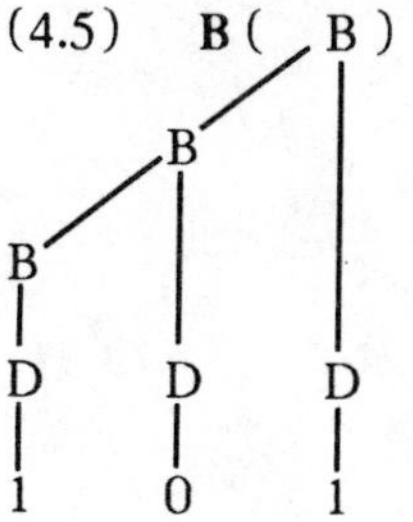

(4.6)

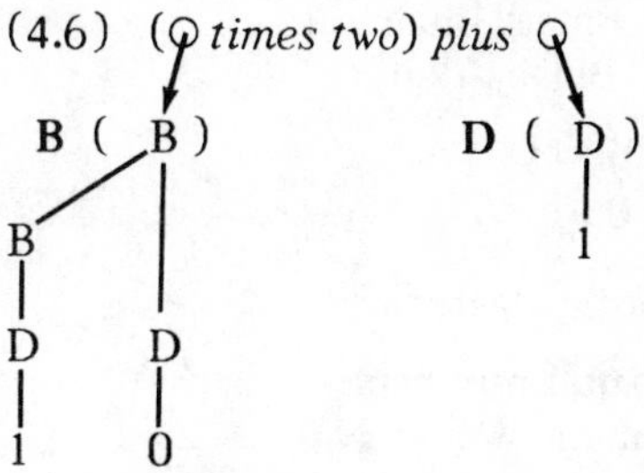

(4.7)

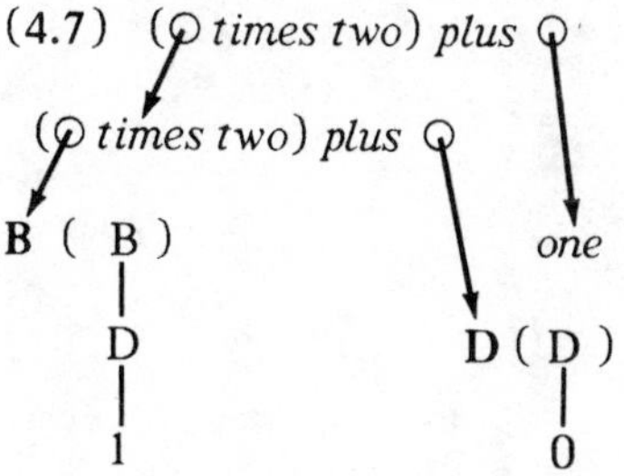

(4.8)

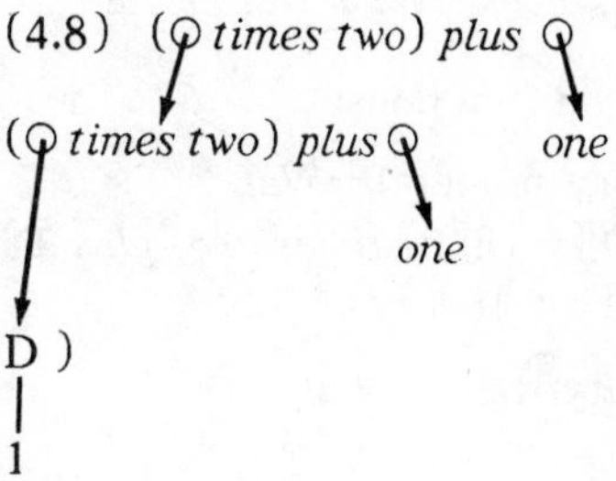

4.2 FORMAT OF A DENOTATIONAL DEFINITION

A *denotational definition* of a language consists of three parts: the abstract syntax definition of the language, the semantic algebras, and the valuation function. As we saw in the previous section, the valuation function is actually a collection of functions, one for each syntax domain. A valuation function **D** for a syntax domain D is listed as a set of equations, one per option in the corresponding BNF rule for D.

Figure 4.1 gives the denotational definition of binary numerals.

The syntax domains are the ones we saw in the previous section. Only one semantic algebra is needed— the algebra of natural numbers *Nat*. Operations *minus* and *div* are not listed in the algebra, because they aren't used in the valuation functions.

It is instructive to determine once again the meaning of the tree in Diagram 4.1. We represent the tree in its linear form ⟦101⟧, using the double brackets to

Figure 4.1

Abstract syntax:

B∈ Binary-numeral
D∈ Binary-digit

B ::= BD | D
D ::= 0 | 1

Semantic algebras:

I. Natural numbers
Domain *Nat* = ℕ
Operations
zero, one, two, $\cdots$: *Nat*
plus, times : *Nat* × *Nat* → *Nat*

Valuation functions:

B: Binary-numeral → *Nat*
B⟦BD⟧ = (**B**⟦B⟧ *times two*) *plus* **D**⟦D⟧
B⟦D⟧ = **D**⟦D⟧

D: Binary-digit → *Nat*
D⟦0⟧ = *zero*
D⟦1⟧ = *one*

---

remind us that it is indeed a tree. We begin with:

B⟦101⟧ = (**B**⟦10⟧ *times two*) *plus* **D**⟦1⟧

The **B**⟦BD⟧ equation of the **B** function divides ⟦101⟧ into its subparts. The linear representation of ⟦101⟧ may not make it clear how to split the numeral into its two subparts. When in doubt, check back with the derivation tree! Checking back, we see that the division was performed correctly. We continue:

(**B**⟦10⟧ *times two*) *plus* **D**⟦1⟧
= (((**B**⟦1⟧ *times two*) *plus* **D**⟦0⟧) *times two*) *plus* **D**⟦1⟧
= (((**D**⟦1⟧ *times two*) *plus* **D**⟦0⟧) *times two*) *plus* **D**⟦1⟧
= (((*one times two*) *plus zero*) *times two*) *plus one*
= *five*

The derivation mimics the top-down tree transformation seen earlier.

The "bottom-up" method also maps ⟦101⟧ to *five*. We write a system of equations that defines the meanings of each of the subtrees in the tree:

D⟦0⟧ = *zero*
D⟦1⟧ = *one*
B⟦1⟧ = D⟦1⟧
B⟦10⟧ = (B⟦1⟧ *times two*) *plus* D⟦0⟧
B⟦101⟧ = (B⟦10⟧ *times two*) *plus* D⟦1⟧

If we treat each D⟦d⟧ and B⟦b⟧ as a variable name as in algebra, we can solve the simultaneous set of equations:

D⟦0⟧ = *zero*
D⟦1⟧ = *one*
B⟦1⟧ = *one*
B⟦10⟧ = *two*
B⟦101⟧ = *five*

Again, we see that the meaning of the tree is *five*.

4.3 A CALCULATOR LANGUAGE

A calculator is a good example of a processor that accepts programs in a simple language as input and produces simple, tangible output. The programs are entered by pressing buttons on the device, and the output appears on a display screen. Consider the calculator pictured in Figure 4.2. It is an inexpensive model with a single "memory cell" for retaining a numeric value. There is also a conditional evaluation feature, which allows the user to enter a form of if-then-else expression.

A sample session with the calculator might go:

```
press  ON
press  ( 4 + 1 2 ) * 2
press  TOTAL                 (the calculator prints 32)
press  1 + LASTANSWER
press  TOTAL                 (the calculator prints 33)
press  IF LASTANSWER + 1 , 0 , 2 + 4
press  TOTAL                 (the calculator prints 6)
press  OFF
```

The calculator's memory cell automatically remembers the value of the previous expression calculated so the value can be used in a later expression. The

Figure 4.2

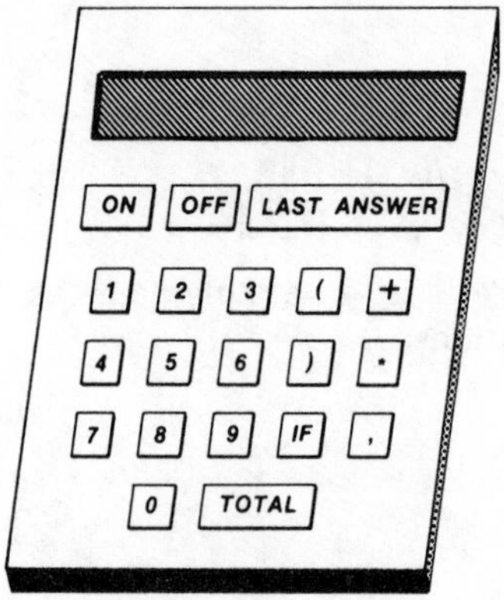

IF and , keys are used to build a conditional expression that chooses its second or third argument to evaluate based upon whether the value of the first is zero or nonzero. An excellent way of understanding the proper use of the calculator is to study the denotational semantics of its input language, which is given in Figure 4.3.

The abstract syntax indicates that a session with the calculator consists of pressing the ON key and entering an expression sequence. An *expression sequence* is one or more expressions, separated by occurrences of TOTAL, terminated by the OFF key. The syntax for an expression follows the usual abstract syntax for arithmetic. Since the words of the language are numerals, no BNF rule is given for the syntax domain Numeral.

The semantic algebras show that the calculator reasons with two kinds of semantic objects: truth values and natural numbers. The phrase $n \in Nat$ in the *Nat* algebra's definition reminds us that all occurrences of identifier n in the valuation equations stand for an element of domain *Nat*. The same holds for the phrase $t \in Tr$. This convention is used in all the remaining semantic definitions in this book.

We can learn much about the calculator language from its semantic algebras. Apparently, the members of *Nat* will be the meanings of numerals and expressions in the calculator language, but *Tr* has no obvious representation of its elements in the syntax. This suggests that the calculator has some internal mechanism for doing logical reasoning, but the full power of that mechanism is not given to the user. This is confirmed by the presence of the *equals* operation in the algebra for *Nat*; the calculator can do arithmetic comparisons, but no

Figure 4.3

Abstract syntax:

P∈ Program
S∈ Expr-sequence
E∈ Expression
N∈ Numeral

P ::= ON S
S ::= E TOTAL S | E TOTAL OFF
E ::= E_1+E_2 | E_1*E_2 | IF E_1 , E_2 , E_3 | LASTANSWER | (E) | N

Semantic algebras:

I. Truth values
Domain $t \in Tr = \mathbb{B}$
Operations
true, false: *Tr*

II. Natural numbers
Domain $n \in Nat$
Operations
zero, one, two, · · · : *Nat*
plus, times : *Nat* × *Nat* → *Nat*
equals : *Nat* × *Nat* → *Tr*

Valuation functions:

P: Program→Nat^*
P⟦ON S⟧ = **S**⟦S⟧(*zero*)

S: Expr-sequence→*Nat* →Nat^*
S⟦E TOTAL S⟧(n) = let n'= **E**⟦E⟧(n) in n' *cons* **S**⟦S⟧(n')
S⟦E TOTAL OFF⟧(n) = **E**⟦E⟧(n) *cons nil*

E: Expression→*Nat* →*Nat*
E⟦E_1+E_2⟧(n) = **E**⟦E_1⟧(n) *plus* **E**⟦E_2⟧(n)
E⟦E_1*E_2⟧(n) = **E**⟦E_1⟧(n) *times* **E**⟦E_2⟧(n)
E⟦IF E_1 , E_2 , E_3⟧(n) = **E**⟦E_1⟧(n) *equals zero* → **E**⟦E_2⟧(n) [] **E**⟦E_3⟧(n)
E⟦LASTANSWER⟧(n) = n
E⟦(E)⟧(n) = **E**⟦E⟧(n)
E⟦N⟧(n) = **N**⟦N⟧

N: Numeral→*Nat* (omitted— maps numeral N to corresponding $n \in Nat$)

---

comparison operator is included in the syntax. Therefore, we must take care to understand the syntactic construct whose semantic equation utilizes the *equals* operation.

There are four valuation functions for the language:

P: Program→*Nat* *
S: Expr-sequence→*Nat* →*Nat* *
E: Expression→*Nat* →*Nat*
N: Numeral→*Nat*

A good part of the calculator's semantics can be understood from studying the functionalities of the valuation functions. The **P** function maps a program to its meaning, which is a list of natural numbers. The reason for using the codomain *Nat* * is found from the syntax: a program has the form [[ON S]], where [[S]] stands for a sequence of expressions. If each expression has a numeric value, then a sequence of them is list of numbers. The list represents the sequence of outputs displayed by the calculator during a session. This is confirmed by the functionality of **S**, which maps an expression sequence and a number to the desired number list. But what is the extra number used for? Recall that the calculator has a memory cell, which retains the value of the most recently evaluated expression. The number is the value in the memory cell. Perhaps the functionality should be written:

S: Expr-sequence→*Memory-cell* →*Nat* *, where *Memory-cell* = *Nat*

Two important features of denotational definitions are expressed in **S**'s functionality. First, the global data structures in a language's processor can be modelled as arguments to the valuation functions. There are no "global variables" for functions, so all such structures must be specified as arguments so that they are of use in the semantics. Second, the meaning of a syntactic construct can be a function. **S**'s functionality states that "the meaning of an expression sequence is a function from a memory cell to a list of numbers." This seems confusing, for we might think that the meaning of an expression sequence is a list of numbers itself and not a function. The point is that the content of the memory cell is needed to evaluate the sequence— the value in the cell may be accessed via the "LASTANSWER" key. The functionality notes the dependence of the value of the expression sequence upon the memory cell.

Let's consider the semantic equations. The equation for **P**[[ON S]] states that the meaning of a program session follows from the meaning of the expression sequence [[S]]. The equation also says that the memory cell is initialized to *zero* when the calculator is turned on. The cell's value is passed as an argument to the valuation function for the sequence.

As indicated by the functionality for **S**, an expression sequence uses the value of the memory cell to compute a list of numbers. The equation for **S**[[E TOTAL S]] describes the meaning of a sequence of two or more expressions: the meaning of the first one, [[E]], is appended to the front of the list of values that follows from ⟦S⟧. We can list the corresponding actions that the calculator would take:

1. Evaluate ⟦E⟧ using cell n , producing value n'.
2. Print n' out on the display.
3. Place n' into the memory cell.
4. Evaluate the rest of the sequence ⟦S⟧ using the cell.

Note how each of these four steps are represented in the semantic equation:

1. is handled by the expression **E**⟦E⟧(n), binding it to the variable n'.
2. is handled by the expression n' *cons* $\cdots$.
3. and 4. are handled by the expression **S**⟦S⟧(n').

Nonetheless, the right-hand side of **S**⟦E TOTAL S⟧ is a mathematical value. Note that the same value is represented by the expression:

E⟦E⟧(n) *cons* **S**⟦S⟧ (**E**⟦E⟧(n))

which itself suggests that ⟦E⟧ be evaluated *twice*. This connection between the structure of function expressions and operational principles will be examined in detail in later chapters. In the meantime, it can be used to help understand the meanings denoted by the function expressions.

The meaning of **S**⟦E TOTAL OFF⟧ is similar. Since ⟦E⟧ is the last expression to be evaluated, the list of subsequent outputs is just *nil*.

Of the semantic equations for expressions, the ones for ⟦LASTANSWER⟧ and ⟦IF E_1, E_2, E_3⟧ are of interest. The ⟦LASTANSWER⟧ operator causes a lookup of the value in the memory cell. The meaning of the IF expression is a conditional. The *equals* operation is used here. The test value, ⟦E_1⟧, is evaluated and compared with *zero*. If it equals *zero*, **E**⟦E_2⟧(n) is taken as the value of the conditional, else **E**⟦E_3⟧(n) is used. Hence, the expression ⟦E_1⟧ in the first position of the conditional takes on a logical meaning in addition to its numeric one. This is a source of confusion in the calculator language and is a possible area for improvement of the language.

One last remark: equations such as **E**⟦(E)⟧(n) = **E**⟦E⟧(n) may also be written as **E**⟦(E)⟧ = λn. **E**⟦E⟧(n), making use of the abstraction notation, or even as **E**⟦(E)⟧ = **E**⟦E⟧ (why?). This will be done in later examples.

A simplification of a sample calculator program is instructional:

P⟦ON 2+1 TOTAL IF LASTANSWER , 2 , 0 TOTAL OFF⟧
= **S**⟦2+1 TOTAL IF LASTANSWER , 2 , 0 TOTAL OFF⟧(*zero*)
= let n'= **E**⟦2+1⟧(*zero*)
    in n' *cons* **S**⟦IF LASTANSWER , 2 , 0 TOTAL OFF⟧(n')

Simplifying **E**⟦2+1⟧(*zero*) leads to the value *three*, and we have:

let n'= *three* in n' *cons* **S**⟦IF LASTANSWER , 2 , 0 TOTAL OFF⟧(n')
= *three cons* **S**⟦IF LASTANSWER , 2 , 0 TOTAL OFF⟧(*three*)

= *three cons* (E⟦IF LASTANSWER , 2 , 0⟧(*three*) *cons nil*)

If we work on the conditional, we see that:

E⟦IF LASTANSWER , 2 , 0⟧(*three*)
= E⟦LASTANSWER⟧(*three*) *equals zero* → E⟦2⟧(*three*) [] E⟦0⟧(*three*)
= *three equals zero* → *two* [] *zero*
= *false* → *two* [] *zero* = *zero*

This gives as the final result the list:

three cons (*zero cons nil*)

Each of the simplification steps preserved the meaning of P⟦2+1 TOTAL IF LASTANSWER , 2 , 0 TOTAL OFF⟧. The purpose of simplification is to produce an equivalent expression whose meaning is more obvious than the original's. The simplification process is of interest in itself, for it shows how the calculator operates on input. If the denotational definition is used as a *specification* for the calculator, the definition plus simplification strategy show a possible *implementation* of the calculator. A simple-minded implementation would use functions, parameters, and an evaluation strategy corresponding to the simplification sequence just seen. It only takes a bit of insight, however, to notice that the numeral argument can be converted into a global memory cell. The derivation of a processor for a language from its denotational specification will be repeatedly touched upon in future chapters.

SUGGESTED READINGS

Jones 1982a; Gordon 1979; Milne & Strachey 1976; Pagan 1981; Stoy 1977; Tennent 1977, 1981

EXERCISES

1. Use the binary numeral semantics in Figure 4.1 to determine the meanings of the following derivation trees:

   a. ⟦0011⟧
   b. ⟦000⟧
   c. ⟦111⟧

2. Here is an alternative abstract syntax for the language of binary numerals:

   $N \in$ Numeral
   $B \in$ Bin-Numeral
   $D \in$ Bin-digit
   $N ::= B$
   $B ::= DB \mid D$
   $D ::= 0 \mid 1$

   Define the valuation function that maps a binary numeral to its value. (Hint: define $\mathbf{P}$: Numeral $\rightarrow$ *Nat* and $\mathbf{B}$: Bin-numeral $\rightarrow$ (*Value* $\times$ *Scale*), where *Value* = *Nat* is the value of the numeral, and *Scale* = { *one*, *two*, *four*, *eight*, $\cdots$ } remembers the scale (physical size) of the numeral.)

3. a. In a fashion similar to that in Figure 4.1, define a denotational semantics for the language of base 8 numerals, Octal. Let **E** be the valuation function **E** : Octal $\rightarrow$ *Nat*.
   b. Prove the following equivalence: $\mathbf{E}[\![015]\!] = \mathbf{B}[\![1101]\!]$.
   c. Construct an algorithm that maps an octal numeral to binary form. Use the respective denotational semantics for Octal and Binary-numeral to prove that your algorithm is correct.

4. Simplify these calculator programs to their meanings in *Nat**:

   a. [[ON 1+(IF LASTANSWER , 4 , 1) TOTAL LASTANSWER TOTAL 5*2 TOTAL OFF]]
   b. [[ON 5 TOTAL 5 TOTAL 10 TOTAL OFF]]
   c. [[ON LASTANSWER TOTAL OFF]]

5. Augment the calculator so that it can compare two values for equality: add an = button to its panel and augment the BNF rule for Expression to read: $E ::= \cdots \mid E_1{=}E_2$

   a. Write the semantic equation for $\mathbf{E}[\![E_1{=}E_2]\!]$.
   b. What changes must be made to the other parts of the denotational definition to accommodate the new construct? Make these changes. Do you think the new version of the calculator is an improvement over the original?

6. Alter the calculator semantics in Figure 4.3 so that the memory cell argument to **S** and **E** becomes a memory *stack*; that is, use *Nat** in place of *Nat* as an argument domain to **S** and **E**.

a. Adjust the semantics so that the last answer is *pushed* onto the memory stack and the LASTANSWER button accesses the top value on the stack.
b. Augment the syntax of the calculator language so that the user can explicitly pop values off the memory stack.

7. Use the denotational definition in Figure 4.3 to guide the coding of a test implementation of the calculator in Pascal (or whatever language you choose). What do the semantic algebras become in the implementation? How are the valuation equations realized? What does the memory cell become? What questions about the implementation *doesn't* the denotational definition answer?

Reuse String algebra in book (pg. 37)

8. Design, in the following stages, a calculator for manipulating character string expressions:

   a. List the semantic algebras that the calculator will need.
   b. List the operations that the calculator will provide to the user.
   c. Define the abstract syntax of these operations.
   d. Define the valuation functions that give meaning to the abstract syntax definition.

   Can these four steps be better accomplished in another order? Is the order even important?

9. If you are familiar with attribute grammars, describe the relationship between a denotational definition of a language and its attribute grammar definition. What corresponds to inherited attributes in the denotational definition? What are the synthesized attributes? Define attribute grammars for the binary numerals language and the calculator language.

10. Consider the compiler-oriented aspects of a denotational definition: if there existed a machine with hardwired instructions *plus*, *times*, and representations of numbers, the definition in Figure 4.1 could be used as a syntax-directed translation scheme for binary numbers to machine code. For example:

$$\mathbf{B}[\![101]\!] = (((\mathit{one\ times\ two})\ \mathit{plus\ zero})\ \mathit{times\ two})\ \mathit{plus\ one}$$

is the "compiled code" for the input program $[\![101]\!]$; the syntax pieces are mapped to their denotations, but no simplifications are performed. The machine would evaluate this program to *five*. With this idea in mind, propose how a compiler for the calculator language of Figure 4.3 might be derived from its denotational definition. Propose a machine for executing compiled calculator programs.

Chapter 5

Imperative Languages

Most sequential programming languages use a data structure that exists independently of any program in the language. The data structure isn't explicitly mentioned in the language's syntax, but it is possible to build phrases that access it and update it. This data structure is called the *store*, and languages that utilize stores are called *imperative*. The fundamental example of a store is a computer's primary memory, but file stores and data bases are also examples. The store and a computer program share an intimate relationship:

1. The store is critical to the evaluation of a phrase in a program. A phrase is understood in terms of how it handles the store, and the absence of a proper store makes the phrase nonexecutable.
2. The store serves as a means of communication between the different phrases in the program. Values computed by one phrase are deposited in the store so that another phrase may use them. The language's sequencing mechanism establishes the order of communication.
3. The store is an inherently "large" argument. Only one copy of store exists at any point during the evaluation.

In this chapter, we study the store concept by examining three imperative languages. You may wish to study any subset of the three languages. The final section of the chapter presents some variants on the store and how it can be used.

5.1 A LANGUAGE WITH ASSIGNMENT

The first example language is a declaration-free Pascal subset. A program in the language is a sequence of *commands*. Stores belong to the domain *Store* and serve as arguments to the valuation function:

$$\mathbf{C}: \text{Command} \rightarrow Store_{\perp} \rightarrow Store_{\perp}$$

The purpose of a command is to produce a new store from its store argument.

However, a command might not terminate its actions upon the store— it can "loop." The looping of a command $[\![C]\!]$ with store s has semantics $\mathbf{C}[\![C]\!]s = \bot$. (This explains why the *Store* domain is lifted: $\bot$ is a possible answer.) The primary property of nontermination is that it creates a nonrecoverable situation. Any commands $[\![C']\!]$ following $[\![C]\!]$ in the evaluation sequence will not evaluate. This suggests that the function $\mathbf{C}[\![C']\!]: Store_\bot \rightarrow Store_\bot$ be strict; that is, given a nonrecoverable situation, $\mathbf{C}[\![C']\!]$ can do nothing at all. Thus, command composition is $\mathbf{C}[\![C_1;C_2]\!] = \mathbf{C}[\![C_2]\!] \circ \mathbf{C}[\![C_1]\!]$.

Figure 5.1 presents the semantic algebras for the imperative language. The *Store* domain models a computer store as a mapping from the identifiers of the

Figure 5.1

I. Truth Values
Domain $t \in Tr = \mathbb{B}$
Operations

$true, false : Tr$
$not : Tr \rightarrow Tr$

II. Identifiers
Domain $i \in Id =$ Identifier

III. Natural Numbers
Domain $n \in Nat = \mathbb{N}$
Operations

$zero, one, \cdots : Nat$
$plus : Nat \times Nat \rightarrow Nat$
$equals : Nat \times Nat \rightarrow Tr$

IV. Store
Domain $s \in Store = Id \rightarrow Nat$
Operations

$newstore : Store$
$newstore = \lambda i.\, zero$
$access : Id \rightarrow Store \rightarrow Nat$
$access = \lambda i.\, \lambda s.\, s(i)$
$update : Id \rightarrow Nat \rightarrow Store \rightarrow Store$
$update = \lambda i.\lambda n.\lambda s.\, [\, i \mapsto n\,]s$

---

language to their values. The operations upon the store include a constant for creating a new store, an operation for accessing a store, and an operation for placing a new value into a store. These operations are exactly those described in Example 3.11 of Chapter 3.

The language's definition appears in Figure 5.2.

The valuation function **P** states that the meaning of a program is a map from an input number to an answer number. Since nontermination is possible, $\perp$ is also a possible "answer," hence the rightmost codomain of **P** is $Nat_\perp$ rather than just *Nat*. The equation for **P** says that the input number is associated with identifier [[A]] in a new store. Then the program body is evaluated, and the answer is extracted from the store at [[Z]].

The clauses of the **C** function are all strict in their use of the store. Command composition works as described earlier. The conditional commands are choice functions. Since the expression $(e_1 \rightarrow e_2 \,[\!]\, e_3)$ is nonstrict in arguments e_2 and e_3, the value of **C**[[**if** B **then** C]]*s* is *s* when **B**[[B]]*s* is *false*, even if **C**[[C]]$s = \perp$. The assignment statement performs the expected update; the [[**diverge**]] command causes nontermination.

The **E** function also needs a store argument, but the store is used in a "read only" mode. **E**'s functionality shows that an expression produces a number, not a new version of store; the store is not updated by an expression. The equation for addition is stated so that the order of evaluation of $[\![E_1]\!]$ and $[\![E_2]\!]$ is not important to the final answer. Indeed, the two expressions might even be evaluated in parallel. A strictness check of the store is not needed, because **C** has already verified that the store is proper prior to passing it to **E**.

Here is the denotation of a sample program with the input *two*:

P[[Z:=1; **if** A=0 **then diverge**; Z:=3.]](*two*)
= let *s* = (*update* [[A]] *two newstore*) in
  let *s'* = **C**[[Z:=1; **if** A=0 **then diverge**; Z:=3]]*s*
  in *access* [[Z]] *s'*

Since (*update* [[A]] *two newstore*) is ([[[A]]↦*two*] *newstore*), that is, the store that maps [[A]] to *two* and all other identifiers to *zero*, the above expression simplifies to:

let *s'* = **C**[[Z:=1; **if** A=0 **then diverge**; Z:=3]] ([[[A]]↦*two*] *newstore*)
in *access* [[Z]] *s'*

From here on, we use s_1 to stand for ([[[A]]↦*two*] *newstore*). Working on the value bound to *s'* leads us to derive:

C[[Z:=1; **if** A=0 **then diverge**; Z:=3]]s_1
= $(\underline{\lambda}s.$ **C**[[**if** A=0 **then diverge**; Z:=3]] (**C**[[Z:=1]]*s*))s_1

The store s_1 is a proper value, so it can be bound to *s*, giving:

Figure 5.2

Abstract syntax:

P∈ Program
C∈ Command
E∈ Expression
B∈ Boolean-expr
I ∈ Identifier
N∈ Numeral

P ::= C.
C ::= C_1;C_2 | **if** B **then** C | **if** B **then** C_1 **else** C_2 | I:=E | **diverge**
E ::= E_1+E_2 | I | N
B ::= E_1=E_2 | ¬ B

Semantic algebras:
(defined in Figure 5.1)

Valuation functions:

P: Program→*Nat* →$Nat_\perp$

$\mathbf{P}[\![C.]\!] = \lambda n.\ \text{let}\ s = (update\ [\![A]\!]\ n\ newstore)\ \text{in}$
$\qquad\qquad\text{let}\ s' = \mathbf{C}[\![C]\!]s\ \text{in}\ (access\ [\![Z]\!]\ s')$

C: Command→$Store_\perp$→$Store_\perp$

$\mathbf{C}[\![C_1;C_2]\!] = \underline{\lambda} s.\ \mathbf{C}[\![C_2]\!]\,(\mathbf{C}[\![C_1]\!]s)$
$\mathbf{C}[\![\textbf{if}\ B\ \textbf{then}\ C]\!] = \underline{\lambda} s.\ \mathbf{B}[\![B]\!]s \to \mathbf{C}[\![C]\!]s\ [\!]\ s$
$\mathbf{C}[\![\textbf{if}\ B\ \textbf{then}\ C_1\ \textbf{else}\ C_2]\!] = \underline{\lambda} s.\ \mathbf{B}[\![B]\!]s \to \mathbf{C}[\![C_1]\!]s\ [\!]\ \mathbf{C}[\![C_2]\!]s$
$\mathbf{C}[\![I{:=}E]\!] = \underline{\lambda} s.\ update\ [\![I]\!]\ (\mathbf{E}[\![E]\!]s)\ s$
$\mathbf{C}[\![\textbf{diverge}]\!] = \underline{\lambda} s.\ \perp$

E: Expression→*Store* →*Nat*

$\mathbf{E}[\![E_1+E_2]\!] = \lambda s.\ \mathbf{E}[\![E_1]\!]s\ \ plus\ \ \mathbf{E}[\![E_2]\!]s$
$\mathbf{E}[\![I]\!] = \lambda s.\ access\ [\![I]\!]\ s$
$\mathbf{E}[\![N]\!] = \lambda s.\ \mathbf{N}[\![N]\!]$

B: Boolean-expr→*Store* →*Tr*

$\mathbf{B}[\![E_1=E_2]\!] = \lambda s.\ \mathbf{E}[\![E_1]\!]s\ \ equals\ \ \mathbf{E}[\![E_2]\!]s$
$\mathbf{B}[\![\neg B]\!] = \lambda s.\ not(\mathbf{B}[\![B]\!]s)$

N: Numeral→*Nat* (*omitted*)

$\mathbf{C}[\![\textbf{if } A{=}0 \textbf{ then diverge}; Z{:=}3]\!](\mathbf{C}[\![Z{:=}1]\!]s_1)$

We next work on $\mathbf{C}[\![Z{:=}1]\!]s_1$:

$$\begin{aligned}
&\mathbf{C}[\![Z{:=}1]\!]s_1\\
&= (\underline{\lambda}s.\ update\ [\![Z]\!]\ (\mathbf{E}[\![1]\!]s)\ s)\ s_1\\
&= update\ [\![Z]\!]\ (\mathbf{E}[\![1]\!]s_1)\ s_1\\
&= update\ [\![Z]\!]\ (\mathbf{N}[\![1]\!])\ s_1\\
&= update\ [\![Z]\!]\ one\ \ s_1\\
&= [\ [\![Z]\!]\mapsto one\ ][\ [\![A]\!]\mapsto two\ ]\,newstore
\end{aligned}$$

which we call s_2. Now:

$$\begin{aligned}
&\mathbf{C}[\![\textbf{if } A{=}0 \textbf{ then diverge}; Z{:=}3]\!]s_2\\
&= (\underline{\lambda}s.\ \mathbf{C}[\![Z{:=}3]\!]\,((\underline{\lambda}s.\ \mathbf{B}[\![A{=}0]\!]s \rightarrow \mathbf{C}[\![\textbf{diverge}]\!]s\ [\!]\ s\ )s\ ))s_2\\
&= \mathbf{C}[\![Z{:=}3]\!]\,((\underline{\lambda}s.\ \mathbf{B}[\![A{=}0]\!]s \rightarrow \mathbf{C}[\![\textbf{diverge}]\!]s\ [\!]\ s\ )s_2)\\
&= \mathbf{C}[\![Z{:=}3]\!]\,(\mathbf{B}[\![A{=}0]\!]s_2 \rightarrow \mathbf{C}[\![\textbf{diverge}]\!]s_2\ [\!]\ s_2)
\end{aligned}$$

Note that $\mathbf{C}[\![\textbf{diverge}]\!]s_2 = (\underline{\lambda}s.\bot)s_2 = \bot$, so nontermination is the result if the test has value *true*. Simplifying the test, we obtain:

$$\begin{aligned}
&\mathbf{B}[\![A{=}0]\!]s_2 = (\lambda s.\ \mathbf{E}[\![A]\!]s\ \ equals\ \ \mathbf{E}[\![0]\!]s\ )s_2\\
&= \mathbf{E}[\![A]\!]s_2\ equals\ \ \mathbf{E}[\![0]\!]s_2\\
&= (access\ [\![A]\!]\ s_2)\ equals\ \ zero
\end{aligned}$$

Examining the left operand, we see that:

$$\begin{aligned}
&access\ [\![A]\!]\ s_2\\
&= s_2[\![A]\!]\\
&= (\ [\ [\![Z]\!]\mapsto one\ ][\ [\![A]\!]\mapsto two\ ]\,newstore\ )\ [\![A]\!]\\
&= (\ [\ [\![A]\!]\mapsto two\ ]\,newstore\ )\ [\![A]\!] \qquad \text{(why?)}\\
&= two
\end{aligned}$$

Thus, $\mathbf{B}[\![A{=}0]\!]s_2 = false$, implying that $\mathbf{C}[\![\textbf{if } A{=}0 \textbf{ then diverge}]\!]s_2 = s_2$. Now:

$$\begin{aligned}
&\mathbf{C}[\![Z{:=}3]\!]s_2\\
&= [\ [\![Z]\!]\mapsto three\ ]s_2
\end{aligned}$$

The denotation of the entire program is:

$$\begin{aligned}
&\text{let } s' = [\ [\![Z]\!]\mapsto three\ ]s_2 \text{ in } access\ [\![Z]\!]\ s'\\
&= access\ [\![Z]\!]\ [\ [\![Z]\!]\mapsto three\ ]s_2\\
&= (\ [\ [\![Z]\!]\mapsto three\ ]s_2)\ [\![Z]\!]\\
&= three
\end{aligned}$$

We obtain a much different denotation when the input number is *zero*:

$\mathbf{P}[\![\text{Z:=1; if A=0 then diverge; Z:=3.}]\!](zero)$
$= \text{let } s' = \mathbf{C}[\![\text{Z:=1; if A=0 then diverge; Z:=3}]\!]s_3 \text{ in } access\,[\![\text{Z}]\!]\,s'$

where $s_3 = [\,[\![\text{A}]\!] \mapsto zero\,]\,newstore$. Simplifying the value bound to s' leads to:

$\mathbf{C}[\![\text{Z:=1; if A=0 then diverge; Z:=3}]\!]s_3$
$= \mathbf{C}[\![\text{if A=0 then diverge; Z:=3}]\!]s_4$

where $s_4 = [\,[\![\text{Z}]\!] \mapsto one\,]s_3$. As for the conditional, we see that:

$\mathbf{B}[\![\text{A=0}]\!]s_4 \rightarrow \mathbf{C}[\![\text{diverge}]\!]s_4 \,[\!]\, s_4$
$= true \rightarrow \mathbf{C}[\![\text{diverge}]\!]s_4 \,[\!]\, s_4$
$= \mathbf{C}[\![\text{diverge}]\!]s_4$
$= (\underline{\lambda} s.\, \bot)s_4$
$= \bot$

So the value bound to s' is $\mathbf{C}[\![\text{Z:=3}]\!]\bot$. But $\mathbf{C}[\![\text{Z:=3}]\!]\bot = (\underline{\lambda} s.\, update\,[\![\text{Z}]\!]\,(\mathbf{E}[\![3]\!]s)\,s)\bot = \bot$. Because of the strict abstraction, the assignment isn't performed. The denotation of the program is:

$\text{let } s' = \bot \text{ in } access\,[\![\text{Z}]\!]\,s'$

which simplifies directly to $\bot$. (Recall that the form (let $x = e_1$ in e_2) represents $(\underline{\lambda} x.\, e_2)e_1$.) The undefined store forces the value of the entire program to be undefined.

The denotational definition is also valuable for proving properties such as program equivalence. As a simple example, we show for distinct identifiers $[\![\text{X}]\!]$ and $[\![\text{Y}]\!]$ that the command $\mathbf{C}[\![\text{X:=0; Y:=X+1}]\!]$ has the same denotation as $\mathbf{C}[\![\text{Y:=1; X:=0}]\!]$. The proof strategy goes as follows: since both commands are functions in the domain $Store_\bot \rightarrow Store_\bot$, it suffices to prove that the two functions are equal by showing that both produce same answers from same arguments. (This is because of the principle of extensionality mentioned in Section 3.2.3.) First, it is easy to see that if the store argument is $\bot$, both commands produce the answer $\bot$. If the argument is a proper value, let us call it s and simplify:

$\mathbf{C}[\![\text{X:=0; Y:=X+1}]\!]s$
$= \mathbf{C}[\![\text{Y:=X+1}]\!](\mathbf{C}[\![\text{X:=0}]\!]s)$
$= \mathbf{C}[\![\text{Y:=X+1}]\!]([\,[\![\text{X}]\!] \mapsto zero\,]s)$
$= update\,[\![\text{Y}]\!]\,(\mathbf{E}[\![\text{X+1}]\!]([\,[\![\text{X}]\!] \mapsto zero\,]s))([\,[\![\text{X}]\!] \mapsto zero\,]s)$
$= update\,[\![\text{Y}]\!]\,one\,[\,[\![\text{X}]\!] \mapsto zero\,]s$
$= [\,[\![\text{Y}]\!] \mapsto one\,][\,[\![\text{X}]\!] \mapsto zero\,]s$

Call this result s_1. Next:

$\mathbf{C}[\![\text{Y:=1; X:=0}]\!]s$

$= \mathbf{C}[\![X{:=}0]\!]\,(\mathbf{C}[\![Y{:=}1]\!]s\,)$
$= \mathbf{C}[\![X{:=}0]\!]\,(\,[\,[\![Y]\!]\mapsto one\,]s\,)$
$= [\,[\![X]\!]\mapsto zero\,][\,[\![Y]\!]\mapsto one\,]s$

Call this result s_2. The two values are defined stores. Are they the *same* store? It is not possible to simplify s_1 into s_2 with the simplification rules. But, recall that stores are themselves functions from the domain $Id \rightarrow Nat$. To prove that the two stores are the same, we must show that each produces the same number answer from the same identifier argument. There are three cases to consider:

1. The argument is $[\![X]\!]$: then $s_1[\![X]\!] = (\,[\,[\![Y]\!]\mapsto one\,]\,[\,[\![X]\!]\mapsto zero\,]s\,)[\![X]\!] = (\,[\,[\![X]\!]\mapsto zero\,]s\,)[\![X]\!] = zero$; and $s_2[\![X]\!] = (\,[\,[\![X]\!]\mapsto zero\,]\,[\,[\![Y]\!]\mapsto one\,]s\,)[\![X]\!] = zero$.
2. The argument is $[\![Y]\!]$: then $s_1[\![Y]\!] = (\,[\,[\![Y]\!]\mapsto one\,][\,[\![X]\!]\mapsto zero\,]s\,)[\![Y]\!] = one$; and $s_2[\![Y]\!] = (\,[\,[\![X]\!]\mapsto zero\,]\,[\,[\![Y]\!]\mapsto one\,]s\,)[\![Y]\!] = (\,[\,[\![Y]\!]\mapsto one\,]s\,)[\![Y]\!] = one$.
3. The argument is some identifier $[\![I]\!]$ other than $[\![X]\!]$ or $[\![Y]\!]$: then $s_1[\![I]\!] = s[\![I]\!]$ and $s_2[\![I]\!] = s[\![I]\!]$.

Since s_1 and s_2 behave the same for all arguments, they are the same function. This implies that $\mathbf{C}[\![X{:=}0;\,Y{:=}X{+}1]\!]$ and $\mathbf{C}[\![Y{:=}1;\,X{:=}0]\!]$ are the same function, so the two commands are equivalent. Many proofs of program properties require this style of reasoning.

5.1.1 Programs Are Functions

The two sample simplification sequences in the previous section were operational-like: a program and its input were computed to an answer. This makes the denotational definition behave like an operational semantics, and it is easy to forget that functions and domains are even involved. Nonetheless, it is possible to study the denotation of a program *without* supplying sample input, a feature that is not available to operational semantics. This broader view emphasizes that the denotation of a program is a *function*.

Consider again the example $[\![Z{:=}1;\,\mathbf{if}\ A{=}0\ \mathbf{then\ diverge};\,Z{:=}3]\!]$. What is its meaning? It's a function from Nat to $Nat_\perp$:

$\mathbf{P}[\![Z{:=}1;\,\mathbf{if}\ A{=}0\ \mathbf{then\ diverge};\,Z{:=}3.]\!]$
$= \lambda n.\ \text{let } s = update\,[\![A]\!]\ n\ newstore \text{ in}$
$\quad \text{let } s' = \mathbf{C}[\![Z{:=}1;\,\mathbf{if}\ A{=}0\ \mathbf{then\ diverge};\,Z{:=}3]\!]s$
$\quad \text{in } access\,[\![Z]\!]\ s'$
$= \lambda n.\ \text{let } s = update\,[\![A]\!]\ n\ newstore \text{ in}$
$\quad \text{let } s' = (\underline{\lambda}s.\,(\underline{\lambda}s.\,\mathbf{C}[\![Z{:=}3]\!]\,(\mathbf{C}[\![\mathbf{if}\ A{=}0\ \mathbf{then\ diverge}]\!]s\,))s\,)(\mathbf{C}[\![Z{:=}1]\!]s\,)$
$\quad \text{in } access\,[\![Z]\!]\ s'$

$$= \lambda n.\ \text{let } s = update\,[\![\text{A}]\!]\ n\ newstore\ \text{ in}$$
$$\text{let } s' = (\underline{\lambda} s.\ (\underline{\lambda} s.\ update\,[\![\text{Z}]\!]\ three\ s\ )$$
$$((\underline{\lambda} s.\ (access\,[\![\text{A}]\!]\ s\ )\ equals\ \ zero \rightarrow (\underline{\lambda} s.\ \bot)s\ [\!]\ s\ )s\ ))$$
$$((\underline{\lambda} s.\ update\,[\![\text{Z}]\!]\ one\ \ s\ )s\ )$$
$$\text{in } access\,[\![\text{Z}]\!]\ s'$$

which can be restated as:

$$\lambda n.\ \text{let } s = update\,[\![\text{A}]\!]\ n\ \ newstore\ \text{ in}$$
$$\text{let } s' = (\text{let } s'_1 = update\,[\![\text{Z}]\!]\ one\ \ s\ \text{ in}$$
$$\text{let } s'_2 = (access\,[\![\text{A}]\!]\ s'_1)\ equals\ \ zero \rightarrow (\underline{\lambda} s.\ \bot)s'_1\ [\!]\ s'_1$$
$$\text{in } update\,[\![\text{Z}]\!]\ three\ \ s'_2)$$
$$\text{in } access\,[\![\text{Z}]\!]\ s'$$

The simplifications taken so far have systematically replaced syntax constructs by their function denotations; all syntax pieces are removed (less the identifiers). The resulting expression denotes the meaning of the program. (A comment: it is proper to be concerned why a phrase such as $\mathbf{E}[\![0]\!]s$ was simplified to *zero* even though the value of the store argument s is unknown. The simplification works because s is an argument bound to $\underline{\lambda} s$. Any undefined stores are "trapped" by $\underline{\lambda} s$. Thus, within the scope of the $\underline{\lambda} s$, all occurrences of s represent defined values.)

The systematic mapping of syntax to function expressions resembles compiling. The function expression certainly does resemble compiled code, with its occurrences of tests, accesses, and updates. But it is still a function, mapping an input number to an output number.

As it stands, the expression does not appear very attractive, and the intuitive meaning of the original program does not stand out. The simplifications shall proceed further. Let s_0 be $(update\,[\![\text{A}]\!]\ n\ \ newstore\ )$. We simplify to:

$$\lambda n.\ \text{let } s' = (\text{let } s'_1 = update\,[\![\text{Z}]\!]\ one\ \ s_0\ \text{ in}$$
$$\text{let } s'_2 = (access\,[\![\text{A}]\!]\ s'_1)\ equals\ \ zero \rightarrow (\underline{\lambda} s.\ \bot)s'_1\ [\!]\ s'_1$$
$$\text{in } update\,[\![\text{Z}]\!]\ three\ \ s'_2)$$
$$\text{in } access\,[\![\text{Z}]\!]\ s'$$

We use s_1 for $(update\,[\![\text{Z}]\!]\ one\ \ s_0)$; the conditional in the value bound to s' is:

$$(access\,[\![\text{A}]\!]\ s_1)\ equals\ \ zero \rightarrow \bot\ [\!]\ s_1$$
$$= n\ \ equals\ \ zero \rightarrow \bot\ [\!]\ s_1$$

The conditional can be simplified no further. We can make use of the following property; "for $e_2 \in Store_\bot$ such that $e_2 \neq \bot$, let $s = (e_1 \rightarrow \bot\ [\!]\ e_2)$ in e_3 equals $e_1 \rightarrow \bot\ [\!]\ [e_2/s]e_3$." (The proof is left as an exercise.) It allows us to state that:

$$\text{let } s'_2 = (n\ \ equals\ \ zero \rightarrow \bot\ [\!]\ s_1)\ \text{in } update\,[\![\text{Z}]\!]\ three\ \ s'_2$$

$$= n \ equals \ zero \rightarrow \bot \ [\,] \ update [\![Z]\!] \ three \ s_1$$

This reduces the program's denotation to:

$$\lambda n. \text{ let } s' = (n \ equals \ zero \rightarrow \bot \ [\,] \ update [\![Z]\!] \ three \ s_1) \text{ in } access [\![Z]\!] \ s'$$

The property used above can be applied a second time to show that this expression is just:

$$\lambda n. \ n \ equals \ zero \rightarrow \bot \ [\,] \ access [\![Z]\!] \ (update [\![Z]\!] \ three \ s_1)$$

which is:

$$\lambda n. \ n \ equals \ zero \rightarrow \bot \ [\,] \ three$$

which is the intuitive meaning of the program!

This example points out the beauty in the denotational semantics method. It extracts the *essence* of a program. What is startling about the example is that the primary semantic argument, the store, disappears completely, because it does not figure in the input-output relation that the program describes. This program does indeed denote a function from *Nat* to $Nat_\bot$.

Just as the replacement of syntax by function expressions resembles compilation, the internal simplification resembles compile-time code optimization. When more realistic languages are studied, such "optimizations" will be useful for understanding the nature of semantic arguments.

5.2 AN INTERACTIVE FILE EDITOR

The second example language is an interactive file editor. We define a *file* to be a list of records, where the domain of records is taken as primitive. The file editor makes use of two levels of store: the primary store is a component holding the file edited upon by the user, and the secondary store is a system of text files indexed by their names. The domains are listed in Figure 5.3.

The edited files are values from the *Openfile* domain. An opened file $r_1, r_2, \cdots, r_{last}$ is represented by two lists of text records; the lists break the file open in the middle:

$$\boxed{r_{i-1} \ \cdots \ r_2 \ r_1} \qquad \boxed{r_i \ r_{i+1} \ \cdots \ r_{last}}$$

r_i is the "current" record of the opened file. Of course, this is not the only representation of an opened file, so it is important that all operations that depend on this representation be grouped with the domain definition. There are a good number of them. *Newfile* represents a file with no records. *Copyin* takes a file from the file system and organizes it as:

Figure 5.3

IV. Text file   Domain $f \in File = Record^*$

V. File system

Domain $s \in File\text{-}system = Id \rightarrow File$

Operations

$access : Id \times File\text{-}system \rightarrow File$

$access = \lambda(i,s).\ s(i)$

$update : Id \times File \times File\text{-}system \rightarrow File\text{-}system$

$update = \lambda(i,f,s).\ [\, i \mapsto f\,]s$

VI. Open file

Domain $p \in Openfile = Record^* \times Record^*$

Operations

$newfile\text{: } Openfile$

$newfile = (nil,nil)$

$copyin : File \rightarrow Openfile$

$copyin = \lambda f.\ (nil,f)$

$copyout : Openfile \rightarrow File$

$copyout = \lambda p.$ "appends $fst(p)$ to $snd(p)$— defined later"

$forwards\text{: } Openfile \rightarrow Openfile$

$forwards = \lambda(front, back).\ null\ back \rightarrow (front, back)$
$\quad [\!]\ ((hd\ back)\ cons\ front,\ (tl\ back))$

$backwards : Openfile \rightarrow Openfile$

$backwards = \lambda(front, back).\ null\ front \rightarrow (front, back)$
$\quad [\!]\ (tl\ front, (hd\ front)\ cons\ back)$

$insert : Record \times Openfile \rightarrow Openfile$

$insert = \lambda(r\ , (front, back)).\ null\ back \rightarrow (front,\ r\ cons\ back)$
$\quad [\!]\ ((hd\ back)\ cons\ front),\ r\ cons\ (tl\ back))$

$delete : Openfile \rightarrow Openfile$

$delete = \lambda(front, back).\ (front,\ (null\ back \rightarrow back\ [\!]\ tl\ back))$

$at\text{-}first\text{-}record\text{: } Openfile \rightarrow Tr$

$at\text{-}first\text{-}record = \lambda(front, back).\ null\ front$

$at\text{-}last\text{-}record : Openfile \rightarrow Tr$

$at\text{-}last\text{-}record = \lambda(front, back).\ null\ back \rightarrow true$
$\quad [\!]\ (null\ (tl\ back) \rightarrow true\ [\!]\ false)$

$isempty : Openfile \rightarrow Tr$

$isempty = \lambda(front, back).\ (null\ front)\ and\ (null\ back)$

$$\qquad \qquad \qquad r_1 \; r_2 \; \cdots \; r_{last}$$

Record r_1 is the current record of the file. Operation *copyout* appends the two lists back together. A definition of the operation appears in the next chapter.

The *forwards* operation makes the record following the current record the new current record. Pictorially, for:

$$r_{i-1} \; \cdots \; r_2 \; r_1 \qquad \qquad r_i \; r_{i+1} \; r_{last}$$

a forwards move produces:

$$r_i \; r_{i-1} \; \cdots \; r_2 \; r_1 \qquad \qquad r_{i+1} \; \cdots \; r_{last}$$

Backwards performs the reverse operation. *Insert* places a record r behind the current record; an insertion of record r' produces:

$$r_i \; \cdots \; r_2 \; r_1 \qquad \qquad r' \; r_{i+1} \; \cdots \; r_{last}$$

The newly inserted record becomes current. *Delete* removes the current record. The final three operations test whether the first record in the file is current, the last record in the file is current, or if the file is empty.

Figure 5.4 gives the semantics of the text editor.

Since all of the file manipulations are done by the operations for the *Openfile* domain, the semantic equations are mainly concerned with trapping unreasonable user requests. They also model the editor's output log, which echoes the input commands and reports errors.

The **C** function produces a line of terminal output and a new open file from its open file argument. For user commands such as **[[newfile]]**, the action is quite simple. Others, such as **[[moveforward]]**, can generate error messages, which are appended to the output log. For example:

C[[delete]](*newfile*)
= let (k',p') = *isempty* (*newfile*) → ("error: file is empty", *newfile*)
　　　　　　　　[] ("", *delete* (*newfile*))
　　in ("delete" *concat* k', p'))
= let (k',p') = ("error: file is empty", *newfile*)
　　in ("delete" *concat* k', p')
= ("delete" *concat* "error: file is empty", *newfile*)
= ("delete error: file is empty", *newfile*)

The **S** function collects the log messages into a list. **S[[quit]]** builds the very end

Figure 5.4

Abstract syntax:

$P \in$ Program-session
$S \in$ Command-sequence
$C \in$ Command
$R \in$ Record
$I \in$ Identifier

P ::= **edit** I **cr** S
S ::= C **cr** S | **quit**
C ::= **newfile** | **moveforward** | **moveback** | **insert** R | **delete**

Semantic algebras:

I. Truth values
Domain $t \in Tr$
Operations
$true, false : Tr$
$and : Tr \times Tr \rightarrow Tr$

II. Identifiers
Domain $i \in Id = $ Identifier

III. Text records
Domain $r \in Record$

IV. - VI. defined in Figure 5.3

VII. Character Strings (defined in Example 3.3 of Chapter 3)

VIII. Output terminal log
Domain $l \in Log = String^*$

Valuation functions:

P: Program-session $\rightarrow$ *File-system* $\rightarrow$ (*Log* $\times$ *File-system*)
$\mathbf{P}[\![\mathbf{edit}\ I\ \mathbf{cr}\ S]\!] = \lambda s.$ let $p = copyin\,(access\,([\![I]\!], s))$ in
$(\text{"edit I"}\ cons\ fst(\mathbf{S}[\![S]\!]p\ ),\ update([\![I]\!],\ copyout\ (snd\ (\mathbf{S}[\![S]\!]p\ )),\ s))$

S: Command-sequence $\rightarrow$ *Openfile* $\rightarrow$ (*Log* $\times$ *Openfile*)
$\mathbf{S}[\![C\ \mathbf{cr}\ S]\!] = \lambda p.$ let $(l', p') = \mathbf{C}[\![C]\!]p$ in $((l'\ cons\ fst(\mathbf{S}[\![S]\!]p')),\ snd\,(\mathbf{S}[\![S]\!]p'))$
$\mathbf{S}[\![\mathbf{quit}]\!] = \lambda p.(\text{"quit"}\ cons\ nil\ , p)$

Figure 5.4 (continued)

$\mathbf{C}$: Command $\rightarrow$ *Openfile* $\rightarrow$ (*String* $\times$ *Openfile*)

$\mathbf{C}[\![\text{newfile}]\!] = \lambda p.$ ("newfile", *newfile*)

$\mathbf{C}[\![\textbf{moveforward}]\!] = \lambda p.$ let $(k',p') =$ *isempty* $(p) \rightarrow$ ("error: file is empty", p)
$\quad [\!]$ (*at-last-record*$(p) \rightarrow$ ("error: at back already", p)
$\quad\quad [\!]$ ("", *forwards*(p)))
in ("moveforward" *concat* k', p'))

$\mathbf{C}[\![\textbf{moveback}]\!] = \lambda p.$ let $(k',p') =$ *isempty* $(p) \rightarrow$ ("error: file is empty", p)
$\quad [\!]$ (*at-first-record*$(p) \rightarrow$ ("error: at front already", p))
$\quad\quad [\!]$ ("", *backwards*(p)))
in ("moveback" *concat* k', p')

$\mathbf{C}[\![\textbf{insert R}]\!] = \lambda p.$ ("insert R", *insert* $(\mathbf{R}[\![\text{R}]\!], p)$)

$\mathbf{C}[\![\textbf{delete}]\!] = \lambda p.$ let $(k',p') =$ *isempty* $(p) \rightarrow$ ("error: file is empty", p)
$\quad [\!]$ ("", *delete* (p)))
in ("delete" *concat* k', p')

---

of this list. The equation for $\mathbf{S}[\![\text{C } \mathbf{cr} \text{ S}]\!]$ deserves a bit of study. It says to:

1. Evaluate $\mathbf{C}[\![\text{C}]\!]p$ to obtain the next log entry l' plus the updated open file p'.
2. Cons l' to the log list and pass p' onto $\mathbf{S}[\![\text{S}]\!]$.
3. Evaluate $\mathbf{S}[\![\text{S}]\!]p'$ to obtain the meaning of the remainder of the program, which is the rest of the log output plus the final version of the updated open file.

The two occurrences of $\mathbf{S}[\![\text{S}]\!]p'$ may be a bit confusing. They do *not* mean to "execute" $[\![\text{S}]\!]$ twice— semantic definitions are functions, and the operational analogies are not always exact. The expression has the same meaning as:

let $(l', p') = \mathbf{C}[\![\text{C}]\!]p$ in let $(l'', p'') = \mathbf{S}[\![\text{S}]\!]p'$ in $(l'$ *cons* $l'', p'')$

The $\mathbf{P}$ function is similar in spirit to $\mathbf{S}$. (One last note: there is a bit of cheating in writing "edit I" as a token, because $[\![\text{I}]\!]$ is actually a piece of abstract syntax tree. A coercion function should be used to convert abstract syntax forms to string forms. This is of little importance and is omitted.)

A small example shows how the log successfully collects terminal output. Let $[\![\text{A}]\!]$ be the name of a nonempty file in the file system s_0.

$\mathbf{P}[\![\textbf{edit} \text{ A } \mathbf{cr}\ \textbf{moveback}\ \mathbf{cr}\ \textbf{delete}\ \mathbf{cr}\ \textbf{quit}]\!]s_0$
$=$ ("edit A" *cons* *fst*$(\mathbf{S}[\![\textbf{moveback}\ \mathbf{cr}\ \textbf{delete}\ \mathbf{cr}\ \textbf{quit}]\!]p_0)$,

$$update([\![A]\!], copyout(snd(\mathbf{S}[\![\textbf{moveback cr delete cr quit}]\!]p_0), s_0))$$
$$\text{where } p_0 = copyin\ (access\ ([\![A]\!], s_0))$$

Already, the first line of terminal output is evident, and the remainder of the program can be simplified. After a number of simplifications, we obtain:

$$(\text{"edit A"}\ cons\ \text{"moveback error: at front already"}$$
$$cons\ fst(\mathbf{S}[\![\textbf{delete cr quit}]\!]p_0)),$$
$$update([\![A]\!], copyout(snd(\mathbf{S}[\![\textbf{delete cr quit}]\!]p_0))))$$

as the second command was incorrect. $\mathbf{S}[\![\textbf{delete cr quit}]\!]p_0$ simplifies to a pair ("delete quit", p_1), for $p_1 = delete(p_0)$, and the final result is:

$$(\text{"edit A moveback error: at front already delete quit"},$$
$$update([\![A]\!], copyout(p_1), s_0))$$

5.2.1 Interactive Input and Partial Syntax

A user of a file editor may validly complain that the above definition still isn't realistic enough, for interactive programs like text editors do not collect all their input into a single program before parsing and processing it. Instead, the input is processed incrementally— one line at a time. We might model incremental output by a series of abstract syntax trees. Consider again the sample program [[**edit** A **cr moveback cr delete cr quit**]]. When the first line [[**edit** A **cr**]] is typed at the terminal, the file editor's parser can build an abstract syntax tree that looks like Diagram 5.1:

(5.1)

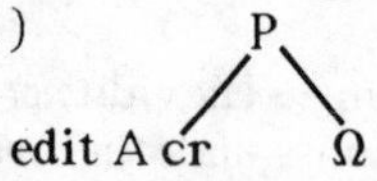

(5.2)

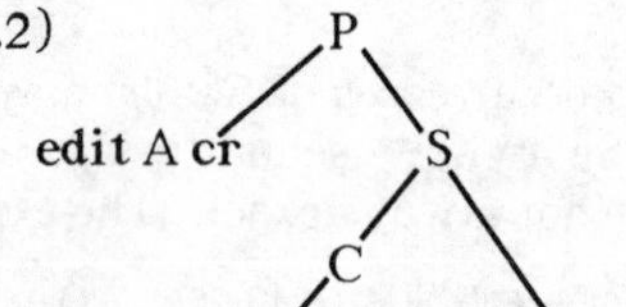

The parser knows that the first line of input is correct, but the remainder, the command sequence part, is unknown. It uses $[\![\Omega]\!]$ to stand in place of the command sequence that follows. The tree in Diagram 5.1 can be pushed through the **P** function, giving $\mathbf{P}[\![\textbf{edit}\ A\ \textbf{cr}\ \Omega]\!]s_0 = (\text{"edit A"}\ cons\ fst(\mathbf{S}[\![\Omega]\!]p_0), update([\![A]\!], copyout(snd(\mathbf{S}[\![\Omega]\!]p_0), s_0)))$ The processing has started, but the entire log and final file system are unknown.

When the user types the next command, the better-defined tree in Diagram 5.2 is built, and the meaning of the new tree is:

$$\mathbf{P}[\![\textbf{edit A cr moveback cr } \Omega]\!] =$$
$$(\text{"edit A" } \textit{cons} \text{ "moveback error: at front already" } \textit{cons } \textit{fst}(\mathbf{S}[\![\Omega]\!]p_0),$$
$$\textit{update}\,([\![\mathrm{A}]\!], \textit{copyout}\,(\textit{snd}\,(\mathbf{S}[\![\Omega]\!]p_0)), s_0))$$

This denotation includes more information than the one for Diagram 5.1; it is "better defined." The next tree is Diagram 5.3:

(5.3)

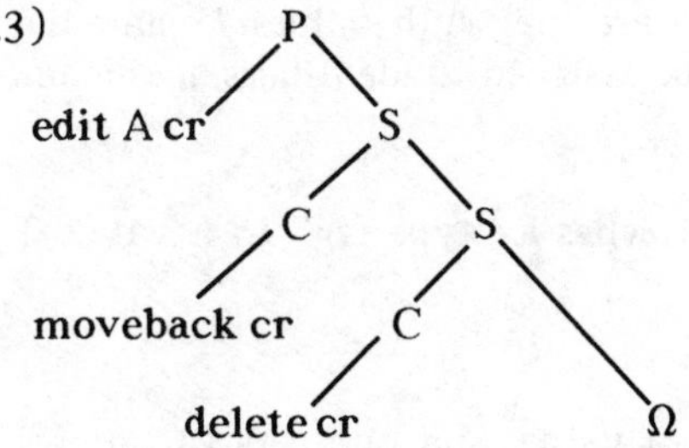

The corresponding semantics can be worked out in a similar fashion. An implementation strategy is suggested by the sequence: an implementation of the valuation function executes under the control of the editor's parser. Whenever the parser obtains a line of input, it inserts it into a partial abstract syntax tree and calls the semantic processor, which continues its logging and file manipulation from the point where it left off, using the new piece of abstract syntax.

This idea can be formalized in an interesting way. Each of the abstract syntax trees was better defined than its predecessor. Let's use the symbol $\sqsubseteq$ to describe this relationship. Thus, $(5.1) \sqsubseteq (5.2) \sqsubseteq (5.3) \sqsubseteq \cdots$ holds for the example. Similarly, we expect that $\mathbf{P}[\![(5.3)]\!]s_0$ contains more answer information than $\mathbf{P}[\![(5.2)]\!]s_0$, which itself has more information than $\mathbf{P}[\![(5.1)]\!]s_0$. If we say that the undefined value $\perp$ has the least answer information possible, we can define $\mathbf{S}[\![\Omega]\!]p = \perp$ for all arguments
p The $\perp$ value stands for undetermined semantic information. Then we have that:

$$(\text{"edit A" } \textit{cons} \perp, \perp)$$
$$\sqsubseteq (\text{"edit A" } \textit{cons} \text{ "moveback error: at front already" } \textit{cons} \perp, \perp)$$
$$\sqsubseteq (\text{"edit A" } \textit{cons} \text{ "moveback error: at front already" } \textit{cons} \text{ "delete" } \textit{cons} \perp, \perp)$$
$$\sqsubseteq \cdots$$

Each better-defined partial tree gives better-defined semantic information. We use these ideas in the next chapter for dealing with recursively defined functions.

5.3 A DYNAMICALLY TYPED LANGUAGE WITH INPUT AND OUTPUT

The third example language is an extension of the one in Section 5.1. Languages like SNOBOL allow variables to take on values from different data types during the course of evaluation. This provides flexibility to the user but requires that type checking be performed at run-time. The semantics of the language gives us insight into the type checking. Input and output are also included in the example.

Figure 5.5 gives the new semantic algebras needed for the language. The value domains that the language uses are the truth values *Tr* and the natural numbers *Nat*. Since these values can be assigned to identifiers, a domain:

$$Storable\text{-}value = Tr + Nat$$

is created. The + domain builder attaches a "type tag" to a value. The *Store* domain becomes:

$$Store = Id \rightarrow Storable\text{-}value$$

The type tags are stored with the truth values and numbers for later reference. Since storable values are used in arithmetic and logical expressions, type errors

Figure 5.5

V. Values that may be stored
  Domain $v \in Storable\text{-}value = Tr + Nat$

VI. Values that expressions may denote
  Domain $x \in Expressible\text{-}value = Storable\text{-}value + Errvalue$
    where $Errvalue = Unit$
  Operations

$check\text{-}expr : (Store \rightarrow Expressible\text{-}value) \times$
$(Storable\text{-}value \rightarrow Store \rightarrow Expressible\text{-}value) \rightarrow (Store \rightarrow Expressible\text{-}value)$

$f_1\ check\text{-}expr\ f_2 = \lambda s.$ cases $(f_1\ s)$ of
  is$Storable\text{-}value(v) \rightarrow (f_2\ v\ s)$
  [] is$Errvalue() \rightarrow$ in$Errvalue()$
  end

VII. Input buffer
  Domain $i \in Input = Expressible\text{-}value^*$
  Operations

$get\text{-}value : Input \rightarrow (Expressible\text{-}value \times Input)$

$get\text{-}value = \lambda i.\ null\ i \rightarrow (inErrvalue(), i)$ [] $(hd\ i, tl\ i)$

Figure 5.5 (continued)

VIII. Output buffer

Domain $o \in Output = (Storable\text{-}value + String)^*$

Operations

$empty : Output$

$empty = nil$

$put\text{-}value : Storable\text{-}value \times Output \to Output$

$put\text{-}value = \lambda(v,o).\ \mathrm{in}Storable\text{-}value(v)\ cons\ o$

$put\text{-}message : String \times Output \to Output$

$put\text{-}message = \lambda(t,o).\ \mathrm{in}String(t)\ cons\ o$

IX. Store

Domain $s \in Store = \mathrm{Id} \to Storable\text{-}value$

Operations

$newstore : Store$

$access : Id \to Store \to Storable\text{-}value$

$update : Id \to Storable\text{-}value \to Store \to Store$

X. Program State

Domain $a \in State = Store \times Input \times Output$

XI. Post program state

Domain $z \in Post\text{-}state = OK + Err$

where $OK = State$

and $Err = State$

Operations

$check\text{-}result : (Store \to Expressible\text{-}value) \times (Storable\text{-}value \to State \to Post\text{-}state_\perp)$
$\to (State \to Post\text{-}state_\perp)$

$f\ check\text{-}result\ \ g = \lambda(s,i,o).\ \mathrm{cases}\ (f\ s)\ \mathrm{of}$

$\qquad \mathrm{is}Storable\text{-}value(v) \to (g\ v\ (s,i,o))$

$\qquad [\!]\ \mathrm{is}Errvalue() \to \mathrm{in}Err(s,\ i,\ put\text{-}message(\text{"type error"},\ o))\ \mathrm{end}$

$check\text{-}cmd : (State \to Post\text{-}state_\perp) \times (State \to Post\text{-}state_\perp) \to (State \to Post\text{-}state_\perp)$

$h_1\ check\text{-}cmd\ \ h_2 = \lambda a.\ \mathrm{let}\ z = (h_1\ a)\ \mathrm{in\ cases}\ z\ \mathrm{of}$

$\qquad \mathrm{is}OK(s,i,o) \to h_2(s,i,o)$

$\qquad [\!]\ \mathrm{is}Err(s,i,o) \to z\ \mathrm{end}$

are possible, as in an attempt to add a truth value to a number. Thus, the values that expressions denote come from the domain:

Expressible-value = *Storable-value* + *Errvalue*

where the domain *Errvalue* = *Unit* is used to denote the result of a type error.

Of interest is the program state, which is a triple of the store and the input and output buffers. The *Post-state* domain is used to signal when an evaluation is completed successfully and when a type error occurs. The tag attached to the state is utilized by the *checkcmd* operation. This operation is the sequencing operation for the language and is represented in infix form. The expression (C⟦C_1⟧ *check-cmd* C⟦C_2⟧) does the following:

1. It gives the current state a to C⟦C_1⟧, producing a post-state z = C⟦C_1⟧a.
2. If z is a proper state a′, and then, if the state component is *OK*, it produces C⟦C_2⟧a'. If z is erroneous, C⟦C_2⟧ is ignored (it is "branched over"), and z is the result.

A similar sequencing operation, *check-result*, sequences an expression with a command. For example, in an assignment ⟦I:=E⟧, ⟦E⟧'s value must be determined before a store update can occur. Since ⟦E⟧'s evaluation may cause a type error, the error must be detected before the update is attempted. Operation *check-result* performs this action. Finally, *check-expr* performs error trapping at the expression level.

Figure 5.6 shows the valuation functions for the language.

You are encouraged to write several programs in the language and derive their denotations. Notice how the algebra operations abort normal evaluation when type errors occur. The intuition behind the operations is that they represent low-level (even hardware-level) fault detection and branching mechanisms. When a fault is detected, the usual machine action is a single branch out of the program. The operations defined here can only "branch" out of a subpart of the function expression, but since all type errors are propagated, these little branches chain together to form a branch out of the entire program. The implementor of the language would take note of this property and produce full jumps on error detection. Similarly, the in*OK* and in*Err* tags would not be physically implemented, as any running program has an *OK* state, and any error branch causes a change to the *Err* state.

5.4 ALTERING THE PROPERTIES OF STORES

The uses of the store argument in this chapter maintain properties 1-3 noted in the introduction to this chapter. These properties limit the use of stores. Of course, the properties are limiting in the sense that they describe typical features of a store in a sequential programming language. It is instructive to relax each

Figure 5.6

Abstract syntax:

P∈ Program
C∈ Command
E∈ Expression
I ∈ Id
N∈ Numeral

P ::= C.
C ::= C_1;C_2 | I:=E | **if** E **then** C_1 **else** C_2 | **read** I | **write** E | **diverge**
E ::= E_1+E_2 | E_1=E_2 | ¬ E | (E) | I | N | **true**

Semantic algebras:

I. Truth values (defined in Figure 5.1)

II. Natural numbers (defined in Figure 5.1)

III. Identifiers (defined in Figure 5.1)

IV. Character strings (defined in Example 3.5 of Chapter 3)

V. - XI. (defined in Figure 5.5)

Valuation functions:

P: Program→*Store* →*Input* →*Post-state*$_\perp$
  P⟦C.⟧ = λs.λi. C⟦C⟧ (s, i, *empty*)

C: Command→*State* →*Post-state*$_\perp$
  C⟦C_1;C_2⟧ = C⟦C_1⟧ *check-cmd* C⟦C_2⟧
  C⟦I:=E⟧ = E⟦E⟧ *check-result* (λv.λ(s,i,o). in*OK*((*update* ⟦I⟧ v s), i, o))
  C⟦**if** E **then** C_1 **else** C_2⟧ = E⟦E⟧ *check-result*
    (λv.λ(s,i,o). cases v of
      is*Tr*(t)→(t →C⟦C_1⟧ [] C⟦C_2⟧)(s,i,o)
      [] is*Nat*(n)→in*Err*(s,i, *put-message*("bad test", o)) end)
  C⟦**read** I⟧ = λ(s,i,o). let (x,i′) = *get-value*(i) in
    cases x of
      is*Storable-value*(v) → in*OK*((*update* ⟦I⟧ v s), i′, o)
      [] is*Errvalue*() → in*Err*(s, i′, *put-message*("bad input", o)) end
  C⟦**write** E⟧ = E⟦E⟧ *check-result* (λv.λ(s,i,o). in*OK*(s, i, *put-value*(v,o)))
  C⟦**diverge**⟧ = λa. ⊥

Figure 5.6 (continued)

E: Expression→*Store*→*Expressible-value*

E⟦E₁+E₂⟧ = E⟦E₁⟧ *check-expr*
(λv. cases v of
isTr(t)→λs. inErrvalue()
[] isNat(n)→E⟦E₂⟧ *check-expr*
(λv'.λs. cases v' of
isTr(t')→inErrvalue()
[] isNat(n')→inStorable-value(inNat(n plus n')) end)
end)

E⟦E₁=E₂⟧ = "similar to above equation"

E⟦¬ E⟧ = E⟦E⟧ *check-expr*
(λv.λs. cases v of
isTr(t)→inStorable-value(inTr(not t))
[] isNat(n)→inErrvalue() end)

E⟦(E)⟧ = E⟦E⟧

E⟦I⟧ = λs. inStorable-value(access ⟦I⟧ s)

E⟦N⟧ = λs. inStorable-value(inNat(N⟦N⟧))

E⟦true⟧ = λs. inStorable-value(inTr(true))

N:Numeral→*Nat* (omitted)

---

of restrictions 1, 3, and 2 in turn and see what character of programming languages result.

5.4.1 Delayed Evaluation

Call-by-value (argument first) simplification is the safe method for rewriting operator, argument combinations when strict functions are used. This point is important, for it suggests that an implementation of the strict function needs an evaluated argument to proceed. Similarly, call-by-name (argument last) simplification is the safe method for handling arguments to nonstrict functions. Here is an example: consider the nonstrict function $f = (\lambda x.\ zero)$ of domain $Nat_\perp \rightarrow Nat_\perp$. If f is given an argument e whose meaning is $\perp$, then $f(e)$ is *zero*. Argument e's simplification may require an infinite number of steps, for it represents a nonterminating evaluation. Clearly, e should not be simplified if given to a nonstrict f.

The *Store*-based operations use only proper arguments and a store can only hold values that are proper. Let's consider how stores might operate with improper values. First, say that expression evaluation can produce both proper and improper values. Alter the *Store* domain to be $Store = Id \rightarrow Nat_{\perp}$. Now improper values may be stored. Next, adjust the *update* operation to be: $update : Id \rightarrow Nat_{\perp} \rightarrow Store \rightarrow Store$, $update = \lambda i.\lambda n.\lambda s.[\, i \mapsto n\,]s$. An assignment statement uses *update* to store the value of an expression [[E]] into the store. If [[E]] represents a "loop forever" situation, then $\mathbf{E}[\![E]\!]s = \perp$. But, since *update* is nonstrict in its second argument, $(update\ [\![I]\!]\ (\mathbf{E}[\![E]\!]s)\ s)$ is defined. From the operational viewpoint, unevaluated or partially evaluated expressions may be stored into s. The form $\mathbf{E}[\![E]\!]s$ need not be evaluated until it is used; the arrangement is called *delayed* (or *lazy*) *evaluation*. Delayed evaluation provides the advantage that the only expressions evaluated are the ones that are actually needed for computing answers. But, once **E**[[E]]'s value is needed, it must be determined with respect to the store that was active when [[E]] was saved. To understand this point, consider this code:

```
begin
    X:=0;
    Y:=X+1;
    X:=4
resultis Y
```

where the block construct is defined as:

$$\mathbf{K}: \text{Block} \rightarrow Store_{\perp} \rightarrow Nat_{\perp}$$

$$\mathbf{K}[\![\textbf{begin}\ \text{C}\ \textbf{resultis}\ \text{E}]\!] = \underline{\lambda} s.\, \mathbf{E}[\![E]\!]\,(\mathbf{C}[\![C]\!]s\,)$$

(Note: **E** now has functionality $\mathbf{E}: \text{Expression} \rightarrow Store_{\perp} \rightarrow Nat_{\perp}$, and it is strict in its store argument.) At the final line of the example, the value of [[Y]] must be determined. The semantics of the example, with some proper store s_0, is:

$$\begin{aligned}
&\mathbf{K}[\![\textbf{begin}\ \text{X:=0; Y:=X+1; X:=4}\ \textbf{resultis}\ \text{Y}]\!]s_0\\
&= \mathbf{E}[\![Y]\!]\,(\mathbf{C}[\![\text{X:=0; Y:=X+1; X:=4}]\!]s_0)\\
&= \mathbf{E}[\![Y]\!]\,(\mathbf{C}[\![\text{Y:=X+1; X:=4}]\!]\,(\mathbf{C}[\![\text{X:=0}]\!]s_0))\\
&= \mathbf{E}[\![Y]\!]\,(\mathbf{C}[\![\text{Y:=X+1; X:=4}]\!]\,(update\,[\![X]\!]\,(\mathbf{E}[\![0]\!]s_0)\ s_0))
\end{aligned}$$

At this point, $(\mathbf{E}[\![0]\!]s_0)$ need not be simplified; a new, proper store, $s_1 = (update\,[\![X]\!]\ \mathbf{E}[\![0]\!]s_0\ s_0)$ is defined regardless. Continuing through the other two commands, we obtain:

$$\begin{aligned}
&s_3 = update\,[\![X]\!]\ (\mathbf{E}[\![4]\!]s_2)\ s_2\\
&\qquad \text{where } s_2 = update\,[\![Y]\!]\ (\mathbf{E}[\![X+1]\!]s_1)\ s_1
\end{aligned}$$

and the meaning of the block is:

$$\mathbf{E}[\![Y]\!]s_3 = access\,[\![Y]\!]\,s_3$$
$$= \mathbf{E}[\![X+1]\!]s_1$$
$$= \mathbf{E}[\![X]\!]s_1\ plus\ one$$
$$= (access\,[\![X]\!]\,s_1)\ plus\ one)$$
$$= \mathbf{E}[\![0]\!]s_0\ plus\ one$$
$$= zero\ plus\ one = one$$

The old version of the store, version s_1, must be retained to obtain the proper value for $[\![X]\!]$ in $[\![X+1]\!]$. If s_3 was used instead, the answer would have been the incorrect *five*.

Delayed evaluation can be carried up to the command level by making the **C**, **E**, and **K** functions nonstrict in their store arguments. The surprising result is that only those commands that have an effect on the output of a program need be evaluated. Convert all strict abstractions $(\underline{\lambda} s.\, e)$ in the equations for **C** in Figure 5.2 to the nonstrict forms $(\lambda s.\, e)$. Redefine *access* and *update* to be:

$$access : \text{Identifier} \to Store_\perp \to Nat_\perp$$
$$access = \lambda i.\underline{\lambda} s.\, s(i)$$
$$update : \text{Identifier} \to Nat_\perp \to Store_\perp \to Store_\perp$$
$$update = \lambda i.\lambda m.\lambda p.\,(\lambda i'.\, i'\ equals\ i \to m\ [\!]\ (access\ i'\ p))$$

Then, regardless of the input store s, the program:

```
begin
    X:=0;
    diverge;
    X:=2
resultis X+1
```

has the value *three*! This is because $\mathbf{C}[\![X{:=}0; \mathbf{diverge}]\!]s = \perp$, and:

$$\mathbf{E}[\![X+1]\!](\mathbf{C}[\![X{:=}2]\!]\perp)$$
$$= \mathbf{E}[\![X+1]\!](update\,[\![X]\!]\,(\mathbf{E}[\![2]\!]\perp)\perp),\ \text{as } \mathbf{C} \text{ is nonstrict}$$
$$= \mathbf{E}[\![X+1]\!](\,[\,[\![X]\!]\mapsto\mathbf{E}[\![2]\!]\perp\,]\perp),\ \text{as } update \text{ is nonstrict}$$
$$= \mathbf{E}[\![X]\!](\,[\,[\![X]\!]\mapsto\mathbf{E}[\![2]\!]\perp\,]\perp)\ plus\ one$$
$$= (access\,[\![X]\!](\,[\,[\![X]\!]\mapsto\mathbf{E}[\![2]\!]\perp\,]\perp))\ plus\ one$$
$$= \mathbf{E}[\![2]\!]\perp\ plus\ one$$
$$= two\ plus\ one,\ \text{as } \mathbf{E} \text{ is nonstrict}$$
$$= three$$

The derivation suggests that only the last command in the block need be evaluated to obtain the answer. Of course, this goes against the normal left-to-right, top-to-bottom sequentiality of command evaluation, so the nonstrict handling of stores requires a new implementation strategy.

5.4.2 Retaining Multiple Stores

Relaxing the strictness condition upon stores means that multiple values of stores must be present in an evaluation. Must an implementation of any of the languages defined earlier in this chapter use multiple stores? At first glance, the definition of addition:

$$\mathbf{E}[\![\mathrm{E}_1 + \mathrm{E}_2]\!] = \lambda s.\, \mathbf{E}[\![\mathrm{E}_1]\!]s \textit{ plus } \mathbf{E}[\![\mathrm{E}_2]\!]s$$

apparently does need two copies of the store to evaluate. Actually, the format is a bit deceiving. An implementation of this clause need only retain one copy of the store s because both $\mathbf{E}[\![\mathrm{E}_1]\!]$ and $\mathbf{E}[\![\mathrm{E}_2]\!]$ use s in a "read only" mode. Since s is not updated by either, the equation should be interpreted as saying that the order of evaluation of the two operands to the addition is unimportant. They may even be evaluated in parallel. The obvious implementation of the store is a global variable that both operands may access.

This situation changes when side effects occur within expression evaluation. If we add the block construct to the Expression syntax domain and define its semantics to be:

$$\mathbf{E}[\![\textbf{begin } \mathrm{C} \textbf{ resultis } \mathrm{E}]\!] = \underline{\lambda} s.\, \text{let } s' = \mathbf{C}[\![\mathrm{C}]\!]s \text{ in } \mathbf{E}[\![\mathrm{E}]\!]s'$$

then expressions are no longer "read only" objects. An implementation faithful to the semantic equation must allow an expression to own a local copy of store. The local store and its values disappear upon completion of expression evaluation. To see this, you should perform the simplification of $\mathbf{C}[\![\mathrm{X}{:=}(\textbf{begin } \mathrm{Y}{:=}\mathrm{Y}+1 \textbf{ resultis } \mathrm{Y})+\mathrm{Y}]\!]$. The incrementation of $[\![\mathrm{Y}]\!]$ in the left operand is unknown to the right operand. Further, the store that gets the new value of $[\![\mathrm{X}]\!]$ is exactly the one that existed prior to the right-hand side's evaluation.

The more conventional method of integrating expression-level updates into a language forces any local update to remain in the global store and thus affect later evaluation. A more conventional semantics for the block construct is:

$$\mathbf{K}[\![\textbf{begin } \mathrm{C} \textbf{ resultis } \mathrm{E}]\!] = \underline{\lambda} s.\, \text{let } s' = \mathbf{C}[\![\mathrm{C}]\!]s \text{ in } (\mathbf{E}[\![\mathrm{E}]\!]s', s')$$

The expressible value and the updated store form a pair that is the result of the block.

5.4.3 Noncommunicating Commands

The form of communication that a store facilitates is the building up of side effects that lead to some final value. The purpose of a command is to advance a computation a bit further by drawing upon the values left in the store by previous commands. When a command is no longer allowed to draw upon the values, the communication breaks down, and the language no longer has a sequential flavor.

Let's consider an example that makes use of multiple stores. Assume there exists some domain D with an operation $combine: D \times D \to D$. If *combine* builds a "higher-quality" D-value from its two D-valued arguments, a useful store-based, noncommunicating semantics might read:

Domain $s \in Store = Id \to D$

C: Command$\to Store_\perp \to Store_\perp$

$\mathbf{C}[\![C_1;C_2]\!] = \underline{\lambda} s.\, join\, (\mathbf{C}[\![C_1]\!]s)\, (\mathbf{C}[\![C_2]\!]s)$

where $join : Store_\perp \to Store_\perp \to Store_\perp$

$join = \underline{\lambda} s_1.\underline{\lambda} s_2.\, (\lambda i.\, s_1(i)\ combine\ s_2(i))$

These clauses suggest parallel but noninterfering execution of commands. Computing is divided between $[\![C_1]\!]$ and $[\![C_2]\!]$ and the partial results are joined using *combine*. This is a nontraditional use of parallelism on stores; the traditional form of parallelism allows interference and uses the single-store model. Nonetheless, the above example is interesting because it suggests that noncommunicating commands can work together to build answers rather than deleting each other's updates.

SUGGESTED READINGS

Semantics of the store and assignment: Barron 1977; Donohue 1977; Friedman et al. 1984; Landin 1965; Strachey 1966, 1968
Interactive systems: Bjørner and Jones 1982; Cleaveland 1980
Dynamic typing: Tennent 1973
Delayed evaluation: Augustsson 1984; Friedman & Wise 1976; Henderson 1980; Henderson & Morris 1976

EXERCISES

1. Determine the denotations of the following programs in $Nat_\perp$ when they are used with the input data value *one*:

a. **P**[[Z:=A.]]
b. **P**[[(**if** A=0 **then diverge else** Y:=A+1);Z:=Y.]]
c. **P**[[**diverge**; Z:=0.]]

2. Determine the denotations of the programs in the previous exercise without any input; that is, give their meanings in the domain $Nat \to Nat_{\perp}$.

3. Give an example of a program whose semantics with respect to Figure 5.2, is the denotation ($\lambda n.\ one$). Does an algorithmic method exist for listing all the programs with exactly this denotation?

4. Show that the following properties hold with respect to the semantic definition of Figure 5.2:

a. **P**[[Z:=0; **if** A=0 **then** Z:=A.]] = **P**[[Z:=0.]]
b. For any C∈ Command, **C**[[**diverge**; C]] = **C**[[**diverge**]]
c. For all E_1, E_2∈ Expression, **E**[[E_1+E_2]] = **E**[[E_2+E_1]]
d. For any B∈ Boolean-expr, C_1, C_2∈ Command,
C[[**if** B **then** C_1 **else** C_2]] = **C**[[**if** ¬ B **then** C_2 **else** C_1]].
e. There exist some B∈ Boolean-expr and C_1, C_2∈ Command such that **C**[[**if** B **then** C_1; **if** ¬ B **then** C_2]] ≠ **C**[[**if** B **then** C_1 **else** C_2]]

(Hint: many of the proofs will rely on the extensionality of functions.)

5. a. Using structural induction, prove the following: for every E∈ Expression in the language of Figure 5.2, for any I∈ Identifier, *E'*∈ Expression, and *s* ∈ *Store*, **E**[[[E'/I]E]]*s* = **E**[[E]](*update* [[I]] **E**[[E']]*s s*).
b. Use the result of part a to prove: for every B∈ Boolean-expr in the language of Figure 5.2, for every I∈ Identifier, *E'*∈ Expression, and *s* ∈ *Store*, **B**[[[E'/I]B]]*s* = **B**[[B]](*update* [[I]] **E**[[E']]*s s*).

6. Say that the *Store* algebra in Figure 5.1 is redefined so that the domain is $s \in Store' = (Id \times Nat)^*$.

a. Define the operations *newstore'*, *access'*, and *update'* to operate upon the new domain. (For this exercise, you are allowed to use a recursive definition for *access'*. The definition must satisfy the properties stated in the solution to Exercise 14, part b, of Chapter 3.) Must the semantic equations in Figure 5.2 be adjusted to work with the new algebra?
b. Prove that the definitions created in part a satisfy the properties: for all $i \in Id$, $n \in Nat$, and $s \in Store'$:

access' i newstore' = *zero*
access' i (*update' i n s*) = *n*
access' i (*update' j n s*) = (*access' i s*), for $j \neq i$

How do these proofs relate the new *Store* algebra to the original? Try to define a notion of "equivalence of definitions" for the class of all *Store* algebras.

7. Augment the Command syntax domain in Figure 5.2 with a **swap** command:

   $C ::= \cdots \mid \mathbf{swap}\ I_1, I_2$

   The action of **swap** is to interchange the values of its two identifier variables. Define the semantic equation for **swap** and prove that the following property holds for any $J \in Id$ and $s \in Store$: $\mathbf{C}[\![\mathbf{swap}\ J, J]\!]s = s$. (Hint: appeal to the extensionality of store functions.)

8. a. Consider the addition of a Pascal-like **cases** command to the language of Figure 5.2. The syntax goes as follows:

   C∈ Command
   G∈ Guard
   E∈ Expression

   $C ::= \cdots \mid \mathbf{case}\ E\ \mathbf{of}\ G\ \mathbf{end}$
   $G ::= N{:}C;\ G \mid N{:}C$

   Define the semantic equation for $\mathbf{C}[\![\mathbf{case}\ E\ \mathbf{of}\ G\ \mathbf{end}]\!]$ and the equations for the valuation function $\mathbf{G}: \text{Guard} \rightarrow (Nat \times Store) \rightarrow Store$. List the design decisions that must be made.

   b. Repeat part a with the rule $G ::= N{:}C \mid G_1; G_2$

9. Say that the command $[\![\mathbf{test}\ E\ \mathbf{on}\ C]\!]$ is proposed as an extension to the language of Figure 5.2. The semantics is:

   $$\mathbf{C}[\![\mathbf{test}\ E\ \mathbf{on}\ C]\!] = \underline{\lambda} s.\ \text{let}\ s' = \mathbf{C}[\![C]\!]s\ \text{in}\ \mathbf{E}[\![E]\!]s'\ \mathit{equals\ zero} \rightarrow s' \,[\!]\, s$$

   What problems do you see with implementing this construct on a conventional machine?

10. Someone proposes a version of "parallel assignment" with semantics:

   $$\mathbf{C}[\![I_1, I_2 := E_1, E_2]\!] = \underline{\lambda} s.\ \text{let}\ s' = (\mathit{update}\ [\![I_1]\!]\ \mathbf{E}[\![E_1]\!]s\ s)$$
   $$\text{in}\ \mathit{update}\ [\![I_2]\!]\ \mathbf{E}[\![E_2]\!]s'\ s'$$

   Show, via a counterexample, that the semantics does not define a true parallel assignment. Propose an improvement. What is the denotation of $[\![J, J := 0, 1]\!]$ in your semantics?

11. In a LUCID-like language, a family of parallel assignments are performed in a construct known as a *block*. The syntax of a block B is:

B ::= **begin** A **end**
A ::= I_{new}:=E | A_1§A_2

The block is further restricted so that all identifiers on the left hand sides of assignments in a block must be distinct. Define the semantics of the block construct.

12. Add the **diverge** construction to the syntax of Expression in Figure 5.2 and say that **E**[[**diverge**]] = $\lambda s. \perp$. How does this addition impact:

    a. The functionalities and semantic equations for **C**, **E**, and **B**?
    b. The definition and use of the operations *update*, *plus*, *equals*, and *not*? What is your opinion about allowing the possibility of nontermination in expression evaluation? What general purpose imperative languages do you know of that guarantee termination of expression evaluation?

13. The document defining the semantics of Pascal claims that the order of evaluation of operands in an (arithmetic) expression is left unspecified; that is, a machine may evaluate the operands in whatever order it pleases. Is this concept expressed in the semantics of expressions in Figure 5.2? However, recall that Pascal expressions may contain side effects. Let's study this situation by adding the construct [[C **in** E]]. Its evaluation first evaluates [[C]] and then evaluates [[E]] using the store that was updated by [[C]]. The store (with the updates) is passed on for later use. Define **E**[[C **in** E]]. How must the functionality of **E** change to accommodate the new construct? Rewrite all the other semantic equations for **E** as needed. What order of evaluation of operands does your semantics describe? Is it possible to specify a truly nondeterminate order of evaluation?

14. For some defined store s_0, give the denotations of each of the following file editor programs, using the semantics in Figure 5.4:

    a. **P**[[**edit** A **cr newfile cr insert** R_0 **cr insert** R_1 **quit**]]s_0. Call the result (log_1, s_1).
    b. **P**[[**edit** A **cr moveforward cr delete cr insert** R_2 **quit**]]s_1, where s_1 is from part a. Call the new result (log_2, s_2).
    c. **P**[[**edit** A **cr insert** R_3 *cr* **quit**]]s_2, where s_2 is from part b.

15. Redo part a of the previous question in the style described in Section 5.2.1, showing the partial syntax trees and the partial denotations produced at each step.

16. Extend the file editor of Figure 5.4 to be a text editor: define the internal structure of the *Record* semantic domain in Figure 5.3 and devise operations for manipulating the words in a record. Augment the syntax of the

language so that a user may do manipulations on the words within individual records.

17. Design a programming language for performing character string manipulation. The language should support fundamental operations for pattern matching and string manipulation and possess assignment and control structure constructs for imperative programming. Define the semantic algebras first and then define the abstract syntax and valuation functions.

18. Design a semantics for the grocery store data base language that you defined in Exercise 6 of Chapter 1. What problems arise because the abstract syntax was defined before the semantic algebras? What changes would you make to the language's syntax after this exercise?

19. In the example in Section 5.3, the *Storable-value* domain is a subdomain of the *Expressible-value* domain; that is, every storable value is expressible. What problems arise when this isn't the case? What problems/situations arise when an expressible value isn't storable? Give examples.

20. In the language of Figure 5.6, what is **P**[[**write** 2; **diverge.**]]? Is this a satisfactory denotation for the program? If not, suggest some revisions to the semantics.

21. Alter the semantics of the language of Figure 5.6 so that an expressible value error causes an error message to be placed into the output buffer immediately (rather than letting the command in which the expressible value is embedded report the message later).

22. Extend the *Storable-value* algebra of Figure 5.5 so that arithmetic can be performed on the (numeric portion of) storable values. In particular, define operations:

    plus' : *Storable-value* × *Storable-value* → *Expressible-value*
    not' : *Storable-value* → *Expressible-value*
    equals' : *Storable-value* × *Storable-value* → *Expressible-value*

    so that the equations in the **E** valuation function can be written more simply, e.g.,

    $$\mathbf{E}[\![E_1 + E_2]\!] = \mathbf{E}[\![E_1]\!]s\ \mathit{check\text{-}expr}\ (\lambda v_1 .\ \mathbf{E}[\![E_2]\!]s\ \mathit{check\text{-}expr}\ (\lambda v_2 .\ v_1\ \mathit{plus'}\ v_2))$$

    Rewrite the other equations of **E** in this fashion. How would the new versions of the storable value operations be implemented on a computer?

23. Alter the semantics of the language of Figure 5.6 so that a variable retains the type of the first identifier that is assigned to it.

24. a. Alter the *Store* algebra in Figure 5.5 so that:

$$Store = Index \rightarrow Storable\text{-}value^*$$
where $Index = Id + Input + Output$
$Input = Unit$
$Output = Unit$

that is, the input and output buffers are kept in the store and indexed by tags. Define the appropriate operations. Do the semantic equations require alterations?

b. Take advantage of the new definition of storage by mapping a variable to a *history* of all its updates that have occurred since the program has been running.

25. Remove the command [[**read** I]] from the language of Figure 5.6 and place the construct [[**read**]] into the syntax of expressions.

a. Give the semantic equation for **E**[[**read**]].
b. Prove that **C**[[**read** I]] = **C**[[I:= **read**]].
c. What are the pragmatic advantages and disadvantages of the new construct?

26. Suppose that the *Store* domain is defined to be $Store = Id \rightarrow (Store \rightarrow Nat)$ and the semantic equation for assignment is:

C[[I:=E]] = $\underline{\lambda}s.\,update$ [[I]] (**E**[[E]]) s

a. Define the semantic equations for the **E** valuation function.
b. How does this view of expression evaluation differ from that given in Figures 5.1 and 5.2? How is the new version like a macroprocessor? How is it different?

27. If you are familiar with data flow and demand-driven languages, comment on the resemblance of the nonstrict version of the **C** valuation function in Section 5.4.1 to these forms of computation.

28. Say that a vendor has asked you to design a simple, general purpose, imperative programming language. The language will include concepts of *expression* and *command*. Commands update the store; expressions do not. The *control structures* for commands include sequencing and conditional choice.

a. What questions should you ask the vendor about the language's design? Which design decisions should you make without consulting the vendor first?

b. Say that you decide to use denotational semantics to define the semantics of the language. How does its use direct and restrict your view of:

i. What the store should be?
ii. How stores are accessed and updated?
iii. What the order of evaluation of command and expression subparts should be?
iv. How the control structures order command evaluation?

29. Programming language design has traditionally worked from a "bottom up" perspective; that is, given a physical computer, a machine language is defined for giving instructions to the computer. Then, a second language is designed that is "higher level" (more concise or easier for humans to use) than the first, and a translator program is written to translate from the second language to the first.

Why does this approach limit our view as to what a programming language should be? How might we break out of this approach by using denotational semantics to design new languages? What biases do we acquire when we use denotational semantics?

Chapter 6

Domain Theory II: Recursively Defined Functions

The examples in Chapter 5 provide strong evidence that denotational semantics is an expressive and convenient tool for language definition. Yet a few gaps remain to be filled. In Figure 5.3, the *copyout* function, which concatenates two lists, is not given. We can specify *copyout* using an iterative or recursive specification, but at this point neither is allowed in the function notation.

A similar situation arises with the semantics of a Pascal-like **while**-loop:

B: Boolean-expression
C: Command
  C ::= ··· | **while** B **do** C | ···

Here is a recursive definition of its semantics: for **B**: Boolean-expression $\rightarrow Store \rightarrow Tr$ and **C**: Command $\rightarrow Store_{\perp} \rightarrow Store_{\perp}$:

$$\mathbf{C}[\![\mathbf{while}\ \mathrm{B}\ \mathbf{do}\ \mathrm{C}]\!] = \underline{\lambda} s.\, \mathbf{B}[\![\mathrm{B}]\!]s \rightarrow \mathbf{C}[\![\mathbf{while}\ \mathrm{B}\ \mathbf{do}\ \mathrm{C}]\!](\mathbf{C}[\![\mathrm{C}]\!]s)\ [\!]\ s$$

Unfortunately, the clause violates a rule of Chapter 3: the meaning of a syntax phrase may be defined only in terms of the meanings of its proper subparts. We avoid this problem by stating:

$$\mathbf{C}[\![\mathbf{while}\ \mathrm{B}\ \mathbf{do}\ \mathrm{C}]\!] = w$$
$$\text{where } w : Store_{\perp} \rightarrow Store_{\perp} \text{ is } \quad w = \underline{\lambda} s.\, \mathbf{B}[\![\mathrm{B}]\!]s \rightarrow w(\mathbf{C}[\![\mathrm{C}]\!]s)\ [\!]\ s$$

But the recursion remains, for the new version exchanges the recursion in the syntax for recursion in the function notation.

We have steadfastly avoided recursion in function definitions because Section 3.3 showed that a recursive definition might not define a unique function. Recall the recursive specification of function $q : Nat \rightarrow Nat_{\perp}$ from Section 3.3:

$$q = \lambda n.\, n\ equals\ zero \rightarrow one\ [\!]\ q(n\ plus\ one)$$

Whatever q stands for, it must map a *zero* argument to *one*. Its behavior for other arguments, however, is not so clear. All the specification requires is that the answer for a nonzero argument n be the same as that for n *plus one*, its successor. A large number of functions satisfy this criterion. One choice is the function that maps *zero* to *one* and all other arguments to $\bot$. We write this function's graph as $\{(zero, one)\}$ (rather than $\{(zero, one), (one, \bot), (two, \bot), \cdots\}$, treating the $(n, \bot)$ pairs as "ghost members"). This choice is a natural one for programming, for it corresponds to what happens when the definition is run as a routine on a machine. But it is not the only choice. The graph $\{(zero, one), (one, four), (two, four), (three, four), \cdots\}$ denotes a function that also has the behavior specified by *q*— *zero* maps to *one* and all other arguments map to the same answer as their successors. In general, any function whose graph is of the form $\{(zero, one), (one, k), (two, k), \cdots\}$, for some $k \in Nat_\bot$, satisfies the specification. For a programmer, the last graph is an unnatural choice for the meaning of *q*, but a mathematician might like a function with the largest possible graph instead, the claim being that a "fuller" function gives more insight. In any case, a problem exists: a recursive specification may not define a unique function, so which one should be selected as *the* meaning of the specification? Since programming languages are implemented on machines, we wish to choose the function that suits operational intuitions. Fortunately, a well-developed theory known as *least fixed point semantics* establishes the meaning of recursive specifications. The theory:

1. Guarantees that the specification has at least one function satisfying it.
2. Provides a means for choosing a "best" function out of the set of all functions satisfying the specification.
3. Ensures that the function selected has a graph corresponding to the conventional operational treatment of recursion: the function maps an argument *a* to a defined answer *b* iff the operational evaluation of the specification with the representation of argument *a* produces the representation of *b* in a finite number of recursive invocations.

Two simple examples of recursive specifications will introduce all the important concepts in the theory. The theory itself is formalized in Sections 6.2 through 6.5. If you are willing to accept that recursive specifications do indeed denote unique functions, you may wish to read only Sections 6.1 and 6.6.

6.1 SOME RECURSIVELY DEFINED FUNCTIONS

Perhaps the best known example of a recursive function specification is the factorial function. Since it is so well understood, it makes an excellent testing ground for the theory. Its specification is $fac: Nat \rightarrow Nat_\bot$ such that:

$$fac(n) = n\ equals\ zero \rightarrow one\ []\ n\ times\ (fac(n\ minus\ one))$$

This specification differs from *q*'s because only one function satisfies the specification: the factorial function, whose graph is $\{(zero, one), (one, one),$

(*two*, *two*), (*three*, *six*), $\cdots$, (*i*, *i*!), $\cdots$ }. The graph will be the key to understanding the meaning of the specification. Note that it is an infinite set. It is often difficult for people to understand infinite objects; we tend to learn about them by considering their finite subparts and building up, step by step, toward the object. We can study the factorial function in this way by evaluating sample arguments with *fac*. Since the function underlying the recursive specification is not formally defined at the moment, an arrow (⇛) will be used when a recursive unfolding is made.

Here is an evaluation using *fac*:

fac(*three*) ⇛ *three equals zero* → *one* [] *three times fac*(*three minus one*)
= *three times fac*(*three minus one*)
= *three times fac*(*two*)
⇛ *three times* (*two equals zero* → *one* [] *two times fac*(*two minus one*))
= *three times* (*two times fac*(*one*))
⇛ *three times* (*two times* (*one equals zero* → *one*
[] *one times fac*(*one minus one*)))
= *three times* (*two times* (*one times fac*(*zero*)))
⇛ *three times* (*two times* (*one times* (*zero equals zero* → *one*
[] *zero times fac*(*zero minus one*))))
= *three times* (*two times* (*one times one*))
= *six*

The recursive unfoldings and simplifications correspond to the conventional operational treatment of a recursive routine. Four unfoldings of the recursive definition were needed to produce the answer. To make the *fac* specification produce an answer *b* from an argument *a*, at most a *finite* number of unfoldings are needed. If an *infinite* number of unfoldings are needed to produce an answer, the evaluation will never be complete. These ideas apply to the specification *q* as well. Only argument *zero* ever produces an answer in a finite number of unfoldings of *q*.

Rather than randomly supplying arguments to *fac*, we use a more systematic method to understand its workings. Our approach is to place a limit on the number of unfoldings of *fac* and see which arguments can produce answers. Here is a summary of *fac*'s behavior broken down in this fashion:

1. *Zero unfoldings*: no argument $n \in Nat$ can produce an answer, for no form *fac*(*n*) can simplify to an answer without the initial unfolding. The corresponding function graph is { }.
2. *One unfolding*: this allows *fac* to be replaced by its body only once. Thus, *fac*(*zero*) ⇛ *zero equals zero* → *one* [] $\cdots$ = *one*, but all other nonzero arguments require further unfoldings to simplify to answers. The graph produced is { (*zero*, *one*) }.
3. *Two unfoldings*: since only one unfolding is needed for mapping argument

zero to *one*, (*zero*, *one*) appears in the graph. The extra unfolding allows argument *one* to evaluate to *one*, for *fac*(*one*) ⇒ *one equals zero* → *one* [] *one times* (*fac*(*one minus one*)) = *one times fac*(*zero*) ⇒ *one times* (*zero equals zero* → *one* [] ···) = *one times one* = *one*. All other arguments require further unfoldings and do not produce answers at this stage. The graph is { (*zero*, *one*), (*one*, *one*) }.

4. $(i+1)$ *unfoldings, for* $i \geq 0$: all arguments with values of i or less will simplify to answers $i!$, giving the graph { (*zero*, *one*), (*one*, *one*), (*two*, *two*), (*three*, *six*), ···, $(i, i!)$ }.

The graph produced at each stage defines a function. In the above example, let fac_i denote the function defined at stage i. For example, $graph(fac_3)$ = { (*zero*, *one*), (*one*, *one*), (*two*, *two*) }. Some interesting properties appear: for all $i \geq 0$, $graph(fac_i) \subseteq graph(fac_{i+1})$. This says that the partial functions produced at each stage are consistent with one another in their answer production. This isn't a startling fact, but it will prove to be important later. Further, for all $i \geq 0$, $graph(fac_i) \subseteq graph(factorial)$, which says that each fac_i exhibits behavior consistent with the ultimate solution to the specification, the factorial function. This implies:

$$\bigcup_{i=0}^{\infty} graph(fac_i) \subseteq graph(factorial)$$

Conversely, if some pair (a,b) is in $graph(factorial)$, then there must be some finite $i > 0$ such that (a,b) is in $graph(fac_i)$ also, as answers are produced in a finite number of unfoldings. (This property holds for *factorial* and its specification, but it may not hold in general. In Section 6.3, we show how to make it hold.) Thus:

$$graph(factorial) \subseteq \bigcup_{i=0}^{\infty} graph(fac_i)$$

and we have just shown:

$$graph(factorial) = \bigcup_{i=0}^{\infty} graph(fac_i)$$

The equality suits our operational intuitions and states that the factorial function can be totally understood in terms of the finite subfunctions $\{ fac_i \mid i \geq 0 \}$.

This example demonstrates the fundamental principle of least fixed point semantics: the meaning of any recursively defined function is exactly the union of the meanings of its finite subfunctions. It is easy to produce a nonrecursive representation of each subfunction. Define each fac_i: $Nat \to Nat_\perp$, for $i \geq 0$, as:

$$fac_0 = \lambda n. \perp$$

$$fac_{i+1} = \lambda n. n \; equals \; zero \to one \; [] \; n \; times \; fac_i(n \; minus \; one), \quad \text{for all } i \geq 0$$

The graph of each fac_i is the one produced at stage i of the *fac* unfolding. The importance is twofold: first, each fac_i is a nonrecursive definition, which suggests that a recursive specification can be understood in terms of a family of nonrecursive ones; and, second, a format common to all the fac_i's can be extracted. Let:

$$F = \lambda f.\lambda n.\, n \ equals \ zero \rightarrow one \,\square\, n \ times \ (f(n \ minus \ one))$$

Each $fac_{i+1} = F(fac_i)$. The nonrecursive $F\colon (Nat \rightarrow Nat_\perp) \rightarrow (Nat \rightarrow Nat_\perp)$ is called a *functional*, because it takes a function as an argument and produces one as a result. Thus:

$$graph\,(factorial) = \bigcup_{i=0}^{\infty} graph\,(F^i(\emptyset))$$

where $F^i = F \circ F \circ \cdots \circ F$, i times, and $\emptyset = (\lambda n.\perp)$. Another important fact is that $graph\,(F(factorial)) = graph\,(factorial)$, which implies $F(factorial) = factorial$, by the extensionality principle. The factorial function is a *fixed point* of F, as the answer F produces from argument *factorial* is exactly *factorial* again.

We can apply the ideas just discussed to the q specification. We use the associated functional $Q\colon (Nat \rightarrow Nat_\perp) \rightarrow (Nat \rightarrow Nat_\perp)$, which is:

$$Q = \lambda g.\lambda n.\, n \ equals \ zero \rightarrow one \,\square\, g\,(n \ plus \ one)$$

Then:

$Q^0(\emptyset) = (\lambda n.\perp)$

$graph\,(Q^0(\emptyset)) = \{\ \}$

$Q^1(\emptyset) = \lambda n.\, n \ equals \ zero \rightarrow one \,\square\, (\lambda n.\perp)(n \ plus \ one)$

$= \lambda n.\, n \ equals \ zero \rightarrow one \,\square\, \perp$

$graph\,(Q^1(\emptyset)) = \{\,(zero, one)\,\}$

$Q^2(\emptyset) = Q(Q(\emptyset))$

$= \lambda n.\, n \ equals \ zero \rightarrow one \,\square\, ((n \ plus \ one) \ equals \ zero \rightarrow one \,\square\, \perp)$

$graph\,(Q^2(\emptyset)) = \{\,(zero, one)\,\}$

At this point a convergence has occurred: for all $i \geqslant 1$, $graph\,(Q^i(\emptyset)) = \{\,(zero, one)\,\}$. It follows that:

$$\bigcup_{i=0}^{\infty} graph\,(Q^i(\emptyset)) = \{\,(zero, one)\,\}$$

Let *qlimit* denote the function that has this graph. It is easy to show that $Q(qlimit) = qlimit$, that is, *qlimit* is a fixed point of Q.

Unlike the specification *fac*, q has many possible solutions. Recall that each one must have a graph of the form $\{\,(zero, one), (one, k), \cdots, (i, k), \cdots\,\}$ for some $k \in Nat_\perp$. Let qk be one of these solutions. We can show that:

1. qk is a fixed point of Q, that is, $Q(qk) = qk$.
2. $graph\,(qlimit) \subseteq graph\,(qk)$.

Fact 1 says that the act of satisfying a specification is formalized by the fixed point property— only fixed points of the associated functional are possible meanings of the specification. Fact 2 states that the solution obtained using the stages of unfolding method is the *smallest* of all the possible solutions. For this reason, we call it the *least fixed point* of the functional.

Now the method for providing a meaning for a recursive specification is complete. Let a recursive specification $f = F(f)$ denote the least fixed point of functional F, that is, the function associated with $\bigcup_{i=0}^{\infty} graph(F^i(\emptyset))$. The three desired properties follow: a solution to the specification exists; the criterion of leastness is used to select from the possible solutions; and, since the method for constructing the function exactly follows the usual operational treatment of recursive definitions, the solution corresponds to the one determined computationally.

The following sections formalize the method.

6.2 PARTIAL ORDERINGS

The theory is formalized smoothly if the subset relation used with the function graphs is generalized to a *partial ordering*. Then elements of semantic domains can be directly involved in the set theoretical reasoning. For a domain D, a binary relation $r \subseteq D \times D$ (or $r: D \times D \rightarrow \mathbb{B}$) is represented by the infix symbol $\sqsubseteq_D$, or just $\sqsubseteq$ if the domain of usage is clear. For $a, b \in D$, we read $a \sqsubseteq b$ as saying "a is less defined than b."

6.1 Definition:

A relation $\sqsubseteq : D \times D \rightarrow \mathbb{B}$ is a partial ordering upon D iff $\sqsubseteq$ is:

1. *reflexive: for all $a \in D$, $a \sqsubseteq a$;*
2. *antisymmetric: for all $a, b \in D$, $a \sqsubseteq b$ and $b \sqsubseteq a$ imply $a = b$.*
3. *transitive: for all $a, b, c \in D$, $a \sqsubseteq b$ and $b \sqsubseteq c$ imply $a \sqsubseteq c$.*

A partial ordering $\sqsubseteq$ on a domain D treats the members of D as if they were sets. In fact, given a set E, we can use $\subseteq$ as a partial ordering upon the members of $\mathbb{P}(E)$. A minimum partial order structure on a domain D is the *discrete* partial ordering, which makes each $d \in D$ less defined than itself and relates no other elements; that is, for all $d, e \in D$, $d \sqsubseteq e$ iff $d = e$.

A partially ordered set of elements can be represented by an acyclic graph, where $x \sqsubseteq y$ when there is an arc from element x to element y and x is beneath y on the page. For example, given $\mathbb{P}(\{\, one, two, three \,\})$, partially ordered by subset inclusion, we draw the graph:

P0 =

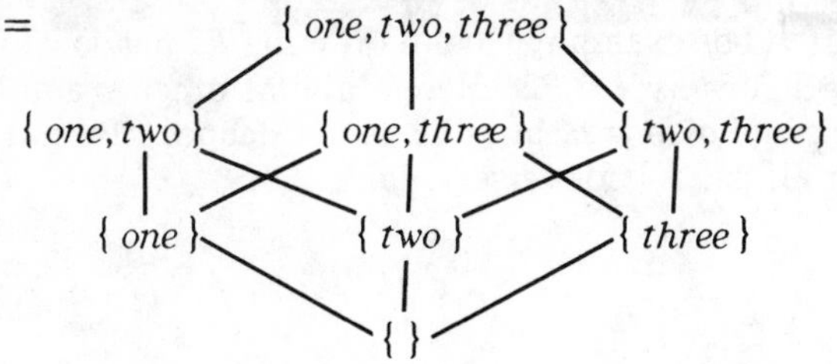

to represent the partial ordering. Taking into account reflexivity, antisymmetry, and transitivity, the graph completely describes the partial ordering. For example, { *two* } ⊑ { *one*, *two* }, { *one* } ⊑ { *one* }, and { } ⊑ { *two*, *three* }.

For the set { a, b, c, d }, the graph:

P1 =

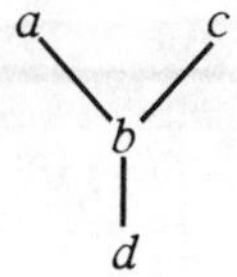

also defines a partial ordering, as does:

P2 = $a \quad b \quad c \quad d$

(the discrete ordering). There is a special symbol to denote the element in a partially ordered domain that corresponds to the empty set.

6.2 Definition:

For partial ordering ⊑ on D, if there exists an element $c \in D$ such that for all $d \in D$, $c \sqsubseteq d$, then c is the least defined element in D and is denoted by the symbol ⊥ (read "bottom").

Partial orderings *P0* and *P1* have bottom elements, but *P2* does not. We also introduce an operation analogous to set union.

6.3 Definition:

For a partial ordering ⊑ on D, for all $a, b \in D$, the expression $a \sqcup b$ denotes the element in D (if it exists) such that:

1. $a \sqsubseteq a \sqcup b$ *and* $b \sqsubseteq a \sqcup b$.
2. *for all* $d \in D$, $a \sqsubseteq d$ *and* $b \sqsubseteq d$ *imply* $a \sqcup b \sqsubseteq d$.

The element $a \sqcup b$ is the *join* of a and b. The join operation produces the smallest element that is larger than both of its arguments. A partial ordering might not have joins for all of its pairs. For example, partial ordering *P2* has joins defined only for pairs (i, i)— $i \sqcup i = i$ for any $i \in P2$. Here are some other examples: for partial ordering *P1*, $c \sqcup d = c$ and $a \sqcup d = a$, but $a \sqcup c$ is not defined. Partial ordering *P0* has joins defined for all pairs. Conversely, for:

$P3 =$

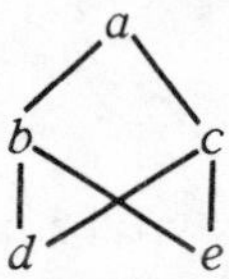

$d \sqcup e$ is *not* defined. Even though all of b, c, and a are better defined than d and e, no one of the three is minimal; since both $b \not\sqsubseteq c$ and $c \not\sqsubseteq b$, neither of the two can be chosen as least.

An intersection-like operation called *meet* is definable in a similar fashion. We write $x \sqcap y$ to denote the best-defined element that is smaller than both x and y. *P0* has meets defined for all pairs of elements. In *P3*, $b \sqcap c$ is not defined for reasons similar to those given for the undefinedness of $d \sqcup e$; $d \sqcap e$ has no value either.

6.4 Definition:

A set D, partially ordered by $\sqsubseteq$, *is a lattice iff for all* $a, b \in D$, *both* $a \sqcup b$ *and* $a \sqcap b$ *exist.*

P0 is a lattice, but *P1*-*P3* are not. For any set E, $\mathbb{P}(E)$ is a lattice under the usual subset ordering: join is set union and meet is set intersection.

The concepts of join and meet are usefully generalized to operate over a (possibly infinite) set of arguments rather than just two.

6.5 Definition:

For a set D partially ordered by $\sqsubseteq$ *and a subset X of D,* $\bigsqcup X$ *denotes the element of D (if it exists) such that:*

1. *for all* $x \in X$, $x \sqsubseteq \bigsqcup X$.
2. *for all* $d \in D$, *if for all* $x \in X$, $x \sqsubseteq d$, *then* $\bigsqcup X \sqsubseteq d$.

The element $\bigsqcup X$ is called the *least upper bound* (*lub*) of X. The definition for *greatest lower bound* (*glb*) of X is similar and is written $\bigsqcap X$.

6.6 Definition:

A set D partially ordered by $\sqsubseteq$ *is a complete lattice iff for all subsets X of D, both* $\bigsqcup X$ *and* $\bigsqcap X$ *exist.*

The standard example of a complete lattice is the powerset lattice $\mathbb{P}(E)$. Any lattice with a finite number of elements must be a complete lattice. Not all lattices are complete, however; consider the set $F = \{ x \mid x \textit{ is a finite subset of } \mathbb{N} \}$ partially ordered by subset inclusion. F is clearly a lattice, as joins and meets of finite sets yield finite sets, but F is not complete, for the lub of the set $S = \{ \{ zero \}, \{ zero, one \}, \{ zero, one, two \}, \cdots \}$ is exactly $\mathbb{N}$, which is not in F.

A complete lattice D must always have a bottom element, for $\bigsqcap D = \bot$. Dually, $\bigsqcup D$ denotes an element represented by $\top$ (*top*).

The definitions of lattice and complete lattice are standard ones and are included for completeness' sake. The theory for least fixed point semantics doesn't require domains to be lattices. The only property needed from partially ordered sets is that lubs exist for those sets representing the subfunction families. This motivates two important definitions.

6.7 Definition:

For a partially ordered set D, a subset X of D is a chain iff X is nonempty and for all $a, b \in X$, $a \sqsubseteq b$ *or* $b \sqsubseteq a$.

A *chain* represents a family of elements that contain information consistent with one another. (Recall the family of functions developed in the stages of unfolding of *fac* in Section 6.1.) Chains can be finite or infinite; in partial order *P1*, $\{ d, b, a \}$ forms a chain, as does $\{ c \}$, but $\{ a, c \}$ does not. The lub of a finite chain is always the largest element in the chain. This does not hold for infinite chains: consider again the set S defined above, which is a chain in both lattice F and complete lattice $\mathbb{P}(\mathbb{N})$.

Since chains abstract the consistent subfunction families, it is important to ensure that such chains always have lubs. A lattice may not have lubs for infinite chains, so ordinary lattices are not suitable. On the other hand, requiring a domain to be a complete lattice is too strong. The compromise settled upon is called a *complete partial ordering*.

6.8 Definition:

1. *A partially ordered set D is a complete partial ordering (cpo) iff every chain in D has a least upper bound in D.*
2. *A partially ordered set D is a pointed complete partial ordering (pointed cpo) iff it is a complete partial ordering and it has a least element.*

The partial orderings *P0* through *P3* are cpos, but only *P0* and *P1* are pointed cpos. The examples suggest that the requirements for being a cpo are quite weak. The solutions for recursive function specifications are found as elements within pointed cpos.

6.3 CONTINUOUS FUNCTIONS

When the partial order relation $\sqsubseteq$ was introduced, $\sqsubseteq$ was read as "is less defined than." For functions, we judged definedness in terms of their graphs: a function f is less defined than a function g if f's graph is a subset of g's. The totally undefined function $(\lambda n. \bot)$ contains no answer-producing information at all, and it is appropriate that its graph is the empty set and that $(\lambda n. \bot) \sqsubseteq f$ for all functions f. The graph representation of a function provides a way to "look inside" the function and judge its information content. In general, any element d of an arbitrary domain D might be thought of as a set-like object, containing "atoms" of information. Then, $\sqsubseteq_D$ can still be thought of as a subset relation, and the least upper bound operator can still be thought of as set union.

Now consider what a function does to its arguments. A function $f: A \to B$ is a transformation agent, converting an element $x \in A$ to some $f(x) \in B$. How should this be accomplished? If x is thought of as a set of "atoms," then f transforms x by mapping x's atoms into the B domain and recombining them there. If $x \sqsubseteq_A y$, an application of f should produce the analogous situation in B. A function $f: A \to B$ is *monotonic* iff for all $x, y \in A$, $x \sqsubseteq_A y$ implies $f(x) \sqsubseteq_B f(y)$. The condition is justified by practical issues in computing: a procedure for transforming a data structure such as an array performs the transformation by altering the array's subparts one at a time, combining them to form a new value. The procedure denotes a monotonic function. Nonmonotonic functions tend to be nasty entities, often impossible to implemement. A famous example of a nonmonotonic function is *program-halts* : $Nat_\bot \to \mathbb{B}$,

$$\textit{program-halts}(x) = \begin{cases} \textit{true} & \text{if } x \neq \bot \\ \textit{false} & \text{if } x = \bot \end{cases}$$

program-halts is nonmonotonic. Consider a proper number n. It is always the case that $\bot \sqsubseteq n$, but it is normally *not* the case that *program-halts*$(\bot) \sqsubseteq$ *program-halts*(n), that is, *false* $\sqsubseteq$ *true*, as *false* is not less defined than *true*— their information contents are disjoint.

For the moment, pretend that an implementation of *program-halts* exists and call its coded procedure PGM-HALTS. PGM-HALTS could see if a program P terminates with its input A, for P represents a function in domain $Nat \to Nat_\bot$, A represents a natural number, so PGM-HALTS(P(A)) returns TRUE or FALSE based upon whether or not P halts with A. It is easy to see how PGM-HALTS might return a TRUE value (it runs P(A) and once P(A) stops and outputs a numeral, it returns TRUE), but how can PGM-HALTS ever tell that P(A) will run forever (that is, be undefined) so that it can return FALSE? There is no obvious solution; in fact, there is no solution at all— this is the famous "halting problem" of computability theory: *program-halts* cannot be implemented on any computing machine.

We require that all the functions used in denotational semantics be monotonic. The requirement guarantees that any family of subfunctions $\perp$, $F(\perp)$, $F(F(\perp))$, $\cdots$, $F^i(\perp)$, $\cdots$ generated by a monotonic functional F is a chain.

A condition stronger than monotonicity is needed to develop least fixed point semantics. Just as the binary join operation was generalized to the lub operation, the monotonicity condition is generalized to *continuity*.

6.9 Definition:

For cpos A and B, a monotonic function $f: A \to B$ is continuous iff for any chain $X \subseteq A$, $f(\bigsqcup X) = \bigsqcup\{ f(x) \mid x \in X \}$.

A continuous function preserves limits of chains. That is, $f(\bigsqcup X)$ contains exactly the same information as that obtained by mapping all the x's to $f(x)$'s and joining the results. The reason that we use continuous functions is that we require the property $graph(\bigsqcup\{ F^i(\emptyset) \mid i \geq 0 \}) \subseteq \bigcup_{i=0}^{\infty} \{ graph(F^i(\emptyset)) \mid i \geq 0 \}$, which was noted in Section 6.1 in the *fac* example.

Continuous functions suggest a strategy for effectively processing objects of infinite size (information content). For some infinite object Y, it may not be possible to place a representation of Y in the computer store, so $f(Y)$ simply isn't computable in the conventional way. But if Y is the least upper bound of a chain $\{ y_i \mid i \in \mathbb{N} \}$ where each y_i has finite size, and f is a continuous function, then each y_i can be successively stored and f applied to each. The needed value $f(Y)$ is built up piece by piece as $f(y_0) \sqcup f(y_1) \sqcup f(y_2) \sqcup \cdots$. Since $\{ f(y_i) \mid i \in \mathbb{N} \}$ constitutes a chain and f is continuous, $f(Y) = \bigsqcup\{ f(y_i) \mid i \in \mathbb{N} \}$. (This was the same process used for determining the graph of the factorial function.) Of course, to completely compute the answer will take an infinite amount of time, but it is reassuring that every piece of the answer $f(Y)$ will appear within a finite amount of time.

Continuity is such an important principle that virtually all of the classical areas of mathematics utilize it in some form.

6.4 LEAST FIXED POINTS

A *functional* is a continuous function $f: D \to D$; usually D is a domain of form $A \to B$, but it doesn't have to be.

6.10 Definition:

For a functional $F: D \to D$ and an element $d \in D$, d is a fixed point of F iff $F(d) = d$. Further, d is the least fixed point of F if, for all $e \in D$, $F(e) = e$ implies $d \sqsubseteq e$.

6.11 Theorem:

If the domain D is a pointed cpo, then the least fixed point of a continuous functional $F: D \to D$ exists and is defined to be $fix\, F = \bigsqcup\{ F^i(\bot) \mid i \geq 0 \}$, where $F^i = F \circ F \circ \cdots \circ F$, i times.

Proof: First, *fix F* is a fixed point of *F*, as

$$\begin{aligned} F(fix\, F) &= F(\bigsqcup\{ F^i(\bot) \mid i \geq 0 \}) \\ &= \bigsqcup\{ F(F^i(\bot)) \mid i \geq 0 \} \text{ by continuity of } F \\ &= \bigsqcup\{ F^i(\bot) \mid i \geq 1 \} \\ &= \bigsqcup\{ F^i(\bot) \mid i \geq 0 \}, \text{ as } F^0(\bot) = \bot \text{ and } \bot \sqsubseteq F(\bot) \\ &= fix\, F \end{aligned}$$

To show *fix F* is least, let $e \in D$ be a fixed point of *F*. Now, $\bot \sqsubseteq e$, and by the monotonicity of *F*, $F^i(\bot) \sqsubseteq F^i(e) = e$, for all $i > 0$, since *e* is a fixed point. This implies $fix\, F = \bigsqcup\{ F^i(\bot) \mid i \geq 0 \} \sqsubseteq e$, showing *fix F* is least. □

This produces the primary result of the chapter:

6.12 Definition:

The meaning of a recursive specification $f = F(f)$ is taken to be fix F, the least fixed point of the functional denoted by F.

Examples of recursive specifications and their least fixed point semantics are given in Section 6.6. First, a series of proofs are needed to show that semantic domains are cpos and that their operations are continuous.

6.5 DOMAINS ARE CPOS

The partial orderings defined in Section 6.3 introduce internal structure into domains. In this section we define the partial orderings for primitive domains and the compound domain constructions. The orderings make the domains into cpos. Our reason for using cpos (rather than pointed cpos) is that we want ordinary sets (which are discretely ordered cpos) to be domains. The lifting construction is the tool we use to make a cpo into a pointed cpo.

What partial ordering should be placed on a primitive domain? Each of a primitive domain's elements is a distinct, atomic answer value. For example, in $\mathbb{N}$, both *zero* and *one* are answer elements, and by no means does *one* contain more information than *zero* (or vice versa). The information is equal in "quantity" but disjoint in value. This suggests that $\mathbb{N}$ has the discrete ordering: $a \sqsubseteq b$ iff $a = b$. We always place the discrete partial ordering upon a primitive domain.

6.13 Proposition:

Any set of elements D with the discrete partial ordering is a cpo, and any operation $f\colon D \to E$ is continuous.

Proof: Trivial, as the only chains in D are sets of one element. □

The partial orderings of compound domains are based upon the orderings of their component domains. Due to its importance in converting cpos into pointed cpos, the partial ordering for the lifting construction is defined first.

6.14 Definition:

For a partially ordered set A, its lifting $A_\perp$ is the set $A \cup \{\perp\}$, partially ordered by the relation $d \sqsubseteq_{A_\perp} d'$ iff $d = \perp$, or $d, d' \in A$ and $d \sqsubseteq_A d'$.

6.15 Proposition:

If A is a cpo, then $A_\perp$ is a pointed cpo. Further, $(\underline{\lambda} x.e) : A_\perp \to B_\perp$ is continuous when $(\lambda x.e) : A \to B_\perp$ is.

Proof: Left as an exercise. □

For the cpo $\mathbb{N}$, the pointed cpo $\mathbb{N}_\perp$ is drawn as:

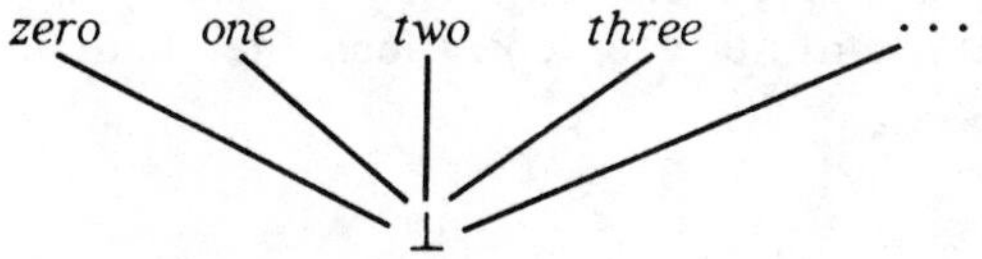

6.16 Definition:

For partially ordered sets A and B, their product $A \times B$ is the set $\{ (a, b) \mid a \in A$ and $b \in B \}$ partially ordered by the relation $(a, b) \sqsubseteq_{A \times B} (a', b')$ iff $a \sqsubseteq_A a'$ and $b \sqsubseteq_B b'$.

6.17 Proposition:

If A and B are (pointed) cpos, then $A \times B$ is a (pointed) cpo, and its associated operation builders are continuous.

Proof: Any chain C in $A \times B$ has the form $C = \{ (a_i, b_i) \mid a_i \in A, b_i \in B, i \in I \}$, for some index set I. By Definition 6.16, both $M = \{ a_i \mid i \in I \}$ and

$N = \{ b_i \mid i \in I \}$ are chains in A and B respectively, with lubs $\bigsqcup M$ and $\bigsqcup N$. That $\bigsqcup C = (\bigsqcup M, \bigsqcup N)$ follows from the definition of lub. Thus $A \times B$ is a cpo, and the pairing operation is continuous. (If A and B are both pointed, $(\bot, \bot)$ is the least element in $A \times B$. This element is distinct from the $\bot$ introduced by lifting.) To show that *fst* is continuous, consider the chain C above:

$$\begin{aligned} &\bigsqcup\{ fst(a_i, b_i) \mid i \in I \} = \bigsqcup\{ a_i \mid i \in I \} \\ &= fst(\bigsqcup\{ a_i \mid i \in I \}, \bigsqcup\{ b_i \mid i \in I \}) \\ &= fst(\bigsqcup\{ (a_i, b_i) \mid i \in I \}). \end{aligned}$$

The proof for *snd* is similar. □

It is straightforward to generalize Definition 6.16 and Proposition 6.17 to products of arbitrary size.

Here is a sample product construction: $\mathbb{B}_\bot \times \mathbb{B}_\bot =$

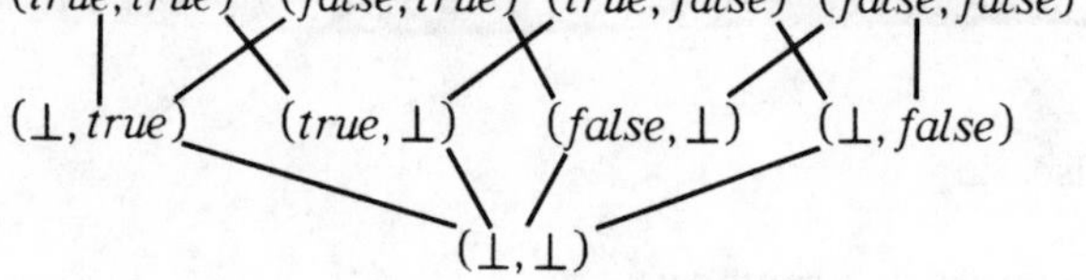

Now that the partial ordering upon products has been established, we can state an important result about the continuity of operations that take arguments from more than one domain.

6.18 Proposition:

A function $f: D_1 \times D_2 \times \cdots \times D_n \rightarrow E$ is continuous iff it is continuous in each of its individual arguments; that is, f is continuous in $D_1 \times D_2 \times \cdots \times D_n$ iff it is continuous in every D_i, for $1 \leq i \leq n$, where the other arguments are held constant.

Proof: The proof is given for $f: D_1 \times D_2 \rightarrow E$; a proof for general products is an extension of this one.

Only if: Let f be continuous. To show f continuous in D_1, set its second argument to some $x \in D_2$. For chain $\{ d_i \mid d_i \in D_1, i \in I \}$, $\bigsqcup\{ f(d_i, x) \mid i \in I \} = f(\bigsqcup\{ (d_i, x) \mid i \in I \})$, as f is continuous; this equals $f(\bigsqcup\{ d_i \mid i \in I \}, \bigsqcup\{ x \}) = f(\bigsqcup\{ d_i \mid i \in I \}, x)$. The proof for D_2 is similar.

If: Let f be continuous in its first and second arguments separately, and let $\{ (a_i, b_i) \mid a_i \in D_1, b_i \in D_2, i \in I \}$ be a chain. Then $f(\bigsqcup\{ (a_i, b_i) \mid i \in I \})$

$= f(\bigsqcup\{ a_i \mid i \in I \}, \bigsqcup\{ b_j \mid j \in I \})$, $= \bigsqcup\{ f(a_i, \bigsqcup\{ b_j \mid j \in I \}) \mid i \in I \}$ by f's continuity on its first argument; this equals $\bigsqcup\{ \bigsqcup\{ f(a_i, b_j) \mid j \in I \} \mid i \in I \}$ $= \bigsqcup\{ f(a_i, b_j) \mid i \in I \text{ and } j \in I \}$ as taking lubs is associative. Now for each pair (a_i, b_j) take $k = \max(i,j)$. For example, if $i \leqslant j$, k is j, and then $(a_i, b_j) \sqsubseteq (a_k, b_k) = (a_j, b_j)$, as $a_i \sqsubseteq a_j$ since $\{ a_i \mid i \in I \}$ is a chain. This implies $f(a_i, b_j) \sqsubseteq f(a_k, b_k)$. Similar reasoning holds when $j \leqslant i$. This means $f(a_i, b_j) \sqsubseteq f(a_k, b_k) \sqsubseteq \bigsqcup\{ f(a_k, b_k) \mid k \in I \}$, implying $\bigsqcup\{ f(a_i, b_j) \mid i \in I, j \in I \}$ $\sqsubseteq \bigsqcup\{ f(a_k, b_k) \mid k \in I \}$. But for all $k \in I$, $f(a_k, b_k)$ is in $\{ f(a_i, b_j) \mid i \in I, j \in I \}$, implying $\bigsqcup\{ f(a_k, b_k) \mid k \in I \} \sqsubseteq \bigsqcup\{ f(a_i, b_j) \mid i \in I, j \in I \}$, and so the lubs are equal. This concludes the proof, since $\bigsqcup\{ f(a_i, b_j) \mid i \in I, j \in I \}$ $= \bigsqcup\{ f(a_k, b_k) \mid k \in I \} = \bigsqcup\{ f(a_i, b_i) \mid i \in I \}$. □

6.19 Definition:

For partial orders A and B, their disjoint union $A + B$ is the set $\{ (zero, a) \mid a \in A \} \cup \{ (one, b) \mid b \in B \}$ partially ordered by the relation $d \sqsubseteq_{A+B} d'$ iff $(d = (zero, a)$, $d' = (zero, a')$, and $a \sqsubseteq_A a')$ or $(d = (one, b)$, $d' = (one, b')$, and $b \sqsubseteq_B b')$.

6.20 Proposition:

If A and B are cpos, then $A + B$ is a cpo, and its associated operation builders are continuous.

Proof: Left as an exercise. □

As an example, $\mathbb{B}_\perp + \mathbb{N}_\perp$ is:

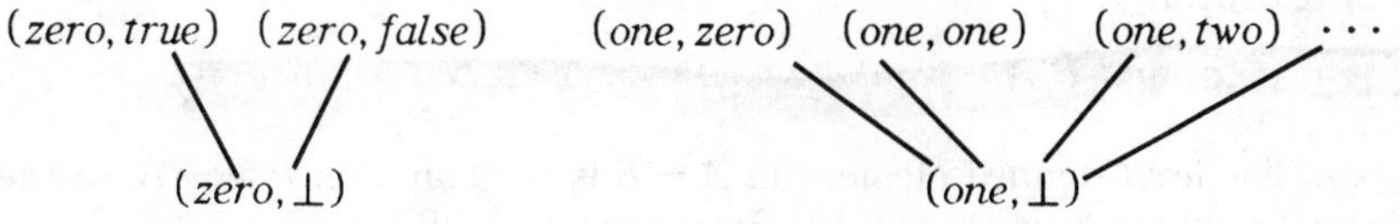

6.21 Definition:

For partially ordered sets A and B, their function space $A \rightarrow B$ is the set of all continuous functions with domain A and codomain B, partially ordered by the relation $f \sqsubseteq_{A \rightarrow B} g$ iff for all $a \in A$, $f(a) \sqsubseteq_B g(a)$.

6.22 Proposition:

If A and B are cpos, then $A \to B$ is a cpo, and its associated operation builders are continuous.

Proof: For the chain $C = \{ f_i : A \to B \mid i \in I \}$, for each $a_j \in A$, the set $A_j = \{ f_i(a_j) \mid i \in I \}$ is a chain in B, due to the partial ordering. Since B is a cpo, $\bigsqcup A_j$ exists for all such j. Use these lubs to define the function $g : A \to B$ such that $g(a_j) = \bigsqcup A_j$ for $a_j \in A$. We first show that g is continuous: for a chain $X = \{ a_j \in A \mid j \in J \}$, $\bigsqcup \{ g(a_j) \mid j \in J \}$ equals $\bigsqcup \{ \bigsqcup \{ f_i(a_j) \mid i \in I \} \mid j \in J \}$ by the definition of g; this value equals $\bigsqcup \{ \bigsqcup \{ f_i(a_j) \mid j \in J \} \mid i \in I \}$ as lubs are associative; this value equals $\bigsqcup \{ f_i(\bigsqcup \{ a_j \mid j \in J \}) \mid i \in I \}$ as each f_i is continuous; and this equals $\bigsqcup \{ f_i(\bigsqcup X) \mid i \in I \} = g(\bigsqcup X)$. That g is the lub of the chain follows by definition of the partial ordering.

To show that function application is continuous, let $g = \bigsqcup \{ f_i : A \to B \mid i \in I \}$; then $\bigsqcup \{ f_i(a) \mid i \in I \} = g(a) = (\bigsqcup \{ f_i \mid i \in I \})(a)$, taking care of the first argument; and $\bigsqcup \{ g(a_j) \mid j \in J \} = g(\bigsqcup \{ a_j \mid j \in J \})$ by the continuity of g, handling the second argument.

Finally, for abstraction, let $\{ e_i \mid i \in I \}$ be a set of expressions such that for any $a \in A$, $\{ [a/x]e_i \mid i \in I \}$ is a chain in B. Then $\{ \lambda x.e_i \mid i \in I \}$ is a chain in $A \to B$ by definition of the partial ordering. Earlier in the proof we saw that $\bigsqcup \{ \lambda x.e_i \mid i \in I \}$ is the function g such that $g(a) = \bigsqcup \{ (\lambda x.e_i)(a) \mid i \in I \} = \bigsqcup \{ [a/x]e_i \mid i \in I \}$. Thus, $g = \lambda a. \bigsqcup \{ [a/x]e_i \mid i \in I \} = \lambda x. \bigsqcup \{ [x/x]e_i \mid i \in I \}$ by renaming the argument identifier; this equals $\lambda x. \bigsqcup \{ e_i \mid i \in I \}$ by definition of substitution. Hence abstraction is continuous. □

6.23 Corollary:

If A is a cpo and B is a pointed cpo, then $A \to B$ is a pointed cpo.

Proof: The least defined element in $A \to B$ is the function $f: A \to B$, defined as $f(a) = b_0$, where b_0 is the least defined element in B. □

The partial ordering on $A \to B$ is known as the *pointwise* ordering, for $f \sqsubseteq g$ iff f produces less-defined answers than g at all argument points. The pointwise ordering formalizes the method of ordering functions based on the subset inclusion of their graphs. As an example, if we represent a function by its graph and not include any argument, answer pairs of the form $(t, \perp)$, the domain $\mathbb{B}_\perp \to \mathbb{B}_\perp$ appears:

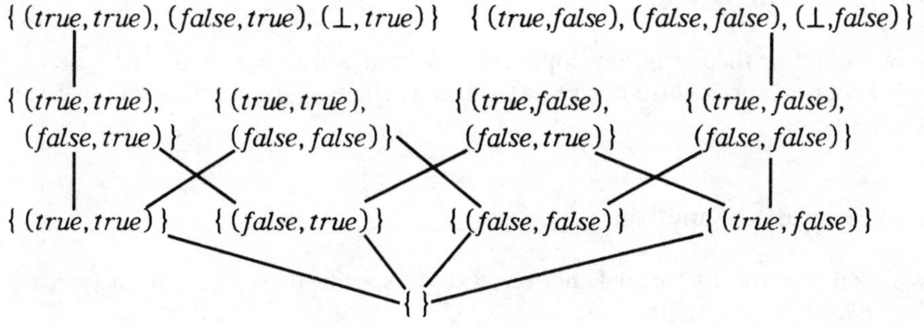

Since $\mathbb{B}_\perp$ is a pointed cpo, so is $\mathbb{B}_\perp \to \mathbb{B}_\perp$. The least element is not the $\perp$ introduced by lifting, but is the proper function $(\lambda t. \perp)$.

The preceding results taken together imply the following.

6.24 Theorem:

Any operation built using function notation is a continuous function.

The least fixed point semantics method operates on pointed cpos. The least element of a domain gives a starting point for building a solution. This starting point need not be the $\perp$ element added by lifting: Proposition 6.17 and Corollary 6.23 show that least elements can naturally result from a compound domain construction. In any case, lifting is an easy way of creating the starting point. In the examples in the next section, the symbol $\perp$ will be used to stand for the least member of a pointed cpo, regardless of whether this element is due to a lifting or not.

We will treat *fix* as an operation builder. (See Theorem 6.11.) For any pointed cpo D and continuous function $F{:}D \to D$, *fix* F denotes the lub of the chain induced from F. From here on, any recursive specification $f = F(f)$ is taken as an abbreviation for $f = \mathit{fix}\ F$.

Since it is important to know if a cpo is pointed, the following rules are handy:

ispointed $(P) =$ *false*, where P is a primitive domain
ispointed $(A \times B) =$ *ispointed* (A) and *ispointed* (B)
ispointed $(A + B) =$ *false*
ispointed $(A \to B) =$ *ispointed* (B)
ispointed $(A_\perp) =$ *true*

6.6 EXAMPLES

Now that the theory is developed, we present a number of old and new recursive function specifications and determine their least fixed point semantics.

6.6.1 Factorial Function

We examine the factorial function and its specification once more. Recall that $fac : Nat \to Nat_\bot$ is defined as:

$$fac = \lambda n.\, n \text{ equals zero} \to one \,[\,]\, n \text{ times } fac(n \text{ minus one})$$

which is an acceptable definition, since $Nat_\bot$ is a pointed cpo, implying that $Nat \to Nat_\bot$ is also. (Here is one small, technical point: the specification should actually read:

$$fac = \lambda n.\, n \text{ equals zero} \to one \,[\,]\, (\text{let } n' = fac(n \text{ minus one}) \text{ in } n \text{ times } n')$$

because *times* uses arguments from *Nat* and not from $Nat_\bot$. We gloss over this point and say that *times* is strict on $Nat_\bot$ arguments.) The induced functional $F: (Nat \to Nat_\bot) \to (Nat \to Nat_\bot)$ is:

$$F = \lambda f.\lambda n.\, n \text{ equals zero} \to one \,[\,]\, n \text{ times } f(n \text{ minus one})$$

The least fixed point semantics of *fac* is $fix\, F = \bigsqcup \{ fac_i \mid i \geqslant 0 \}$, where:

$$fac_0 = (\lambda n.\, \bot) = \bot \in Nat \to Nat_\bot$$
$$fac_{i+1} = F(fac_i) \text{ for } i \geqslant 0$$

These facts have been mentioned before. What we examine now is the relationship between *fix F* and the operational evaluation of *fac*. First, the fixed point property says that $fix\, F = F(fix\, F)$. This identity is a useful simplification rule. Consider the denotation of the phrase $(fix\, F)(three)$. Why does this expression stand for *six*? We use equals-for-equals substitution to simplify the original form:

$$(fix\, F)(three)$$
$$= (F(fix\, F))(three), \text{ by the fixed point property}$$
$$= ((\lambda f.\lambda n.\, n \text{ equals zero} \to one \,[\,]\, n \text{ times } f(n \text{ minus one}))(fix\, F))(three)$$
$$= (\lambda n.\, n \text{ equals zero} \to one \,[\,]\, n \text{ times } (fix\, F)(n \text{ minus one}))(three)$$

We see that the fixed point property justifies the recursive unfolding rule that was informally used in Section 6.1.

Rather than expanding $(fix\, F)$ further, we bind *three* to *n*:

$$= three \text{ equals zero} \to one \,[\,]\, three \text{ times } (fix\, F)(three \text{ minus one})$$

$= three\ times\ (fix\ F)(two)$
$= three\ times\ (F\ (fix\ F))(two)$
$= three\ times\ ((\lambda f.\lambda n.\ n\ equals\ zero \rightarrow one\ [\!]\ n\ times\ f(n\ minus\ one))(fix\ F))(two)$
$= three\ times\ (\lambda n.n\ equals\ zero \rightarrow one\ [\!]\ n\ times\ (fix\ F)(n\ minus\ one))(two)$

The expression $(fix\ F)$ can be expanded at will:

$= three\ times\ (two\ times\ (fix\ F)(one))$
. . .
$= three\ times\ (two\ times\ (one\ times\ (fix\ F)(zero)))$
. . .
$= six$

6.6.2 Copyout Function

The interactive text editor in Figure 5.3 utilized a function called *copyout* for converting an internal representation of a file into an external form. The function's definition was not specified because it used recursion. Now we can alleviate the omission. The domains $File = Record^*$ and $Openfile = Record^* \times Record^*$ were used. Function *copyout* converts an open file into a file by appending the two record lists. A specification of $copyout : Openfile \rightarrow File_\perp$ is:

$$copyout = \lambda(front, back).\ null\ front \rightarrow back$$
$$[\!]\ copyout\ ((tl\ front), ((hd\ front)\ cons\ back))$$

It is easy to construct the appropriate functional F; *copyout* has the meaning $(fix\ F)$. You should prove that the function $F^i(\perp)$ is capable of appending list pairs whose first component has length $i-1$ or less. This implies that the lub of the $F^i(\perp)$ functions, $(fix\ F)$, is capable of concatenating all pairs of lists whose first component has finite length.

Here is one more remark about *copyout*: its codomain was stated above as $File_\perp$, rather than just *File*, as originally given in Figure 5.3. The new codomain was used because least fixed point semantics requires that the codomain of any recursively defined function be pointed. If we desire a recursive version of *copyout* that uses *File* as its codomain, we must apply the results of Exercise 14 of Chapter 3 and use a primitive recursive-like definition. This is left as an important exercise. After you have studied all of the examples in this chapter, you should determine which of them can be handled *without* least fixed point semantics by using primitive recursion. The moral is that least fixed point semantics is a powerful and useful tool, but in many cases we can deal quite nicely without it.

6.6.3 Double Recursion

Least fixed point semantics is helpful for understanding recursive specifications that may be difficult to read. Consider this specification for $g : Nat \rightarrow Nat_\perp$:

$$g = \lambda n.\, n\ equals\ zero \rightarrow one\ [\!]\ (g(n\ minus\ one)\ plus\ g(n\ minus\ one))\ minus\ one$$

The appropriate functional F should be obvious. We gain insight by constructing the graphs for the first few steps of the chain construction:

$$graph\,(F^0(\perp)) = \{\ \}$$
$$graph\,(F^1(\perp)) = \{\ (zero, one)\ \}$$
$$graph\,(F^2(\perp)) = \{\ (zero, one),\ (one, one)\ \}$$
$$graph\,(F^3(\perp)) = \{\ (zero, one),\ (one, one),\ (two, one)\ \}$$

You should be able to construct these graphs yourself and verify the results. For all $i \geq 0$, $graph\,(F^{i+1}(\perp)) = \{\ (zero, one), (one, one), \cdots, (i, one)\ \}$, implying $(fix\ F) = \lambda n.\, one$. The recursive specification disguised a very simple function.

6.6.4 Simultaneous Definitions

Some recursive specifications are presented as a collection of mutually recursive specifications. Here is a simple example of an f: $Nat \rightarrow Nat_\perp$ and a $g : Nat \rightarrow Nat_\perp$ such that each function depends on the other to produce an answer:

$$f = \lambda x.\, x\ equals\ zero \rightarrow g(zero)\ [\!]\ f(g(x\ minus\ one))\ plus\ two$$
$$g = \lambda y.\, y\ equals\ zero \rightarrow zero\ [\!]\ y\ times\ f(y\ minus\ one)$$

Identifier g is free in f's specification and f is free in g's. Attempting to solve f's or g's circularity separately creates a problem, for there is no guarantee that f is defined without a well-defined function for g, and no function for g can be produced without a function for f. This suggests that the least fixed points for f and g be formed simultaneously. We build a functional over *pairs*:

$$F : ((Nat \rightarrow Nat_\perp) \times (Nat \rightarrow Nat_\perp)) \rightarrow ((Nat \rightarrow Nat_\perp) \times (Nat \rightarrow Nat_\perp)),$$
$$F = \lambda(f,g).\, (\ \lambda x.\, x\ equals\ zero \rightarrow g(zero)\ [\!]\ f(g(x\ minus\ one))\ plus\ two,$$
$$\lambda y.\, y\ equals\ zero \rightarrow zero\ [\!]\ y\ times\ f(y\ minus\ one)\ )$$

A pair of functions (α, β) is sought such that $F(\alpha, \beta) = (\alpha, \beta)$.

We build a chain of function pairs. Here are the graphs that are produced by the chain construction (note that $\perp$ stands for the pair $((\lambda n.\, \perp), (\lambda n.\, \perp))$):

$$F^0(\perp) = (\ \{\ \}, \{\ \}\ )$$
$$F^1(\perp) = (\ \{\ \}, \{\ (zero, zero)\ \}\ )$$
$$F^2(\perp) = (\ \{\ (zero, zero)\ \}, \{\ (zero, zero)\ \}\ )$$

$F^3(\bot) = (\ \{\ (zero, zero), (one, two)\ \}, \{\ (zero, zero), (one, zero)\ \}\ )$
$F^4(\bot) = (\ \{\ (zero, zero), (one, two), (two, two)\ \},$
$\{\ (zero, zero), (one, zero), (two, four)\ \}\ )$
$F^5(\bot) = (\ \{\ (zero, zero), (one, two), (two, two)\ \},$
$\{\ (zero, zero), (one, zero), (two, four), (three, six)\ \}\ )$

At this point, the sequence converges: for all $i>5$, $F^i(\bot) = F^5(\bot)$. The solution to the mutually recursive pair of specifications is *fix F*, and $f = fst(fix\ F)$ and $g = snd(fix\ F)$.

Any finite set of mutually recursive function definitions can be handled in this manner. Thus, the least fixed point method is powerful enough to model the most general forms of computation, such as general recursive equation sets and flowcharts.

6.6.5 The While-Loop

Recall that a specification of the semantics of a **while**-loop is:

$\mathbf{C}[\![\mathbf{while}\ \mathrm{B}\ \mathbf{do}\ \mathrm{C}]\!] = \underline{\lambda} s.\ \mathbf{B}[\![\mathrm{B}]\!]s \rightarrow \mathbf{C}[\![\mathbf{while}\ \mathrm{B}\ \mathbf{do}\ \mathrm{C}]\!]\,(\mathbf{C}[\![\mathrm{C}]\!]s)\ [\!]\ s$

The definition is restated in terms of the *fix* operation as:

$\mathbf{C}[\![\mathbf{while}\ \mathrm{B}\ \mathbf{do}\ \mathrm{C}]\!] = fix(\lambda f.\underline{\lambda} s.\ \mathbf{B}[\![\mathrm{B}]\!]s \rightarrow f(\mathbf{C}[\![\mathrm{C}]\!]s)\ [\!]\ s)$

The functional used in this definition is interesting because it has functionality $Store_\bot \rightarrow Store_\bot$, where $Store = Id \rightarrow Nat$.

Let's consider the meaning of the sample loop command $\mathbf{C}[\![\mathbf{while}\ \mathrm{A}{>}0\ \mathbf{do}\ (\mathrm{A}{:=}\mathrm{A}-1;\ \mathrm{B}{:=}\mathrm{B}+1)]\!]$. We let $test = \mathbf{B}[\![\mathrm{A}{>}0]\!]$ and $adjust = \mathbf{C}[\![\mathrm{A}{:=}\mathrm{A}-1;\ \mathrm{B}{:=}\mathrm{B}+1]\!]$. The functional is:

$F = \lambda f.\underline{\lambda} s.\ test\ s \rightarrow f(adjust\ s)\ [\!]\ s$

As is our custom, we work through the first few steps of the chain construction, showing the graphs produced at each step:

$graph\,(F^0(\bot)) = \{\ \}$
$graph\,(F^1(\bot)) = \{\ (\{\ ([\![\mathrm{A}]\!], zero), ([\![\mathrm{B}]\!], zero), \cdots\ \},$
$\{\ ([\![\mathrm{A}]\!], zero), ([\![\mathrm{B}]\!], zero), \cdots\ \}), \cdots,$
$(\{\ ([\![\mathrm{A}]\!], zero), ([\![\mathrm{B}]\!], four), \cdots\ \},$
$\{\ ([\![\mathrm{A}]\!], zero), ([\![\mathrm{B}]\!], four), \cdots\ \}), \cdots\ \}.$

The graph for $F^1(\bot)$ is worth studying carefully. Since the result is a member of $Store_\bot \rightarrow Store_\bot$, the graph contains pairs of function graphs. Each pair shows a store prior to its "loop entry" and the store after "loop exit." The members shown in the graph at this step are those stores whose [[A]] value equals *zero*. Thus, those stores that already map [[A]] to *zero* fail the test upon loop entry and exit immediately. The store is left unchanged. Those stores that require loop processing are mapped to $\perp$:

$$
\begin{aligned}
&graph\,(F^2(\perp)) = \\
&\quad \{\ (\{\,([\![A]\!], zero), ([\![B]\!], zero), \cdots\},\ \{\,([\![A]\!], zero), ([\![B]\!], zero), \cdots\,\}), \cdots, \\
&\quad (\{\,([\![A]\!], zero), ([\![B]\!], four), \cdots\},\ \{\,([\![A]\!], zero), ([\![B]\!], four)), \cdots\,\}), \cdots, \\
&\quad (\{\,([\![A]\!], one), ([\![B]\!], zero), \cdots\},\ \{\,([\![A]\!], zero), ([\![B]\!], one), \cdots\,\}), \cdots, \\
&\quad (\{\,([\![A]\!], one), ([\![B]\!], four), \cdots\},\ \{\,([\![A]\!], zero), ([\![B]\!], five), \cdots\,\}), \cdots\ \}.
\end{aligned}
$$

Those input stores that require one or fewer iterations to process appear in the graph. For example, the fourth illustrated pair denotes a store that has [[A]] set to *one* and [[B]] set to *four* upon loop entry. Only one iteration is needed to reduce [[A]] down to *zero*, the condition for loop exit. In the process [[B]] is incremented to *five*:

$$
\begin{aligned}
&graph\,(F^3(\perp)) = \\
&\quad \{\ (\{\,([\![A]\!], zero), ([\![B]\!], zero), \cdots\},\ \{\,([\![A]\!], zero), ([\![B]\!], zero), \cdots\,\}), \cdots, \\
&\quad (\{\,([\![A]\!], zero), ([\![B]\!], four), \cdots\},\ \{\,([\![A]\!], zero), ([\![B]\!], four), \cdots\,\}), \cdots, \\
&\quad (\{\,([\![A]\!], one), ([\![B]\!], zero), \cdots\},\ \{\,([\![A]\!], zero), ([\![B]\!], one), \cdots\,\}), \cdots, \\
&\quad (\{\,([\![A]\!], one), ([\![B]\!], four), \cdots\},\ \{\,([\![A]\!], zero), ([\![B]\!], five), \cdots\,\}), \\
&\quad (\{\,([\![A]\!], two), ([\![B]\!], zero), \cdots\},\ \{\,([\![A]\!], zero), ([\![B]\!], two), \cdots\,\}), \cdots, \\
&\quad (\{\,([\![A]\!], two), ([\![B]\!], four), \cdots\},\ \{\,([\![A]\!], zero), ([\![B]\!], six), \cdots\,\}), \cdots\ \}.
\end{aligned}
$$

All stores that require two iterations or less for processing are included in the graph. The graph of $F^{i+1}(\perp)$ contains those pairs whose input stores finish processing in i iterations or less. The least fixed point of the functional contains mappings for those stores that conclude their loop processing in a finite number of iterations.

The **while**-loop's semantics makes a good example for restating the important principle of least fixed point semantics: the meaning of a recursive specification is totally determined by the meanings of its finite subfunctions. Each subfunction can be represented nonrecursively in the function notation. In this case:

$$
\begin{aligned}
\mathbf{C}[\![\textbf{while } B \textbf{ do } C]\!] = \bigsqcup\{\ & \underline{\lambda} s.\, \perp, \\
& \underline{\lambda} s.\mathbf{B}[\![B]\!]s \rightarrow \perp [\!]\ s, \\
& \underline{\lambda} s.\, \mathbf{B}[\![B]\!]s \rightarrow (\mathbf{B}[\![B]\!](\mathbf{C}[\![C]\!]s) \rightarrow \perp [\!]\ \mathbf{C}[\![C]\!]s)\ [\!]\ s, \\
& \underline{\lambda} s.\, \mathbf{B}[\![B]\!]s \rightarrow (\mathbf{B}[\![B]\!](\mathbf{C}[\![C]\!]s) \rightarrow \\
& \qquad\qquad (\mathbf{B}[\![B]\!](\mathbf{C}[\![C]\!](\mathbf{C}[\![C]\!]s)) \rightarrow \perp [\!]\ \mathbf{C}[\![C]\!](\mathbf{C}[\![C]\!]s)) \\
& \qquad\qquad [\!]\ \mathbf{C}[\![C]\!]s) \\
& \quad [\!]\ s,\ \cdots\ \}
\end{aligned}
$$

The family of expressions makes apparent that iteration is an unwinding of a loop body; this corresponds to the operational view. Can we restate this idea even more directly? Recall that **C⟦diverge⟧** $= \underline{\lambda}s.\, \bot$. Substituting the commands into the set just constructed gives us:

C⟦while B do C⟧ $= \bigsqcup\{$ **C⟦diverge⟧**,
  C⟦if B then diverge else skip⟧,
  C⟦if B then (C; if B then diverge else skip) else skip⟧,
  C⟦if B then (C; if B then
    (C; if B then diverge else skip)
   else skip) else skip⟧, $\cdots$ $\}$

A family of finite noniterative programs represents the loop. It is easier to see what is happening by drawing the abstract syntax trees:

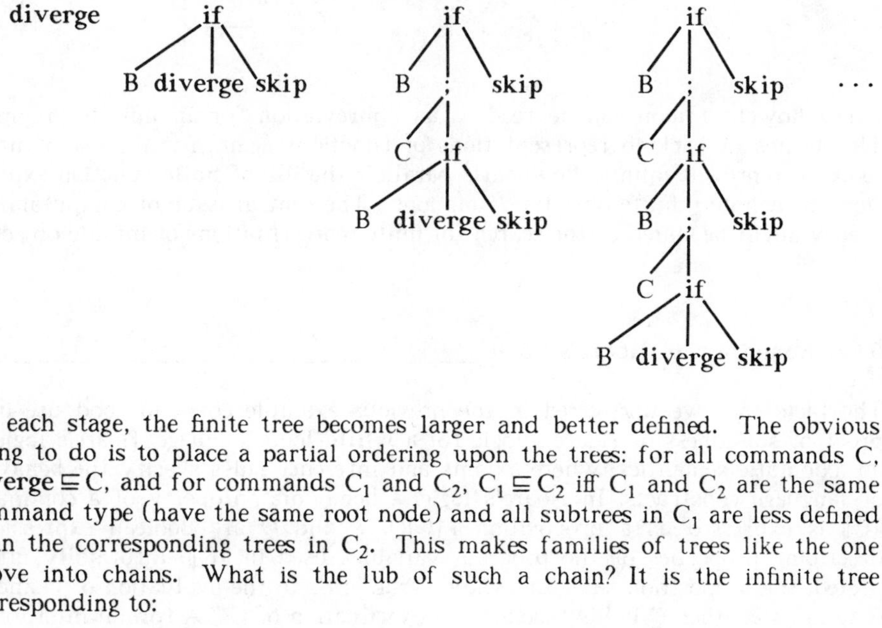

At each stage, the finite tree becomes larger and better defined. The obvious thing to do is to place a partial ordering upon the trees: for all commands C, **diverge** $\sqsubseteq$ C, and for commands C_1 and C_2, $C_1 \sqsubseteq C_2$ iff C_1 and C_2 are the same command type (have the same root node) and all subtrees in C_1 are less defined than the corresponding trees in C_2. This makes families of trees like the one above into chains. What is the lub of such a chain? It is the infinite tree corresponding to:

if B then (C; if B then (C; if B then (C; $\cdots$ **) else skip) else skip) else skip**

Draw this tree, and define $L =$ **if B then (C;** L **) else skip**. The **while**-loop example has led researchers to study languages that contain infinite programs that are represented by recursive definitions, such as L. The goal of such studies is to determine the semantics of recursive and iterative constructs by studying their circularity at the syntax level. The fundamental discovery of this research is that, whether the recursion is handled at the syntax level or at the semantics level, the result is the same: **C**[[**while** B **do** C]] = **C**[[L]]. An introduction to this approach is found in Guessarian (1981). We stay with resolving circularity in the semantics, due to our large investment in the existing forms of abstract syntax, structural induction, and least fixed point semantics. Finally, the infinite tree L is abbreviated:

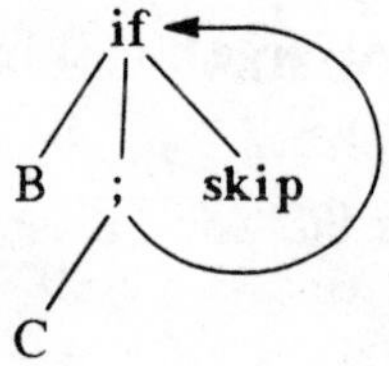

or

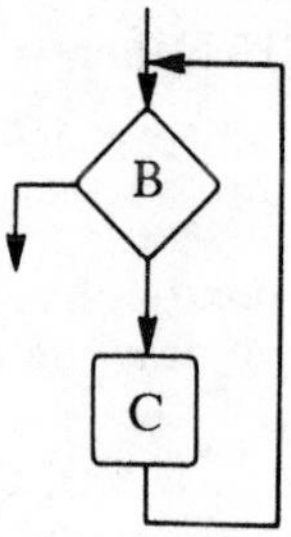

Every flowchart loop can be read as an abbreviation for an infinite program. This brings us back to representations of functions again, for the use of finite loops to represent infinite flowcharts parallels the use of finite function expressions to denote infinite objects— functions. The central issue of computability theory might be stated as the search for finite representations of infinite objects.

6.6.6 Soundness of Hoare's Logic

The facts that we uncovered in the previous example come to good use in a proof of soundness of Hoare's logic for a **while**-loop language. Hoare's logic is an axiomatic semantics, where axioms and inference rules specify the behavior of language constructs. In Hoare's logic, a behavioral property of a command [[C]] is expressed as a proposition $P\{C\}Q$. P and Q are Boolean expressions describing properties of the program variables used in [[C]]. Informally interpreted, the proposition says "if P holds true prior to the evaluation of C and if C terminates, then Q holds true after the evaluation of C." A formal interpretation of the proposition using denotational semantics is: "$P\{C\}Q$ is valid iff for all $s \in$ *Store*, **B**[[P]]s = *true* and **C**[[C]]$s \neq \perp$ imply **B**[[Q]](**C**[[C]]s) = *true*."

Figure 6.1 presents Hoare's logic for commands in Figure 5.2 augmented by the **while**-loop. Lack of space prevents us from specifying some example propositions and performing their verification. But we will show that the axiom and rules in the figure are *sound*; that is, if the antecedent propositions to a rule are valid, then the consequent of the rule is also valid. The significance of the

Figure 6.1

a) $[E/x]P\{x{:=}E\}P$

b) $\dfrac{P\{C_1\}Q,\ \ Q \textit{ implies } R,\ \ R\{C_2\}S}{P\{C_1;C_2\}S}$

c) $\dfrac{B \textit{ and } P\{C_1\}Q,\ \ (\textit{not } B) \textit{ and } P\{C_2\}Q}{P\{\textbf{if } B \textbf{ then } C_1 \textbf{ else } C_2\}Q}$

d) $\dfrac{P \textit{ and } B\{C\}P}{P\{\textbf{while } B \textbf{ do } C\}(\textit{not } B) \textit{ and } P}$

soundness proof is that the axiom and rules are more than empty definitions—they are theorems with respect to the language's denotational semantics. Thus, the axiomatic definition is complementary to the denotational one in the sense described in the Introduction.

Here is the proof of soundness:

1. *Axiom a*: For arbitrary Boolean expressions P and Q, identifier $[\![x]\!]$, and expression $[\![E]\!]$, we must show that $\mathbf{B}[\![[E/x]P]\!]s = \textit{true}$ and $\mathbf{C}[\![x{:=}E]\!]s \neq \bot$ imply that $\mathbf{B}[\![P]\!][\,[\![x]\!] \mapsto \mathbf{E}[\![E]\!]s]s = \textit{true}$. But this claim was proved in Exercise 5 of Chapter 5.
2. *Rule b*: We assume each of the three antecedents of the rule to be valid. To show the consequent, we are allowed to assume $\mathbf{B}[\![P]\!]s = \textit{true}$ and $\mathbf{C}[\![C_1;C_2]\!]s \neq \bot$; we must prove that $\mathbf{B}[\![S]\!](\mathbf{C}[\![C_1;C_2]\!]s) = \textit{true}$. First, note that $\mathbf{C}[\![C_1;C_2]\!]s \neq \bot$ implies that both $\mathbf{C}[\![C_1]\!]s \neq \bot$ and $\mathbf{C}[\![C_2]\!](\mathbf{C}[\![C_1]\!]s) \neq \bot$. By the validity of $P\{C_1\}Q$ and $\mathbf{C}[\![C_1]\!]s \neq \bot$, we have $\mathbf{B}[\![Q]\!](\mathbf{C}[\![C_1]\!]s) = \textit{true}$. From Q *implies* R, we obtain $\mathbf{B}[\![R]\!](\mathbf{C}[\![C_1]\!]s) = \textit{true}$. Finally, by the validity of $R\{C_2\}S$ and $\mathbf{C}[\![C_2]\!](\mathbf{C}[\![C_1]\!]s) \neq \bot$, we get $\mathbf{B}[\![S]\!](\mathbf{C}[\![C_2]\!](\mathbf{C}[\![C_1]\!]s)) = \mathbf{B}[\![S]\!](\mathbf{C}[\![C_1;C_2]\!]s) = \textit{true}$.
3. *Rule c*: The proof is straightforward and is left as an exercise.
4. *Rule d*: We assume the antecedent B *and* $P\{C\}P$ is valid. We also assume that $\mathbf{B}[\![P]\!]s = \textit{true}$ and $\mathbf{C}[\![\textbf{while } B \textbf{ do } C]\!]s \neq \bot$. We must show $\mathbf{B}[\![(\textit{not } B) \textit{ and } P]\!](\mathbf{C}[\![\textbf{while } B \textbf{ do } C]\!]s) = \textit{true}$. The following abbreviations will prove helpful to the proof:

$$F = \lambda f.\underline{\lambda} s.\ \mathbf{B}[\![B]\!]s \rightarrow f(\mathbf{C}[\![C]\!]s)\ [\!]\ s$$

$$F_i = (F \circ F \circ \cdots \circ F)(\underline{\lambda} s.\bot),\ \ F \text{ repeated } i \text{ times}$$

$$\mathbf{C}[\![\mathrm{C}]\!]^i = \mathbf{C}[\![\mathrm{C}]\!] \circ \mathbf{C}[\![\mathrm{C}]\!] \circ \cdots \circ \mathbf{C}[\![\mathrm{C}]\!],\ \mathbf{C}[\![\mathrm{C}]\!] \text{ repeated } i \text{ times}$$

Since $\mathbf{C}[\![\textbf{while}\ \mathrm{B}\ \textbf{do}\ \mathrm{C}]\!]s = \bigsqcup\{F_i(s) \mid i \geqslant 0\} \neq \bot$, there must exist some $k \geqslant 0$ such that $F_k(s) \neq \bot$. Pick the least such k that satisfies this property. (There must be a least one, for the F_i's form a chain.) Further, k is greater than *zero*, for F_0 is $(\underline{\lambda}s.\bot)$. Hence, $F_k(s) = \mathbf{B}[\![\mathrm{B}]\!]s \rightarrow F_{k-1}(\mathbf{C}[\![\mathrm{C}]\!]s) [\!] s$. If $\mathbf{B}[\![\mathrm{B}]\!]s =$ *false*, then k must be *one*; if $\mathbf{B}[\![\mathrm{B}]\!]s =$ *true*, then $F_k(s) = F_{k-1}(\mathbf{C}[\![\mathrm{C}]\!]s)$. This line of reasoning generalizes to the claim that $F_k(s) = F_1(\mathbf{C}[\![\mathrm{C}]\!]^{k-1}s)$, which holds because F_k is the least member of the F_i's that maps s to a non-$\bot$ value.

Let $s^* = \mathbf{C}[\![\mathrm{C}]\!]^{k-1}s$. Now $F_1(s^*) = \mathbf{B}[\![\mathrm{B}]\!]s^* \rightarrow F_0(s^*) [\!] s^*$. Clearly, $\mathbf{B}[\![\mathrm{B}]\!]s^*$ must be *false* and $F_1(s^*) = s^*$, else $F_k(s) = F_1(s^*) = F_0(\mathbf{C}[\![\mathrm{C}]\!]s^*) = (\underline{\lambda}s.\bot)(\mathbf{C}[\![\mathrm{C}]\!]^k s) = \bot$, which would be a contradiction. So we have that $\mathbf{B}[\![\mathrm{B}]\!]s^* = \mathbf{B}[\![\mathrm{B}]\!](F_k\, s) =$ *false*.

Now consider $\mathbf{B}[\![P]\!]s$: by assumption, it has value *true*. By using the assumption that B *and* $P\{\mathrm{C}\}P$ is valid, we can use reasoning like that taken in the previous paragraph to prove for $0 \leqslant i \leqslant k$ that $\mathbf{B}[\![P]\!](\mathbf{C}[\![\mathrm{C}]\!]^i s) =$ *true*. Hence, $\mathbf{B}[\![(\textit{not}\ \mathrm{B})\ \textit{and}\ P]\!]s^* = \mathbf{B}[\![(\textit{not}\ \mathrm{B})\ \textit{and}\ P]\!](F_k\, s) =$ *true*.

Now we complete the proof. We know that $F_k \sqsubseteq \mathit{fix}\, F = \mathbf{C}[\![\textbf{while}\ \mathrm{B}\ \textbf{do}\ \mathrm{C}]\!]$. Hence, $F_k(s) \sqsubseteq \mathbf{C}[\![\textbf{while}\ \mathrm{B}\ \textbf{do}\ \mathrm{C}]\!]s$, and *true* $= \mathbf{B}[\![(\textit{not}\ \mathrm{B})\ \textit{and}\ P]\!](F_k\, s) \sqsubseteq \mathbf{B}[\![(\textit{not}\ \mathrm{B})\ \textit{and}\ P]\!](\mathbf{C}[\![\textbf{while}\ \mathrm{B}\ \textbf{do}\ \mathrm{C}]\!]s)$ by the monotonicity of $\mathbf{B}[\![(\textit{not}\ \mathrm{B})\ \textit{and}\ P]\!]$. But this implies that $\mathbf{B}[\![(\textit{not}\ \mathrm{B})\ \textit{and}\ P]\!](\mathbf{C}[\![\textbf{while}\ \mathrm{B}\ \textbf{do}\ \mathrm{C}]\!]s) =$ *true*, because $\mathbb{B}$ is discretely ordered.

6.7 REASONING ABOUT LEAST FIXED POINTS

We use mathematical induction to reason about numbers and structural induction to reason about derivation trees. An induction principle is useful for reasoning about recursively specified functions. Since the meaning of a recursively specified function is the limit of the meanings of its finite subfunctions, the *fixed point induction principle* proves a property about a recursively defined function by proving it for its finite subfunctions: if all the subfunctions have the property, then the least fixed point must have it as well.

We begin by formalizing the notion of "property" as an *inclusive predicate*. A predicate P is a (not necessarily continuous) function from a domain D to $\mathbb{B}$.

6.25 Definition:

A predicate $P: D \rightarrow \mathbb{B}$ is inclusive iff for every chain $C \subseteq D$, if $P(c) =$ true for every $c \in C$, then $P(\bigsqcup C) =$ true also.

We only work with inclusive predicates.

Say that for a recursively defined function $f: A \to B$, $f = F(f)$, we wish to show that $P(f)$ holds true. If P is an inclusive predicate, then we can use the fact that $f = fix\ F$ as follows:

1. Show that $P(\bot)$ holds, for $\bot \in A \to B$.
2. Assuming for arbitrary $i \geq 0$, that $P(F^i(\bot))$ holds, show that $P(F^{i+1}(\bot))$ holds.

Mathematical induction guarantees that for all $n \geq 0$, $P(F^n(\bot))$ holds. Since P is inclusive, we have that $P(fix\ F)$ holds.

A more elegant form of this reasoning is fixed point induction.

6.26 Definition:

The fixed point induction principle: For a pointed cpo D, a continuous functional $F : D \to D$, and an inclusive predicate $P: D \to \mathbb{B}$, if:

1. $P(\bot)$ holds.

2. For arbitrary $d \in D$, when $P(d)$ holds, then $P(F(d))$ holds.

then $P(fix\ F)$ holds as well.

The proof of the validity of the fixed point induction principle is left as an exercise.

Fixed point induction helps us to show that the g function defined in the example of Section 6.6.3 is indeed the constant function that maps its arguments to *one*.

6.27 Proposition:

For all $n \in Nat$, $g(n) \neq \bot$ implies $g(n) = one$.

Proof: We use fixed point induction on the predicate $P(f)$ = "for all $n \in Nat$, $f(n) \neq \bot$ implies $f(n) = one$." For the basis step, we must show that $P(\lambda m.\bot)$ holds. For an arbitrary $n \in Nat$, $(\lambda m.\bot)(n) = \bot$, so the claim is vacuously satisfied. For the inductive step, we assume the inductive hypothesis $P(f)$ and show $P(F(f))$. For an arbitrary $n \in Nat$, we must consider the following two cases to determine the value of $F(f)(n)$:

1. n equals *zero*: then $F(f)(n) = one$, and this satisfies the claim.
2. n is greater than *zero*: then $F(f)(n)$ = $(f(n\ minus\ one)\ plus\ f(n\ minus\ one))\ minus\ one$. Consider the value of $f(n\ minus\ one)$:

   a. If it is $\bot$, then since *plus* and *minus* are strict, $F(f)(n) = \bot$, and the claim is vacuously satisifed.

   b. If it is non-$\bot$, then by the inductive hypothesis $f(n\ minus\ one) = one$, and simple arithmetic shows that $F(f)(n) = one$. □

How do we know that the predicate we just used is inclusive? It is difficult to see how the logical connectives "for all," "implies," "and," "$\neq$," etc., all fit together to make an inclusive predicate. The following criterion is helpful.

6.28 Proposition:

(Manna, Ness, & Vuillemin 1972) Let f be a recursively defined function that we wish to reason about. A logical assertion P is an inclusive predicate if P has the form:

$$\text{for all } d_1 \in D_1, \cdots, d_m \in D_m, \ \underset{j=1}{\overset{n}{\text{AND}}} \ (\underset{k=1}{\overset{p}{\text{OR}}} \ Q_{jk})$$

for $m \geq 0$, $n \geq 0$, $p \geq 0$, where Q_{jk} can be either:

1. *A predicate using only $d_1, \cdots, d_m$ as free identifiers.*
2. *An expression of form $E_1 \sqsubseteq E_2$, where E_1 and E_2 are function expressions using only $f, d_1, \cdots, d_m$ as free identifiers.*

So an inclusive predicate can be a universally quantified conjunction of disjunctions. Here is an example: "for all $n \in Nat$, $(\perp \sqsubseteq f(n))$ and $(n$ *equals one* or $f(n) \sqsubseteq$ *zero*)." By using the following logical equivalences (among others) we can show that a large variety of predicates are inclusive:

$(E_1 \sqsubseteq E_2)$ and $(E_2 \sqsubseteq E_1)$ iff $(E_1 = E_2)$
$(P_1$ implies $P_2)$ iff $((\text{not } P_1) \text{ or } P_2)$
$(\text{not}(\text{not } P_1))$ iff P_1
$(P_1$ or $(P_2$ and $P_3))$ iff $((P_1 \text{ or } P_2) \text{ and } (P_1 \text{ or } P_3))$

For example, the predicate used in the proof of Proposition 6.27 is inclusive because we can use the logical equivalences just mentioned to place the predicate in the form specified in Proposition 6.28. The proof of Proposition 6.27 was conducted with the predicate in its original form, but it's important to verify that the predicate is convertible to an inclusive one.

Fixed point induction is primarily useful for showing equivalences of program constructs. Here is one example: we define the semantics of a **repeat**-loop to be:

$$\mathbf{C}[\![\mathbf{repeat}\ \mathrm{C}\ \mathbf{until}\ \mathrm{B}]\!] = \mathit{fix}(\lambda f.\underline{\lambda} s.\ \mathrm{let}\ s' = \mathbf{C}[\![\mathrm{C}]\!]s\ \mathrm{in}\ \mathbf{B}[\![\mathrm{B}]\!]s' \rightarrow s' \,[\!]\, (f\,s'))$$

6.29 Proposition:

For any command $[\![\mathrm{C}]\!]$ *and Boolean expression* $[\![\mathrm{B}]\!]$, $\mathbf{C}[\![\mathrm{C};\ \mathbf{while}\ \neg\,\mathrm{B}\ \mathbf{do}\ \mathrm{C}]\!] = \mathbf{C}[\![\mathbf{repeat}\ \mathrm{C}\ \mathbf{until}\ \mathrm{B}]\!]$.

Proof: The fixed point induction must be performed over the two recursive definitions simultaneously. The predicate we use is:

$$P(f, g) = \text{"for all } s \in Store_{\perp},\ f(\mathbf{C}[\![C]\!]s) = (g\ s)\text{"}$$

For the basis step, we must show that $P((\lambda s.\perp), (\lambda s.\perp))$ holds, but this is obvious. For the inductive step, the inductive hypothesis is $P(f, g)$, and we must show that $P(F(f), G(g))$ holds, where:

$$F = (\lambda f.\underline{\lambda} s.\ \mathbf{B}[\![\neg B]\!]s \rightarrow f(\mathbf{C}[\![C]\!]s)\ [\!]\ s)$$
$$G = (\lambda f.\underline{\lambda} s.\ \text{let } s' = \mathbf{C}[\![C]\!]s \text{ in } \mathbf{B}[\![B]\!]s' \rightarrow s'\ [\!]\ (f\ s'))$$

For an arbitrary $s \in Store_{\perp}$, if $s = \perp$, then $F(f)(\mathbf{C}[\![C]\!]\perp) = \perp = G(g)(\perp)$, because $\mathbf{C}[\![C]\!]$, $F(f)$, and $G(g)$ are all strict. (The fact that $\mathbf{C}[\![C]\!]$ is strict for any $C \in$ Command requires a small, separate proof and is left as an exercise.) On the other hand, if $s \neq \perp$, then consider the value of $\mathbf{C}[\![C]\!]s$. If it is $\perp$, then again $F(f)(\perp) = \perp = (\text{let } s' = \perp \text{ in } \mathbf{B}[\![B]\!]s' \rightarrow s'\ [\!]\ (g\ s'))) = G(g)(\perp)$. So say that $\mathbf{C}[\![C]\!]s$ is some defined store s_0. We have that:

$$F(f)(s_0) = \mathbf{B}[\![\neg B]\!]s_0 \rightarrow f(\mathbf{C}[\![C]\!]s_0)\ [\!]\ s_0 = \mathbf{B}[\![B]\!]s_0 \rightarrow s_0\ [\!]\ f(\mathbf{C}[\![C]\!]s_0)$$

and

$$G(g)(s) = \mathbf{B}[\![B]\!]s_0 \rightarrow s_0\ [\!]\ (g\ s_0)$$

By the inductive hypothesis, it follows that $f(\mathbf{C}[\![C]\!]s_0) = (g\ s_0)$. This implies that $F(f)(s_0) = G(g)(s)$, which completes the proof. □

SUGGESTED READINGS

Least fixed points: Bird 1976; Guessarian 1981; Kleene, 1952; Park 1969; Manna 1974; Manna, Ness, & Vuillemin 1972; Manna & Vuillemin 1972; Rogers 1967

Complete partial orderings: Birkhoff 1967; Gierz, et al. 1980; Kamimura & Tang 1983, 1984a; Milner 1976; Plotkin 1982; Reynolds 1977; Scott 1976, 1980a, 1982a; Wadsworth 1978

EXERCISES

1. Simplify the following expressions to answer forms or explain at some point in the simplification why no final answer will ever be found:

   a. $f(three)$, for f defined in Section 6.6.4.

   b. $f(four)$, for f defined in Section 6.6.4.

   c. $\mathbf{C}[\![$**while** X>0 **do** (Y:=X; X:=X−1)$]\!]s_0$, for $s_0 = [\,[\![X]\!] \mapsto two\,]newstore$, for the **while**-loop defined in Section 6.6.5.

d. $\mathbf{C}[\![$**while** X>0 **do** Y:=X$]\!]$*newstore*, for the while-loop defined in Section 6.6.5.

2. For each of the recursively defined functions that follow:

   i. Build the functional F associated with the definition.
   ii. Show the (graph) set representations of $F^0(\varnothing)$, $F^1(\varnothing)$, $F^2(\varnothing)$, and $F^i(\varnothing)$, for $\varnothing = \lambda n.\bot$.
   iii. Define $\bigcup_{i=0}^{\infty} graph(F^i(\varnothing))$.
   iv. Attempt to give a nonrecursively defined function whose denotation is the value in part iii.

   a. $f: Nat \times Nat \to Nat_\bot$,
      $f(m,n) = m\ equals\ zero \to n\ [\!]\ one\ plus\ f(m\ minus\ one, n)$
   b. $g: Nat_\bot \to Nat_\bot$, $g = \underline{\lambda} n.\ n\ plus\ (n\ equals\ zero \to zero\ [\!]\ g(g(n\ minus\ one)))$
   c. (Ackermann's function) $A: Nat \times Nat \to Nat_\bot$,
      $A(m,n) = m\ equals\ zero \to n$
      $[\!]\ n\ equals\ zero \to A(m\ minus\ one, one)$
      $[\!]\ A(m\ minus\ one, A(m,n))$
   d. $f: Nat \times Nat \to Nat_\bot$, $g: Nat \to Tr_\bot$,
      $f(m,n) = g(n) \to m\ [\!]\ f(m\ minus\ two, n\ minus\ two)$
      $g(m) = m\ equals\ zero \to true\ [\!]\ m\ equals\ one \to false\ [\!]\ g(m\ minus\ two)$

3. Recall that $newstore = (\lambda i.\ zero)$.

   a. Without using fixed point induction, prove that $\mathbf{C}[\![$**while** A>0 **do** A:=A−1$]\!]s_0 = newstore$, where $s_0 = [[\![A]\!] \mapsto two]newstore$.
   b. Use fixed point induction to show that $\mathbf{C}[\![$**while**A=0 **do** B:=1$]\!]$*newstore* $= \bot$.

4. a. For the function g defined in Section 6.6.3, why can't we prove the property "for all $n \in Nat$, $g(n) = one$" using fixed point induction?
   b. Prove the above property using mathematical induction. (Hint: first prove "for all $n \in Nat$, $(F^{n+1}(\lambda n.\bot))(n) = one$.")
   c. Based on your experiences in part b, suggest a proof strategy for proving claims of the form: "for all $n \in Nat$, $f(n) \neq \bot$." Will your strategy generalize to argument domains other than *Nat*?

5. Use the logical equivalences given in Section 5.4 to formally show that the following predicates are inclusive for $f: Nat \to Nat_\bot$

   a. $P(f) =$ "for all $n \in Nat$, $f(n) \neq \bot$ implies $f(n) \sqsubseteq zero$"
   b. $P(f,g) =$ "for all $n \in Nat$, $f(n) \neq \bot$ implies $f(n) = g(n)$"

Give counterexamples that show that these predicates are *not* inclusive:

c. $P(f)=$ "there exists an $n \in Nat$, $f(n) = \bot$"
d. "$P(f) = f(zero) \neq (\lambda n.n)$," for $f: Nat \to (Nat \to Nat_{\bot})$

6. For the recursively defined function:

$$factoo(m,n) = m\ equals\ zero \to n\ [\!]\ factoo(m\ minus\ one, m\ times\ n)$$

prove the property that for all $n \in Nat$, $fac(n) = factoo(n, one)$, where fac is defined in Section 6.6.1:

a. Using fixed point induction.
b. Using mathematical induction.

When is it appropriate to use one form of reasoning over the other?

7. For the functional $F: (Nat \to Nat_{\bot}) \to (Nat \to Nat_{\bot})$,

$$F = \lambda f.\lambda m.\ m\ equals\ zero \to one\ [\!]\ m\ equals\ one \to f(m\ plus\ two)\ [\!]\ f(m\ minus\ two)$$

prove that all of these functions are fixed points of F:

a. $\lambda n.\ one$
b. $\lambda n.\ ((n\ mod\ two)\ equals\ zero) \to one\ [\!]\ two$
c. $\lambda n.\ ((n\ mod\ two)\ equals\ zero) \to one\ [\!]\ \bot$

Which of the three is the least fixed point (if any)?

8. Prove the following properties for all B∈ Boolean-expr and C∈ Command:

a. **C**[[**while** B **do** C]] = **C**[[**if** B **then** C; **while** B **do** C **else skip**]]
b. **C**[[**repeat** C **until** B]] = **C**[[C; **if** B **then skip else repeat** C **until** B]]
c. **C**[[**while** B **do** C]] = **C**[[(**while** B **do** C); **if** B **then** C]]
d. **C**[[**if** B **then repeat** C **until** ¬ B]] = **C**[[**while** B **do** C]]

where the **while**-loop is defined in Section 6.6.5, the **repeat**-loop is defined in Section 6.7, and **C**[[**skip**]] = $\underline{\lambda}s.\ s$.

9. Formulate Hoare-style inference rules and prove their soundness for the following commands:

a. [[**if** B **then** C]] from Figure 5.2.
b. [[**diverge**]] from Figure 5.2.
c. [[**repeat** C **until** B]] from Section 6.7.

10. A language designer has proposed a new control construct called **entangle.** It satifies this equality:

C[[**entangle** B **in** C]] = **C**[[**if** B **then** (C; (**entangle** B **in** C); C) **else** C]]

a. Define a semantics for **entangle.** Prove that the semantics satisfies the above property.
b. Following the pattern shown in Section 6.6.5, draw out the family of approximate syntax trees for [[**entangle** B **in** C]].
c. Comment why the **while**- and **repeat**-loop control constructs are easily implementable on a computer while **entangle** is not.

11. Redraw the semantic domains listed in exercise 4 of Chapter 3, showing the partial ordering on the elements.

12. For cpos D and E, show that for any $f, g : D \rightarrow E$, $f \sqsubseteq_{D \rightarrow E} g$ iff (for all $a_1, a_2 \in A$, $a_1 \sqsubseteq_A a_2$ implies $f(a_1) \sqsubseteq_B g(a_2)$).

13. Why is $fix\ F : D \rightarrow E$ continuous when $F : (D \rightarrow E) \rightarrow (D \rightarrow E)$ is?

14. Show that D^* is a cpo when D is and that its associated operations are continuous.

15. Show that the operation $(\_ \rightarrow \_ [\!] \_) : Tr \times D \times D \rightarrow D$ is continuous.

16. Show that the composition of continuous functions is a continuous function.

17. The cpos D and E are *order isomorphic* iff there exist continuous functions $f: D \rightarrow E$ and $g: E \rightarrow D$ such that $g \circ f = id_D$ and $f \circ g = id_E$. Thus, order isomorphic cpos are in 1-1, onto, order preserving correspondence. Prove that the following pairs of cpos are order isomorphic. (Let A, B, and C be arbitrary cpos.)

a. $\mathbb{N}$ and $\mathbb{N} + \mathbb{N}$
b. $\mathbb{N}$ and $\mathbb{N} \times \mathbb{N}$
c. $A \times B$ and $B \times A$
d. $A + B$ and $B + A$
e. $Unit \rightarrow A$ and A
f. $(Unit \times A) \rightarrow B$ and $A \rightarrow B$
g. $(A \times B) \rightarrow C$ and $A \rightarrow (B \rightarrow C)$

18. Let A and B be cpos, and let $\prod_{a:A} B$ be the usual A-fold product of B elements. Define $apply : A \times (\prod_{a:A} B) \rightarrow B$ to be the indexing operation; that is, $apply(a,p) = p \downarrow a$.

a. Show that the product is order isomorphic with the set of *all* functions with domain A and codomain B.
b. Given that the semantic domain $A \rightarrow B$ contains just the *continuous*

functions from A to B, propose a domain construction for the infinite product above that is order isomorphic with $A \rightarrow B$.

19. Researchers in semantic domain theory often work with *bounded complete ω-algebraic cpos*. Here are the basic definitions and results:

An element $d \in D$ is *finite* iff for all chains $C \subseteq D$, if $d \sqsubseteq \bigsqcup C$, then there exists some $c \in C$ such that $d \sqsubseteq c$. Let $\mathbf{fin}D$ be the set of finite elements in D.

a. Describe the finite elements in:

i. $\mathbb{N}$
ii. $\mathbb{P}(\mathbb{N})$, the powerset of $\mathbb{N}$ partially ordered by $\subseteq$
iii. $\mathbb{N} \rightarrow \mathbb{N}_\perp$ (hint: work with the graph representations of the functions)
iv. $D+E$, where D and E are cpos
v. $D \times E$, where D and E are cpos
vi. $D_\perp$, where D is a cpo

A cpo D is *algebraic* if, for every $d \in D$, there exists a chain $C \subseteq \mathbf{fin}D$ such that $\bigsqcup C = d$. D is *ω-algebraic* if $\mathbf{fin}D$ has at most a countably infinite number of elements.

b. Show that the cpos in parts i through vi of part a are ω-algebraic, when D and E represent ω-algebraic cpos.
c. Show that $\mathbb{N} \rightarrow \mathbb{N}$ is algebraic but is not ω-algebraic.
d. For algebraic cpos D and E, prove that a monotonic function from $\mathbf{fin}D$ to $\mathbf{fin}E$ can be uniquely extended to a continuous function in $D \rightarrow E$. Prove that $D \rightarrow E$ is order isomorphic to the partially ordered set of monotonic functions from $\mathbf{fin}D$ to $\mathbf{fin}E$. Next, show that a function that maps from algebraic cpo D to algebraic cpo E and is continuous on $\mathbf{fin}D$ to $\mathbf{fin}E$ need not be continuous on D to E.

A cpo D is *bounded complete* if, for all $a, b \in D$, if there exists a $c \in D$ such that $a \sqsubseteq c$ and $b \sqsubseteq c$, then $a \sqcup b$ exists in D.

e. Show that the following cpos are bounded complete ω-algebraic:

i. The cpos in parts i through vi in part b, where D and E represent bounded complete ω-algebraic cpos.
ii. $D \rightarrow E$, where D and E are bounded complete ω-algebraic cpos and E is pointed. (Hint: first show that for any $d \in \mathbf{fin}D$ and $e \in \mathbf{fin}E$ that the "step function" $(\lambda a.\,(d \sqsubseteq a) \rightarrow e \,[\!]\, \perp)$ is a finite element in $D \rightarrow E$. Then show that any $f: D \rightarrow E$ is the lub of a chain whose elements are finite joins of step functions.)

For a partially ordered set E, a nonempty set $A \subseteq E$ is an *ideal* if:

i. For all $a, b \in E$, if $a \in A$ and $b \sqsubseteq a$, then $b \in A$.
ii. For all $a, b \in A$, there exists some $c \in A$ such that $a \sqsubseteq c$ and $b \sqsubseteq c$.

f. For an algebraic cpo D, let $\mathbf{id}D = \{ A \mid A \subseteq \mathbf{fin} D$ *and* A *is an ideal* $\}$. Show that the partially ordered set $(\mathbf{id}D, \subseteq)$ is order isomorphic with D.

20. We gain important insights by applying *topology* to domains. For a cpo D, say that a set $U \subseteq D$ is a *Scott-open set* iff:

    i. It is closed upwards: for all $a \in U$, $b \in D$, if $a \sqsubseteq b$, then $b \in U$.
    ii. It contains a lub only if it contains a "tail" of the chain: for all chains $C \subseteq D$, if $\bigsqcup C \in U$, then there exists some $c \in C$ such that $c \in U$.

    A collection of sets $S \subseteq \mathbb{P}(D)$ is a *topology on D* iff:

    i. Both $\{\,\}$ and D belong to S.
    ii. For any $R \subseteq S$, $\bigcup R \in S$, that is, S is closed under arbitrary unions.
    iii. For any $U, V \in S$, $U \cap V \in S$, that is, S is closed under binary intersections.

    a. Show that for any cpo D that the collection of Scott-open sets forms a topology on D.
    b. Describe the Scott-open sets for these cpos: Nat, $Tr_\perp$, $Tr_\perp \times Tr_\perp$, $Nat \rightarrow Nat$, $Nat \rightarrow Nat_\perp$.
    c. Show that every element $d \in D$ is characterized by a unique collection of Scott-open sets, that is, prove that for all distinct $d, e \in D$, there exists some Scott-open set $U \subseteq D$ such that $(d \in U$ *and* $e \notin U)$ or $(e \in U$ *and* $d \notin U)$. (Hint: first show that the set $D - \{ e \mid e \sqsubseteq d \}$, for any $d \in D$, is Scott-open; use this result in your proof.)

    Part c says that the Scott-open sets have the T_0*-separation property*. Because of this result, we treat the Scott-open sets as "detectable properties" of D-elements. Each element is identified by the properties that it satisfies.

    d. Show that for all $d, e \in D$, $d \sqsubseteq e$ iff for all open sets $U \subseteq D$, $d \in U$ implies $e \in U$.

    A function $f: D \rightarrow E$ is *topologically continuous* iff for all open sets $U \subseteq E$, $f^{-1}(U)$ is open in D. That is, a set of answer values share a property only because their corresponding arguments also share a property.

    e. Prove that a function $f: D \rightarrow E$ is chain-continuous (see Definition 6.9) iff it is topologically continuous (with respect to the Scott-topologies on D and E).

21. Section 6.1 is a presentation of Kleene's *first recursion theorem*, which states that the meaning of a recursive specification $f = F(f)$ that maps arguments in $\mathbb{N}$ to answers in $\mathbb{N}$ (or nontermination) is exactly the union of the $F^i(\emptyset)$ approximating functions. The proof of the theorem (see Kleene 1952, or Rogers 1967) doesn't mention continuity or pointed cpos. Why do we require these concepts for Chapter 6?

Chapter 7

Languages with Contexts

Virtually all languages rely on some notion of context. The context in which a phrase is used influences its meaning. In a programming language, contexts are responsible for attributing meanings to identifiers. There are several possible notions of a programming language context; let's consider two of them. The first, a simplistic view, is that the store establishes the context for a phrase. The view works with the languages studied in Chapter 5, but it does suggest that the context within the block

```
begin
    integer X; integer Y;
    Y:=0;
    X:=Y;
    Y:=1;
    X:=Y+1
end
```

is constantly changing. This is counterintuitive; surely the declarations of the identifiers X and Y establish the context of the block, and the commands within the block operate within that context. A second example,

```
begin integer X;
    X:=0;
    begin real X;
        X:=1.5
    end;
    X:=X+1
end
```

shows that the meaning of an identifier isn't just its storable value. In this example, there are two distinct definitions of X. The outer X denotes an *integer* object, while the inner X is a *real* object. These objects are different; X happens to be the name used for both of them. Any potential ambiguities in using X are handled by the scope rules of ALGOL60. The "objects" mentioned are in actuality computer storage locations, and the primary meaning of an ALGOL60 identifier is the location bound to it. The version of context we choose to use is the set of identifier, storage location pairs that are accessible at a textual position. Each position in the program resides within a unique context, and the context can be determined without running the program.

In denotational semantics, the context of a phrase is modelled by a value called an *environment*. Environments possess several distinctive properties:

1. As mentioned, an environment establishes a context for a syntactic phrase, resolving any ambiguities concerning the meaning of identifiers.
2. There are as many environment values as there are distinct contexts in a program. Multiple environments may be maintained during program evaluation.
3. An environment is (usually) a static object. A phrase uses the same environment each time it is evaluated with the store.

An environment argument wasn't needed for the languages in Chapter 5, because the programs in the languages used exactly one environment. The single environment was "pasted onto" the store, giving a map from identifiers to storable values. In this chapter, that simple model is split apart into two separate components, the environment and the store.

The primary real-life example of an environment is a complier's symbol table. A compiler uses a symbol table to translate a source program into compiled code. The symbol table contains an entry for each identifier in the program, listing the identifier's data type, its mode of usage (variable, constant, parameter, . . .), and its relative location in the run-time computer store. Since a block-structured language allows multiple uses of the same identifier, the symbol table is responsible for resolving naming conflicts. The schemes for implementation are many: one is to keep a different symbol table for each block of the program (the portions in common between blocks may be shared); another is to build the table as a single stack, which is incremented and decremented upon respective entry and exit for a block. Symbol tables may be entirely compile-time objects, as in ALGOL68 and standard Pascal, or they can be run-time objects, as in SNOBOL4, or they can be used in both phases, as in ALGOL60.

Those portions of a semantics definition that use an environment to resolve context questions are sometimes called the *static semantics*. The term traditionally describes compile-time actions such as type-checking, scope resolution, and storage calculation. Static semantics may be contrasted with the "real" production of meaning, which takes the name *dynamic semantics*. Code generation and execution comprise the implementation-oriented version of dynamic semantics. In general, the separation of static from dynamic semantics is rarely clear cut, and we will not attempt formal definitions here.

Environments are used as arguments by the valuation functions. The meaning of a command is now determined by the function:

$$\mathbf{C}\colon \text{Command} \to \mathit{Environment} \to \mathit{Store} \to \mathit{Store}_{\bot}$$

The meaning of a command as a $Store \rightarrow Store_\perp$ function is determined once an environment establishes the context for the command. An environment belongs to the domain

$$Environment = Identifier \rightarrow Denotable\text{-}value$$

The *Denotable-value* domain contains all the values that identifiers may represent. This domain varies widely from language to language and its structure largely determines the character of the language.

In this chapter, we study language features whose semantics are understood in terms of environments. These features include declarations, block structure, scoping mechanisms, recursive bindings, and compound data structures. The concepts are presented within the framework of two languages: an imperative block-structured language and an applicative language.

7.1 A BLOCK-STRUCTURED LANGUAGE

The basic principles and uses of environments are seen in the semantics of a simple block-structured language. The language is similar to the one defined in Figure 5.2, but includes declarations and blocks. The new semantic domains are listed in Figure 7.1.

The more realistic store requires a primitive domain of storage locations, and the locations domain is listed first. The operations are the same as in the algebra in Example 3.4 of Chapter 3: *first-locn* is a constant, marking the first usable location in a store; *next-locn* maps a location to its immediate successor in a store; *equal-locn* checks for equality of two values; and *lessthan-locn* compares two locations and returns a truth value based on the locations' relative values.

The collection of values that identifiers may represent is listed next. Of the three components of the *Denotable-value* domain, the *Location* domain holds the denotations of variable identifiers, the *Nat* domain holds the meanings of constant identifiers, and the *Errvalue* domain holds the meaning for undeclared identifiers.

For this language, an environment is a pair. The first component is the function that maps identifiers to their denotable values. The second component is a location value, which marks the extent of the store reserved for declared variables. In this example, the environment takes the responsibility for assigning locations to variables. This is done by the *reserve-locn* operation, which returns the next usable location. Although it is not made clear by the algebra, the structure of the language will cause the locations to be used in a stack-like fashion. The *emptyenv* must be given the location marking the beginning of usable space in the store so that it can build the initial environment.

The store is a map from storage locations to storable values, and the operations are the obvious ones. Errors during evaluation are possible, so the store

Figure 7.1

V. Storage locations

Domain $l \in Location$

Operations

$\mathit{first\text{-}locn} : Location$

$\mathit{next\text{-}locn} : Location \rightarrow Location$

$\mathit{equal\text{-}locn} : Location \rightarrow Location \rightarrow Tr$

$\mathit{lessthan\text{-}locn} : Location \rightarrow Location \rightarrow Tr$

VI. Denotable values

Domain $d \in \mathit{Denotable\text{-}value} = Location + Nat + Errvalue$

where $Errvalue = Unit$

VII. Environment: a map to denotable values and the maximum store location

Domain $e \in Environment = (Id \rightarrow \mathit{Denotable\text{-}value}) \times Location$

Operations

$emptyenv : Location \rightarrow Environment$

$emptyenv = \lambda l.\, ((\lambda i.\, \mathrm{in}Errvalue\,()), l)$

$accessenv : Id \rightarrow Environment \rightarrow \mathit{Denotable\text{-}value}$

$accessenv = \lambda i.\lambda(map, l).\, map(i)$

$updateenv : Id \rightarrow \mathit{Denotable\text{-}value} \rightarrow Environment \rightarrow Environment$

$updateenv = \lambda i.\lambda d.\lambda(map, l).\, ([\, i \mapsto d\,]map, l)$

$\mathit{reserve\text{-}locn} : Environment \rightarrow (Location \times Environment)$

$\mathit{reserve\text{-}locn} = \lambda(map, l).\, (l, (map, \mathit{next\text{-}locn}(l)))$

VIII. Storable values

Domain $v \in \mathit{Storable\text{-}value} = Nat$

IX. Stores

Domain $s \in Store = Location \rightarrow \mathit{Storable\text{-}value}$

Operations

$access : Location \rightarrow Store \rightarrow \mathit{Storable\text{-}value}$

$access = \lambda l.\lambda s.\, s(l)$

$update : Location \rightarrow \mathit{Storable\text{-}value} \rightarrow Store \rightarrow Store$

$update = \lambda l.\lambda v.\lambda s.\, [\, l \mapsto v\,]s$

X. Run-time store, labeled with status of computation

Domain $p \in Poststore = OK + Err$

where $OK = Err = Store$

Figure 7.1 (continued)

Operations

$return : Store \rightarrow Poststore$

$return = \lambda s.\ \mathrm{in}OK(s)$

$signalerr : Store \rightarrow Poststore$

$signalerr = \lambda s.\ \mathrm{in}Err(s)$

$check : (Store \rightarrow Poststore_{\perp}) \rightarrow (Poststore_{\perp} \rightarrow Poststore_{\perp})$

$check\ f = \underline{\lambda} p.\ \text{cases } p \text{ of}$

$\quad \mathrm{is}OK(s) \rightarrow (f\ s)$

$\quad [\!]\ \mathrm{is}Err(s) \rightarrow p \text{ end}$

---

will be labeled with the status of the evaluation. The *check* operation uses the tags to determine if evaluation should continue.

Figure 7.2 defines the block-structured language and its semantics.

Since the *Denotable-value* domain contains both natural numbers and locations, denotable value errors may occur in a program; for example, an identifier with a number denotation might be used where an identifier with a location denotation is required. An identifier with an erroneous denotable value always induces an error. Expressible value errors occur when an expressible value is inappropriately used.

The **P** valuation function requires a store and a location value, the latter marking the beginning of the store's free space. The **K** function establishes the context for a block. The **D** function augments an environment. The composition of declarations parallels the composition of commands. A constant identifier declaration causes an environment update, where the identifier is mapped to its numeral value in the environment. The denotation of a variable declaration is more involved: a new location is reserved for the variable. This location, l', plus the current environment, e', are used to create the environment in which the variable $[\![I]\!]$ binds to in*Location*(l').

Of the equations for the **C** function, the one for composition deserves the most study. First, consider the *check* operation. If command $\mathbf{C}[\![C_1]\!]e$ maps a store into an erroneous post-store, then *check* traps the error and prevents $\mathbf{C}[\![C_2]\!]e$ from altering the store. This would be implemented as a branch around the code for $[\![C_2]\!]$. The environment is also put to good use: commands $[\![C_1]\!]$ and $[\![C_2]\!]$ are both evaluated in the context represented by e. This point is important, for $[\![C_1]\!]$ could be a block with local declarations. It would need its own

Figure 7.2

Abstract syntax:

P∈ Program
K∈ Block
D∈ Declaration
C∈ Command
E∈ Expression
B∈ Boolean-expr
I ∈ Identifier
N∈ Numeral

P ::= K.
K ::= **begin** D; C end
D ::= D_1;D_2 | **const** I=N | **var** I
C ::= C_1;C_2 | I:=E | **while** B **do** C | K
E ::= E_1+E_2 | I | N

Semantic algebras:

I.-III. Natural numbers, truth values, identifiers
(defined in Figure 5.1)

IV. Expressible values
Domain *x* ∈ *Expressible-value* = *Nat* + *Errvalue*
where *Errvalue* = *Unit*

V.-X. (defined in Figure 7.1)

Valuation functions:

P: Program→ *Location* → *Store* → $Poststore_{\perp}$
P[[K.]] = λ*l*. **K**[[K]](*emptyenv l*)

K: Block→ *Environment* → *Store* → $Poststore_{\perp}$
K[[**begin** D;C **end**]] = λ*e*. **C**[[C]](**D**[[D]]*e*)

D: Declaration→ *Environment* → *Environment*
D[[D_1;D_2]] = **D**[[D_2]] ∘ **D**[[D_1]]
D[[**const** I=N]] = *updateenv* [[I]] in*Nat*(**N**[[N]])
D[[**var** I]] = λ*e*.let (*l'*,*e'*) = (*reserve-locn e*) in (*updateenv* [[I]] in*Location*(*l'*) *e'*)

C: Command → *Environment* → *Store* → $Poststore_{\perp}$
C[[C_1;C_2]] = λ*e*. (*check* (**C**[[C_2]] *e*)) ∘ (**C**[[C_1]] *e*)

Figure 7.2 (continued)

$\mathbf{C}[\![\mathrm{I{:=}E}]\!] = \lambda e.\lambda s.$ cases $(accessenv\ [\![\mathrm{I}]\!]\ e)$ of
  is$Location(l) \to$ (cases $(\mathbf{E}[\![\mathrm{E}]\!]e\ s)$ of
    is$Nat(n) \to (return\ (update\ l\ n\ s))$
    [] is$Errvalue() \to (signalerr\ s)$ end)
  [] is$Nat(n) \to (signalerr\ s)$
  [] is$Errvalue() \to (signalerr\ s)$ end
$\mathbf{C}[\![$**while** B **do** C$]\!] = \lambda e.\ fix(\lambda f.\lambda s.$ cases $(\mathbf{B}[\![\mathrm{B}]\!]e\ s)$ of
  is$Tr(t) \to (t \to (check\ f) \circ (\mathbf{C}[\![\mathrm{C}]\!]e)\ [\!]\ return\ )(s)$
  [] is$Errvalue() \to (signalerr\ s)$ end)
$\mathbf{C}[\![\mathrm{K}]\!] = \mathbf{K}[\![\mathrm{K}]\!]$

E: Expression $\to$ *Environment* $\to$ *Store* $\to$ *Expressible-value*
$\mathbf{E}[\![\mathrm{E}_1 + \mathrm{E}_2]\!] = \lambda e.\lambda s.$ cases $(\mathbf{E}[\![\mathrm{E}_1]\!]e\ s)$ of
  is$Nat(n_1) \to$ (cases $(\mathbf{E}[\![\mathrm{E}_2]\!]e\ s)$ of
    is$Nat(n_2) \to$ in$Nat(n_1\ plus\ n_2)$
    [] is$Errvalue() \to$ in$Errvalue()$ end)
  [] is$Errvalue() \to$ in$Errvalue()$ end
$\mathbf{E}[\![\mathrm{I}]\!] = \lambda e.\lambda s.$ cases $(accessenv\ [\![\mathrm{I}]\!]\ e)$ of
  is$Location(l) \to$ in$Nat(access\ l\ s)$
  [] is$Nat(n) \to$ in$Nat(n)$
  [] is$Errvalue() \to$ in$Errvalue()$ end
$\mathbf{E}[\![\mathrm{N}]\!] = \lambda e.\lambda s.$ in$Nat(\mathbf{N}[\![\mathrm{N}]\!])$

B: Boolean-expr $\to$ *Environment* $\to$ *Store* $\to (Tr + Errvalue)$ (omitted)

N: Numeral $\to$ *Nat* (omitted)

---

local environment to process its commands. However, $\mathbf{C}[\![\mathrm{C}_2]\!]$ retains its own copy of e, so the environments created within $\mathbf{C}[\![\mathrm{C}_1]\!]$ do not affect $\mathbf{C}[\![\mathrm{C}_2]\!]$'s version. (Of course, whatever alterations $\mathbf{C}[\![\mathrm{C}_1]\!]e$ makes upon the store are passed to $\mathbf{C}[\![\mathrm{C}_2]\!]e$.) This language feature is called *static scoping*. The context for a phrase in a statically scoped language is determined solely by the textual position of the phrase. One of the benefits of static scoping is that any identifier declared within a block may be referenced only by the commands within that block. This makes the management of storage locations straightforward. So-called *dynamically scoped* languages, whose contexts are not totally determined by textual position, will be studied in a later section.

The meaning of an expression supplied with an environment and store is an expressible value. Error checking also occurs at the expression level, as an undeclared identifier might be used in an expression.

A key feature of this language, as well as other strongly typed languages, is that environment processing can proceed independently of store processing. That is, the denotation P⟦P⟧ can be simplified without the values of the initial base location l and the initial store s (see Section 5.1.1 of chapter 5). The result is a smaller function expression that contains no occurrences of environment arguments nor of the *cases* expressions that check denotable and expressible value tags. The simplifications correspond to the declaration and type-checking actions that occur in a compiler.

The following example demonstrates this point. Since the value of the run-time store is not known, we do no simplification on any operations from the algebras *Store* and *Poststore*. Expressions using these operations are "frozen"— their evaluation is delayed until run-time. The static semantics analysis of a program is presented in Figure 7.3.

The diagrammatic form:

$$\begin{array}{c}(\cdots E \cdots)\\ \downarrow\\ E'\end{array}$$

represents the simplification of expression E to E' and its replacement in the larger expression, giving $(\cdots E' \cdots)$. Notice how the environment arguments distribute throughout the commands and their subparts without interfering with the frozen *check* $(\lambda s. \cdots)$ expression forms. All *Denotable-value* and *Expressible-value* labels are consumed by the *cases* expressions. As simplification proceeds, environment arguments disappear, variables map to their location values, and constants reveal their natural number values. The final expression can be read more easily if reverse function composition is used: let $f\,!\,g$ stand for $g \circ f$. Then the result is:

$$\begin{array}{l}
\lambda l.\ (\lambda s.\, return\ (update\ l\ (one\ plus\ two)\ s))\\
\quad !\ (check\ (fix(\lambda f.\lambda s.\\
\qquad\quad ((access\ l\ s)\ equals\ zero \rightarrow\\
\qquad\qquad (\lambda s.\, return\ (update\,(next\text{-}locn\ l)\ (access\ l\ s)\ s\,))\ !\ (check\, f)\\
\qquad\qquad [\!]\ return\\
\qquad\quad)\ s\,))\\
\quad !\ (check\ (\lambda s.\, return\ (update\ l\ one\ s))))
\end{array}$$

The expression rightly resembles a series of machine code instructions, parameterized on a store's base address l. In Chapter 10, we study the mapping of expressions such as this one into object code for a real machine.

Figure 7.3

Let D_0 = **const** A=1
D_1 = **var** X
$C_0 = C_1;C_2;C_3$
C_1 = X:=A+2
C_2 = **begin var** A;C_4 **end**
C_3 = X:=A
C_4 = **while** X=0 **do** A:=X

P⟦**begin** $D_0;D_1;C_0$ **end**⟧

↓

$\lambda l.$ **K**⟦**begin** $D_0;D_1$:C_0 **end**⟧(*emptyenv l*)

let this be e_0

↓

C⟦C_0⟧(**D**⟦$D_0;D_1$⟧e_0)

↓

D⟦D_1⟧(**D**⟦**const** A=1⟧e_0)

↓

(*updateenv* ⟦A⟧ in*Nat*(*one*) e_0)

let this be e_1= (*map*,*l*)

↓

D⟦**var** X⟧e_1

↓

let (l',e')= (*reserve-locn* e_1) in · · ·

↓

(*l*, (*map*, (*next-locn l*)))

e_2

↓

(*updateenv* ⟦X⟧ in*Location* (*l*) e_2)

e_3

↓

(*check* (**C**⟦$C_2;C_3$⟧e_3)) ∘ (**C**⟦X:=A+2⟧e_3)

↓

$\lambda s.$ cases (*accessenv* ⟦X⟧ e_3) of · · · end

↓

in*Location* (*l*)

↓ ↓

Figure 7.3 (continued)

cases ($\mathbf{E}[\![\text{A+2}]\!]e_3\ s$) of · · · end

in*Nat*(*one plus two*)

return (*update* l (*one plus two*) s)

(*check* ($\mathbf{C}[\![\text{C}_3]\!]e_3$)) ∘ ($\mathbf{C}[\![$**begin var** A; C_4 **end**$]\!]e_3$)

$\mathbf{C}[\![\text{C}_4]\!](\mathbf{D}[\![$**var** A$]\!]e_3)$

(*updateenv* $[\![\text{A}]\!]$ in*Location* (*next-locn* l) e_4)

e_5

$\mathbf{C}[\![$**while** X=0 **do**A:=X$]\!]e_5$

fix($\lambda f.\ \lambda s.$ cases ($\mathbf{B}[\![\text{X=0}]\!]e_5\ s$) of · · · end

in*Tr* ((*access* l s) *equals zero*)

((*access* l s) *equals zero* →
(*check* f) ∘ ($\mathbf{C}[\![\text{A:=X}]\!]e_5$) [] *return*) s

$\lambda s.$ *return* (*update* (*next-locn* l) (*access* l s) s)

$\mathbf{C}[\![\text{X:=A}]\!]e_3$

$\lambda s.$ *return* (*update* l *one* s)

7.1.1 Stack-Managed Storage

The store of a block-structured language is used in a stack-like fashion— locations are bound to identifiers sequentially using *nextlocn*, and a location bound to an identifier in a local block is freed for re-use when the block is exited. The re-use of locations happens automatically due to the equation for $\mathbf{C}[\![\text{C}_1;\text{C}_2]\!]$. Any locations bound to identifiers in $[\![\text{C}_1]\!]$ are reserved by the environment built from e for $\mathbf{C}[\![\text{C}_1]\!]$, but $\mathbf{C}[\![\text{C}_2]\!]$ re-uses the original e (and its original location marker), effectively deallocating the locations.

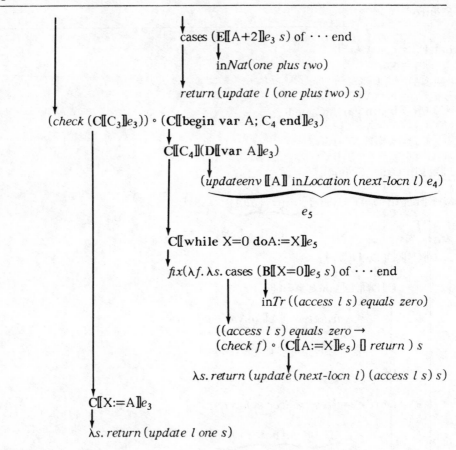

Stack-based storage is a significant characteristic of block-structured programming languages, and the *Store* algebra deserves to possess mechanisms for stack-based allocation and deallocation. Let's move the storage calculation mechanism over to the store algebra. Figure 7.4 presents one of many possible results.

The new store domain uses the (*Location* → *Storable-value*) component as the data space of the stack, and the *Location* component indicates the amount of storage in use— it is the "stack top marker." Operations *access* and *update* verify that any reference to a storage location is a valid one, occurring at an active location beneath the stack top. The purposes of *mark-locn* and *allocate-locn* should be clear; the latter is the run-time version of the environment's *reserve-locn* operation. The *deallocate-locns* operation releases stack storage from the stack top to the value indicated by its argument.

Freed from storage management, the environment domain takes the form *Environment* = *Id* → *Denotable-value*. The operations are adjusted accordingly, and the operation *reserve-locn* is dropped. (This is left as an easy exercise.) If the environment leaves the task of storage calculation to the store operations, then processing of declarations requires the store as well as the environment. The functionality of the valuation function for declarations becomes:

Figure 7.4

IX′. Stack-based store

Domain *Store* = (*Location* → *Storable-value*) × *Location*

Operations

access : *Location* → *Store* → (*Storable-value* + *Errvalue*)

$access = \lambda l.\lambda(map, top).\ l\ lessthan\text{-}locn\ top \rightarrow \text{in}Storable\text{-}value(map\ l)\ [\!]\ \text{in}Errvalue()$

update : *Location* → *Storable-value* → *Store* → *Poststore*

$update = \lambda l.\lambda v.\lambda(map, top).\ l\ lessthan\text{-}locn\ top \rightarrow \text{in}OK([l \mapsto v]map, top)\ [\!]\ \text{in}Err(map, top)$

mark-locn : *Store* → *Location*

$mark\text{-}locn = \lambda(map, top).\ top$

allocate-locn : *Store* → *Location* × *Poststore*

$allocate\text{-}locn = \lambda(map, top).\ (top,\ \text{in}OK(map, next\text{-}locn(top)))$

deallocate-locns : *Location* → *Store* → *Poststore*

$deallocate\text{-}locns = \lambda l.\lambda(map, top).\ (l\ lessthan\text{-}locn\ top)\ or\ (l\ equal\text{-}locn\ top) \rightarrow \text{in}OK(map, l)\ [\!]\ \text{in}Err(map, top)$

$\mathbf{D}$: Declaration $\rightarrow$ *Environment* $\rightarrow$ *Store* $\rightarrow$ (*Environment* $\times$ *Poststore*)

$\mathbf{D}[\![\mathbf{var}\ \mathrm{I}]\!] = \lambda e.\lambda s.\ \mathrm{let}\ (l, p) = (\mathit{allocate\text{-}locn}\ s)$
$\quad\quad \mathrm{in}\ ((\mathit{updateenv}\ [\![\mathrm{I}]\!]\ \mathrm{in}\mathit{Location}(l)\ e), p)$

$\mathbf{D}[\![\mathrm{D}_1;\mathrm{D}_2]\!] = \lambda e.\lambda s.\ \mathrm{let}\ (e', p) = (\mathbf{D}[\![\mathrm{D}_1]\!]e\ s)\ \mathrm{in}\ (\mathit{check}\ \mathbf{D}[\![\mathrm{D}_2]\!]e')(p)$

where *check* : (*Store* $\rightarrow$(*Environment* $\times$ *Poststore*)) $\rightarrow$(*Poststore* $\rightarrow$(*Environment* $\times$ *Poststore*)) behaves like its namesake in Figure 7.1. This version of declaration processing makes the environment into a run-time object, for the binding of location values to identifiers cannot be completed without the run-time store. Contrast this with the arrangement in Figure 7.2, where location binding is computed by the environment operation *reserve-locn*, which produced a result relative to an arbitrary base address. A solution for freeing the environment from dependence upon *allocate-locn* is to provide it information about storage management strategies, so that the necessary address calculations can be performed independently of the value of the run-time store. This is left as an exercise.

The **K** function manages the storage for the block:

$\mathbf{K}[\![\mathbf{begin}\ \mathrm{D;C}\ \mathbf{end}]\!] = \lambda e.\lambda s.\ \mathrm{let}\ l = \mathit{mark\text{-}locn}\ s\ \mathrm{in}$
$\quad \mathrm{let}\ (e', p) = \mathbf{D}[\![\mathrm{D}]\!]e\ s\ \mathrm{in}$
$\quad \mathrm{let}\ p' = (\mathit{check}\ (\mathbf{C}[\![\mathrm{C}]\!]e'))(p)$
$\quad \mathrm{in}\ (\mathit{check}\ (\mathit{deallocate\text{-}locns}\ l))(p')$

The *deallocate-locns* operation frees storage down to the level held by the store prior to block entry, which is (*mark-locn s*).

7.1.2 The Meanings of Identifiers

The notion of context can be even more subtle than we first imagined. Consider the Pascal assignment statement X:=X+1. The meaning of X on the right-hand side of the assignment is decidedly different from X's meaning on the left-hand side. Specifically, the "left-hand side value" is a location value, while the "right-hand side value" is the storable value associated with that location. Apparently the context problem for identifiers is found even at the primitive command level.

One way out of this problem would be to introduce two environment arguments for the semantic function for commands: a left-hand side one and a right-hand side one. This arrangement is hardly natural; commands are the "sentences" of a program, and sentences normally operate in a single context. Another option is to say that any variable identifier actually denotes a pair of values: a location value and a storable value. The respective values are called the identifier's *L-value* and *R-value*. The L-value for a variable is kept in the environment, and the R-value is kept in the store. We introduce a valuation function **I**: *Id* → *Environment* → *Store* → (*Location* × *Storable-value*). In practice, the **I** function is split into two semantic functions **L**: *Id* → *Environment* → *Location* and **R**: *Id* → *Environment* → *Store* → *Storable-value* such that:

$$\mathbf{L}[\![\mathrm{I}]\!] = \mathit{accessenv}\ [\![\mathrm{I}]\!]$$
$$\mathbf{R}[\![\mathrm{I}]\!] = \mathit{access} \circ \mathit{accessenv}\ [\![\mathrm{I}]\!].$$

We restate the semantic equations using variables as:

$$\mathbf{C}[\![\mathrm{I{:=}E}]\!] = \lambda e.\lambda s.\ \mathit{return}\ (\mathit{update}\ (\mathbf{L}[\![\mathrm{I}]\!]e)\ (\mathbf{E}[\![\mathrm{E}]\!]e\ s)\ s)$$
$$\mathbf{E}[\![\mathrm{I}]\!] = \mathbf{R}[\![\mathrm{I}]\!]$$

The definitions are a bit simplistic because they assume that all identifiers are variables. Constant identifiers can be integrated into the scheme — a declaration such as $[\![$const A=N$]\!]$ suggests $\mathbf{L}[\![\mathrm{A}]\!]e=$ in*Errvalue*(). (What should $(\mathbf{R}[\![\mathrm{A}]\!]e\ s)$ be?)

Yet another view to take is that the R-value of a variable identifier is a function of its L-value. The "true meaning" of a variable is its L-value, and a "coercion" occurs when a variable is used on the right-hand side of an assignment. This coercion is called *dereferencing*. We formalize this view as:

J: Id → *Environment* → *Denotable-value*

$$\mathbf{J}[\![\mathrm{I}]\!] = \lambda e.\ (\mathit{accessenv}\ [\![\mathrm{I}]\!]\ e)$$

$$\mathbf{C}[\![\mathrm{I{:=}E}]\!] = \lambda e.\lambda s.\ \mathit{return}\ (\mathit{update}\ (\mathbf{J}[\![\mathrm{I}]\!]e)\ (\mathbf{E}[\![\mathrm{E}]\!]e\ s)\ s\ )$$
$$\mathbf{E}[\![\mathrm{I}]\!] = \lambda e.\lambda s.\ \mathit{dereference}\ (\mathbf{J}[\![\mathrm{I}]\!]e)\ s$$

where *dereference*: *Location* → *Store* → *Storable-value*

dereference = *access*

An identifier's meaning is just its denotable value. Those identifiers with locations as their meanings (the variables) are dereferenced when an expressible value is needed. This is the view that was taken in the previous sections.

The implicit use of dereferencing is so common in general purpose programming languages that we take it for granted, despite the somewhat unorthodox appearance of commands such as X=X+1 in FORTRAN. Systems-oriented programming languages such as BCPL, Bliss, and C use an explicit dereferencing operator. For example, in BCPL expressible values include locations, and the appropriate semantic equations are:

$$\mathbf{E}[\![\mathrm{I}]\!] = \lambda e.\lambda s.\ \ \mathrm{in}\mathit{Location}(\mathbf{J}[\![\mathrm{I}]\!]e)$$
$$\mathbf{E}[\![@\ \mathrm{E}]\!] = \lambda e.\lambda s.\ \mathrm{cases}\ (\mathbf{E}[\![\mathrm{E}]\!]e\ s)\ \mathrm{of}$$
$$\mathrm{is}\mathit{Location}(l) \to (\mathit{dereference}\ l\ s)$$
$$[\!]\ \cdots\ \mathrm{end}$$

The @ symbol is the dereferencing operator. The meaning of X:=X+1 in BCPL is decidedly different from that of X:=@X+1.

7.2 AN APPLICATIVE LANGUAGE

The next example language using environments is an *applicative language*. An applicative language contains no variables. All identifiers are constants and can be given attributes but once, at their point of definition. Without variables, mechanisms such as assignment are superfluous and are dropped. Arithmetic is an applicative language. Another example is the minimal subset of LISP known as "pure LISP." The function notation that we use to define denotational definitions can also be termed an applicative language. Since an applicative language has no variables, its semantics can be specified without a *Store* domain. The environment holds the attributes associated with the identifiers.

The language that we study is defined in Figure 7.5. It is similar to pure LISP. A program in the language is just an expression. An expression can be a LET definition; a LAMBDA form (representing a function routine with parameter I); a function application; a list expression using CONS, HEAD, TAIL, or NIL; an identifier; or an atomic symbol. We learn much about the language by examining its semantic domains. *Atom* is a primitive answer domain and its internal structure will not be considered. The language also contains a domain of functions, which map denotable values to denotable values; a denotable value can be a function, a list, or an atom. For the first time, we encounter a semantic domain defined in terms of itself. By substitution, we see that:

$$\mathit{Denotable\text{-}value} = ((\mathit{Denotable\text{-}value} \rightarrow \mathit{Denotable\text{-}value}) + \mathit{Denotable\text{-}value}^* + \mathit{Atom} + \mathit{Error})_\perp$$

A solution to this mathematical puzzle exists, but to examine it now would distract us from the study of environments, so the discussion is saved for Chapter 11. Perhaps you sensed that this semantic problem would arise when you read the abstract syntax. The syntax allows LAMBDA forms to be arguments to other LAMBDA forms; a LAMBDA form can even receive itself as an argument! It is only natural that the semantic domains have the ability to mimic this self-applicative behavior, so recursive domain definitions result.

E determines the meaning of an expression with the aid of an environment. The meaning of an expression is a denotable value. An atom, list, or even a function can be a legal "answer." The LET expression provides a definition mechanism for augmenting the environment and resembles the declaration construct in Figure 7.2. Again, static scoping is used. Functions are created by the LAMBDA construction. A function body is evaluated in the context that is active at the point of function definition, augmented by the binding of an actual parameter to the binding identifier. This definition is also statically scoped.

Figure 7.5

Abstract syntax:

E∈ Expression
A∈ Atomic-symbol
I ∈ Identifier

E ::= LET I = E_1 IN E_2 | LAMBDA (I) E | E_1 E_2 |
E_1 CONS E_2 | HEAD E | TAIL E | NIL | I | A | (E)

Semantic algebras:

I. Atomic answer values
Domain *a* ∈ *Atom*
Operations
(omitted)

II. Identifiers
Domain *i* ∈ *Id* = Identifier
Operations
(usual)

III. Denotable values, functions, and lists
Domains *d* ∈ *Denotable-value* = $(Function + List + Atom + Error)_\bot$
f ∈ *Function* = *Denotable-value* → *Denotable-value*
t ∈ *List* = *Denotable-value**
Error = *Unit*

IV. Expressible values
Domain *x* ∈ *Expressible-value* = *Denotable-value*

V. Environments
Domain *e* ∈ *Environment* = *Id* → *Denotable-value*
Operations

accessenv : *Id* → *Environment* → *Denotable-value*
accessenv = $\lambda i.\lambda e.\, e\,(i)$

updateenv : *Id* → *Denotable-value* → *Environment* → *Environment*
updateenv = $\lambda i.\lambda d.\lambda e.\,[\, i \mapsto d\,]e$

Valuation functions:

E: Expression→*Environment* →*Expressible-value*

E⟦LET I=E_1 IN E_2⟧ = λe. E⟦E_2⟧(*updateenv* ⟦I⟧ (E⟦E_1⟧*e*) *e*)

E⟦LAMBDA (I) E⟧ = λe. in*Function*(λd. E⟦E⟧(*updateenv* ⟦I⟧ *d e*))

Figure 7.5 (continued)

$$
\begin{aligned}
&E\llbracket E_1\ E_2 \rrbracket = \lambda e.\ \text{let } x = (E\llbracket E_1 \rrbracket e) \text{ in cases } x \text{ of}\\
&\qquad \text{is}Function(f) \rightarrow f(E\llbracket E_2 \rrbracket e)\\
&\qquad \square\ \text{is}List(t) \rightarrow \text{in}Error()\\
&\qquad \square\ \text{is}Atom(a) \rightarrow \text{in}Error()\ \square\ \text{is}Error() \rightarrow \text{in}Error() \text{ end}\\
&E\llbracket E_1 \text{ CONS } E_2 \rrbracket = \lambda e.\ \text{let } x = (E\llbracket E_2 \rrbracket e) \text{ in cases } x \text{ of}\\
&\qquad \text{is}Function(f) \rightarrow \text{in}Error()\\
&\qquad \square\ \text{is}List(t) \rightarrow \text{in}List(E\llbracket E_1 \rrbracket e\ cons\ t)\\
&\qquad \square\ \text{is}Atom(a) \rightarrow \text{in}Error()\ \square\ \text{is}Error() \rightarrow \text{in}Error() \text{ end}\\
&E\llbracket \text{HEAD } E \rrbracket = \lambda e.\ \text{let } x = (E\llbracket E \rrbracket e) \text{ in cases } x \text{ of}\\
&\qquad \text{is}Function(f) \rightarrow \text{in}Error()\\
&\qquad \square\ \text{is}List(t) \rightarrow (null\ t \rightarrow \text{in}Error()\ \square\ (hd\ t))\\
&\qquad \square\ \text{is}Atom(a) \rightarrow \text{in}Error()\ \square\ \text{is}Error() \rightarrow \text{in}Error() \text{ end}\\
&E\llbracket \text{TAIL } E \rrbracket = \lambda e.\ \text{let } x = (E\llbracket E \rrbracket e) \text{ in cases } x \text{ of}\\
&\qquad \text{is}Function(f) \rightarrow \text{in}Error()\\
&\qquad \square\ \text{is}List(t) \rightarrow (null\ t \rightarrow \text{in}Error()\ \square\ \ \text{in}List(tl\ t))\\
&\qquad \square\ \text{is}Atom(a) \rightarrow \text{in}Error()\ \square\ \text{is}Error() \rightarrow \text{in}Error() \text{ end}\\
&E\llbracket \text{NIL} \rrbracket = \lambda e.\ \text{in}List(nil)\\
&E\llbracket I \rrbracket = accessenv\ \llbracket I \rrbracket\\
&E\llbracket A \rrbracket = \lambda e.\ \text{in}Atom(A\llbracket A \rrbracket)\\
&E\llbracket (E) \rrbracket = E\llbracket E \rrbracket
\end{aligned}
$$

A: Atomic-symbol $\rightarrow$ *Atom* (omitted)

7.2.1 Scoping Rules

The applicative language uses static scoping; that is, the context of a phrase is determined by its physical position in the program. Consider this sample program (let a_0 and a_1 be sample atomic symbols):

```
LET F = a0 IN
  LET F = LAMBDA (Z) F CONS Z  IN
    LET Z = a1 IN
      F(Z CONS NIL)
```

The occurrence of the first F in the body of the function bound to the second F refers to the atom a_0— the function is not recursive. The meaning of the entire expression is the same as (LAMBDA (Z) a_0 CONS Z) (a_1 CONS NIL)'s, which equals (a_0 CONS (a_1 CONS NIL))'s. Figure 7.6 contains the derivation.

An alternative to static scoping is *dynamic scoping*, where the context of a phrase is determined by the place(s) in the program where the phrase's value is required. The most general form of dynamic scoping is macro definition and invocation. A definition LET I=E binds identifier I to the *text* E; E is not assigned a context until its value is needed. When I's value is required, the context where I appears is used to acquire the text that is bound to it. I is replaced by the text, and the text is evaluated in the existing context. Here is a small example (the ⇛ denotes an evaluation step):

```
LET X = a0 IN
 LET Y = X CONS NIL IN
  LET X = X CONS Y IN  Y

⇛(X is bound to a0)
  LET Y = X CONS NIL IN
   LET X = X CONS Y IN  Y

⇛(X is bound to a0)
  (Y is bound to  X CONS NIL)
  LET X = X CONS Y IN  Y

⇛(X is bound to a0)
  (Y is bound to  X CONS NIL)
  (X is bound to  X CONS Y)
  Y

⇛(X is bound to a0)
  (Y is bound to  X CONS NIL)
  (X is bound to  X CONS Y)
  X CONS NIL

⇛(X is bound to a0)
  (Y is bound to  X CONS NIL)
  (X is bound to  X CONS Y)
  (X CONS Y) CONS NIL

⇛(X is bound to a0)
  (Y is bound to  X CONS NIL)
```

Figure 7.6

Let $E_0 = \text{LET F} = a_0 \text{ IN } E_1$
$E_1 = \text{LET F} = \text{LAMBDA (Z) F CONS Z IN } E_2$
$E_2 = \text{LET Z} = a_1 \text{ IN F(Z CONS NIL)}$

$$\mathbf{E}[\![E_0]\!]e_0$$

$$\downarrow$$

$$\mathbf{E}[\![E_1]\!]\underbrace{(\mathit{updateenv}\, [\![F]\!]\, (\mathbf{E}[\![a_0]\!]e_0)\; e_0)}_{e_1}$$

$$\downarrow$$

$$\mathbf{E}[\![E_2]\!]\underbrace{(\mathit{updateenv}\, [\![F]\!]\, (\mathbf{E}[\![\text{LAMBDA (Z) F CONS Z}]\!]e_1)\; e_1)}_{e_2}$$

$$\downarrow$$

$$\mathbf{E}[\![\text{F(Z CONS NIL)}]\!]\underbrace{(\mathit{updateenv}\, [\![Z]\!]\, (\mathbf{E}[\![a_1]\!]e_2)\; e_2)}_{e_3}$$

$$\downarrow$$

let $x = (\mathbf{E}[\![F]\!]e_3)$ in cases x of $\cdots$ end

$$\downarrow$$

$$\mathbf{E}[\![\text{LAMBDA (Z) F CONS Z}]\!]e_1$$
$$= \text{in}\mathit{Function}(\lambda d.\, \mathbf{E}[\![\text{F CONS Z}]\!](\mathit{updateenv}\, [\![Z]\!]\, d\; e_1))$$

$$\downarrow$$

$$(\lambda d.\; \cdots)(\mathbf{E}[\![\text{Z CONS NIL}]\!]e_3)$$

$$\downarrow$$

$$\mathbf{E}[\![\text{F CONS Z}]\!]\underbrace{(\mathit{updateenv}\, [\![Z]\!]\, (\mathbf{E}[\![\text{Z CONS NIL}]\!]e_3)\; e_1)}_{e_4}$$

$$\downarrow$$

let $x = (\mathbf{E}[\![Z]\!]e_4)$ in cases x of $\cdots$ end

$$\downarrow$$

$$(\mathit{accessenv}\, [\![Z]\!]\, e_4) = \mathbf{E}[\![\text{Z CONS NIL}]\!]e_3 = \text{in}\mathit{List}(\text{in}\mathit{Atom}(a_1)\; \mathit{cons}\; \mathit{nil})$$

$$\downarrow$$

$$\text{in}\mathit{List}((\mathbf{E}[\![F]\!]e_4)\; \mathit{cons}\; (\text{in}\mathit{Atom}(a_1)\; \mathit{cons}\; \mathit{nil}))$$

$$\downarrow$$

$$(\mathit{accessenv}\, [\![F]\!]\, e_4) = (e_4[\![F]\!]) = (e_1[\![F]\!])$$
$$= (\mathbf{E}[\![a_0]\!]e_0) = \text{in}\mathit{Atom}(a_0)$$

$$\downarrow$$

$$\text{in}\mathit{List}(\text{in}\mathit{Atom}(a_0)\; \mathit{cons}\; (\text{in}\mathit{Atom}(a_1)\; \mathit{cons}\; \mathit{nil}))$$

(X is bound to X CONS Y)
(X CONS (X CONS NIL)) CONS NIL

$\Rightarrow \cdots$

and the evaluation unfolds forever.

This form of dynamic scoping can lead to evaluations that are counterintuitive. The version of dynamic scoping found in LISP limits dynamic scoping just to LAMBDA forms. The semantics of ⟦LAMBDA (I) E⟧ shows that the construct is evaluated within the context of its application to an argument (and not within the context of its definition).

We use the new domain:

Function = *Environment* → *Denotable-value* → *Denotable-value*

and the equations:

E⟦LAMBDA (I) E⟧ = λe. in*Function*($\lambda e'.\lambda d$. **E**⟦E⟧ (*updateenv* ⟦I⟧ d e'))
E⟦E_1 E_2⟧ = λe. let x = (**E**⟦E_1⟧e) in cases x of
  is*Function*(f) → (f e (**E**⟦E_2⟧e))
  [] is*List*(t) → in*Error*()
  [] is*Atom*(a) → in*Error*()
  [] is*Error*() → in*Error*() end

The example in Figure 7.6 is redone using dynamic scoping in Figure 7.7.

The differences between the two forms of scoping become apparent from the point where **E**⟦F(Z CONS NIL)⟧ is evaluated with environment e_3. The body bound to ⟦F⟧ evaluates with environment e_3 and not e_1. A reference to ⟦F⟧ in the body stands for the function bound to the second ⟦F⟧ and not the atom bound to the first.

Since the context in which a phrase is evaluated is not associated with the phrase's textual position in a program, dynamically scoped programs can be difficult to understand. The inclusion of dynamic scoping in LISP is partly an historical accident. Newer applicative languages, such as ML, HOPE, and Scheme, use static scoping.

7.2.2 Self-Application

The typeless character of the applicative language allows us to create programs that have unusual evaluations. In particular, a LAMBDA expression can accept itself as an argument. Here is an example: LET X= LAMBDA (X) (X X) IN (X X). This program does nothing more than apply the LAMBDA form bound to X to itself. For the semantics of Figure 7.5 and a hypothetical environment e_0:

Figure 7.7

$E\llbracket E_0 \rrbracket e_0$

$\downarrow$

$\cdots$

$\downarrow$

$(E\llbracket F(Z \text{ CONS NIL}) \rrbracket e_3)$

where $e_3 = (\mathit{updateenv}\ \llbracket Z \rrbracket\ (E\llbracket a_1 \rrbracket e_2)\ e_2)$
$e_2 = (\mathit{updateenv}\ \llbracket F \rrbracket\ (E\llbracket \text{LAMBDA (Z) F CONS Z} \rrbracket e_1)\ e_1)$
$e_1 = (\mathit{updateenv}\ \llbracket F \rrbracket\ (E\llbracket a_0 \rrbracket e_0)\ e_0)$.

$\downarrow$

let $x = (E\llbracket F \rrbracket e_3)$ in cases x of $\cdots$ end

$\downarrow$

$\mathit{accessenv}\ \llbracket F \rrbracket\ e_3$

$\downarrow$

$E\llbracket \text{LAMBDA (Z) F CONS Z} \rrbracket e_1$

$\downarrow$

$\text{in}\mathit{Function}(\lambda e'.\lambda d.\ E\llbracket \text{F CONS Z} \rrbracket\ (\mathit{updateenv}\ \llbracket Z \rrbracket\ d\ e'))$

$\downarrow$

$(\lambda e'.\lambda d. \cdots)\ e_3\ (E\llbracket \text{Z CONS NIL} \rrbracket e_3)$

$\downarrow$

$E\llbracket \text{F CONS Z} \rrbracket \underbrace{(\mathit{updateenv}\ \llbracket Z \rrbracket\ (E\llbracket \text{Z CONS NIL} \rrbracket e_3)\ e_3)}_{e_4}$

$\downarrow$

let $x = (E\llbracket Z \rrbracket e_4)$ in cases x of $\cdots$ end

$\downarrow$

$\mathit{accessenv}\ \llbracket Z \rrbracket\ e_4$
$= E\llbracket \text{Z CONS NIL} \rrbracket e_3$
$\cdots$
$= \text{in}\mathit{List}(\text{in}\mathit{Atom}(a_1)\ \mathit{cons}\ \mathit{nil})$

$\downarrow$

$\text{in}\mathit{List}(E\llbracket F \rrbracket e_4\ \mathit{cons}\ (\text{in}\mathit{Atom}(a_1)\ \mathit{cons}\ \mathit{nil}))$

$\downarrow$

$\mathit{accessenv}\ \llbracket F \rrbracket\ e_4$
$= E\llbracket \text{LAMBDA (Z) F CONS Z} \rrbracket e_1$
$= \text{in}\mathit{Function}(\lambda e'.\lambda d. \cdots)$

$\downarrow$

$\text{in}\mathit{List}(\text{in}\mathit{Function}(\lambda e'.\lambda d. \cdots)\ \mathit{cons}\ \text{in}\mathit{Atom}(a_1)\ \mathit{cons}\ \mathit{nil})$

$$\begin{aligned}
&\mathrm{E}[\![\text{LET X} = \text{LAMBDA (X) (X X) IN (X X)}]\!]e_0\\
&= \mathrm{E}[\![\text{(X X)}]\!]e_1, \text{ where } e_1 = (\mathit{updateenv}\,[\![\text{X}]\!]\,(\mathrm{E}[\![\text{LAMBDA (X) (X X)}]\!]e_0)\; e_0)\\
&= \mathrm{E}[\![\text{LAMBDA (X) (X X)}]\!]e_0\;(\mathrm{E}[\![\text{X}]\!]e_1)\\
&= (\lambda d.\, \mathrm{E}[\![\text{(X X)}]\!](\mathit{updateenv}\,[\![\text{X}]\!]\; d\; e_0))(\mathrm{E}[\![\text{X}]\!]e_1)\\
&= \mathrm{E}[\![\text{(X X)}]\!](\mathit{updateenv}\,[\![\text{X}]\!]\,(\mathrm{E}[\![\text{LAMBDA (X) (X X)}]\!]e_0)\; e_0)\\
&= \mathrm{E}[\![\text{(X X)}]\!]e_1
\end{aligned}$$

The simplification led to an expression that is identical to the one that we had four lines earlier. Further simplification leads back to the same expression over and over.

A couple of lessons are learned from this example. First, simplification on semantic expressions is not guaranteed to lead to a constant that is "the answer" or "true meaning" of the original program. The above program has *some* meaning in the *Denotable-value* domain, but the meaning is unclear. The example points out once more that we are using a *notation* for representing meanings and the notation has shortcomings. These shortcomings are not peculiar to this particular notation but exist in some inherent way in all such notations for representing functions. The study of these limitations belongs to computability theory.

The second important point is that a circular derivation was produced without a recursive definition. The operational properties of a recursive definition $f = \alpha(f)$ are simulated by defining a function $h(g) = \alpha(g(g))$ and letting $f = h(h)$. A good example of this trick is a version of the factorial function:

$$f(p) = \lambda x.\, \mathit{if}\ x{=}0\ \mathit{then}\ 1\ \mathit{else}\ x * ((p\,(p))(x-1))$$
$$\mathit{fac} = f(f)$$

The recursiveness in the applicative language stems from the recursive nature of the *Denotable-value* domain. Its elements are in some fundamental way "recursive" or "infinite." The nature of an element in a recursively defined semantic domain is more difficult to understand than the recursive specification of an element in a nonrecursive domain. Chapter 11 examines this question in detail.

Finally, it is conceivable that the meaning of the example program is $\perp$— the simplification certainly suggests that no semantic information is contained in the program. In fact, this is the case, but to *prove* it so is nontrivial. Any such proof needs knowledge of the method used to build the domain that satisfies the recursive domain specification.

7.2.3 Recursive Definitions

Now we add a mechanism for defining recursive LAMBDA forms and give it a simple semantics with the *fix* operation. We add two new clauses to the abstract syntax for expressions:

$$\text{E} ::= \ldots \mid \text{LETREC I} = \text{E}_1 \text{ IN E}_2 \mid \text{IFNULL E}_1 \text{ THEN E}_2 \text{ ELSE E}_3$$

The LETREC clause differs from the LET clause because all occurrences of identifier I in E_1 refer to the I being declared. The IF clause is an expression conditional for lists, which will be used to define useful recursive functions on lists.

First, the semantics of the conditional construct is:

$$\begin{aligned}
&\text{E}[\![\text{IFNULL E}_1 \text{ THEN E}_2 \text{ ELSE E}_3]\!] = \lambda e.\ \text{let } x = (\text{E}[\![\text{E}_1]\!]e) \text{ in cases } x \text{ of}\\
&\quad \text{is}Function(f) \rightarrow \text{in}Error()\\
&\quad [\,]\ \text{is}List(t) \rightarrow ((null\ t) \rightarrow (\text{E}[\![\text{E}_2]\!]e)\ [\,]\ (\text{E}[\![\text{E}_3]\!]e))\\
&\quad [\,]\ \text{is}Atom(a) \rightarrow \text{in}Error()\\
&\quad [\,]\ \text{is}Error() \rightarrow \text{in}Error()\ \text{end}
\end{aligned}$$

The semantics of the LETREC expression requires a recursively defined *environment*:

$$\begin{aligned}
&\text{E}[\![\text{LETREC I} = \text{E}_1 \text{ IN E}_2]\!] = \lambda e.\ \text{E}[\![\text{E}_2]\!]e'\\
&\quad \text{where } e' = updateenv\ [\![\text{I}]\!]\ (\text{E}[\![\text{E}_1]\!]e')\ e
\end{aligned}$$

$\text{E}[\![\text{E}_2]\!]$ requires an environment that maps $[\![\text{I}]\!]$ to $\text{E}[\![\text{E}_1]\!]e'$ for some e'. But to support recursive invocations, e' must contain the mapping of $[\![\text{I}]\!]$ to $\text{E}[\![\text{E}_1]\!]e'$ as well. Hence e' is defined in terms of itself. This situation is formally resolved with least fixed point semantics. We write:

$$\text{E}[\![\text{LETREC I} = \text{E}_1 \text{ IN E}_2]\!] = \lambda e.\ \text{E}[\![\text{E}_2]\!](fix\ (\lambda e'.\ updateenv\ [\![\text{I}]\!]\ (\text{E}[\![\text{E}_1]\!]e')\ e\ ))$$

The functional $G = (\lambda e'.\ updateenv\ [\![\text{I}]\!]\ (\text{E}[\![\text{E}_1]\!]e')\ e)\ :\ Environment \rightarrow Environment$ generates the family of subfunctions approximating the recursive environment. This family is:

$$\begin{aligned}
G^0 &= \lambda i.\ \bot\\
G^1 &= updateenv\ [\![\text{I}]\!]\ (\text{E}[\![\text{E}_1]\!](G^0))\ e\\
&= updateenv\ [\![\text{I}]\!]\ (\text{E}[\![\text{E}_1]\!]\ (\lambda i.\ \bot))\ e\\
G^2 &= updateenv\ [\![\text{I}]\!]\ (\text{E}[\![\text{E}_1]\!](G^1))\ e\\
&= updateenv\ [\![\text{I}]\!]\ (\text{E}[\![\text{E}_1]\!]\ (updateenv\ [\![\text{I}]\!]\ (\text{E}[\![\text{E}_1]\!](\lambda i.\ \bot))\ e\ ))\ e\\
&\ldots\\
G^{i+1} &= updateenv\ \ (\text{E}[\![\text{E}_1]\!](G^i\ ))\ e
\end{aligned}$$

Each subenvironment G^{i+1} produces a better-defined meaning for $[\![\text{I}]\!]$ than its predecessor G^i and acts like e otherwise. A subenvironment G^{i+1} is able to handle i recursive references to $[\![\text{I}]\!]$ in $[\![\text{E}_1]\!]$ before becoming exhausted and producing $\bot$. The limit of the chain of subenvironments is an environment that can handle an unlimited number of recursive references. Rest assured that you don't need to remember all these details to define and use recursive environments. We give the details to demonstrate that fixed point theory has intuitive and practical applications.

Now consider this example:

LETREC F = LAMBDA (X) IFNULL X THEN NIL ELSE a_0 CONS F(TAIL X)
IN F(a_1 CONS a_2 CONS NIL)

Function F transforms a list argument into a list of the same length containing only a_0 atoms. The value of the above expression is the same as (a_0 CONS a_0 CONS NIL). Figure 7.8 shows the simplification. References to $[\![F]\!]$ in E_1 and E_2 are resolved by the recursive environment.

Now that we have seen several examples, comments about the LET construct are in order. The purpose of LET is similar to that of the constant declaration construct in Figure 7.2. In fact, $\mathbf{E}[\![\text{LET I} = E_1 \text{ IN } E_2]\!]$ equals $\mathbf{E}[\![\,[E_1/\,I\,]E_2\,]\!]$, where $[\![\,[E_1/\,I\,]E_2\,]\!]$ denotes the physical substitution of expression $[\![E_1]\!]$ for all free occurrences of $[\![I]\!]$ in $[\![E_2]\!]$, with renaming of the identifiers in $[\![E_2]\!]$ as needed. (The proof of this claim is left as an exercise.) As an example:

LET X = a_0 IN
LET Y = X CONS NIL IN
(HEAD Y) CONS X CONS NIL

rewrites to the simpler program:

LET Y = a_0 CONS NIL IN
(HEAD Y) CONS a_0 CONS NIL

which rewrites to:

(HEAD (a_0 CONS NIL)) CONS a_0 CONS NIL

which rewrites to:

a_0 CONS a_0 CONS NIL

These rewriting steps preserve the semantics of the original program. The rewritings are a form of computing, just like the computing done on an arithmetic expression.

The LETREC construct also possesses a substitution principle: for $[\![\text{LETREC I} = E_1 \text{ IN } E_2]\!]$, all free occurrences of $[\![I]\!]$ in $[\![E_2]\!]$ are replaced by $[\![E_1]\!]$, *and* to complete the substitution, any free occurrences of $[\![I]\!]$ in the resulting expression are also replaced (until they are completely eliminated). Of course, the number of substitutions is unbounded: LETREC I= α(I) IN β(I) writes to $\beta(\alpha(\text{I}))$, then to $\beta(\alpha(\alpha(\text{I})))$, then to $\beta(\alpha(\alpha(\alpha(\text{I}))))$ $\cdots$, and so on. This is expected, since the environment that models the recursion uses *fix* to generate a similar chain of semantic values. Complete substitution isn't feasible for producing answers in a finite amount of time, so the substitutions must be perfomed more cautiously: occurrences of $[\![I]\!]$ in $[\![E_2]\!]$ are replaced by $[\![E_1]\!]$ only when absolutely needed to complete the simplification of $[\![E_2]\!]$. This strategy matches the conventional

Figure 7.8

Let $E_0 =$ LAMBDA (X) E_1
$E_1 =$ IFNULL X THEN NIL ELSE a_0 CONS F(TAIL X)
$E_2 =$ F(a_1 CONS a_2 CONS NIL).

$\mathbf{E}[\![\text{LETREC F} = E_0 \text{ IN } E_2]\!]e_0$

$\downarrow$

$\mathbf{E}[\![E_2]\!]e_1$

where $e_1 = \mathit{fix}\, G$
$G = (\mathit{fix}(\lambda e'.\mathit{update}\, [\![\text{F}]\!]\, (\mathbf{E}[\![E_0]\!]e')\, e_0))$

$\downarrow$

$\mathbf{E}[\![\text{F}(a_1 \text{ CONS } a_2 \text{ CONS NIL})]\!]e_1$

$\downarrow$

let $x = (\mathbf{E}[\![\text{F}]\!](\mathit{fix}\, G))$ in cases x of $\cdots$ end

$\downarrow$

$\mathit{accessenv}\, [\![\text{F}]\!]\, (\mathit{fix}\, G)$
$= (\mathit{fix}\, G)[\![\text{F}]\!]$
$= G\, (\mathit{fix}\, G)[\![\text{F}]\!]$
$= (\mathit{updateenv}\, [\![\text{F}]\!]\, (\mathbf{E}[\![E_0]\!](\mathit{fix}\, G))\, e_0)\, [\![\text{F}]\!]$
$= \mathbf{E}[\![\text{LAMBDA (X) } E_1]\!](\mathit{fix}\, G)$
$= \text{in}\mathit{Function}(\lambda d.\, \mathbf{E}[\![E_1]\!](\mathit{updateenv}\, [\![\text{X}]\!]\, d\, e_1))$

$\downarrow$

$\mathbf{E}[\![E_1]\!](\underbrace{\mathit{updateenv}\, [\![\text{X}]\!]\, (\mathbf{E}[\![a_1 \text{ CONS } a_2 \text{ CONS NIL}]\!]e_1)\, e_1}_{e_2})$

$\downarrow$

$\mathbf{E}[\![\text{IFNULL X THEN NIL ELSE } a_0 \text{ CONS F(TAIL X)}]\!]e_2$

$\downarrow$

let $x = (\mathbf{E}[\![\text{X}]\!]e_2)$ in cases x of $\cdots$ end

$\downarrow$

$\mathbf{E}[\![a_1 \text{ CONS } a_2 \text{ CONS NIL}]\!]e_1$

$\downarrow$

$\text{in}\mathit{List}(\text{in}\mathit{Atom}(a_1)\, \mathit{cons} \cdots)$

$\downarrow$

$\mathit{null}\, (\text{in}\mathit{Atom}(a_1)\, \mathit{cons} \cdots) \rightarrow \mathbf{E}[\![\text{NIL}]\!]e_2\ [\!]\ \mathbf{E}[\![a_0 \text{ CONS F(TAIL X)}]\!]e_2$

$\downarrow$

$\mathbf{E}[\![a_0 \text{ CONS F(TAIL X)}]\!]e_2$

$\downarrow$

Figure 7.8 (continued)

let $x = (\mathbf{E}[\![\mathrm{F(TAIL\ X)}]\!]e_2)$ in cases x of $\cdots$ end

  let $x = (\mathbf{E}[\![\mathrm{F}]\!]e_2)$ in cases x of $\cdots$ end

    $\mathit{accessenv}\,[\![\mathrm{F}]\!]\,e_2 = e_1[\![\mathrm{F}]\!] = (\mathit{fix}\,G)[\![\mathrm{F}]\!]$

    $\cdots$

    $= G\,(\mathit{fix}\,G)[\![\mathrm{F}]\!] = \mathrm{in}\mathit{Function}(\lambda d.\,\mathbf{E}[\![\mathrm{E}_1]\!] \cdots)$

  $\mathbf{E}[\![\mathrm{E}_1]\!](\mathit{updateenv}\,[\![\mathrm{X}]\!]\,(\mathbf{E}[\![\mathrm{TAIL\ X}]\!]e_2)\,e_1)$

  $\mathrm{in}\mathit{List}(\mathrm{in}\mathit{Atom}(a_0)\ \mathit{cons}\ \mathit{nil})$

$\mathrm{in}\mathit{List}(\mathbf{E}[\![\mathrm{a}_0]\!]e_2\ \mathit{cons}\ (\mathrm{in}\mathit{Atom}(\mathrm{a}_0)\ \mathit{cons}\ \mathit{nil}))$

$\mathrm{in}\mathit{List}(\mathrm{in}\mathit{Atom}(a_0)\ \mathit{cons}\ \mathrm{in}\mathit{Atom}(a_0)\ \mathit{cons}\ \mathit{nil})$

approach for evaluating calls of recursively defined functions.

These examples suggest that computation upon applicative programs is just substitution. Since the environment is tied to the semantics of substitution, it is directly involved in the execution and is a run-time structure in an implementation of the applicative language. The pre-execution analysis seen in Section 7.1 will not eliminate occurrences of environment arguments in the denotations of applicative programs. Like the *Store* algebra of Figure 7.1, these expressions are "frozen" until run-time.

7.3 COMPOUND DATA STRUCTURES

Both imperative and applicative languages use compound data structures—values that can be structurally decomposed into other values. The applicative language used lists, which are compound structures built with CONS and NIL and decomposed with HEAD and TAIL. Another favorite compound structure for applicative languages is the tuple, which is built with a tupling constructor and decomposed with indexing operations. The semantics of these objects is straightforward: finite lists of A elements belong to the A^* domain, and tuples of $A, B, C, \ldots$ elements are members of the product space $A \times B \times C \times \cdots$.

The problems with modelling compound structures increase with imperative languages, as variable forms of the objects exist, and an object's subcomponents can be altered with assignment. For this reason, we devote this section to studying several versions of array variables.

What is an array? We say that it is a collection of homogeneous objects indexed by a set of scalar values. By *homogeneous*, we mean that all of the components have the same structure. This is not absolutely necessary; languages such as SNOBOL4 allow array elements' structures to differ. But homogeneity makes the allocation of storage and type-checking easier to perform. Consequently, compiler-oriented languages insist on homogeneous arrays so that these tasks can be performed by the compiler. The disassembly operation on arrays is indexing. The indexing operation takes an array and a value from the index set as arguments. The index set is *scalar*, that is, a primitive domain with relational and arithmetic-like operations, so that arithmetic-like expressions represent index values for the indexing operation. Normally, the index set is restricted by lower and upper bounds.

The first version of array that we study is a linear vector of values. Let some primitive domain *Index* be the index set; assume that it has associated relational operations *lessthan*, *greaterthan*, and *equals*. The array domain is:

$$1DArray = (Index \to Location) \times Lower\text{-}bound \times Upper\text{-}bound$$
$$\text{where } Lower\text{-}bound = Upper\text{-}bound = Index$$

The first component of an array maps indexes to the locations that contain the storable values associated with the array. The second and third components are the lower and upper bounds allowed on indexes to the array. You are left with the exercise of defining the indexing operation.

The situation becomes more interesting when multidimensional arrays are admitted. Languages such as ALGOL60 allow arrays to contain other arrays as components. For example, a three-dimensional array is a vector whose components are two-dimensional arrays. The hierarchy of multidimensional arrays is defined as an infinite sum. For simplicity, assume the index set for each dimension of indexing is the same domain *Index*. We define:

$$1DArray = (Index \to Location) \times Index \times Index$$

and for each $n \geqslant 1$:

$$(n+1)DArray = (Index \to nDArray) \times Index \times Index$$

so that the domain of multidimensional arrays is:

$$a \in MDArray = \sum_{m=1}^{\infty} mDArray$$

$$\begin{aligned} &= ((Index \to Location) \times Index \times Index) \\ &\quad + ((Index \to ((Index \to Location) \times Index \times Index)) \times Index \times Index) \\ &\quad + ((Index \to ((Index \to ((Index \to Location) \times Index \times Index)) \times Index \\ &\qquad \times Index)) \times Index \times Index) \\ &\quad + \cdots \end{aligned}$$

The definition says that a one-dimensional array maps indexes to locations, a two-dimensional array maps indexes to one-dimensional arrays, and so on. Any $a \in MDArray$ has the form in$kDArray\,(map, lower, upper)$ for some $k \geqslant 1$, saying that a is a k-dimensional array.

The indexing operation for multidimensional arrays is:

$$access\text{-}array : Index \rightarrow MDArray \rightarrow (Location + MDArray + Errvalue)$$

$$\begin{aligned} access\text{-}array = \lambda i.\lambda r.\ &\text{cases } r \text{ of} \\ &\text{is}1DArray(a) \rightarrow index_1\ a\ i \\ &[]\ \text{is}2DArray(a) \rightarrow index_2\ a\ i \\ &\ldots \\ &[]\ \text{is}kDArray(a) \rightarrow index_k\ a\ i \\ &\cdots \text{end} \end{aligned}$$

where, for all $m \geqslant 1$, $index_m$ abbreviates the expression:

$$\begin{aligned} &\lambda(map, lower, upper).\lambda i.\ (i\ lessthan\ lower) \\ &\quad or\ (i\ greaterthan\ upper) \rightarrow \text{in}Errvalue()\ []\ mInject(map\ (i)) \end{aligned}$$

where $mInject$ abbreviates the expressions:

$$1Inject = \lambda l.\ \text{in}Location(l)$$

$$\ldots$$

$$(n{+}1)Inject = \lambda a.\ \text{in}MDArray(\ \text{in}nDArray(a))$$

The *access-array* operation is represented by an infinite function expression. But, by using the pair representation of disjoint union elements, the operation is convertible to a finite, computable format. The operation performs a one-level indexing upon an array a, returning another array if a has more than one dimension. We define no *update-array* operation; the store-based operation *update* is used in combination with the *access-array* operation to complete an assignment to a location in an array.

Unfortunately, the straightforward model just seen is clumsy to use in practice, as realistic programming languages allow arrays to be built from a variety of components, such as numbers, record structures, sets, and so on. A nested array could be an array of records containing arrays. Here is a Pascal-like syntax for such a system of data type declarations:

T∈ Type-structure
S∈ Subscript

T ::= **nat** | **bool** | **array** [N_1..N_2] **of** T | **record** D **end**
D ::= D_1;D_2 | **var** I:T
C ::= . . . | I[S]:=E | . . .
E ::= . . . | I[S] | . . .
S ::= E | E,S

We provide a semantics for this type system. First, we expand the *Denotable-value* domain to read:

$$\begin{aligned}&\mathit{Denotable\text{-}value} = (\mathit{Natlocn} + \mathit{Boollocn} + \mathit{Array} + \mathit{Record} + \mathit{Errvalue})_\bot\\ &\quad \text{where } l \in \mathit{Natlocn} = \mathit{Boollocn} = \mathit{Location}\\ &\qquad a \in \mathit{Array} = (\mathit{Nat} \rightarrow \mathit{Denotable\text{-}value}) \times \mathit{Nat} \times \mathit{Nat}\\ &\qquad r \in \mathit{Record} = \mathit{Environment} = \mathit{Id} \rightarrow \mathit{Denotable\text{-}value}\end{aligned}$$

Each component in the domain corresponds to a type structure. The recursiveness in the syntax definition motivates the recursiveness of the semantic domain.

The valuation function for type structures maps a type structure expression to storage allocation actions. The *Store* algebra of Figure 7.4 is used with the *Poststore* algebra of Figure 7.1 in the equations that follow.

$$\mathbf{T}: \text{Type-structure} \rightarrow \mathit{Store} \rightarrow (\mathit{Denotable\text{-}value} \times \mathit{Poststore})$$

$$\mathbf{T}[\![\mathbf{nat}]\!] = \lambda s.\ \text{let } (l,p) = (\mathit{allocate\text{-}locn}\ s) \text{ in } (\text{in}\mathit{Natlocn}(l), p)$$

$$\mathbf{T}[\![\mathbf{bool}]\!] = \lambda s.\ \text{let } (l,p) = (\mathit{allocate\text{-}locn}\ s) \text{ in } (\text{in}\mathit{Boollocn}(l), p)$$

$$\begin{aligned}&\mathbf{T}[\![\mathbf{array}\ [\mathrm{N}_1..\mathrm{N}_2]\ \mathbf{of}\ \mathrm{T}]\!] = \lambda s.\ \text{let } n_1 = \mathbf{N}[\![\mathrm{N}_1]\!] \text{ in let } n_2 = \mathbf{N}[\![\mathrm{N}_2]\!]\\ &\quad \text{in } n_1\ \mathit{greaterthan}\ n_2 \rightarrow (\text{in}\mathit{Errvalue}(), (\mathit{signalerr}\ s))\\ &\qquad [\!]\ \mathit{get\text{-}storage}\ n_1\ (\mathit{empty\text{-}array}\ n_1\ n_2)\ s\end{aligned}$$

where

$$\begin{aligned}&\mathit{get\text{-}storage}: \mathit{Nat} \rightarrow \mathit{Array} \rightarrow \mathit{Store} \rightarrow (\mathit{Denotable\text{-}value} \times \mathit{Poststore})\\ &\mathit{get\text{-}storage} = \lambda n.\lambda a.\lambda s.\ n\ \mathit{greater}\ n_2 \rightarrow (\text{in}\mathit{Array}(a), \mathit{return}\ s)\\ &\qquad [\!]\ \text{let } (d,p) = \mathbf{T}[\![\mathrm{T}]\!]s\\ &\qquad \text{in } (\mathit{check}\ (\mathit{get\text{-}storage}\ (n\ \mathit{plus}\ \mathit{one})\ (\mathit{augment\text{-}array}\ n\ d\ a)))(p)\end{aligned}$$

and

$$\begin{aligned}&\mathit{augment\text{-}array}: \mathit{Nat} \rightarrow \mathit{Denotable\text{-}value} \rightarrow \mathit{Array} \rightarrow \mathit{Array}\\ &\mathit{augment\text{-}array} = \lambda n.\lambda d.\lambda(\mathit{map}, \mathit{lower}, \mathit{upper}).\ ([n \mapsto d\ ]\mathit{map}, \mathit{lower}, \mathit{upper})\\ &\mathit{empty\text{-}array}: \mathit{Nat} \rightarrow \mathit{Nat} \rightarrow \mathit{Array}\\ &\mathit{empty\text{-}array} = \lambda n_1.\lambda n_2.((\lambda n.\ \text{in}\mathit{Errvalue}()), n_1, n_2)\end{aligned}$$

$$\mathbf{T}[\![\mathbf{record}\ \mathrm{D}\ \mathbf{end}]\!] = \lambda s.\ \text{let } (e,p) = (\mathbf{D}[\![\mathrm{D}]\!]\ \mathit{emptyenv}\ s) \text{ in } (\text{in}\mathit{Record}(e), p)$$

The heart of the strategy for creating an array value is *get-storage*, which iterates from the lower bound of the array to the upper bound, allocating the proper amount of storage for a component at each iteration. The component is inserted into the array by the *augment-array* operation.

A declaration activates the storage allocation strategy specificed by its type structure:

$\mathbf{D}$: Declaration $\rightarrow$ *Environment* $\rightarrow$ *Store* $\rightarrow$ (*Environment* $\times$ *Poststore*)
$\mathbf{D}[\![D_1;D_2]\!] = \lambda e.\lambda s.$ let $(e', p) = (\mathbf{D}[\![D_1]\!]e\ s)$ in $(check\ (\mathbf{D}[\![D_2]\!]e'))(p)$
$\mathbf{D}[\![$var I:T$]\!] = \lambda e.\lambda s.$ let $(d, p) = \mathbf{T}[\![T]\!]s$ in $((updateenv\ [\![I]\!]\ d\ e), p)$

Now assume that the operation *access-array* : *Nat* $\rightarrow$ *Array* $\rightarrow$ *Denotable-value* has been defined. (This is left as an easy exercise.) Array indexing is defined in the semantic equations for subscripts:

$\mathbf{S}$: Subscript $\rightarrow$ *Array* $\rightarrow$ *Environment* $\rightarrow$ *Store* $\rightarrow$ *Denotable-value*
$\mathbf{S}[\![E]\!] = \lambda a.\lambda e.\lambda s.$ cases $(\mathbf{E}[\![E]\!]e\ s)$ of
 . . .
 [] is*Nat*$(n) \rightarrow access\text{-}array\ n\ a$
 . . . end
$\mathbf{S}[\![E,S]\!] = \lambda a.\lambda e.\lambda s.$ cases $(\mathbf{E}[\![E]\!]e\ s)$ of
 . . .
 [] is*Nat*$(n) \rightarrow$ (cases $(access\text{-}array\ n\ a)$ of
 . . .
 [] is*Array*$(a') \rightarrow \mathbf{S}[\![S]\!]a'\ e\ s$
 . . . end)
 . . . end

A version of first order array assignment is:

$\mathbf{C}[\![I[S]{:=}E]\!] = \lambda e.\lambda s.$ cases $(accessenv\ [\![I]\!]\ e)$ of
 . . .
 [] is*Array*$(a) \rightarrow$ (cases $(\mathbf{S}[\![S]\!]a\ e\ s)$ of
 . . .
 [] is*Natlocn*$(l) \rightarrow$ (cases $(\mathbf{E}[\![E]\!]e\ s)$ of
 . . .
 [] is*Nat*$(n) \rightarrow return\ (update\ l\ $ in*Nat*$(n)\ s)$
 . . . end)
 . . . end)
 . . . end

As usual, a large amount of type-checking is required to complete the assignment, and an extra check ensures that the assignment is first order; that is, the left-hand side $[\![$ I[S] $]\!]$ denotes a location and not an array.

The final variant of array assignment we examine is the most general. The array is heterogeneous (its components can be elements of different structures), its dimensions and index ranges can change during execution, and by using a recursive definition, it can possess itself as an element. Variants on this style of array are found in late binding languages such as APL, SNOBOL4, and TEMPO, where pre-execution analysis of arrays yields little.

The domain of heterogeneous arrays is the domain *Array* just defined in the previous example, but the operations upon the domain are relaxed to allow more freedom. Since an array is a denotable value, the usual methods for accessing and updating a heterogeneous array are generalized to methods for handling all kinds of denotable values. A first order denotable value is just a degenerate array. The *access-value* operation fetches a component of a denotable value. It receives as its first argument a list of indexes that indicates the path taken to find the component.

```
access-value : Nat* → Denotable-value → Denotable-value
access-value = λnlist.λd.
    null nlist → d
    [] (cases d of
        isNatlocn(l) → inErrvalue()
        . . .
        [] isArray(map, lower, upper) →
            let n = hd nlist in
            (n lessthan lower ) or (n greaterthan upper ) → inErrvalue()
                [] (access-value (tl nlist ) (map n ))
        . . . end)
```

The operation searches through the structure of its denotable value argument until the component is found. An empty index list signifies that the search has ended. A nonempty list means that the search can continue if the value is an array. If so, the array is indexed at position (*hd nlist*) and the search continues on the indexed component.

The updating operation follows a similar strategy, but care must be taken to preserve the outer structure of an array while the search continues within its subparts. The argument *new-value* is inserted into the array *current-value* at index *nlist:*

```
update-value : Nat* → Denotable-value → Denotable-value → Denotable-value
update-value = λnlist.λnew-value λcurrent-value .
    null nlist → new-value
    [] (cases current-value of
        isNatlocn(l) → inErrvalue()
        . . .
        [] isArray(map, lower, upper) →
            let n = hd nlist in
            let new-lower = (n lessthan lower → n [] lower) in
```

let *new-upper* = (*n greaterthan upper* → *n* [] *upper*)
in *augment-array n* (*update-value* (*tl nlist*) *new-value* (*map n*))
(*map*, *new-lower*, *new-upper*)

...

[] is*Errvalue*() → *augment-array n* (*update-value* (*tl nlist*) *new-value*
in*Errvalue*())) (*empty-array n n*)

··· end)

where

augment-array : *Nat* → *Denotable-value* → *Array* → *Denotable-value*

augment-array = λ*n*.λ*d*.λ(*map*, *lower*, *upper*).in*Array*([*i* ↦ *d*]*map*, *lower*, *upper*)

If an index list causes a search deeper into an array structure than what exists, the "is*Errvalue*() → ··· " clause creates another dimension to accommodate the index list. Thus an array can grow extra dimensions. If an index from the index list falls outside of an array's bounds, the "is*Array*(···) → ··· " clause expands the arrays's bounds to accommodate the index. Thus an array can change its bounds. The outer structure of a searched array is preserved by the *augment-array* operation, which inserts the altered component back into the structure of the indexed array. Note that *update-value* builds a new denotable value; it does not alter the store. A separate dereferencing step is necessary to cause conventional assignment.

The exercises continue the treatment of this and other kinds of array.

SUGGESTED READINGS

Semantics of block structure: Henhapl & Jones 1982; Landin 1965; Meyer 1983; Mosses 1974; Oles 1985; Reynolds 1981; Strachey 1968

Semantics of applicative languages: Abelson & Sussman 1985; Gordon 1973, 1975; Muchnick & Pleban 1982; Reynolds 1970; Steele & Sussman 1978

Semantics of compound data structures: Abelson & Sussman 1985; Andrews & Henhapl 1982; Gordon 1979; Jones & Muchnick 1978; Tennent 1977

EXERCISES

1. a. Let the domain *Location* be *Nat*. (Thus, *first-locn* = *zero*, *next-locn* = (λ*l*. *l plus one*), etc.) Using the strategy of *not* simplifying away occurrences of *access*, *update*, *check*, or *return*, simplify P⟦**begin var** A; A:=2; **begin var** B; B:=A+1 **end end**⟧ as far as possible.

b. Let the result of part a be called *Object-code*. Do *one* step of simplification to the expression *Object-code*(*zero*).
c. Let the result of part b be called *Loaded-object-code*. Simplify the expression *Loaded-object-code*(*newstore*) to a post-store value.

2. Extend the language in Figure 7.2 to include declarations of variables of Boolean type; that is:

   D ::= · · · | **bool var** I

   and expressions of Boolean type:

   E ::= · · · | **true** | ¬ E

   Adjust the semantic algebras and the semantic equations to accommodate the extensions.

3. Augment the language of Figure 7.2 to include procedures:

   D ::= · · · | **proc** I=C

   and procedure invocations:

   C ::= · · · | **call** I

   Now augment the *Denotable-value* domain with the summand *Proc* = *Store*→*Poststore*$_\perp$ to accommodate procedures.

   a. If the semantics of procedure definition is written **D**[[**proc** I=C]] = λ*e*.(*updateenv* [[I]] in*Proc*(**C**[[C]]*e*) *e*), write the semantic equation for **C**[[**call** I]]. What kind of scoping is used?
   b. Say that the domain *Proc* is changed to be *Proc* = *Environment* →*Store* →*Poststore*$_\perp$. Write the semantic equations for procedure definition and invocation. What kind of scoping is used?

4. a. For the semantics of Figure 7.2, show that there exist identifiers I and J and a command C such that **B**[[**begin var** I; **var** J; C **end**]] ≠ **B**[[**begin var** J; **var** I; C **end**]].
   b. Revise the language's semantics so that for all identifiers I and J and command C, the above inequality becomes an equality. Using structural induction, prove this.
   c. Does the semantics you defined in part b support the equality **B**[[**begin var** I; I:=I **end**]] = *return*?

5. a. Define the semantics of the ALGOL60 **for**-loop.
   b. Define the semantics of the Pascal **for**-loop. (Recall that the loop index may not be altered within the loop's body.)

6. It is well known that the environment object in Figure 7.2 can be implemented as a single global stack. Where is the stack concept found in the semantic equations?

7. The semantics in Figure 7.2 is somewhat simple minded in that the block [[**begin var** A; **const** A=0; C **end**]] has a nonerroneous denotation.

   a. What is [[A]]'s denotation in [[C]]?
   b. Adjust the semantics of declarations so that redeclaration of identifiers in a block produces an error denotation for the block.

8. Use structural induction to prove that the semantics in Figure 7.2 is constructed so that if any command in a program maps a store to an erroneous post-store, then the denotation of the entire program is exactly that erroneous post-store.

9. a. Add to the language of Figure 7.2 the declaration [[**var** I:=E]]. What problems arise in integrating the new construct into the existing valuation function **D** for declarations?
   b. Attempt to handle the problems noted in part a by using a new declaration valuation function:

   $$\mathbf{D}: \text{Declaration} \rightarrow \mathit{Environment} \rightarrow (\mathit{Store} \rightarrow \mathit{Poststore})$$
   $$\rightarrow (\mathit{Environment} \times (\mathit{Store} \rightarrow \mathit{Poststore}))$$

   $$\mathbf{B}[\![\mathbf{begin}\ \mathrm{D};\mathrm{C}\ \mathbf{end}]\!] = \lambda e.\ \mathrm{let}\ (e', c) = \mathbf{D}[\![\mathrm{D}]\!]e\ \mathit{return}\ \mathrm{in}\ ((\mathit{check}\ \mathbf{C}[\![\mathrm{C}]\!]e') \circ c)$$

   Write the semantic equations for $\mathbf{D}[\![\mathrm{D}_1;\mathrm{D}_2]\!]$ and $\mathbf{D}[\![\mathbf{var}\ \mathrm{I}{:=}\mathrm{E}]\!]$ in the new format.

10. Make the needed adjustments so that the stack-based store model of Figure 7.4 can be used with the semantics of Figure 7.2.

11. A design deficiency of the language in Figure 7.2 is its delayed reporting of errors. For example, a denotable value error occurs in the assignment [[B:=A+1]] when [[A]] is not previously declared. The error is only reported when the run-time store is mapped to an erroneous post-store. The error reporting need not be delayed until run-time: consider the valuation function $\mathbf{C}: \text{Command} \rightarrow \mathit{Environment} \rightarrow \mathit{Compiled\text{-}code}$, where $\mathit{Compiled\text{-}code} = (\mathit{Store} \rightarrow \mathit{Poststore}) + \mathit{Error\text{-}message}$. Rewrite the semantics of Figure 7.2 using the new form of **C** so that an expressible value or denotable value error in a command leads to an *Error-message* denotation.

12. Extend the language of Figure 7.2 with pointers. In particular, set

    Denotable-value = *Natlocn* + *Ptrlocn* + *Nat* + *Errvalue*
    where *Natlocn* = *Location* (locations that hold numbers)
    Ptrlocn = *Location* (locations that hold pointers)
    Errvalue = *Unit*.

Augment the syntax of the language and give the semantics of pointer declaration, dereferencing, assignment, and dynamic storage allocation. How does the integration of pointers into the language change the stack-based storage model?

13. Augment the file editor language of Figure 5.4 with environments by introducing the notion of *window* into the editor. A user of the file editor can move from one window to another and be able to manipulate more than one file concurrently during a session.

14. Give an example of a programming language whose notion of R-value for an identifier is not a function of the identifier's L-value.

15. Using the semantic definition of Figure 7.5, determine the denotations of the following expressions:

    a. [[LET N = a_0 IN LET N = N CONS NIL IN TAIL N]]
    b. [[LET G = LAMBDA (X) X IN LET G = LAMBDA (Y) (G Y) IN (G a_0)]]
    c. [[LET F = LAMBDA(X) (X X) IN LET G = (F F) IN a_0]]

    Redo parts a through c using the LISP-style dynamic scoping semantics of Section 7.2.1.

16. Using structural induction, prove the following claim for the semantics of Figure 7.5: for all I∈ Identifier, E_1, E_2∈ Expression, E[[LET I = E_1 IN E_2]] = E[[[E_1/I]E_2]].

17. a. Using the semantics of the LETREC construct in Section 7.2.3, determine the denotations of the following examples:

    i. [[LETREC APPEND = LAMBDA (L1) LAMBDA (L2)
    IFNULL L1 THEN L2 ELSE (HEAD L1) CONS (APPEND
    (TAIL L1) L2) IN APPEND (a_0 CONS NIL) (a_1 CONS NIL)]]
    ii. [[LETREC L = a_0 CONS L IN HEAD L]]
    iii. [[LETREC L = HEAD L IN L]]

    b. Reformulate the semantics of the language so that a defined denotation for part ii above is produced. Does the new semantics practice "lazy evaluation"?

18. In LISP, a denotable value may be CONSed to any other denotable value (not just a list), producing a *dotted pair*. For example, [[A CONS (LAMBDA (I) I)]] is a dotted pair. Reformulate the semantics in Figure 7.5 to allow dotted pairs. Redo the denotations of the programs in exercises 15 and 17.

19. Formulate a semantics for the applicative language of Section 7.2 that uses macro substitution-style dynamic scoping.

20. Define the appropriate construction and destruction constructs for the record structure defined in Section 7.3. Note that the denotation of a record is a "little environment." Why does this make a block construct such as the Pascal **with** statement especially appropriate? Define the semantics of a **with**-like block statement.

21. a. Integrate the domain of one-dimensional arrays *1DArray* into the language of Figure 7.2. Define the corresponding assembly and disassembly operations and show the denotations of several example programs using the arrays.
    b. Repeat part a with the domain of multidimensional arrays *MDArray*.
    c. Repeat part a with the Pascal-like type system and domain of arrays *Array*.

22. After completing Exercise 21, revise your answers to handle arrays whose bounds are set by expressions calculated at runtime, e.g., for part c above use: T ::= $\cdots$ | **array** [E_1..E_2] **of** T

23. After completing Exercise 21, adjust the semantics of the assignment statement [[I:=E]] so that:

    a. If [[I]] is an array denotable value and (**E**[[E]]*e s*) is an expressible value from the same domain as the array's components, then a copy of (**E**[[E]]*e s*) is assigned to each of the array's components;
    b. If [[I]] is an array denotable value and (**E**[[E]]*e s*) is an array expressible value of "equivalent type," then the right-hand side value is bound to the left-hand side value.

24. Rewrite the valuation function for type structures so that it uses the *Environment* and *Store* algebras of Figure 7.1; that is, **T**: Type-structure → *Environment* → (*Denotable-value* × *Environment*), and the valuation function for declarations reverts to the **D**: Declaration → *Environment* → *Environment* of Figure 7.2. Which of the two versions of **T** and **D** more closely describes type processing in a Pascal compiler? In a Pascal interpreter? Which version of **T** do you prefer?

25. Consider the domain of one-dimensional arrays; the denotations of the arrays might be placed in the environment (that is, an array is a denotable value) or the store (an array is a storable value). Show the domain algebras and semantic equations for both treatments of one-dimensional arrays. Comment on the advantages and disadvantages of each treatment with respect to understandability and implementability.

26. In FORTRAN, an array is treated as a linear allocation of storage locations; the lower bound on an array is always *one*. Define the domain of one dimensional FORTRAN arrays to be *Location* × *Nat* (that is, the location of the first element in the array and the upper bound of the array). Show the corresponding operations for allocating storage for an array, indexing, and updating an array.

27. Strachey claimed that the essential characteristics of a language are delineated by its *Denotable-value*, *Expressible-value*, and *Storable-value* domains.

    a. Give examples of programming languages such that:

        i. Every expressible value is storable but is not necessarily denotable; every storable value is expressible but is not necessarily denotable; a denotable value is not necessarily expressible or storable.

        ii. Every denotable value is expressible and storable; every storable value is expressible and denotable; an expressible value is not necessarily denotable or storable.

        iii. Every denotable value is expressible and storable; every expressible value is denotable and storable; every storable value is denotable and expressible.

    b. Repeat part a with *Expressible-value* = $(Nat + Tr + Location + Expressible\text{-}value^*)_\perp$; with *Expressible-value* = $((Id \rightarrow Expressible\text{-}value) + Nat)_\perp$.

    c. Pick your favorite general purpose programming language and list its denotable, expressible, and storable value domains. What limitations of the language become immediately obvious from the domains' definitions? What limitations are *not* obvious?

28. Language design is often a process of consolidation, that is, the integration of desirable features from other languages into a new language. Here is a simple example. Say that you wish to integrate the notion of imperative updating, embodied in the language in Figure 7.2, with the notion of value-returning construct, found in the language of Figure 7.5. That is, you desire an imperative language in which every syntactic construct has an associated expressible value (see ALGOL68 or full LISP).

    a. Design such a language and give its denotational semantics. Does the language's syntax look more like the language in Figure 7.2 or 7.5?

    b. Repeat part a so that the new language appears more like the other figure (7.5 or 7.2) than the language in part a did. Comment on how the characteristics of the two languages were influenced by your views of the languages' syntax definitions.

    Attempt this exercise once again by:

c. Integrating an imperative-style data structure, the array, with an expression-based, applicative notation like that of Figure 7.5.
d. Integrating an applicative-style list structure with a command-based, imperative notation like that of Figure 7.2.

29. The function notation used for denotational semantics definitions has its limitations, and one of them is its inability to simply express the Pascal-style hierarchy of data-type. If you were asked to define an imperative programming language with simple and compound data-types, and you knew nothing of the ALGOL/Pascal tradition, what kinds of data-types would you be led to develop if you used denotational semantics as a design tool? What pragmatic advantages and disadvantages do you see in this approach?

Chapter 8

Abstraction, Correspondence, and Qualification

The title of this chapter refers to three language design principles proposed by Tennent. We also study a fourth principle, *parameterization*. Many important language constructs are derived from the principles: subroutines, parameters, block-structuring constructs, and encapsulation mechanisms. Denotational semantics is a useful tool for analyzing the design principles and the constructs that they derive. The language in Figure 8.1 is used as a starting point. We apply each of the principles to the language and study the results.

8.1 ABSTRACTION

The first design principle is the principle of abstraction. Programmers sometimes use the term *abstraction* for a specification that hides some irrelevant computational details. In Chapter 3 we used the term to describe a function expression of form $(\lambda x.M)$. The usage is appropriate, for the expression specifies a function, hiding the details regarding the value x that is used in M. We also gave abstractions names, e.g., $square = (\lambda n.\ n\ times\ n)$. The name enhances the abstraction's worth, for we can refer to the abstraction by mentioning its name, e.g., $square(two)$.

Most programming languages support the creation of named expressions; a Pascal procedure is an abstraction of a command. We execute the command by mentioning its name. Both a *definition* mechanism and an *invocation* mechanism are necessary. Tennent coined the noun *abstract* to describe a named expression that is invoked by mentioning its name. An abstract has both a *name* and a *body*. If its body is an expression from a syntax domain B, the abstract can be invoked by using its name any place in a program where a B-expression is syntactically legal.

The *principle of abstraction* states that any syntax domain of a language may have definition and invocation mechanisms for abstracts.

A Pascal procedure is an example of a *command abstract*. We might also create expression abstracts, declaration abstracts, type abstracts, and so on. Let

Figure 8.1

Abstract syntax:

P∈ Program
D∈ Declaration
T∈ Type-structure
C∈ Command
E∈ Expression
L∈ Identifier-L-value
S∈ Subscript
I ∈ Identifier
N∈ Numeral

P ::= C.
D ::= D_1;D_2 | **var** I:T
T ::= **nat** | **array** [N_1..N_2] **of** T | **record** D **end**
C ::= C_1;C_2 | L:=E | **begin** D;C **end** | · · ·
E ::= E_1+E_2 | I | IS | N | · · ·
L ::= I | IS
S ::= [E] | .I | [E]S | .IS

⟦**define** I=V⟧ be an abstract. ⟦I⟧ is the abstract's name and ⟦V⟧ is its body. The denotable value of ⟦I⟧ is V⟦V⟧. If V⟦V⟧ is a function denotation, then are the arguments to the function provided at the point of definition of the abstract or at the point of its invocation? This is an important question and we study its answer through an example.

We augment the language in Figure 8.1 with definition and invocation mechanisms for command abstracts, which we call *procedures.* The definition mechanism is added to the BNF rule for declarations:

D ::= D_1;D_2 | **var** I:T | **proc** I=C

and the invocation mechanism appears in the rule for commands:

C ::= C_1;C_2 | L:=E | **begin** D;C **end** | I | · · ·

Recall that the valuation function used in Chapter 7 for commands has functionality C: Command →*Environment* →*Store* →*Poststore*$_\perp$. The denotation of the abstract's body can be any of the following:

1. $\mathbf{C}[\![C]\!]$: *Environment* → *Store* → *Poststore*$_\perp$: the environment and store that are used with the body are the ones that are active at the point of invocation. This corresponds to *dynamic scoping*.
2. $(\mathbf{C}[\![C]\!]e)$: *Store* → *Poststore*$_\perp$: the environment active at the point of definition is bound to the body, and the store that is used is the one active at the point of invocation. This corresponds to *static scoping*.
3. $(\mathbf{C}[\![C]\!]e\ s) \in$ *Poststore*$_\perp$: the procedure is completely evaluated at the point of definition, and $[\![I]\!]$ is bound to a constant *Poststore*$_\perp$ value. This option is unknown in existing languages for command abstracts.

These three options list the possible *scoping mechanisms* for command abstracts. For now, let us choose option 2 and define the semantic domain of procedures to be *Proc* = *Store* → *Poststore*$_\perp$. The denotations of procedure identifiers come from *Proc*:

Denotable-value = *Natlocn* + *Array* + *Record* + *Proc*

The semantic equations for procedure definition and invocation are:

$\mathbf{D}[\![\text{proc I=C}]\!] = \lambda e.\lambda s.\ ((\mathit{updateenv}\ [\![I]\!]\ \text{in}\mathit{Proc}(\mathbf{C}[\![C]\!]e)\ e), (\mathit{return}\ s))$

$\mathbf{C}[\![I]\!] = \lambda e.\lambda s.\ \text{cases}\ (\mathit{accessenv}\ [\![I]\!]\ e)\ \text{of}$
$\quad \text{is}\mathit{Natlocn}(l) \rightarrow (\mathit{signalerr}\ s)$
$\quad \ldots$
$\quad [\,]\ \text{is}\mathit{Proc}(q) \rightarrow (q\ s)\ \text{end}$

(Recall that **D**: Declaration → *Environment* → *Store* → (*Environment* × *Poststore*).) Since we chose static scoping, $(\mathbf{C}[\![C]\!]e)$ is bound to $[\![I]\!]$ in the environment, and the store is supplied at invocation-time. The definitions of the other two options are left as exercises.

Similar issues arise for expression abstracts (*functions*). For:

D ::= · · · | **fcn** I=E
E ::= E_1+E_2 | · · · | I

an ALGOL68-like constant definition results when the environment and store are bound at the point of definition. If just the environment is bound at the point of definition, a FORTRAN-style function results. If neither are bound at the point of definition, a text macro definition results.

An interesting hybrid of procedure and function is the *function procedure*, which is a command abstract that is invoked by an Expression-typed identifier. This construct is found in Pascal. The function procedure must return an expressible value as its result. A possible syntax for a function procedure is:

D ::= · · · | **fcnproc** I= C **resultis** E

Its inclusion causes a profound change in the semantics of expressions, for an expression can now alter the value of the store. Further, an invoked function procedure might not terminate. The valuation function for expressions must take the form:

$$\mathbf{E}: \text{Expression} \rightarrow \textit{Environment} \rightarrow \textit{Store} \rightarrow (\textit{Expressible-value} \times \textit{Poststore})_{\perp}$$

If we use static scoping, the equations for definition and invocation are:

D[[**fcnproc** I= C **resultis** E]] = $\lambda e.\lambda s.$ ((*updateenv* [[I]]
  in*Fcn-proc*((*check* (E[[E]]e)) ∘ (C[[C]]e)) *e*), (*return s*))
  where *check* : (*Store* → (*Expressible-value* × *Poststore*)$_\perp$)
    → (*Poststore* → (*Expressible-value* × *Poststore*)$_\perp$)
  traps errors and nontermination

E[[I]] = $\lambda e.\lambda s.$ cases (*accessenv* [[I]] *e*) of
  is*Natlocn*(*l*) → ((*access l s*), (*return s*))
  . . .
  [] is*Fcn-proc*(*f*) → (*f s*) end

All of the other semantic equations for the **E** function must be revised to cope with the complications arising from side effects and nontermination. This is left as an exercise.

Declaration abstractions follow the pattern seen thus far for commands and expressions. The syntax is:

D ::= D_1;D_2 | **var** I:T | · · · | **module** I=D | I

We call the new construct a *module*. The invocation of a module activates the declarations in the module's body. Since there is no renaming of declarations, multiple invocations of the same module in a block cause a redefinition error.

We also have type abstracts:

D ::= · · · | **type** I=T
T ::= **nat** | · · · | I

The definition and invocation of type abstracts follow the usual pattern:

D[[**type** I=T]] = $\lambda e.\lambda s.$ ((*updateenv* [[I]] in*Type*(T[[T]]e) *e*), (*return s*))
  T : Type-structure → *Environment* → *Store* → (*Denotable-value* × *Poststore*)
  T[[I]] = $\lambda e.\lambda s.$ cases (*accessenv* [[I]] *e*) of
    is*Natlocn*(*l*) → (in*Errvalue*(), (*signalerr s*))
    . . .
    [] is*Type*(*v*) → (*v s*) end

An issue raised by type abstraction is: when are two variables equivalent in type? There are two possible answers. The first, *structure equivalence*, states that two variables are type-equivalent if they have identical storage structures. Structure equivalence is used in ALGOL68. The second, *occurrence equivalence*, also known as *name equivalence*, states that two variables are type-equivalent if they are defined with the same occurrence of a type expression. A version of occurrence equivalence is used in Pascal. Consider these declarations:

```
type M = nat;
type N = array [1..3] of M;
var A: nat;
var B: M;
var C: M;
var D: N;
var E: array [2..4] of nat
```

Variables A and B are structure-equivalent but not occurrence-equivalent, because they are defined with different occurrences of type expressions, A with **nat** and B with M. Variables B and C are both structure- and occurrence-equivalent; C and D are neither. Variables D and E are clearly not occurrence-equivalent, but are they structure-equivalent? The two have the same structure in the *store* but have unequal structures, due to different range bounds, in the *environment*. The question has no best answer. A similar problem exists for two variable record structures that differ only in their components' selector names or in the ordering of their components. The semantics of declaration and assignment given in Chapter 7 naturally enforces structure equivalence on types.

If we wish to define the semantics of these variants of type-checking, we must add more information to the denotable values. For arrays, the domain

$$Array = (Index \rightarrow Denotable\text{-}value) \times Index \times Index$$

is inadequate for occurrence equivalence checking and barely adequate for structure equivalence checking. (Why?) A formal description of either kind of equivalence checking is not simple, and the complexity found in the semantic definitions is mirrored in their implementations. The area is still a subject of active research.

8.1.1 Recursive Bindings

The semantics of a recursively defined abstract is straightforward; for the hypothetical abstract:

D ::= · · · | **rec abs** I=M | · · ·

where **abs** could be **proc**, **fcn**, **class**, or whatever, a statically scoped, recursive version is:

$$\mathbf{D}[\![\mathbf{rec\ abs\ I{=}M}]\!] = \lambda e.\lambda s.\,(e', (return\ s))$$
$$\text{where } e' = (updateenv\ [\![\mathrm{I}]\!]\ \mathrm{in}M(\mathbf{M}[\![\mathrm{M}]\!]e')\ e)$$

As we saw in Chapter 7, the recursively defined environment e' causes a reference to identifier [[I]] in [[M]] to be resolved with e'. This produces a recursive invocation.

What sort of abstracts make good use of recursive bindings? Certainly procedures do. Perhaps the most important aspect of recursive invocations is the means for terminating them. In this regard, the **if-then-else** command serves well, for it makes it possible to choose whether to continue the recursive invocations or not. We can increase the utility of recursive expression and type abstracts by adding conditional constructs to their domains:

$$\mathrm{E} ::= \mathrm{E}_1{+}\mathrm{E}_2 \mid \cdots \mid \textbf{if } \mathrm{E}_1 \textbf{ then } \mathrm{E}_2 \textbf{ else } \mathrm{E}_3$$
$$\mathrm{T} ::= \textbf{nat} \mid \cdots \mid \textbf{if } \mathrm{E} \textbf{ then } \mathrm{T}_1 \textbf{ else } \mathrm{T}_2$$

Some applications are given in the exercises.

8.2 PARAMETERIZATION

Abstracts usually carry parameters, which are dummy identifiers that are replaced by values when the abstract is invoked. The dummy identifiers are the *formal parameters* and the expressions that replace them are the *actual parameters*. If a formal parameter [[I]] is used in an abstract's body in positions where a B-construct is syntactically allowed, then the actual parameter bound to [[I]] must be an expression from the B syntax domain. Abstracts may have expression parameters, command parameters, type parameters, and so on.

The *principle of parameterization* states that a formal parameter to an abstract may be from any syntax domain. The denotation of an abstract's body [[V]] parameterized on identifiers $[\![\mathrm{I}_1]\!], \cdots, [\![\mathrm{I}_n]\!]$ is a function of form $(\lambda p_1. \cdots .\lambda p_n.\, \mathbf{V}[\![\mathrm{V}]\!] \cdots)$. What are the denotations of the actual parameters? There are a number of options, and an example is the best means for study.

All parameterized abstracts in this section use only one parameter. Consider a procedure, parameterized on a member of the Expression domain, defined by the syntax:

$$\mathrm{D} ::= \cdots \mid \textbf{proc } \mathrm{I}_1(\mathrm{I}_2){=}\mathrm{C}$$
$$\mathrm{C} ::= \mathrm{C}_1;\mathrm{C}_2 \mid \cdots \mid \mathrm{I(E)}$$

If the abstract is statically scoped, then the domain of procedures is $Proc = Param \rightarrow Store \rightarrow Poststore_{\perp}$. The semantics of the abstract is:

$\mathbf{D}[\![\text{proc } \mathrm{I}_1(\mathrm{I}_2)\text{=C}]\!] = \lambda e.\lambda s.((\mathit{updateenv}\ [\![\mathrm{I}_1]\!]$
$\quad \mathrm{in}\mathit{Proc}(\lambda a.\ \mathbf{C}[\![\mathrm{C}]\!](\mathit{updateenv}\ [\![\mathrm{I}_2]\!]\ a\ e))\ e),\ (\mathit{return}\ s)).$

$\mathbf{C}[\![\mathrm{I(E)}]\!] = \lambda e.\lambda s.\ \text{cases}\ (\mathit{accessenv}\ [\![\mathrm{I}]\!]\ e)\ \text{of}$
$\quad \mathrm{is}\mathit{Natlocn}(l) \rightarrow (\mathit{signalerr}\ s)$
$\quad \cdots$
$\quad [\!]\ \mathrm{is}\mathit{Proc}(q) \rightarrow (q\ (\cdots \mathbf{E}[\![\mathrm{E}]\!] \cdots)\ s)$
$\quad \text{end}$

The expression $(\cdots \mathbf{E}[\![\mathrm{E}]\!] \cdots)$ represents the denotation of the actual parameter, a member of domain *Param*. Recall that E: Expression →*Environment* →*Store* →*Expressible-value* is the functionality of the valuation function for expressions. The options for the denotation of the actual parameter are:

1. $(\mathbf{E}[\![\mathrm{E}]\!]e\ s) \in$ *Expressible-value*: the actual parameter is evaluated with the environment and store active at the point of invocation. This is implemented as *call-by-value*.
2. $(\mathbf{E}[\![\mathrm{E}]\!]e)$: *Store* →*Expressible-value*: the actual parameter is given the invocation environment, but it uses the stores active at the occurrences of its corresponding formal parameter in the procedure body. This is implemented as ALGOL60-style *call-by-name*.
3. $\mathbf{E}[\![\mathrm{E}]\!]$: *Environment* →*Store* →*Expressible-value*: the actual parameter uses the environment and the store active at the occurrences of its corresponding formal parameter in the procedure. This is implemented as *call-by-text*.
4. A fourth option used in some languages is to take the actual parameter domain *Param* to be *Location*. This is implemented as *call-by-reference*. Call-by-reference transmission presents a problem when a nonvariable expression is used as an actual parameter. Since the denotation must be a location value, the usual strategy is to allocate a new location that holds the expressible value of the parameter. This problem is a result of improper language design. A solution is to make an explicit distinction in the language's syntax definition between Identifier L-values and Identifier R-values, as we did in Figure 2.1. A call-by-reference parameter is not an expressible value, but the denotation of an L-value construct, and identifiers that are Expression parameters are R-value constructs.

We conducted the above analysis assuming that expression evaluation always terminated; that is, *Expressible-value* had no $\perp$ element. When nontermination of actual parameter evaluation is a possibility, then each of the four options mentioned above may evaluate their actual parameter expressions in two ways:

1. *Immediate evaluation*: the value of the actual parameter is calculated before its binding to the formal parameter. This is described by making *a*'s binding strict in:

$$\mathbf{D}[\![\mathbf{proc}\ I_1(I_2){=}\ C]\!] = \lambda e.\lambda s.((updateenv\ [\![I_1]\!]$$
$$inProc(\underline{\lambda} a.\ \mathbf{C}[\![C]\!](updateenv\ [\![I_2]\!]\ a\ e))\ e),\ (return\ s))$$

2. *Delayed evaluation*: the value of the actual parameter need be calculated only upon its use in the body of the procedure. In this case, the semantic equation for procedure definition is left in its original form— the value, whether it be proper or improper, is bound into the procedure's environment.

The term *call-by-value* is normally used to mean immediate evaluation to an expressible value, while *call-by-need* and *lazy evaluation* are used to mean delayed evaluation to an expressible value. (The difference between the latter two is that, once an evaluation of an argument does proceed, call-by-need is required to finish it, whereas lazy evaluation need only evaluate the argument to the point that the required subpart of the argument is produced.) Most applications of options 2 through 4 use immediate evaluation. The parameter domain and strictness questions can be raised for all syntactic domains of actual parameters. You should consider these issues for command, declaration, and type parameters to procedures and functions.

One of the more interesting parameterized abstracts is the parameterized type expression. For syntax:

D ::= · · · | **type** $I_1(I_2)$=T | · · ·
T ::= · · · | I(T) | · · ·

type structures such as:

```
type STACKOF(T) = record
        var ST: array [1..k] of T;
        var TOP: nat
    end
```

can be written. An invocation such as **var** X: STACKOF(**nat**) allocates storage for the two components of the record: X.ST refers to an array of k number variables, and X.TOP refers to a number variable. The semantics of parameterized type abstractions is left as an exercise.

8.2.1 Polymorphism and Typing

An operation is *polymorphic* if its argument can be from more than one semantic domain. The answer it produces is dependent upon the domains of its arguments. As an example, a general purpose addition operation might produce an integer sum from two integer arguments and a rational sum from two rational arguments. This operation might be assigned functionality:

$$(\mathit{Integer} \times \mathit{Integer}) \cup (\mathit{Rational} \times \mathit{Rational}) \to \mathit{Integer} \cup \mathit{Rational}$$

Unfortunately, the dependence of the codomain on the domain isn't clearly stated in this description. The graph of the operation is the union of the integer addition and rational addition operations. Polymorphic operations do not fit cleanly into the domain theory of Chapter 3, and our semantic notation does not include them.

Polymorphism does appear in general purpose programming languages. Strachey distinguished between two kinds: *ad hoc polymorphism* (also called *overloading*) and *parametric polymorphism*. An ad hoc polymorphic operator "behaves differently" for arguments of different types, whereas a parametric polymorphic operation "behaves the same" for all types. (We won't attempt more specific definitions because the concepts have proved notoriously difficult to formalize.) In Pascal, a typed language, the + symbol is overloaded, because it performs integer addition, floating point addition, and set union, all unrelated operations. A Pascal compiler determines the context in which the operator appears and associates a specific meaning with +. In contrast, the **hd** operator in Edinburgh ML is parametric. It can extract the head integer from a list of integers, the head character from a list of characters, and, in general, the head α from an α-list. **hd** is a general purpose function, and it is implemented as a general purpose operation. Regardless of the type of argument, the same structural manipulation of a list is performed.

The denotational semantics of an overloaded operator is straightforward to express. Here is a semantic equation for the Pascal addition expression:

$$
\begin{array}{l}
\mathbf{E}[\![\mathrm{E}_1 + \mathrm{E}_2]\!] = \lambda e.\lambda s.\ \text{cases}\ (\mathbf{E}[\![\mathrm{E}_1]\!]e\,s)\ \text{of} \\
\quad \text{is}\mathit{Nat}(n_1) \to (\text{cases}\ (\mathbf{E}[\![\mathrm{E}_2]\!]e\,s)\ \text{of} \\
\qquad\qquad\qquad \text{is}\mathit{Nat}(n_2) \to \text{in}\mathit{Nat}(n_1\ \mathit{plus}\ n_2) \\
\qquad\qquad\qquad \cdots\ \text{end}) \\
\quad \cdots \\
\quad [\!]\ \text{is}\mathit{Rat}(r_1) \to (\text{cases}\ (\mathbf{E}[\![\mathrm{E}_2]\!]e\,s)\ \text{of} \\
\qquad\qquad\qquad \cdots \\
\qquad\qquad\qquad [\!]\ \text{is}\mathit{Rat}(r_2) \to \text{in}\mathit{Rat}(r_1\ \mathit{addrat}\ r_2) \\
\qquad\qquad\qquad \cdots\ \text{end}) \\
\quad \cdots \\
\quad [\!]\ \text{is}\mathit{Set}(t_1) \to \cdots\ \text{in}\mathit{Set}(t_1\ \mathit{union}\ t_2) \cdots \\
\quad \cdots\ \text{end}
\end{array}
$$

A pre-execution analysis like that performed in Figure 7.3 can determine which of *plus*, *addrat*, or *union* is the denotation of the +.

Parametric polymorphic operations are more difficult to handle; we give one method for doing so. Consider the **hd** operator again. In ML, numbers, lists, tuples, sums, function spaces, and the like, are all data types. Its expressible value domain balloons to:

$$Exprval = (Nat + Exprval^* + (Exprval \times Exprval) + (Exprval + Exprval) + (Exprval \rightarrow Exprval) + Errvalue)_\perp$$

The **hd** operator manipulates an expressible value list:

$$\mathbf{E}[\![\mathbf{hd}\ \mathrm{E}]\!] = \lambda e.\ \text{let } x = \mathbf{E}[\![\mathrm{E}]\!]e \text{ in cases } x \text{ of}$$
$$\text{is}Nat(n) \rightarrow \text{in}Errvalue()$$
$$[]\ \text{is}Exprval^*(l) \rightarrow hd\ l$$
$$[]\ \cdots \text{ end}$$

The disadvantage of this formulation is that *Nat*-lists such as (*two cons one cons nil*) become in*Exprval**(in*Nat*(*two*) *cons* in*Nat*(*one*) *cons nil*). We would prefer that **hd** operate directly upon *Nat*-lists, *Nat*×*Nat*-lists, and the like, but both theoretical problems (mathematically, the **hd** operation literally becomes too "large" to be well defined) and notational problems (try to define **hd** in the existing semantic notation) arise. The *real* problem lies in our version of domain theory. Our domains live in a rigid hierarchy, and there exists no "universal domain" that includes all the others as subdomains. If a universal domain U did exist, we could define a single operation $hd' : U \rightarrow U$ that maps those elements of U that "look like" α-lists to elements in U that "look like" α-values. Then $\mathbf{E}[\![\mathbf{hd}\ \mathrm{E}]\!] = \lambda e.\ hd'(\mathbf{E}[\![\mathrm{E}]\!]e)$. A number of researchers, most notably McCracken and Reynolds, have developed domain theories for universal domains and parametric polymorphism.

We next consider polymorphic parameterized abstracts. The parameterized abstracts in the previous section are untyped— no restrictions (beyond syntax domain compatibility) are placed on the formal and actual parameters. This is the version of abstraction used in untyped languages such as BCPL and LISP. If the untyped version of parameterized abstract is used in a typed language such as Pascal, the abstraction acts polymorphically. Consider a command abstract whose denotation lies in the domain $Proc = Expressible\text{-}value \rightarrow Store \rightarrow Poststore_\perp$. A procedure's actual parameter can be an integer, a truth value, an array, or whatever else is a legal expressible value.

However, a typed programming language like Pascal requires that formal parameters be labeled with type expressions. The expression acts as a precondition or guard: only actual parameters whose type structures match the formal parameter's are allowed as arguments. The advantages of typing— pre-execution type equivalence verification, increased user understanding of abstracts, and efficient execution— are well known.

We use the syntax

D ::= ⋯ | **proc** $\mathrm{I}_1(\mathrm{I}_2{:}\mathrm{T})$=C
C ::= ⋯ | I(E) | ⋯

for procedures that receive actual parameters from the Expression syntax domain. The value bound to $[\![I_2]\!]$ must have type structure $[\![T]\!]$.

The semantics of typed parameters can be handled in two ways: (1) the type information can guard entry to the abstract at invocation; (2) the abstract's denotation is restricted at definition to a function whose domain is exactly that specified by the type. To define the first version, we use a valuation function:

$$\mathbf{T'}: \text{Type-structure} \to \mathit{Environment} \to (\mathit{Expressible\text{-}value} + \mathit{Errvalue})$$

such that $(\mathbf{T'}[\![T]\!]e\ x)$ determines whether or not x has data type $[\![T]\!]$. If it does, the result is in$\mathit{Expressible\text{-}value}(x)$; otherwise it is in$\mathit{Errvalue}()$. $\mathbf{T'}$ is a type-equivalence checker. The semantics of statically scoped procedure declaration is:

$$\begin{aligned}
&\mathbf{D}[\![\text{proc } I_1(I_2{:}T){=}C]\!] = \lambda e.\lambda s.\ ((\mathit{updateenv}\ [\![I_1]\!]\\
&\qquad \text{in}\mathit{Proc}(\lambda x.\ \text{cases } (\mathbf{T'}[\![T]\!]e\ x) \text{ of}\\
&\qquad\qquad\qquad \text{is}\mathit{Expressiblevalue}(x) \to \mathbf{C}[\![C]\!](\mathit{updateenv}\ [\![I]\!]\ x\ e)\\
&\qquad\qquad\qquad [\!]\ \text{is}\mathit{Errvalue}() \to \mathit{signalerr}\quad \text{end})\\
&\qquad e),\ (\mathit{return}\ s)).
\end{aligned}$$

The second version fragments the *Proc* domain by making it into a family of procedure domains:

$$\begin{aligned}
&\mathit{Nat\text{-}proc} = \mathit{Nat} \to \mathit{Store} \to \mathit{Poststore}_\perp\\
&\mathit{Array\text{-}proc} = \mathit{Array} \to \mathit{Store} \to \mathit{Poststore}_\perp\\
&\mathit{Record\text{-}proc} = \mathit{Record} \to \mathit{Store} \to \mathit{Poststore}_\perp
\end{aligned}$$

For simplicity, we give only three kinds of parameter domains. (You are given the problem of formulating a complete hierarchy of domains for Pascal.) Another version of the $\mathbf{T'}$ function is needed. First, we define:

$$\begin{aligned}
&\mathit{Type\text{-}tag} = \mathit{Nat\text{-}tag} + \mathit{Array\text{-}tag} + \mathit{Record\text{-}tag} + \mathit{Err\text{-}tag}\\
&\qquad \text{where } \mathit{Nat\text{-}tag} = \mathit{Array\text{-}tag} = \mathit{Record\text{-}tag} = \mathit{Err\text{-}tag} = \mathit{Unit}
\end{aligned}$$

Each non-*Err-tag* corresponds to one of the parameter domains. The valuation function $\mathbf{T'}: \text{Type-structure} \to \mathit{Environment} \to \mathit{Type\text{-}tag}$ maps the formal parameter's type information to a type tag value in the obvious fashion. A declaration of a typed procedure has semantics:

$$\begin{aligned}
&\mathbf{D}[\![\text{proc } I_1(I_2{:}T){=}C]\!] = \lambda e.\lambda s.\ \text{cases } (\mathbf{T'}[\![T]\!]e) \text{ of}\\
&\qquad \text{is}\mathit{Nat\text{-}tag}() \to\\
&\qquad\qquad ((\mathit{updateenv}\ [\![I_1]\!]\ \text{in}\mathit{Nat\text{-}proc}(\lambda n.\ \mathbf{C}[\![C]\!](\mathit{updateenv}\ [\![I_2]\!]\\
&\qquad\qquad\qquad \text{in}\mathit{Nat}(n)\ e))\ e),\ (\mathit{return}\ s))\\
&\qquad \text{is}\mathit{Array\text{-}tag}() \to
\end{aligned}$$

$((updateenv\ [\![I_1]\!]\ \text{in}Array\text{-}proc(\lambda a.\ \mathbf{C}[\![C]\!](updateenv\ [\![I_2]\!]$
$\text{in}Array(a)\ e))\ e),\ (return\ s))$
$\text{is}Record\text{-}tag() \rightarrow$ (similar to above)
$\text{is}Err\text{-}tag() \rightarrow (e, (signalerr\ s))$
end

This semantics explicity restricts the abstract's argument domain by selecting a particular function at the point of definition. More specific information exists about the data type of the parameter, and a more thorough pre-execution analysis can be performed.

Both of these two description methods have drawbacks. You are left with the problem of finding a better solution to parameter-type enforcement.

8.3 CORRESPONDENCE

The *principle of correspondence* is simply stated: for any parameter binding mechanism, there may exist a corresponding definition mechanism, and vice versa. That is, if elements from a domain D may be denotable values of formal parameter identifiers, then elements from D may be denotable values of declared identifiers, and vice versa. Since an environment is a map from identifiers to denotable values, and a declared identifier is used no differently than a parameter identifier, the correspondence principle makes full use of the semantic domains.

The correspondence between the two forms of binding becomes clear when their semantic equations are compared. Consider once again a statically scoped command abstract with a single parameter; let D be the domain of parameter denotations. Equations for definition and invocation read:

$$\mathbf{D}[\![\textbf{proc}\ I_1(I_2){=}C]\!] = \lambda e.\lambda s.\ ((updateenv\ [\![I_1]\!]\ \text{in}Proc(\lambda d.\ \mathbf{C}[\![C]\!](updateenv\ [\![I_2]\!]\ \text{in}D(d)\ \ e))\ \ e),\ \ (return\ \ s))$$

$$\mathbf{C}[\![I(M)]\!] = \lambda e.\lambda s.\ \text{cases}\ (accessenv\ [\![I]\!]\ e)\ \text{of}\ \ldots\ [\,]\ \text{is}Proc(q) \rightarrow q\,(\cdots \mathbf{M}[\![M]\!] \cdots)\ s\ \cdots\ \text{end}$$

We see that $\text{in}D(\cdots \mathbf{M}[\![M]\!] \cdots)$ is bound to $[\![I_2]\!]$ in $[\![C]\!]$'s environment. We can build a definition construct with similar semantics:

$$\mathbf{D}[\![\textbf{define}\ I{=}M]\!] = \lambda e.\lambda s.\ ((updateenv\ [\![I]\!]\ \text{in}D(\cdots \mathbf{M}[\![M]\!] \cdots)\ e),\ (return\ \ s))$$

Thus, $\mathbf{C}[\![\textbf{begin proc}\ I(I'){=}C;\ I(M)\ \textbf{end}]\!] = \mathbf{C}[\![\textbf{begin define}\ I'{=}M;\ C\ \textbf{end}]\!]$ for phrases $[\![M]\!]$ and $[\![C]\!]$ that contain no free occurrences of $[\![I]\!]$. The questions we raised in Section 8.2 regarding the domains of formal parameters now apply to declared identifiers as well.

The correspondence principle may also be practiced in the other direction. When we consider the definition form for variables:

$$\mathbf{D}[\![\mathbf{var}\ \mathrm{I{:}T}]\!] = \lambda e.\lambda s.\ \mathrm{let}\ (d, p) = (\mathbf{T}[\![\mathrm{T}]\!] e\, s)\ \mathrm{in}\ ((\mathit{updateenv}\ [\![\mathrm{I}]\!]\ d\ e), p)$$

we see that the value bound to $[\![\mathrm{I}]\!]$ is an activated type denotation; that is, a reference to newly allocated storage, rather than an expressible value. (Perhaps we should write variable definitions as $[\![\mathrm{I} = \mathbf{ref}\ \mathrm{T}]\!]$.) The corresponding binding mechanism is:

$$\mathbf{D}[\![\mathbf{proc}\ \mathrm{I}_1(\mathrm{I}_2) = \mathrm{C}]\!] = \lambda e.\lambda s.((\mathit{updateenv}\ [\![\mathrm{I}]\!]$$
$$\mathrm{in}\mathit{Proc}(\lambda d.\ \mathbf{C}[\![\mathrm{C}]\!](\mathit{updateenv}\ [\![\mathrm{I}]\!]\ d\ e))\ e,\ (\mathit{return}\ s))$$

$$\mathbf{C}[\![\mathrm{I(T)}]\!] = \lambda e.\lambda s.\ \mathrm{cases}\ (\mathit{accessenv}\ [\![\mathrm{I}]\!]\ e)\ \mathrm{of}$$
$$\cdots$$
$$[\,]\ \mathrm{is}\mathit{Proc}(q) \rightarrow \mathrm{let}\ (d, p) = (\mathbf{T}[\![\mathrm{T}]\!] e\, s)\ \mathrm{in}\ (\mathit{check}\ (q\ d))(p)$$
$$\cdots\ \mathrm{end}$$

Storage for a data object of type $[\![\mathrm{T}]\!]$ is allocated when the procedure is invoked, and a reference to the storage is the denotation bound to the parameter. This form of parameter transmission allocates local variables for a procedure. You should study the differences between the version of $\mathbf{C}[\![\mathrm{I(T)}]\!]$ given above and the version induced by the correspondence principle from $[\![\mathbf{type}\ \mathrm{I{=}T}]\!]$.

The principle of parameterization can be derived from the principles of abstraction and correspondence by first uniformly generating all possible abstraction forms and then deriving the parameter forms corresponding to the definitions.

8.4 QUALIFICATION

The *principle of qualification* is that every syntax domain may have a block construct for admitting local declarations. The language of Figure 8.1 already has a block construct in the Command domain. Blocks for the other domains take on similar forms:

E ::= · · · | **begin** D **within** E **end** | · · ·
D ::= · · · | **begin** D_1 **within** D_2 **end** | · · ·
T ::= · · · | **begin** D **within** T **end** | · · ·

and so on. For a syntax domain M, the semantics of an M-block $[\![\mathbf{begin}\ \mathrm{D}\ \mathbf{within}\ \mathrm{M}\ \mathbf{end}]\!]$ is $\mathbf{M}[\![\mathrm{M}]\!]$ with an environment augmented by the definitions [[D]]. The definitions' scope extends no further than [[M]]. Assuming the usual static scoping, we state the semantics of the M-block as:

$$\mathbf{M}: \mathrm{M} \rightarrow \mathit{Environment} \rightarrow \mathit{Store} \rightarrow (\mathit{M} \times \mathit{Poststore})$$

$$\mathbf{M}[\![\mathbf{begin}\ \mathrm{D}\ \mathbf{within}\ \mathrm{M}\ \mathbf{end}]\!] = \lambda e.\lambda s.\ \mathrm{let}\ (e',p) = (\mathbf{D}[\![\mathrm{D}]\!]e\,s)\ \mathrm{in}\ (\mathit{check}\,(\mathbf{M}[\![\mathrm{M}]\!]e'))(p)$$

This format applies to Command blocks, Expression blocks, Type blocks, and so on. A technical problem arises for Declaration blocks. The scope of local definitions [[D_1]] of block [[**begin** D_1 **within** D_2 **end**]] should extend only as far as [[D_2]], but the **D** valuation function defined in Figure 7.2 processes its environment argument as if it were a store— the additions to the environment are retained beyond the scope of the declaration block. A solution is to make the denotation of a declaration be a list of binding pairs:

$$\mathbf{D}: \mathrm{Declaration} \rightarrow \mathit{Environment} \rightarrow \mathit{Store} \rightarrow ((\mathrm{Identifier} \times \mathit{Denotable\text{-}value})^{*} \times \mathit{Poststore})$$

Thus, ($\mathbf{D}[\![\mathrm{D}]\!]e\,s$) denotes the bindings (and the post-store) defined by [[D]] and not the environment that results when those bindings are added to e. **D**'s definition and the semantics of declaration blocks are left as exercises.

A number of useful constructions result from the the qualification principle. For example, a Declaration block used within a Declaration abstract creates a Modula-style **module.** Here is an example that models a natural number-containing stack:

```
module STACK-OF-NAT =
    begin
        var ST: array [1..k] of nat;
        var TOP: nat
    within
        proc PUSH(I: nat) = if TOP=k then skip
            else (TOP:=TOP+1; ST[TOP]:=I);
        proc POP = if TOP=0 then skip else TOP:=TOP−1;
        fcn TOP = if TOP=0 then error else ST[TOP];
        proc INITIALIZE = TOP:=0
    end
```

The declaration **var** STACK-OF-NAT creates procedures PUSH, POP, TOP, INITIALIZE, and function TOP. The variables ST and TOP are local definitions that are hidden from outside access.

Type blocks are also useful. First, recall that the syntax of a record structure is:

T ::= ··· | record D end | ···

Since the body of a record is a declaration, records of variables, procedures, functions, or whatever are allowed. These make semantic sense as well, for *Record* = *Identifier* → *Denotable-value* and *Denotable-value* = (*Natlocn* + *Array* + *Record* + *Proc* + ··· $)_\perp$. Since Type blocks allow local variables to a type structure, we can create a SIMULA-style *class*. Here is an example of a type definition for a stack class parameterized on the element type:

```
type STACK-OF(X) =
    begin
        var ST: array[1..k] of X;
        var TOP: nat
    within record
        proc PUSH(I:X) =  ··· (as before)
        proc POP = ···
        fcn TOP = ···
        proc INITIALIZE = ···
    end
end
```

A definition **var** A: STACK-OF(**nat**) creates a record with components A.PUSH, A.POP, A.TOP, and A.INITIALIZE. One technical point must be resolved: the type parameter X has two roles in the definition. It induces storage allocation in the definition **var** ST: **array** [1..k] **of** X and it does type equivalence checking in **proc** PUSH(I:X). Both the T and T' valuation functions are needed.

8.5 ORTHOGONALITY

The introduction to this chapter stated that the abstraction, parameterization, correspondence, and qualification principles were tools for programming language design. Any programming language can be uniformly extended along the lines suggested by the principles to produce a host of user conveniences. The design principles encourage the development of an *orthogonal* language.

What is orthogonality? A precise definition is difficult to produce, but languages that are called *orthogonal* tend to have a small number of core concepts and a set of ways of uniformly combining these concepts. The semantics of the combinations are uniform; no special restrictions exist for specific instances of combinations. Here are two examples. First, the syntax domain Expression is an example of a core concept. An expression should have equal rights and uniform semantics in all contexts where it can be used. In

ALGOL68, any legal member of Expression may be used as an index for an array; e.g., "A[4+(F(X)-1)]" is acceptable. The semantics of the expression interacts uniformly with the semantics of the array-indexing operation, regardless of what the expression is. This does not hold in FORTRAN IV, where there are restrictions on which forms of Expression can be used as indexes— the expression $4 + (F(X) - 1)$ is too complex to be a FORTRAN array index. The semantics of expressions is not uniformly handled by the FORTRAN-indexing operation. A second example is the specification of a result type for a function. In Pascal, only values from the scalar types can be results from function procedures. In contrast, ML allows a function to return a value from any legal type whatsoever.

Orthogonality reduces the mental overhead for understanding a language. Because it lacks special cases and restrictions, an orthogonal language definition is smaller and its implementation can be organized to take advantage of the uniformity of definition. The principles introduced in this chapter provide a methodology for introducing orthogonal binding concepts. In general, the denotational semantics method encourages the orthogonal design of a language. A valuation function assigns a uniform meaning to a construct regardless of its context. Further, the semantic domains and function notation encourage uniform application of concepts— if *some* members of a semantic domain are processed by an operation, then arrangements must be made to handle *all* of them. The compactness of a language's denotational definition can be taken as a measure of the degree of the language's orthogonality.

SUGGESTED READINGS

Semantics of abstraction and parameterization: Berry 1981; Gordon 1979; Plotkin 1975; Tennent 1977b

Semantics of qualification and correspondence: Ganzinger 1983; Goguen & Parsaye-Ghomi 1981; Tennent 1977b, 1981

Polymorphism & typing: Demers, Donohue, & Skinner 1978; Kahn, MacQueen, & Plotkin 1984; McCracken 1984; MacQueen & Sethi 1982; Reynolds 1974, 1981, 1985

EXERCISES

1. Describe the different scoping mechanisms possible for the Declaration, Type-structure, Identifier-L-value, and Subscript abstracts derived from Figure 8.1. Write the semantic equations for the various scoping mechanisms and give examples of use of each of the abstracts.

2. Consider the interaction of differently scoped abstracts:
   a. Which forms of scoping of expression abstracts are compatible with statically scoped command abstracts? With dynamically scoped command abstracts?
   b. Repeat part a for differently scoped declaration abstracts and command abstracts; for differently scoped type abstracts and command abstracts; for differently scoped declaration abstracts and expression abstracts.

3. Apply the abstraction principle to the language in Figure 5.2 to create command abstracts. Define the semantics of command abstracts in each of the two following ways:
   a. The denotations of command abstracts are kept in a newly created semantic argument, the environment. Since variable identifiers are used as arguments to the store, what problems arise from this semantics? Show how the problems are solved by forcing variable identifiers to map to location values in the environment.
   b. The denotations of command abstracts are kept in the store; that is, $Store = \text{Identifier} \rightarrow (Nat + Proc)_{\perp}$, where $Proc = Store_{\perp} \rightarrow Store_{\perp}$. What advantages and drawbacks do you see in this semantics?

4. Consider the interaction of parameter-passing mechanisms and scoping mechanisms. Using their semantic definitions as a guide, comment on the pragmatics of each of the parameter transmission methods in Section 8.2 with statically scoped command abstracts; with dynamically scoped command abstracts.

5. In addition to those mentioned in Section 8.2, there are other parameter transmission methods for expressions. Define the semantics of:
   a. Pascal-style call-by-value: the actual parameter is evaluated to an expressible value, a new location is allocated, and the expressible value is placed in the new location's cell. Assignment to the new location is allowed within the abstract's body.
   b. PL/1-style call-by-value-result: an Identifier-L-value parameter is evaluated to a location. The value in that location is copied into a newly allocated cell. Upon the termination of the abstract, the value in the new cell is copied into the location that the actual parameter denotes.
   c. Imperative call-by-need: like ALGOL60-style call-by-name, except that the first time that the actual parameter is evaluated to an expressible value, that value becomes the value associated with the parameter in all subsequent uses. (That is, for the first use of the parameter in the abstract, the parameter behaves like a call-by-name parameter. Thereafter, it behaves like a call-by-value parameter.)

What are the pragmatics of these parameter-passing mechanisms?

6. Define the syntax and semantics of a command abstract that takes a tuple of parameters.

7. An alternative to defining recursive abstracts via recursively defined environments is defining them through the store. Let:

$$Store = Location \rightarrow (Nat + \cdots + Proc + \cdots)_{\perp}$$
$$\text{where } Proc = Store \rightarrow Poststore_{\perp}$$

be a version of store that holds command abstracts. For **D**: Declaration → *Environment* → *Store* → (*Environment* × *Poststore*), let:

$$\mathbf{D}[\![\mathbf{proc}\ \mathrm{I} = \mathrm{C}]\!] = \lambda e.\ \lambda s.\ \text{let } (l, p) = \mathit{allocate\text{-}locn}\ s \text{ in}$$
$$\text{let } e' = \mathit{updateenv}\ [\![\mathrm{I}]\!]\ l\ e$$
$$\text{in } (e', (\mathit{check}(\mathit{return} \circ (\mathit{update}\ l\ \mathrm{in}Proc(\mathbf{C}[\![\mathrm{C}]\!]e'))))(p))$$

be the semantics of procedure declaration.

   a. Write the semantic equation for procedure invocation. Explain the mechanics of recursive invocation. Why is it that recursive calls can occur, but *fix* does not appear in the semantics of declaration? Under what circumstances does the use of [[I]] in [[C]] *not* cause a recursive invocation?
   b. Suggest how this semantics might be extended to allow self-modifying procedures.

8. A variation on expression parameters that was not mentioned in Section 8.2 is the following: $(\lambda e.\ \mathbf{E}[\![\mathrm{E}]\!]e\ s)$: *Environment* → *Expressible-value*.

   a. Revise the semantic equations to fit this form. Explain how this would be implemented.
   b. Show why this form of parameter transmission could easily lead to access errors in the store.

9. Revise the list-processing language given in Figure 7.5 to be typed:

   i. Set the domain *Atom* to be *Nat*.
   ii. Assign to each well-formed member of the Expression syntax domain a type. For example, [[1]] has type "**nat**," [[1 CONS NIL]] has type "**nat list**," and [[(LAMBDA (X: **nat list**) (HEAD X))]] has type "**nat list** → **nat**."

   a. Alter the language's semantics so that the data typing is enforced; that is, ill-typed expressions have an erroneous denotable value.
   b. What is the data type of [[NIL]]? Is the construct overloaded or is it parametrically polymorphic?

c. Are there any expressions that have well-defined denotations in the untyped language but have erroneous denotations in the typed language? (Hint: consider the example of self-application in Section 7.2.2.)
d. Which constructs in the language could be profitably made polymorphic?
e. Are the recursively defined semantic domains absolutely needed to give a denotational semantics to the typed language? (Hint: consider your answer to part c and study the hierarchy *MDArray* in Section 7.3.)

10. Install occurrence equivalence type-checking into the semantics of an imperative language that uses the definition structures of Figure 8.1.

11. a. Define the semantics of these constructs:

$$E ::= \cdots \mid \textbf{if } E_1 \textbf{ then } E_2 \textbf{ else } E_3$$
$$T ::= \cdots \mid \textbf{if } E \textbf{ then } T_1 \textbf{ else } T_2$$

b. Define the semantics of these abstracts:

$$D ::= \cdots \mid \textbf{rec fcn } I_1(I_2) = E \mid \textbf{rec type } I_1(I_2) = T$$

for expression parameters I_2.
c. Give examples of useful recursively defined functions and types using the constructs defined in parts a and b.

12. Add parameterized command abstracts to the language of Figure 5.6 but do *not* include data type information for the formal parameters to the abstracts. In Section 8.2.1, it was suggested that this form of abstract appears to be polymorphic to the user. Why is this form of polymorphism appropriate for this particular language? But why do the polymorphic abstracts have limited utility in this example? How must the language's core operation set be extended to make good use of the polymorphism? Make these extensions and define their semantics.

13. Here is an example of a parameterized abstract in which formal parameters are parameterized on other formal parameters: $[\![\textbf{proc} \text{ stack}(T; op: T \rightarrow T); C]\!]$.

a. Show how this example is derived from the correspondence principle.
b. Give a denotational semantics to this example.

14. Formalize the semantics of the principle of correspondence.

15. Give the semantics of the Expression, Declaration, and Type blocks listed in Section 8.4.

16. What form of parameter transmission is induced by the correspondence principle from the ALGOL68 variable declaration ⟦**loc int** I:=E⟧?

17. For each language listed below, apply the design principles described in this chapter. For each principle, document your design decisions regarding syntax, semantics, and pragmatics.

    a. The calculator language in Figure 4.3.
    b. The imperative language in Figures 5.1 and 5.2.
    c. The applicative language in Figure 7.5.

18. Using the language in Figure 7.2:

    a. Use the principle of abstraction to develop expression and command abstract definition constructs. Give their semantics.
    b. Use the principle of correspondence to develop the corresponding parameter forms and parameter transmission mechanisms for the abstracts. Give their semantics.
    c. What other forms of parameters and parameter transmission would we obtain if part b was redone using the principle of parameterization? Give their semantics.

19. Milne has proposed a variety of composition operations for declarations. Three of them are:

    a. ⟦D_1 **and** D_2⟧: the declarations in ⟦D_1⟧ and ⟦D_2⟧ are evaluated simultaneously, and the resulting bindings are the union of the two.
    b. ⟦D_1 **within** D_2⟧: ⟦D_1⟧'s bindings are given to ⟦D_2⟧ for local use. The bindings that result are just ⟦D_2⟧'s.
    c. ⟦D_1; D_2⟧: ⟦D_1⟧'s bindings are passed on to ⟦D_2⟧. The result is ⟦D_2⟧'s bindings unioned with those bindings of ⟦D_1⟧ that are not superceded by ⟦D_2⟧'s.

    Define the semantics of these forms of composition, paying careful attention to erroneous forms of composition (e.g., in part a, ⟦D_1⟧ and ⟦D_2⟧ share a common identifier).

20. Use the version of **T**: Type-structure → *Environment* → (*Denotable-value* × *Environment*) defined in Exercise 24 of Chapter 7 with the version of **D**: Declaration → *Environment* → *Environment* in Figure 7.1 of Chapter 7 to redefine all of the examples of the language design principles in Chapter 8. Describe the pragmatics of the new definitions versus the ones in Chapter 8.

21. The design principles in this chapter set useful bounds for language extension. Nonetheless, economy of design is another valuable feature of a programming language. After you have worked either Exercise 17 or 18,

comment on the pragmatics of the constructs you have derived. Which of the new constructs are better discarded? Why aren't language design and formal semantics definition the same thing?

Chapter 9

Control as a Semantic Domain

The sequencing found in programs' denotations is somewhat illusionary. Sequencing is an operational concept, and function definitions contain no actual "sequencing," regardless of their format. The sequencing is suggested by the simplification strategies for function notation. A simplification step corresponds roughly to an operational evaluation step, and the order in which the simplifications occur suggests an operational semantics. More than one simplification strategy may be acceptable, however, so the operational ideas do not predominate the definition.

The style of denotational semantics we have been using is called *direct semantics*. Direct semantics definitions tend to use lower-order expressions (that is, nonfunctional values and functions on them) and emphasize the compositional structure of a language. The equation:

$$\mathbf{E}[\![E_1+E_2]\!] = \lambda s.\, \mathbf{E}[\![E_1]\!]s \textit{ plus } \mathbf{E}[\![E_2]\!]s$$

is a good example. The equation gives a simple exposition of side-effect-free addition. The order of evaluation of the operands isn't important, and any simplification strategy works fine. One of the aims of the denotational semantics method is to make the meanings of program constructs clear without relying on operational mechanisms, and in this regard direct semantics performs well.

Languages designed for low-level or general application confront their users with the concept of control. *Control* might be defined as the evaluation ordering of a program's constructs. A language that promotes control as a primary feature provides the user with the ability to affect the control; that is, to change the order of evaluation. Control is an argument that the user can seize and alter. An example of a control argument is the stack of activation records maintained in support of an executing program. The stack contains the sequencing information that "drives" the program, and altering the stack alters the program's future order of evaluation.

The semantic argument that models control is called a *continuation*. Continuations were first developed for modelling unrestricted branches ("gotos") in general purpose languages, but their utility in developing nonstandard evaluation orderings has made them worthy of study in their own right. This chapter presents a number of forms of continuations and their uses.

9.1 CONTINUATIONS

We begin with a small example that uses a control argument. Consider an imperative language similar to the one in Figure 7.2 augmented with a FORTRAN-like **stop** command. The evaluation of a **stop** in a program causes a branch to the very end of the program, cancelling the evaluation of all remaining statements. The output store that the program produces is the one that is supplied as an argument to **stop.** The semantics of a **stop** command can be handled within direct semantics by applying the technique used in Figure 7.1 to trap error values, but we wish to model the change of control more directly. We add a control stack argument to the semantic function. The control stack keeps a list of all the commands that need to be evaluated. The valuation function repeatedly accesses the stack, popping off the top command and executing it. An empty stack means that evaluation is complete, and a **stop** command found at the top of the stack causes the remainder of the stack to be discarded. The valuation function for commands has functionality:

$$\mathbf{C}: \text{Command} \to \mathit{Environment} \to \mathit{Control\text{-}stack} \to \mathit{Store} \to \mathit{Store}_\perp$$

where $c \in \mathit{Control\text{-}stack} = (\mathit{Control\text{-}stack} \to \mathit{Store} \to \mathit{Store}_\perp)^*$. The expression $(\mathbf{C}[\![\mathrm{C}]\!]e\,c\,s)$ resembles an interpreter-like configuration where $(\mathbf{C}[\![\mathrm{C}]\!]e)$ is the control stack top, c is the remainder of the stack, and s is the usual store argument. A fragment of the $\mathbf{C}$ function reads:

$$\mathbf{C}[\![\mathrm{C}_1;\mathrm{C}_2]\!] = \lambda e.\lambda c.\lambda s.\, \mathbf{C}[\![\mathrm{C}_1]\!]e\ ((\mathbf{C}[\![\mathrm{C}_2]\!]e)\ \mathit{cons}\ c)\ s$$
$$\mathbf{C}[\![\mathrm{I}{:=}\mathrm{E}]\!] = \lambda e.\lambda c.\lambda s.\, (\mathit{hd}\ c)\ (\mathit{tl}\ c)\ (\mathit{update}\ (\mathit{accessenv}\ [\![\mathrm{I}]\!]\ e)\ (\mathbf{E}[\![\mathrm{E}]\!]e\ s)\ s)$$
$$\cdots$$
$$\mathbf{C}[\![\mathbf{stop}]\!] = \lambda e.\lambda c.\lambda s.\, s$$

We obtain a neat definition for the **while**-loop:

$$\mathbf{C}[\![\mathbf{while}\ \mathrm{B}\ \mathbf{do}\ \mathrm{C}]\!] = \lambda e.\lambda c.\lambda s.\, \mathbf{B}[\![\mathrm{B}]\!]e\ s \to \mathbf{C}[\![\mathrm{C}]\!]e\ ((\mathbf{C}[\![\mathbf{while}\ \mathrm{B}\ \mathbf{do}\ \mathrm{C}]\!]e)\ \mathit{cons}\ c)\ s\ [\!]\ (\mathit{hd}\ c)\ (\mathit{tl}\ c)\ s$$

which makes clear that control returns to the top of the loop after evaluating the loop's body.

Whenever the c stack is popped, $(\mathit{hd}\ c)$ is always given $(\mathit{tl}\ c)$ as its argument. The simplification steps are shortened if the semantics of $[\![\mathrm{C}_1;\mathrm{C}_2]\!]$ is written so that $(\mathbf{C}[\![\mathrm{C}_2]\!]e)$ takes c as an argument at "push-time." The stack can be replaced by a function. This new function is a (*command*) *continuation*. Its domain is $c \in \mathit{Cmdcont} = \mathit{Store} \to \mathit{Store}_\perp$. The language fragment now reads:

$\mathbf{C}$: Command $\rightarrow$ *Environment* $\rightarrow$ *Cmdcont* $\rightarrow$ *Cmdcont*

$\mathbf{C}[\![C_1;C_2]\!] = \lambda e.\lambda c.\,\mathbf{C}[\![C_1]\!]e\ (\mathbf{C}[\![C_2]\!]e\ c)$

$\mathbf{C}[\![I{:=}E]\!] = \lambda e.\lambda c.\lambda s.\ c\ (update\ (accessenv\ [\![I]\!])\ (\mathbf{E}[\![E]\!]e\ s)\ s)$

$\mathbf{C}[\![\mathbf{stop}]\!] = \lambda e.\lambda c.\lambda s.\ s$

$\mathbf{C}[\![\mathbf{if}\ B\ \mathbf{then}\ C_1\ \mathbf{else}\ C_2]\!] = \lambda e.\lambda c.\ choose\ (\mathbf{B}[\![B]\!]e)\ (\mathbf{C}[\![C_1]\!]e\ c)\ (\mathbf{C}[\![C_2]\!]e\ c)$

$\mathbf{C}[\![\mathbf{while}\ B\ \mathbf{do}\ C]\!] = \lambda e.\lambda c.\ fix(\lambda c'.\ choose\ (\mathbf{B}[\![B]\!]e)\ (\mathbf{C}[\![C]\!]e\ c')\ c)$

where $choose$: $(Store \rightarrow Tr) \rightarrow Cmdcont \rightarrow Cmdcont \rightarrow Cmdcont$

$choose\ b\ c_1\ c_2 = \lambda s.\,(b\ s) \rightarrow (c_1\ s)\ []\ (c_2\ s)$

The continuation argument *c* represents the "remainder of the program" in each of the clauses. The **while**-loop equation is now a least fixed point over the continuation argument rather than the store, for the loop problem is stated as "how does the remainder of the program appear if the **while**-loop can reappear in it an unbounded number of times?" Comparing this equation with the one defined using the control stack will make things clear.

Figure 9.1 shows a program and its continuation semantics. The nested continuation resembles a form of left-to-right function composition that can be overridden when an extraordinary condition (e.g., a **stop** command) occurs. Herein lies the utility of continuations, for normal function composition could not be overidden in a direct semantics definition.

The abstractions in the semantic equations are all nonstrict. The continuations eliminate the need for strict abstractions on the store arguments. You can see the reason in the definition for the **while**-loop: the value of $(\mathbf{C}[\![\mathbf{while}\ B\ \mathbf{do}\ C]\!]e\ c\ s)$ is undefined, iff all finite expansions of the loop map *s* to undefined, iff *c* is not applied to any store in any finite expansion. The remainder of the program (that is, *c*) is never reached when a "loop forever" situation is encountered. A semantic equation $\mathbf{C}[\![C]\!] = \lambda c.\lambda s.\ c(\cdots s \cdots)$ defines a construct $[\![C]\!]$ that is guaranteed to terminate, for *c* is applied to the updated store. An equation $\mathbf{C}[\![C]\!] = \lambda c.\lambda s.\,(\cdots)\,c\,s$ defines a construct whose termination is not guaranteed, so both *c* and *s* are carried along for use by $(\cdots)$.

Since a continuation represents a program's complete computation upon a store, the continuation may contain some final "cleaning up" instructions that produce a final output. For example, the *finish* continuation used in Figure 9.1 might also be defined as *finish* = ($\lambda s.$ "*done*"), which would make all the command continuations into mappings from stores to character strings. The general form of the command continuation domain is:

$c \in Cmdcont = Store \rightarrow Answer$

where *Answer* can be the domain of stores, output buffers, messages, or whatever. This generalization makes continuations especially suitable for handling unusual outputs.

Figure 9.1

Let $C_0 = C_1;C_2;\mathbf{stop};C_1$
$C_1 = X{:=}1$
$C_2 = \mathbf{while}\ X{>}0\ \mathbf{do}\ C_3$
$C_3 = X{:=}X-1$

$\mathbf{C}[\![C_0]\!]e_1\ \mathit{finish}\ s_1$

where $e_1 = (\mathit{updateenv}\ [\![X]\!]\ l_0\ e_0)$
and $\mathit{finish} = (\lambda s.\, s)$

$\downarrow$

$\mathbf{C}[\![C_1]\!]e_1\ (\mathbf{C}[\![C_2;\mathbf{stop};C_1]\!]e_1\ \mathit{finish})\ s_1$

$\downarrow$

$(\lambda c.\lambda s.\, c\,(\mathit{update}\,(\mathit{accessenv}\ [\![X]\!]\ e_1)\ (\mathbf{E}[\![1]\!]e_1\ s)\ s))\ (\mathbf{C}[\![C_2;\mathbf{stop};C_1]\!]e_1\ \mathit{finish})\ s_1$

$\downarrow$

$(\mathbf{C}[\![C_2]\!]e_1\ (\mathbf{C}[\![\mathbf{stop};C_1]\!]e_1\ \mathit{finish}))\ \underbrace{(\mathit{update}\ l_0\ \mathit{one}\ s_1)}_{s_2}$

$\downarrow$

$\mathit{fix}\,F\ s_2$

where $F = \lambda c'.\mathit{choose}\,(\mathbf{B}[\![X{>}0]\!]e_1)\ (\mathbf{C}[\![C_3]\!]e_1\ c')\ c_1$
where $c_1 = \mathbf{C}[\![\mathbf{stop};C_1]\!]e_1\ \mathit{finish}$

$\downarrow$

$(\mathbf{B}[\![X{>}0]\!]e_1\ s_2) \to (\mathbf{C}[\![C_3]\!]e_1\ (\mathit{fix}\ F)\ s_2)\ []\ (c_1\ s_2)$

$\downarrow$

$\mathbf{C}[\![C_3]\!]e_1\ (\mathit{fix}\ F)\ s_2$

$\downarrow$

$(\mathit{fix}\ F)\ \underbrace{(\mathit{update}\ l_0\ \mathit{zero}\ s_2)}_{s_3}$

$\downarrow$

$(\mathbf{B}[\![X{>}0]\!]e_1\ s_3) \to (\mathbf{C}[\![C_3]\!]e_1\ (\mathit{fix}\ F)\ s_3)\ []\ (c_1\ s_3)$

$\downarrow$

$(c_1\ s_3)$

$\downarrow$

$\mathbf{C}[\![\mathbf{stop}]\!]e_1\ (\mathbf{C}[\![C_1]\!]e_1\ \mathit{finish})\ s_3$

$\downarrow$

s_3

9.1.1 Other Levels of Continuations

The semantic equations defined in the previous section show that the command valuation function can be written in continuation style and coexist with other valuation functions written in the direct style. Nonetheless, let's consider representing the valuation function for expressions in the continuation style. Recall that E: Expression → *Environment* → *Store* → *Expressible-value* is the functionality of the valuation function. In continuation form, expression evaluation breaks into explicit steps. In terms of the control stack analogy, an *expression continuation* resembles a stack of evaluation steps for computing the value of an expression. Expression continuations for some expressions will create intermediate values that must be saved along the way. This suggests:

$k \in \mathit{Exprcont} = \mathit{Expressible\text{-}value} \to \mathit{Store} \to \mathit{Answer}'$

The expressible value argument to an expression continuation is the intermediate value of the partially evaluated expression. The *Answer'* domain will be considered shortly.

The semantic equations for some of the expression constructs read as follows:

$$\begin{aligned}
&\mathbf{E}\colon \text{Expression} \to \mathit{Environment} \to \mathit{Exprcont} \to \mathit{Store} \to \mathit{Answer}' \\
&\mathbf{E}[\![\mathrm{E}_1{+}\mathrm{E}_2]\!] = \lambda e.\lambda k.\, \mathbf{E}[\![\mathrm{E}_1]\!]e\, (\lambda n_1.\, \mathbf{E}[\![\mathrm{E}_2]\!]e\, (\lambda n_2.\, k(n_1\ \mathit{plus}\ n_2))) \\
&\mathbf{E}[\![\mathrm{I}]\!] = \lambda e.\lambda k.\lambda s.\, k(\mathit{access}\,(\mathit{accessenv}\,[\![\mathrm{I}]\!]\, e)\, s)\, s \\
&\mathbf{E}[\![\mathrm{N}]\!] = \lambda e.\lambda k.\, k(\mathbf{N}[\![\mathrm{N}]\!])
\end{aligned}$$

Notice how the steps in the addition expression are spelled out by the nested continuation: $[\![\mathrm{E}_1]\!]$ evaluates and binds to n_1; $[\![\mathrm{E}_2]\!]$ evaluates and binds to n_2; and k, the subsequent evaluation, carries on with $(n_1\ \mathit{plus}\ n_2)$.

How do the expression continuations integrate with the command continuations? The answer is tied to the structure of *Answer'*. If the ultimate answer of an expression is the value of the expression, that is, *Answer'* = *Expressible-value*, then two different levels of control result: expression level control and command level control. The interface between the two is a bit awkward:

$$\begin{aligned}
&\mathbf{C}[\![\mathrm{I}{:=}\mathrm{E}]\!] = \lambda e.\,\lambda c.\,\lambda s.\, c(\mathit{update}\,(\mathit{accessenv}\,[\![\mathrm{I}]\!]\, e)\,(\mathbf{E}[\![\mathrm{E}]\!]e\, \mathit{fin}\ s)\, s) \\
&\qquad \text{where } \mathit{fin} \in \mathit{Exprcont} \ \text{ is } \mathit{fin} = \lambda n.\lambda s.\, n
\end{aligned}$$

If *Answer'* = *Answer*, then the two levels of control integrate nicely:

$$\mathbf{C}[\![\mathrm{I}{:=}\mathrm{E}]\!] = \lambda e.\lambda c.\lambda s.\, \mathbf{E}[\![\mathrm{E}]\!]e\, (\lambda n.\lambda s'.\, c(\mathit{update}\,(\mathit{accessenv}\,[\![\mathrm{I}]\!]\, e)\, n\, s'))\, s$$

Now *Exprcont* = *Expressible-value* → *Cmdcont*, which makes clear that the purpose of a series of expression evaluation steps is to produce a value and return back to the level of command control. In an implementation, the code for evaluating expressions exists on the same control stack as the code for evaluating commands.

In a similar fashion, continuations can be introduced into the other evaluation functions of a language. Even the operations of the semantic algebras can be converted. As an example, a completely sequentialized version of assignment reads:

$$\mathbf{C}[\![\mathrm{I}{:=}\mathrm{E}]\!] = \lambda e.\lambda c.\ accessenv'\ [\![\mathrm{I}]\!]\, e\ (\lambda l.\ \mathbf{E}[\![\mathrm{E}]\!] e\ (\lambda n.\ update'\ l\ n\ c))$$

where

$accessenv'$: Identifier $\rightarrow$ *Environment* $\rightarrow$ (*Location* $\rightarrow$ *Cmdcont*) $\rightarrow$ *Cmdcont*

$accessenv' = \lambda i.\lambda e.\lambda m.\ m(e(i))$

and $update'$: *Location* $\rightarrow$ *Expressible-value* $\rightarrow$ *Cmdcont* $\rightarrow$ *Cmdcont*

$update' = \lambda l.\lambda n.\lambda c.\lambda s.\ c([\, l \mapsto n\,]s)$

An assignment statement determines its left-hand-side value first, then its right-hand-side value, and then the update.

Figure 9.5 shows a complete imperative language using command and expression continuations.

9.2 EXCEPTION MECHANISMS

We can use continuations to develop exception-handling mechanisms. An *exception handler* is a procedure that is invoked when an extraordinary situation occurs that cannot be handled by the usual order of evaluation. Control transfers to the handler procedure, which adjusts the state so that computation may resume. Exception handlers of various forms can be found in PL/1, ML, CLU, Ada, Scheme, and many other languages.

On the invocation of an exception handler, the continuation that owns the store surrenders the store to the handler, which is also a continuation. The handler repairs the store and relinquishes control to a continuation representing some remainder of the computation. Figure 9.2 presents a simple version that meshes with the language in Section 9.1.

An exception is signaled by [[**raise** I]], which discards the existing continuation and extracts the continuation for [[I]] from the environment. The handler [[**on** I **do** C]] applies its body to the store and yields control to the continuation that represents the commands following the enclosing **begin**-**end** block.

It is disconcerting that the continuation c in the configuration (**C**[[**raise** I]]$e\ c\ s$) is discarded. It suggests that the complete plan of evaluation is abandoned when an exception handler is invoked. Actually, this is not true: the continuation assigned to the handler "overlaps" the one that was discarded; the commands following the current active block are evaluated as planned. You are left with the exercise of revising the definition so that this property is explicit.

Figure 9.2

Abstract syntax:

D ∈ Declaration
C ∈ Command
I ∈ Identifier

D ::= D_1;D_2 | · · · | **on** I **do** C
C ::= **begin** D;C **end** | · · · | **raise** I

Semantic algebras:

I. Program outputs
Domain $Answer = (Store + String)_\perp$

II. Command continuations
Domain $c \in Cmdcont = Store \to Answer$
Operations
$fin : Cmdcont$
$fin = \lambda s.\ \text{in}Store(s)$

$err : Cmdcont$
$err = \lambda s.\ \text{in}String(\text{"error"})$

III. Denotable values
Domain $Denotable\text{-}value = Cmdcont + Nat + \cdots$

IV. Environments
Domain $e \in Environment = \text{Identifier} \to Denotable\text{-}value$
Operations (usual)

Valuation functions:

D: Declaration $\to Environment \to Cmdcont \to Environment$

$\mathbf{D}[\![D_1;D_2]\!] = \lambda e.\lambda c.\ \mathbf{D}[\![D_2]\!]\ (\mathbf{D}[\![D_1]\!]e\ c)\ c$

$\mathbf{D}[\![\textbf{on}\ \text{I}\ \textbf{do}\ \text{C}]\!] = \lambda e.\lambda c.\ update\ [\![\text{I}]\!]\ \ \text{in}Cmdcont(\mathbf{C}[\![\text{C}]\!]e\ c)\ \ e$

C: Command $\to Environment \to Cmdcont \to Cmdcont$

$\mathbf{C}[\![\textbf{begin}\ \text{D;C}\ \textbf{end}]\!] = \lambda e.\lambda c.\ \mathbf{C}[\![\text{C}]\!]\ (\mathbf{D}[\![\text{D}]\!]e\ c)\ c$

$\mathbf{C}[\![\textbf{raise}\ \text{I}]\!] = \lambda e.\lambda c.\ \text{cases}\ (accessenv\ [\![\text{I}]\!]\ e)\ \text{of}$
$\quad \text{is}Cmdcont(c) \to c$
$\quad [\,]\ \text{is}Nat(n) \to err$
$\quad [\,]\ \cdots\ \text{end}$

9.3 BACKTRACKING MECHANISMS

A useful variant of exception handling is the "undoing" of evaluation steps back to a configuration that is "safe." This version of exception handling is called *backtracking*. Backtracking is an integral feature of programming languages designed for heuristic problem-solving: if a problem solving strategy fails, a backtrack is taken to a configuration that allows an alternative strategy to be applied. These "strategies" are continuations.

We integrate a backtracking facility into a language by using a *failure continuation*. The continuation representing the usual evaluation sequence is called the *success continuation*. The failure continuation is invoked when backtracking is needed. Maintenance of the failure continuation is done by certain constructs in the language: exception-handler definitions, choice constructs, cut points, and so on. Figure 9.3 presents a programming language that resembles a propositional version of PROLOG.

The success continuation is built from the subgoals in the conjunctive construct $[\![C_1,C_2]\!]$. The failure continuation is updated by the choice construct $[\![C_1$ **or** $C_2]\!]$, which chooses the strategy indicated by goal $[\![C_1]\!]$ and saves alternative strategy $[\![C_2]\!]$ in the failure continuation; and by the break point construct [[**cut**]], which disallows backtracking past the point marked by the break point. The success continuation is applied when an endpoint [[**succeedwith** F]] is encountered, and the store is updated about the achievement. Similarly, the

Figure 9.3

Abstract syntax:

P∈ Program
D∈ Declaration
C∈ Command
I ∈ Identifier
F∈ Primitive-operator

P ::= D. ?C

D ::= D_1.D_2 | I ←C

C ::= C_1,C_2 | C_1 **or** C_2 | I | **succeedwith** F | **fail** | **cut**

Semantic algebras:

I. Program outputs
Domain *Answer* = *Store* + *String*

II. Stores
Domain *s* ∈ *Store*

Figure 9.3 (continued)

III. Continuations

Domain $c \in$ *Cmdcont* = *Store* → *Answer*

$fc \in$ *Failure-cont* = *Cmdcont*

$sc \in$ *Success-cont* = *Failure-cont* → *Cmdcont*

Operations

succeeded : *Success-cont*

succeeded = $\lambda fc.\lambda s.$ in*Store*(s)

failed : *Failure-cont*

failed = $\lambda s.$ in*String*("failure")

IV. Evaluation strategies

Domain *Strategy* = *Success-cont* → *Failure-cont* → *Cmdcont*

V. Environments

Domain $e \in$ *Environment* = Identifier → *Strategy*

Operations

emptyenv : *Environment*

emptyenv = $\lambda i.\,(\lambda sc.\lambda fc.\,fc)$

accessenv : Identifier → *Environment* → *Strategy* (usual)

updateenv : Identifier → *Strategy* → *Environment* → *Environment* (usual)

Valuation functions:

P: Program → *Cmdcont*

$\mathbf{P}[\![\mathrm{D.\ ?C}]\!] = \mathbf{C}[\![\mathrm{C}]\!]\,(\mathbf{D}[\![\mathrm{D}]\!]\,emptyenv)\ succeeded\ failed$

D: Declaration → *Environment* → *Environment*

$\mathbf{D}[\![\mathrm{D}_1.\mathrm{D}_2]\!] = \mathbf{D}[\![\mathrm{D}_2]\!] \circ \mathbf{D}[\![\mathrm{D}_1]\!]$

$\mathbf{D}[\![\mathrm{I} \leftarrow \mathrm{C}]\!] = \lambda e.\ updateenv\,[\![\mathrm{I}]\!]\,(\mathbf{C}[\![\mathrm{C}]\!]e)\,e$

C: Command → *Environment* → *Strategy*

$\mathbf{C}[\![\mathrm{C}_1,\mathrm{C}_2]\!] = \lambda e.\lambda sc.\ \mathbf{C}[\![\mathrm{C}_1]\!]e\,(\mathbf{C}[\![\mathrm{C}_2]\!]e\,sc)$

$\mathbf{C}[\![\mathrm{C}_1 \text{ or } \mathrm{C}_2]\!] = \lambda e.\lambda sc.\lambda fc.\lambda s.\ \mathbf{C}[\![\mathrm{C}_1]\!]e\ sc\,(\lambda s'.\,\mathbf{C}[\![\mathrm{C}_2]\!]e\ sc\ fc\ s)\ s$

$\mathbf{C}[\![\mathrm{I}]\!] = accessenv\ [\![\mathrm{I}]\!]$

$\mathbf{C}[\![\textbf{succeedwith}\ \mathrm{F}]\!] = \lambda e.\lambda sc.\lambda fc.\ \lambda s.\ sc\ fc\ (\mathbf{F}[\![\mathrm{F}]\!]s)$

$\mathbf{C}[\![\textbf{fail}]\!] = \lambda e.\lambda sc.\lambda fc.\ fc$

$\mathbf{C}[\![\textbf{cut}]\!] = \lambda e.\lambda sc.\lambda fc.\ sc\ failed$

F: Primitive-operator → *Store* → *Store* (omitted)

failure continuation is applied when a [[**fail**]] construct is encountered. The **or** construct saves the store in its failure continuation so that the updates done in an unsuccessful strategy are undone. This treatment of the store violates the usual "sequentiality" of store processing, and you are left with the exercise of finding an alternative semantics that is "sequential."

9.4 COROUTINE MECHANISMS

Section 9.3 generalized from using one continuation to two; now we generalize to a family of them. A system of continuations that activate one another can be used to design a *coroutine system.* Unlike a subroutine, a coroutine need not complete all the steps in its continuation before relinquishing control to another. A program configuration carries along a collection of partially completed continuations, representing the coroutines in the system. Let us call this collection a *coroutine environment*. When a coroutine is invoked, the current active continuation is saved in the coroutine environment. The invoked continuation is selected from the coroutine environment and placed in control of the configuration.

A language supporting coroutines is presented in Figure 9.4.

In addition to the usual command continuation domain and the newly introduced coroutine environment domain, a domain of coroutine continuations is needed to handle the coroutine environment. The *resume* operation invokes a coroutine by storing the current coroutine continuation and extracting the invoked one. The identifier carried in the coroutine environment is set to the name of the coroutine now in control of the configuration.

9.5 UNRESTRICTED BRANCHING MECHANISMS

We can generalize the coroutine mechanism so that it does not save the continuation of the calling coroutine when another coroutine is invoked. This creates the form of branching known as the **goto.** Without the promise to resume a coroutine at its point of release, the domain of coroutine environments becomes unnecessary, and the coroutine continuation domain becomes the command continuation domain. From here on, we speak not of coroutines, but of labeled commands; the [[**resume** I]] command is now [[**goto** I]].

The continuation associated with a label is kept in the usual environment, which is a static object (unlike the coroutine environment), because the command continuation associated with a label is determined by the label's textual position in the program. We handle a branch by placing the continuation associated with the destination label in control: $\mathbf{C}[\![\mathbf{goto}\ \mathrm{I}]\!] = \lambda e.\lambda c.\, accessenv\, [\![\mathrm{I}]\!]\, e$.

Figure 9.4

Abstract syntax:

B∈ Block
D∈ Declaration
C∈ Command
I ∈ Identifier

B ::= D; **initiate** I
D ::= D_1;D_2 | **coroutine** I=C
C ::= C_1;C_2 | **resume** I | I:=E

Semantic algebras:

I. Command continuations
Domain *Cmdcont* = *Store* → $Answer_\perp$

II. Coroutine continuations and the environments holding them
Domains $c \in$ *Coroutine-cont* = *Coroutine-env* → *Cmdcont*
$e \in$ *Coroutine-env* = $(($Identifier → *Coroutine-cont*$) \times$ Identifier$)_\perp$

Operations

quit : *Coroutine-cont*

err : *Coroutine-cont*

empty-env : Identifier→*Coroutine-env*
empty-env = $\lambda i. ((\lambda i'. err), i)$

initialize : Identifier →*Coroutine-cont* →*Coroutine-env* →*Coroutine-env*
initialize = $\lambda i.\lambda c.\lambda e.$ let $(map, caller) = e$ in $([\, i \mapsto c\,]map, caller)$

resume : Identifier →*Coroutine-cont* →*Coroutine-env* →*Cmdcont*
resume = $\lambda i.\lambda c.\lambda e.$ let $(map, caller) = e$ in
let $map' = [\, caller \mapsto c\,]map$
in $(map'\ i)\ (map', i)$

Valuation functions:

B: Block →*Cmdcont*

B⟦D; **initiate** I⟧ = *resume* ⟦I⟧ *quit* (**D**⟦D⟧(*empty-env* ⟦I⟧))

D: Declaration →*Coroutine-env* →*Coroutine-env*

D⟦D_1;D_2⟧ = **D**⟦D_2⟧ ∘ **D**⟦D_1⟧

D⟦**coroutine** I=C⟧ = *initialize* ⟦I⟧ (**C**⟦C⟧ *quit*)

C: Command →*Coroutine-cont* →*Coroutine-env* →*Cmdcont*

C⟦C_1;C_2⟧ = **C**⟦C_1⟧ ∘ **C**⟦C_2⟧

C⟦**resume** I⟧ = *resume* ⟦I⟧

C⟦I:=E⟧ = $\lambda c.\lambda e.\lambda s.\ c\ e\ (update$ ⟦I⟧ $($**E**⟦E⟧$s)\ s)$

Figure 9.5 presents a definition for a language with unrestricted branches.

So far we have ignored mutual recursion in invocations, but we must now confront the issue if backwards branches are to be allowed. What does a branch continuation look like? Since continuations model the remainder of a program, a continuation for a label $[\![\mathrm{I}]\!]$ must not only contain the denotation for the one command labeled by $[\![\mathrm{I}]\!]$, but the denotation of the remainder of the program that follows $[\![\mathrm{I}]\!]$: if $[\![\mathrm{I}]\!]$ labels command $[\![\mathrm{C}_i]\!]$, the continuation c_i associated with $[\![\mathrm{I}]\!]$ is $(\mathbf{C}[\![\mathrm{C}_i]\!]e\, c_{i+1})$, where c_{i+1} is the continuation for the commands that follow $[\![\mathrm{C}_i]\!]$.

Now consider a block with n distinct labels: $[\![\textbf{begin}\ \mathrm{D};\ \mathrm{I}_1{:}\mathrm{C}_1;\ \mathrm{I}_2{:}\mathrm{C}_2; \cdots \mathrm{I}_n{:}\mathrm{C}_n\ \textbf{end}]\!]$. The continuations are:

$$
\begin{aligned}
c_1 &= (\mathbf{C}[\![\mathrm{C}_1]\!]e'\, c_2)\\
c_2 &= (\mathbf{C}[\![\mathrm{C}_2]\!]e'\, c_3)\\
&\cdots\\
c_{n-1} &= (\mathbf{C}[\![\mathrm{C}_{n-1}]\!]e'\, c_n)\\
c_n &= (\mathbf{C}[\![\mathrm{C}_n]\!]e'\, c)
\end{aligned}
$$

$$
\begin{aligned}
\text{where } e' = {} & (\mathit{updateenv}\, [\![\mathrm{I}_1]\!]\ \mathrm{in}\mathit{Cmdcont}(c_1)\\
& \quad (\mathit{updateenv}\, [\![\mathrm{I}_2]\!]\ \mathrm{in}\mathit{Cmdcont}(c_2)\\
& \qquad \cdots\\
& \qquad\quad (\mathit{updateenv}\, [\![\mathrm{I}_n]\!]\ \mathrm{in}\mathit{Cmdcont}(c_n)\, (\mathbf{D}[\![\mathrm{D}]\!]e)) \cdots))
\end{aligned}
$$

Each c_i possesses the environment that contains the denotations of all the labels. But to define the environment, each c_i must be defined. The mutual recursion is resolved by the *fix* operation. The least fixed point is an n-tuple of continuations, one for each label. The denotation of the entire block is the continuation associated with the first label.

You are encouraged to construct example programs and determine their denotations. A program for computing the factorial function is given a denotation in Figure 9.6. (Assume that semantic equations $\mathbf{E}[\![\mathrm{E}_1 * \mathrm{E}_2]\!]$ and $\mathbf{E}[\![\mathrm{E}_1 - \mathrm{E}_2]\!]$ for multiplication and subtraction are added to the language. The equations have the same format as the one for addition, using operations *mult* and *sub* respectively instead of *add*.) The denotation in Figure 9.6 is simplified to the stage where all abstract syntax pieces and environment arguments have been written away. The denotation of the factorial program is the first component of the least fixed point of a functional; the functional maps a triple of command continuations to a triple of command continuations. Examining the functional's body, we see that component number i of the triple is the denotation of the commands labeled by identifier Li in the program. A jump to label Lk has the denotation $(\mathit{ctuple}{\downarrow}k)$. Each component of the tuple is a deeply nested continuation whose actions upon the store can be read from left to right. The actions are low level and resemble conventional assembly language instructions. This feature is exploited in the next chapter.

Figure 9.5

Abstract syntax:

P∈ Program
B∈ Block
D∈ Declaration
C∈ Command
E∈ Expression
I ∈ Identifier
N∈ Numeral

P ::= B.
B ::= **begin** D; I_1:C_1; I_2:C_2; · · · ; I_n :C_n **end**
D ::= D_1;D_2 | **const** I=E | **var** I
C ::= C_1;C_2 | I:=E | **if** E **then** C_1 **else** C_2 | **while** E **do** C | B | **goto** I
E ::= E_1+E_2 | I | N | **do** C **resultis** E | (E)

Semantic algebras:

I.-V. Natural numbers, truth values, locations, identifiers, and character strings (as usual)

VI. Semantic outputs
Domain $a \in$ *Answer* = $(OK + Err)_\perp$
where *OK* = *Store* and *Err* = *String*

VII.-IX. Expressible, denotable, and storable values
Domains $n \in$ *Exprval* = *Storable-value* = *Nat*
$d \in$ *Denotable-value* = *Nat* + *Location* + *Cmdcont* + *Errvalue*
where *Errvalue* = *Unit*

X. Environments
Domain $e \in$ *Environment* = (Identifier → *Denotable-value*) × *Location*
Operations
(defined in Figure 7.1)

XI. Stores
Domain $s \in$ *Store* = *Location* → *Storable-value*
Operations
(defined in Figure 7.1)

XII. Command continuations
Domain $c \in$ *Cmdcont* = *Store* → *Answer*

Figure 9.5 (continued)

Operations

$finish : Cmdcont$

$finish = \lambda s.\ \text{in}OK(s)$

$error : String \rightarrow Cmdcont$

$error = \lambda t.\lambda s.\ \text{in}Err(t)$

XIII. Expression continuations

Domain $k \in Exprcont = Exprval \rightarrow Cmdcont$

Operations

$return\text{-}value : Exprval \rightarrow Exprcont \rightarrow Cmdcont$

$return\text{-}value = \lambda n.\lambda k.\ k(n)$

$save\text{-}arg = (Exprcont \rightarrow Cmdcont) \rightarrow (Exprval \rightarrow Exprcont) \rightarrow Exprcont$

$save\text{-}arg = \lambda f.\lambda g.\lambda n.\ f(g\,n)$

$add : Exprcont \rightarrow Exprval \rightarrow Exprval \rightarrow Cmdcont$

$add = \lambda k.\lambda n_1.\lambda n_2.\ k(n_1\ plus\ n_2)$

$fetch : Location \rightarrow Exprcont \rightarrow Cmdcont$

$fetch = \lambda l.\lambda k.\lambda s.\ k(access\ l\ s)\ s$

$assign : Location \rightarrow Cmdcont \rightarrow Exprcont$

$assign = \lambda l.\lambda c.\lambda n.\lambda s.\ c(update\ l\ n\ s)$

$choose : Cmdcont \rightarrow Cmdcont \rightarrow Exprcont$

$choose = \lambda c_1.\lambda c_2.\lambda n.\ n\ greaterthan\ zero \rightarrow c_1\ []\ c_2$

Valuation functions:

P: Program $\rightarrow$ *Location* $\rightarrow$ *Cmdcont*

$\mathbf{P}[\![B.]\!] = \lambda l.\ \mathbf{B}[\![B]\!]\ (emptyenv\ l)\ finish$

B: Block $\rightarrow$ *Environment* $\rightarrow$ *Cmdcont* $\rightarrow$ *Cmdcont*

$\mathbf{B}[\![\mathbf{begin}\ D; I_1{:}C_1; I_2{:}C_2; \cdots; I_n{:}C_n\ \mathbf{end}]\!] =$

$$\begin{aligned}\lambda e.\lambda c.\ (fix(\lambda ctuple.\ (\ &(\mathbf{C}[\![C_1]\!]e'\ (ctuple\downarrow 2)),\\ &(\mathbf{C}[\![C_2]\!]e'\ (ctuple\downarrow 3)),\\ &\cdots,\\ &(\mathbf{C}[\![C_n]\!]e'\ c)\ )\ ))\downarrow 1\end{aligned}$$

where $e' = (updateenv\ [\![I_1]\!]\ \text{in}Cmdcont(ctuple\downarrow 1)$

$(updateenv\ [\![I_2]\!]\ \text{in}Cmdcont(ctuple\downarrow 2)$

$\cdots$

$(updateenv\ [\![I_n]\!]\ \text{in}Cmdcont(ctuple\downarrow n)\ (\mathbf{D}[\![D]\!]e))\cdots))$

Figure 9.5 (continued)

D: Declaration → *Environment* → *Environment*
  (defined in Figure 7.2)

C: Command → *Environment* → *Cmdcont* → *Cmdcont*

$\mathbf{C}[\![C_1;C_2]\!] = \lambda e.\, \mathbf{C}[\![C_1]\!]e \circ \mathbf{C}[\![C_2]\!]e$

$\mathbf{C}[\![I{:=}E]\!] = \lambda e.\lambda c.$ cases $(accessenv\ [\![I]\!]\ e)$ of
  is*Nat*$(n) \to error$ "const used on lhs"
  [] is*Location*$(l) \to \mathbf{E}[\![E]\!]e\,(assign\ l\ c)$
  [] is*Cmdcont*$(c) \to error$ "label used on lhs"
  [] is*Errvalue*$() \to error$ "lhs undeclared"
  end

$\mathbf{C}[\![\textbf{if } E \textbf{ then } C_1 \textbf{ else } C_2]\!] = \lambda e.\lambda c.\, \mathbf{E}[\![E]\!]e\ (choose\ (\mathbf{C}[\![C_1]\!]e\,c)\ (\mathbf{C}[\![C_2]\!]e\,c))$

$\mathbf{C}[\![\textbf{while } E \textbf{ do } C]\!] = \lambda e.\lambda c.\, fix(\lambda c'.\, \mathbf{E}[\![E]\!]e\ (choose\ (\mathbf{C}[\![C]\!]e\,c')\ c))$

$\mathbf{C}[\![B]\!] = \mathbf{B}[\![B]\!]$

$\mathbf{C}[\![\textbf{goto } I]\!] = \lambda e.\lambda c.$ cases $(accessenv\ [\![I]\!]\ e)$ of
  is*Nat*$(n) \to error$ "const used as label"
  [] is*Location*$(l) \to error$ "var used as label"
  [] is*Cmdcont*$(c') \to c'$
  [] is*Errvalue*$() \to error$ "unknown id"
  end

E: Expression → *Environment* → *Exprcont* → *Cmdcont*

$\mathbf{E}[\![E_1{+}E_2]\!] = \lambda e.\lambda k.\, \mathbf{E}[\![E_1]\!]e\ (save\text{-}arg\ (\mathbf{E}[\![E_2]\!]e)\ (add\ k))$

$\mathbf{E}[\![I]\!] = \lambda e.\lambda k.$ cases $(accessenv\ [\![I]\!]\ e)$ of
  is*Nat*$(n) \to return\text{-}value\ n\ k$
  [] is*Location*$(l) \to fetch\ l\ k$
  [] is*Cmdcont*$(c) \to error$ "label used in expr"
  [] is*Errvalue*$() \to error$ "undeclared iden"
  end

$\mathbf{E}[\![N]\!] = \lambda e.\lambda k.\, return\text{-}value\ (\mathbf{N}[\![N]\!])\ k$

$\mathbf{E}[\![\textbf{do } C \textbf{ resultis } E]\!] = \lambda e.\lambda k.\, \mathbf{C}[\![C]\!]e\ (\mathbf{E}[\![E]\!]e\ k)$

$\mathbf{E}[\![(E)]\!] = \mathbf{E}[\![E]\!]$

N: Numeral → *Nat* (omitted)

Figure 9.6

```
P[[begin const A=a ; var X; var TOTAL; var FAC;
    L1: X:=A; TOTAL:=1; goto L2;
    L2: while X do (TOTAL:=TOTAL*X; X:=X-1);
    L3: FAC:=TOTAL
    end.]] =

λl. (fix(λctuple.
    ( return-value a
        ( assign l
          ( return-value one
            ( assign next-locn(l)
              ( ctuple↓2) )))),
    fix(λc'. ( fetch l
        ( choose
            ( fetch next-locn(l)
              (save-arg (fetch l)
                ( mult
                  ( assign next-locn(l)
                    ( fetch l
                      ( save-arg (return-value one)
                        ( sub
                          ( assign l
                            c' ))))))))
            (ctuple↓3) ))),
    ( fetch next-locn(l)
        ( assign (next-locn(next-locn(l)))
          finish ))
    ) ) ↓1
```

9.6 THE RELATIONSHIP BETWEEN DIRECT AND CONTINUATION SEMANTICS

A question of interest is the exact relationship between a language's direct semantics definition and its continuation semantics definition. We would like to prove that the two definitions map the same program to equal denotations. But, since the internal structures of the semantics definitions are so dissimilar, the proof can be quite difficult. A related question is whether or not we can derive a continuation semantics definition for a language from its direct semantics definition. Both questions are studied in the following example.

Let $\mathbf{C}_D$: Command $\rightarrow Store_{\perp} \rightarrow Store_{\perp}$ be a valuation function written in direct semantics style. Say that we desire a valuation function $\mathbf{C}_C$: Command $\rightarrow Cmdcont \rightarrow Cmdcont$, $Cmdcont = Store_\perp \rightarrow Store_\perp$, in continuation style such that $\mathbf{C}_D$ is equivalent to $\mathbf{C}_C$. The equivalence can be stated as $\mathbf{C}_D\llbracket \mathrm{C} \rrbracket = \mathbf{C}_C\llbracket \mathrm{C} \rrbracket(\lambda s.\, s)$. But this property will be difficult to prove by induction. Recall that in Section 9.1 we saw the format $\mathbf{C}_C\llbracket \mathrm{C} \rrbracket = \lambda c.\lambda s.\, c(f(s))$ for a terminating command $\llbracket \mathrm{C} \rrbracket$ that performs f to the store. Since $\mathbf{C}_D\llbracket \mathrm{C} \rrbracket$ describes $\llbracket \mathrm{C} \rrbracket$'s actions in isolation, the equality:

$$\mathbf{C}_C\llbracket \mathrm{C} \rrbracket c\, s = c(\mathbf{C}_D\llbracket \mathrm{C} \rrbracket s)$$

holds. This equality generalizes the earlier definition of equivalence; it is called a *congruence*, and two definitions that satisfy a congruence are called *congruent*.

What about a command that might not terminate? Then $\mathbf{C}_D\llbracket \mathrm{C} \rrbracket s$ might be $\perp$, so what should $\mathbf{C}_C\llbracket \mathrm{C} \rrbracket c\, s$ be? If we require *strict* continuations, then the congruence still holds: $\mathbf{C}_C\llbracket \mathrm{C} \rrbracket c\, s = c(\mathbf{C}_D\llbracket \mathrm{C} \rrbracket s) = c(\perp) = \perp$. Sethi and Tang (1980) suggest that a continuation semantics for a simple language be derived from its direct semantics definition by *defining* $\mathbf{C}_C\llbracket \mathrm{C} \rrbracket c\, s = c(\mathbf{C}_D\llbracket \mathrm{C} \rrbracket s)$ for each construct $\llbracket \mathrm{C} \rrbracket$ in the language. We then apply an inductive hypothesis to simplify $c(\mathbf{C}_D\llbracket \mathrm{C} \rrbracket s)$ into a more satisfactory form. Some derivations follow.

First, for $\mathbf{C}_D\llbracket \mathrm{C}_1;\mathrm{C}_2 \rrbracket = \underline{\lambda} s.\, \mathbf{C}_D\llbracket \mathrm{C}_2 \rrbracket(\mathbf{C}_D\llbracket \mathrm{C}_1 \rrbracket s)$, define:

$$\begin{aligned}&\mathbf{C}_C\llbracket \mathrm{C}_1;\mathrm{C}_2 \rrbracket = \lambda c.\underline{\lambda} s.\, c(\mathbf{C}_D\llbracket \mathrm{C}_1;\mathrm{C}_2 \rrbracket s)\\ &= \lambda c.\underline{\lambda} s.\, c(\mathbf{C}_D\llbracket \mathrm{C}_2 \rrbracket(\mathbf{C}_D\llbracket \mathrm{C}_1 \rrbracket s))\end{aligned}$$

Since $\mathbf{C}_D\llbracket \mathrm{C}_1 \rrbracket s \in Store_\perp$, we can use the inductive hypothesis that $\mathbf{C}_C\llbracket \mathrm{C}_2 \rrbracket c\, s = c(\mathbf{C}_D\llbracket \mathrm{C}_2 \rrbracket s)$ to obtain the value $\lambda c.\underline{\lambda} s.\, \mathbf{C}_C\llbracket \mathrm{C}_2 \rrbracket c\,(\mathbf{C}_D\llbracket \mathrm{C}_1 \rrbracket s)$. But $\mathbf{C}_C\llbracket \mathrm{C}_2 \rrbracket c$ is a command continuation, so we apply the inductive hypothesis for $\llbracket \mathrm{C}_1 \rrbracket$ to obtain $\lambda c.\underline{\lambda} s.\, \mathbf{C}_C\llbracket \mathrm{C}_1 \rrbracket(\mathbf{C}_C\llbracket \mathrm{C}_2 \rrbracket c)\, s$. By extensionality and the inductive hypothesis that $\mathbf{C}_C\llbracket \mathrm{C}_2 \rrbracket$ is strict, we obtain:

$$\mathbf{C}_C\llbracket \mathrm{C}_1;\mathrm{C}_2 \rrbracket = \mathbf{C}_C\llbracket \mathrm{C}_1 \rrbracket \circ \mathbf{C}_C\llbracket \mathrm{C}_2 \rrbracket$$

Second, for $\mathbf{C}_D\llbracket \textbf{if}\ \mathrm{E}\ \textbf{then}\ \mathrm{C}_1\ \textbf{else}\ \mathrm{C}_2 \rrbracket = \underline{\lambda} s.\, \mathbf{B}\llbracket \mathrm{B} \rrbracket s \rightarrow \mathbf{C}_D\llbracket \mathrm{C}_1 \rrbracket s\ [\!]\ \mathbf{C}_D\llbracket \mathrm{C}_2 \rrbracket s$, we define:

$$\begin{aligned}&\mathbf{C}_C\llbracket \textbf{if}\ \mathrm{E}\ \textbf{then}\ \mathrm{C}_1\ \textbf{else}\ \mathrm{C}_2 \rrbracket = \lambda c.\underline{\lambda} s.\, c(\mathbf{C}_D\llbracket \textbf{if}\ \mathrm{E}\ \textbf{then}\ \mathrm{C}_1\ \textbf{else}\ \mathrm{C}_2 \rrbracket s)\\ &= \lambda c.\underline{\lambda} s.\, c(\mathbf{B}\llbracket \mathrm{B} \rrbracket s \rightarrow \mathbf{C}_D\llbracket \mathrm{C}_1 \rrbracket s\ [\!]\ \mathbf{C}_D\llbracket \mathrm{C}_2 \rrbracket s)\end{aligned}$$

$\mathbf{B}\llbracket \mathrm{B} \rrbracket s$ is a defined truth value, so a cases analysis gives the value $\lambda c.\underline{\lambda} s.\, \mathbf{B}\llbracket \mathrm{B} \rrbracket s \rightarrow c(\mathbf{C}_D\llbracket \mathrm{C}_1 \rrbracket s)\ [\!]\ c(\mathbf{C}_D\llbracket \mathrm{C}_2 \rrbracket s)$. By the inductive hypothesis for $\llbracket \mathrm{C}_1 \rrbracket$ and $\llbracket \mathrm{C}_2 \rrbracket$, we obtain:

$$\mathbf{C}_C\llbracket \textbf{if}\ \mathrm{E}\ \textbf{then}\ \mathrm{C}_1\ \textbf{else}\ \mathrm{C}_2 \rrbracket = \lambda c.\underline{\lambda} s.\, \mathbf{B}\llbracket \mathrm{B} \rrbracket s \rightarrow \mathbf{C}_C\llbracket \mathrm{C}_1 \rrbracket c\, s\ [\!]\ \mathbf{C}_C\llbracket \mathrm{C}_2 \rrbracket c\, s$$

Deriving the continuation semantics for a **while**-loop is a bit more involved. For $\mathbf{C}_D\llbracket \textbf{while}\ \mathrm{E}\ \textbf{do}\ \mathrm{C} \rrbracket = fix(\lambda f.\underline{\lambda} s.\, \mathbf{B}\llbracket \mathrm{B} \rrbracket s \rightarrow f(\mathbf{C}_D\llbracket \mathrm{C} \rrbracket s)\ [\!]\ s)$, we define:

$$\mathbf{C}_C\llbracket \textbf{while}\ \mathrm{E}\ \textbf{do}\ \mathrm{C} \rrbracket = \lambda c.\underline{\lambda} s.\, c(\mathbf{C}_D\llbracket \textbf{while}\ \mathrm{E}\ \textbf{do}\ \mathrm{C} \rrbracket s)$$

The presence of *fix* thwarts our attempts at simplification. Let:

$$F_D = \lambda f.\underline{\lambda} s.\, \mathbf{B}[\![\mathrm{B}]\!]s \rightarrow f(\mathbf{C}_D[\![\mathrm{C}]\!]s) \,[\!]\, s$$

We hope to find a corresponding functional F_C such that $(\mathit{fix}\, F_C)c\, s = c((\mathit{fix}\, F_D)s)$. Even though we haven't a clue as to what F_C should be, we begin constructing a fixed point induction proof of this equality and derive F_C as we go. The admissible predicate we use is:

$$P(f_C, f_D) = \text{"for all } c \in \mathit{Cmdcont} \text{ and } s \in \mathit{Store}_\perp,\ (f_C\, c\, s) = c(f_D\, s)\text{"}$$

where $f_C\colon \mathit{Cmdcont} \rightarrow \mathit{Cmdcont}$ and $f_D\colon \mathit{Store}_\perp \rightarrow \mathit{Store}_\perp$.

For the basis step, we have $f_C = (\lambda c.\underline{\lambda} s.\perp)$ and $f_D = (\underline{\lambda} s.\perp)$; the proof follows immediately from strictness. For the inductive step, the inductive hypothesis is $(f_C\, c\, s) = c(f_D\, s)$; we wish to prove that $(F_C f_C)\, c\, s = c((F_D f_D)s)$, deriving F_C in the process. We derive:

$$\begin{aligned}
&c((F_D f_D)s)\\
&= c((\underline{\lambda} s.\, \mathbf{B}[\![\mathrm{B}]\!]s \rightarrow f_D(\mathbf{C}_D[\![\mathrm{C}]\!]s) \,[\!]\, s)s)\\
&= c(\mathbf{B}[\![\mathrm{B}]\!]s \rightarrow f_D(\mathbf{C}_D[\![\mathrm{C}]\!]s) \,[\!]\, s)
\end{aligned}$$

when s is proper. This equals:

$$\begin{aligned}
&\mathbf{B}[\![\mathrm{B}]\!]s \rightarrow c(f_D(\mathbf{C}_D[\![\mathrm{C}]\!]s)) \,[\!]\, (c\, s), \text{ by distributing } c \text{ across the conditional}\\
&= \mathbf{B}[\![\mathrm{B}]\!]s \rightarrow (f_C\, c)(\mathbf{C}_D[\![\mathrm{C}]\!]s) \,[\!]\, (c\, s), \text{ by the inductive hypothesis}\\
&= \mathbf{B}[\![\mathrm{B}]\!]s \rightarrow \mathbf{C}_C[\![\mathrm{C}]\!](f_C\, c)s \,[\!]\, (c\, s)
\end{aligned}$$

by the structural induction hypothesis on $\mathbf{C}_D[\![\mathrm{C}]\!]$, because $(f_C\, c) \in \mathit{Cmdcont}$. If we let:

$$F_C = \lambda g.\lambda c.\underline{\lambda} s.\, \mathbf{B}[\![\mathrm{B}]\!]s \rightarrow \mathbf{C}_C[\![\mathrm{C}]\!](g\, c)\, s \,[\!]\, (c\, s)$$

then we are finished:

$$\mathbf{C}_C[\![\textbf{while}\ \mathrm{E}\ \textbf{do}\ \mathrm{C}]\!] = \mathit{fix}(\lambda g.\lambda c.\underline{\lambda} s.\, \mathbf{B}[\![\mathrm{B}]\!]s \rightarrow \mathbf{C}_C[\![\mathrm{C}]\!](g\, c)\, s \,[\!]\, (c\, s))$$

The definition of **while** used in Figure 9.5 can be proved equal to this one with another fixed point induction proof.

The continuation semantics $\mathbf{C}_C$ is congruent to $\mathbf{C}_D$ because it was defined directly from the congruence predicate. The proof of congruence is just the derivation steps read backwards. Few congruences between semantic definitions are as easy to prove as the one given here. Milne and Strachey (1976), Reynolds (1974b), and Stoy (1981) give examples of nontrivial semantics definitions and proofs of congruence.

SUGGESTED READINGS

Continuations: Abdali 1975; Jensen 1978; Mazurkiewicz 1971; Milne & Strachey 1976; Strachey & Wadsworth 1974; Stoy 1977

Control mechanisms: Bjørner & Jones 1982; Friedman et al. 1984; Jones 1982b; Reynolds 1972; Strachey & Wadsworth 1974

Congruences between definitions: Meyer & Wand 1985; Morris 1973; Milne & Strachey 1976; Royer 1985; Reynolds 1974b; Sethi & Tang 1980; Stoy 1981

EXERCISES

1. Add to the syntax of the language in Figure 7.2 the command **exitblock**, which causes a forward branch to the end of the current block.

   a. Without using continuations, integrate the **exitblock** construct into the semantics with as little fuss as possible. (Hint: adjust the *Poststore* domain and *check* operation.)
   b. Rewrite the semantics in continuation style and handle **exitblock** by discarding the current continuation and replacing it by another.
   c. Repeat parts a and b for an **exitloop** command that causes a branch out of the innermost loop; for a **jump** L command that causes a forward branch to a command labeled by identifier L.

2. Convert the operations in the *Nat*, *Environment*, and *Store* algebras of Figure 7.1 into continuation style.

   a. Modify the *access* operation so that an access of an uninitialized storage cell leads directly to an error message.
   b. Introduce a division operation that handles division by zero with an error message.
   c. Rewrite the semantic equations in Figure 7.2 to use the new algebras.

3. A language's control features can be determined from the continuation domains that it uses.

   a. Propose the forms of branching mechanisms that will likely appear when a semantic definition uses each of the following domains:

      i. *Declaration-cont* = *Environment* → *Cmdcont*
      ii. *Denotable-value-cont* = *Denotable-value* → *Cmdcont*
      iii. *Nat-cont* = *Nat* → *Cmdcont*
      iv. *Location-cont* = *Location* → *Exprcont*

b. A reasonable functionality for the continuation version of natural number addition is *add* : *Nat* → *Nat-cont*. For each of parts i through iv, propose operations that use the continuation domain defined.

4. Newcomers to the continuation semantics method often remark that the denotation of a program appears to be "built backwards."

   a. How does this idea relate to the loading of a control stack prior to interpretation? To the compilation of a program?
   b. Notice that the semantic equations of Figure 9.5 do not mention any *Store*-valued objects. Consider replacing the *Cmdcont* algebra by a version of the *Store* algebra; formulate operations for the domain *Cmdcont* = *Store*. Do programs in the new semantics "compute backwards"?
   c. Jensen (1978) noted a strong resemblance between continuation style semantics and weakest precondition semantics (Dijkstra 1976). Let Pred be the syntax domain of predicate calculus expressions. The symbols "B" and "p" stand for elements of Pred. Here is the weakest precondition semantics of a small language:

$$\mathrm{wp}([\![C_1;C_2]\!], p) = \mathrm{wp}([\![C_1]\!], \mathrm{wp}([\![C_2]\!],p))$$
$$\mathrm{wp}([\![I{:=}E]\!], p) = [E/I]p$$
$$\mathrm{wp}([\![\textbf{if } B \textbf{ then } C_1 \textbf{ else } C_2]\!], p) = ([\![B]\!] \textit{ and } \mathrm{wp}([\![C_1]\!], p)) \quad \textit{or } ((\textit{not}[\![B]\!]) \textit{ and } \mathrm{wp}([\![C_2]\!], p))$$
$$\mathrm{wp}([\![\textbf{while } B \textbf{ do } C]\!], p) = (\text{there exists } i \geqslant 0 \text{ such that } H_i(p))$$
$$\text{where } H_0(p) = (\textit{not}([\![B]\!]) \textit{ and } p)$$
$$\text{and } H_{i+1}(p) = \mathrm{wp}([\![\textbf{if } B \textbf{ then } C \textbf{ else skip}]\!], H_i(p))$$
$$\text{and } \mathrm{wp}([\![\textbf{skip}]\!], p) = p$$

   Now consider the continuation semantics of the language. In particular, let **P** : Pred → *Predicate* be the valuation function for predicates, where *Predicate* = *Store* → *Tr'* and *Tr'* = $\textit{Unit}_\perp$. Let *true* : *Tr'* be () and *false* : *Tr'* be ⊥. Define *Cmdcont* = *Predicate*. Using the semantic equations in Section 9.1, show that $\mathbf{C}[\![C]\!]p = \mathbf{P}(\mathrm{wp}([\![C]\!], p))$.

5. Rework the semantics of Figure 9.5 so that a distinction is made between compile-time errors and run-time computations. In particular, create the following domains:

   Pgmcont = *Compile-err* + (*Location* → *Computation*)
   Cmdcont = *Compile-err* + *Computation*
   Exprcont = *Compile-err* + (*Expressible-value* → *Computation*)
   Compile-err = *String*
   Computation = *Store* → *Answer*

$$Answer = (Store + Run\text{-}err)_{\bot}$$
$$Run\text{-}err = String$$

Formulate the semantics so that a denotable or expressible value error in a program [[P]] implies that **P**[[P]] = in*Compile-err*(t), for some message t, and a type-correct program has denotation **P**[[P]] = in(*Location*→*Computation*)(f).

6. Design an imperative language that establishes control at the expression level but not at the command level. That is, the **E** valuation function uses expression continuations, but the **C** valuation function is in direct semantics style. What pragmatic advantages and disadvantages do you see?

7. Apply the principles of abstraction, parameterization, correspondence, and qualification to the language in Figure 9.5.

8. PL/1 supports exception handlers that are invoked by machine level faults. For example, a user can code the handler [[**on zerodivide do** C]], which is raised automatically when a division by zero occurs.

   a. Add the zero division exception handler to the language defined by Figures 9.2 and 9.5.
   b. The user can disable an exception handler by the command [[**no** I]], where [[I]] is the name of an exception handler, either built in or user defined. Add this feature to the language.

9. In ML, exception handlers are dynamically scoped. Revise the definition in Figure 9.2 to use dynamic scoping of handlers. How does this affect the raising of exceptions and exits from blocks? (Consider exceptions raised from within invoked procedures.)

10. One form of coroutine structure places a hierarchy on the coroutines; a coroutine can "own" other coroutines. Call these the *parent* and *child* coroutines, respectively. Child coroutines are declared local to the parent, and only a parent can call a child. A child coroutine can pause and return control to its parent but can not resume its siblings or other nonrelated coroutines. Design a language with hierarchical coroutines.

11. Modify the semantics of the backtracking language in Figure 9.3 so that the commands can recursively invoke one another.

12. Extend the list processing language in Figure 7.6 to allow jumps in expression evaluation. Augment the syntax of expressions by:

    E ::= · · · | **catch** E | **throw** E

    The [[**catch** E]] construct is the intended destination of any [[**throw** E′]]

evaluated within [[E]]. The value catch produces is the value of [[E′]]. Evaluation of [[throw E]] aborts normal evaluation and the value of [[E]] is communicated to the nearest enclosing [[catch]]. Give the semantics of these constructs.

13. Derive the continuation semantics corresponding to the direct semantics of expressions, using the method in Section 9.6 and the congruence $\mathbf{E}_C[\![\mathrm{E}]\!]k\ s = k(\mathbf{E}_D[\![\mathrm{E}]\!]s)\ s$, for:

    a. The **E** valuation function in Figure 5.2.
    b. The **E** valuation function in Figure 7.6.

14. Prove that the direct and continuation semantics of the language in Section 9.6 are also congruent in an operational sense: prove that $\mathbf{C}_D[\![\mathrm{C}]\!]s$ simplifies to s' iff $\mathbf{C}_C[\![\mathrm{C}]\!]c\ s$ simplifies to $c(s')$.

15. Consider the conditions under which a designer uses continuation domains in a language definition.

    a. What motivates their introduction into the definition?
    b. Under what conditions should some valuation functions map to continuations and others to noncontinuation values?
    c. What characteristics of a language *must* result if continuation domains are placed in the language definition?
    d. Are languages with continuation definitions easier to reason about (e.g., in program equivalence proofs) than languages with direct definitions?
    e. What freedom of choice of implementations is lost when continuation domains are used?

Chapter 10

Implementation of Denotational Definitions

A language's implementation should be guided by its semantics definition. In this chapter, we survey techniques for deriving a compiler from a language's semantics and examine some of the existing automated tools for compiler generation. We also consider issues regarding the correctness of implementations.

10.1 A GENERAL METHOD OF IMPLEMENTATION

In the previous chapters, we saw many examples of programs that were mapped to their dentotations and simplified to answers. The simplifications resemble the computational steps that occur in a conventional implementation. They suggest a simple, general implementation technique: treat the semantic notation as a "machine language" and implement an evaluator for the semantic notation. The denotational equations translate a program to its denotation, and the evaluator applies simplification rules to the denotation until all possible simplifications are performed.

As an example, consider the semantic definition in Figure 5.2. The translation of the program [[Z:=A+1]] is the expression:

$$
\begin{aligned}
&\mathrm{P}[\![\mathrm{Z}{:=}\mathrm{A}{+}1]\!] = \\
&\lambda n.\ \mathrm{let}\ s = (\mathit{update}\,[\![\mathrm{A}]\!]\ n\ \mathit{newstore})\ \mathrm{in} \\
&\qquad \mathrm{let}\ s' = (\underline{\lambda s}.\ \mathit{update}\,[\![\mathrm{Z}]\!]\ (\lambda s.\ (\lambda s.\ \mathit{access}\,[\![\mathrm{A}]\!]\ s)s\ \mathit{plus}\ (\lambda s.\ \mathit{one})s)s\ \ s)s \\
&\qquad \mathrm{in}\ (\mathit{access}\,[\![\mathrm{Z}]\!]\ s')
\end{aligned}
$$

(We have not bothered to expand the *Store* algebra operators to their underlying function forms, e.g., *access* to $(\lambda i.\lambda s.\ s(i))$. This keeps the overall expression readable. Also, *Store*-level operations are often treated specially.) The expression is applied to its run-time data, say the number *four*, and is given to the evaluator, which applies the simplification rules. The number *five* is the simplified result and is the output of the evaluator.

Let's call this approach the *compile-evaluate* method. There is a simple variation on the method. The example in Section 5.1 suggests that we can simultaneously translate a program into its denotation and evaluate it with its run-time arguments. For example, the expression $\mathbf{P}[\![\mathrm{Z{:=}A{+}1}]\!]\,\mathit{four}$ is translated to the intermediate form:

$$(\lambda n.\ \text{let } s = (\mathit{update}\,[\![\mathrm{A}]\!]\,n\ \mathit{newstore})\ \text{in}$$
$$\text{let } s' = \mathbf{C}[\![\mathrm{Z{:=}A{+}1}]\!]s\ \text{in}\ (\mathit{access}\,[\![\mathrm{Z}]\!]\ s'))\mathit{four}$$

which is simplified to the expression:

$$\text{let } s' = \mathbf{C}[\![\mathrm{Z{:=}A{+}1}]\!]([\,[\![\mathrm{A}]\!] \mapsto \mathit{four}]\mathit{newstore})\ \text{in}\ (\mathit{access}\,[\![\mathrm{Z}]\!]\ s')$$

which is translated to the expression:

$$\text{let } s' = (\underline{\lambda} s.\ \mathit{update}\,[\![\mathrm{Z}]\!]\ \mathbf{E}[\![\mathrm{A{+}1}]\!]s\ s)([\,[\![\mathrm{A}]\!] \mapsto \mathit{four}]\mathit{newstore})\ \text{in}\ (\mathit{access}\,[\![\mathrm{Z}]\!]\ s')$$

which is simplified to:

$$\text{let } s' = \mathit{update}\,[\![\mathrm{Z}]\!]\ (\mathbf{E}[\![\mathrm{A{+}1}]\!]([\,[\![\mathrm{A}]\!] \mapsto \mathit{four}]\mathit{newstore}))\ \ ([\,[\![\mathrm{A}]\!] \mapsto \mathit{four}]\mathit{newstore})$$
$$\text{in}\ (\mathit{access}\,[\![\mathrm{Z}]\!]\ s')$$

and so on. The result is again *five*. This is an interpreter approach; the denotational definition and evaluator interact to map a source program directly to its output value. The compile-evaluate method is more commonly used by the existing systems that implement semantic definitions. It is closer in spirit to a conventional compiler-based system and seems to be more amenable to optimizations.

10.1.1 The SIS and SPS Systems

Two compiler generator systems based on the compile-evaluate method are Mosses's Semantics Implementation System (SIS) and Wand's Semantics Prototyping System (SPS). SIS was the first compiler generating system based on denotational semantics. Figure 10.1 shows the components and data flow of the system.

SIS consists of a parser generator and an encoder generator. The parser generator produces an SLR(1) parser from an input BNF definition coded in a notation called GRAM. The semantic definition, coded in DSL, is read by the encoder generator, which produces an *encoder*, that is, a translator from abstract syntax trees to "LAMB-denotations." A source program is parsed by the parser and is translated by the encoder. The source program's denotation plus its input values are passed to the evaluator for simplification. The definitions of run-time operations (such as the operations from the *Store* algebra) are supplied at this

Figure 10.1

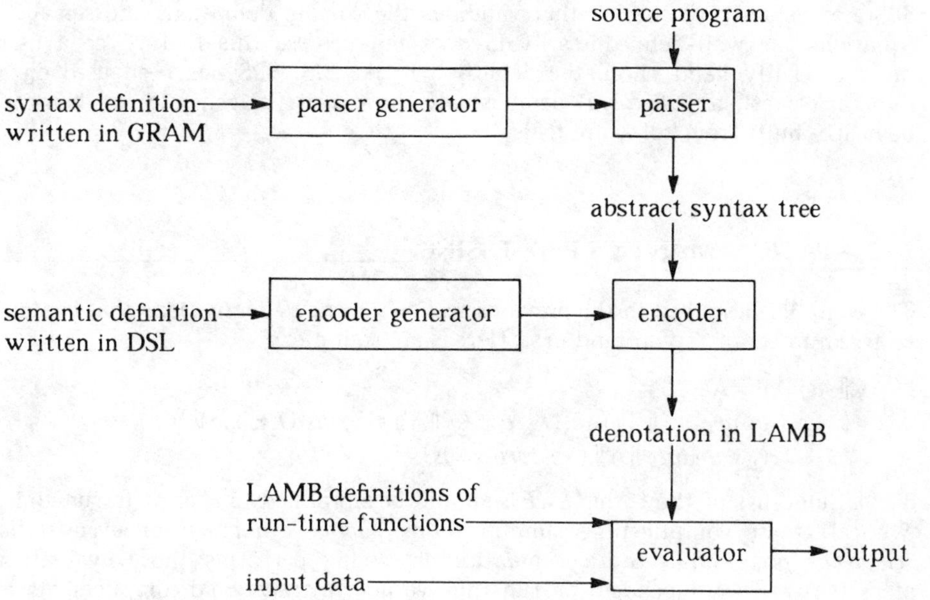

time. The evaluator uses a *call-by-need* simplification strategy: an expression $(\lambda x.M)N$ simplifies to M, and the binding (x, N) is retained by the evaluator in an environment table. When an occurrence of x is encountered in M, N is fetched from the table, simplified to its value v, and used for x. The binding (x,v) replaces (x, N) in the table. This strategy handles combinations more efficiently than the usual textual substitution method.

SIS is coded in BCPL. It has been used to implement a number of test languages. Its strengths include its simplicity and generality— virtually any denotational definition can be implemented using SIS. The system's primary weakness is its inefficiency: the generated compilers are large and the compiled programs run slowly. Nonetheless, SIS is an important example of an automated system that produces a *correct* compiler from a language's formal specification. It has inspired many researchers to develop more efficient and specialized systems.

Wand's SPS system is based on existing software tools. The system's parser generator is the YACC parser generator. A language definition is stated as a

YACC-coded grammar with the denotational semantics equations appended to the grammar rules. The semantics equations are coded in Scheme, a LISP-like programming language that resembles function notation. The SPS evaluator is just the Scheme interpreter, which evaluates denotations relatively efficiently. SPS also uses a type checker that validates the domain definitions and semantic equations for well-definedness. (SIS does not possess this feature, so a user must carefully hand check the definition.) Like SIS, SPS has been used on a number of test languages. It demonstrates how a useful generator system can be neatly built from software tools.

10.2 STATIC SEMANTICS PROCESSING

The compiler described in the previous section generates denotations that contain a large number of trivial bindings. Here is an example:

$$\mathbf{C}[\![\mathrm{A{:=}0;B{:=}A{+}1}]\!] =$$
$$\underline{\lambda} s.\,(\underline{\lambda} s.\, update\,[\![\mathrm{B}]\!]\,(\lambda s.\,(\lambda s.\, access\,[\![\mathrm{A}]\!]\,s)s\ plus\ (\lambda s.\, one)s)s\ s)$$
$$((\underline{\lambda} s.\, update\,[\![\mathrm{A}]\!]\,(\lambda s.\, zero)s\ s)s)$$

Trivial bindings of the form $(\lambda s.\,E)s$ should be simplified to E prior to run-time. We call these compile-time simplifications *partial evaluation* or even *static semantics processing*. Static semantics processing performs those evaluation steps that are not dependent on run-time values. In traditional compilers, static semantics processing includes declaration processing, type checking, and constant folding.

How do we determine which simplifications to perform? We call an expression *unfrozen* if it can be simplified before run-time. A *frozen* expression may not be simplified. Once we decide which semantic algebras define run-time values, we freeze the operations in those algebras. An example of an algebra that is typically frozen is the *Store* algebra. The algebras of truth values and numbers are frozen if the evaluation of Boolean and arithmetic expressions is left until run-time. (In compilers that do constant folding, *Tr* and *Nat* are unfrozen.)

During static semantics processing, we simplify each subexpression of a denotation as far as possible until we encounter a frozen operation, then we are forced to stop. Say that the *Store* and *Nat* algebras are frozen in the above example. Then the subexpression $(\underline{\lambda} s.\, update\,[\![\mathrm{A}]\!]\,(\lambda s.\, zero)s\ s)s$ simplifies to $(update\,[\![\mathrm{A}]\!]\ zero\ s)$, but no further, because *update* is a frozen operation. The simplified subexpression itself is now "frozen." Frozen subexpressions impact other simplifications; a combination $(\lambda x.\,M)N$, where N is a frozen subexpression, is not simplified. (But M itself may be simplified.) Also, some static semantics simplifiers refuse to simplify $(\lambda x.\,M)N$ if unfrozen N is a nonconstant or nonidentifier and occurs free in M more than once, for the resulting expression would be larger, not smaller, than the original.

For the above example with the *Store* and *Nat* algebras frozen, static semantics produces:

$$\underline{\lambda}s.\,(\underline{\lambda}s.update\,[\![B]\!]\,((access\,[\![A]\!]\,s)\;plus\;one)\;s)\,(update\,[\![A]\!]\;zero\;s)$$

which is the expected "machine code" for the command.

Static semantics processing is most useful for simplifying denotations that contain environment arguments. Recall the block-structured language in Section 7.1. Environments process declarations, reserve storage, and map identifiers to denotable values. Environment-related actions are traditionally performed at compile-time. The example in that section showed that the denotation of a program can be simplified to a point where all references to environment arguments disappear. The simplifications are exactly those that would be performed during static semantics processing, because the *Environment* algebra is unfrozen.

The SIS system does static semantics processing. However, SIS does not freeze any expressions; it simplifies every possible subexpression. The method works because the definitions of the frozen operators (such as the *Store*-based ones) are not supplied until run-time. Thus, any expression using a run-time operation is not simplifiable.

10.3 THE STRUCTURE OF THE EVALUATOR

We use the equalities in Section 3.5 to simplify expressions. From here on, we treat the equalities as *rewriting rules*. An equality $M=N$ induces a rewriting rule $M \Rightarrow N$; an occurrence of M in an expression is *reduced* (simplified) to N by the rule. For example, $(\lambda x.\, M)N \Rightarrow [N/x]M$ is a rewriting rule, and is in fact a rather famous one, called the *β-rule*. An expression whose structure matches the left hand side of a rewriting rule is a *redex*, and the expression that results from reducing a redex is called its *contractum*. We write $E_1 \Rightarrow E_2$ if expression E_1 rewrites to E_2 in one step and write $E_1 \Rightarrow^* E_2$ if zero or more steps are used. An expression that contains no redexes is in *normal form*. We say that an expression *has a normal form* if it can be reduced to an expression in normal form. Not all expressions have normal forms (e.g., $(\lambda x.\, x\,x)(\lambda x.\, x\,x)$, where $x \in G = G \rightarrow G$). An important feature of the rules for function notation is that if an expression does have a normal form then it is unique. This property follows from the *confluence* (Church-Rosser) property: if $E_1 \Rightarrow^* E_2$ and $E_1 \Rightarrow^* E_3$, then some E_4 exists such that $E_2 \Rightarrow^* E_4$ and $E_3 \Rightarrow^* E_4$.

An evaluator applies rewriting rules to its argument until a normal form (if it exists) is reached. The evaluator should apply the rules in a fashion that is sufficient for achieving a normal form. (For example, $(\lambda y.\, zero)\ ((\lambda x.\, x\,x)\ (\lambda x.\, x\,x))$ has the normal form *zero*, but perpetually reducing the argument $(\lambda x.\, x\,x)(\lambda x.\, x\,x)$ will never produce it.) A strategy sufficient for reducing an expression to normal form is the *leftmost-outermost method*: at each reduction step, we reduce the leftmost redex that is not contained within another redex. (We make the statement that the leftmost-outermost method is sufficient with the understanding that a combination $(\underline{\lambda}x.\,M)N$, where N itself is a function, argument combination, should be "read backwards" as "$N(M.x\underline{\lambda})$." Recall that a strict abstraction requires a proper argument, hence its argument must be reduced until its proper structure— a pair, injection, abstraction, number, or whatever— appears. Then the β-reduction is made.) Here is a leftmost-outermost reduction:

$$
\begin{aligned}
&(\lambda x.\,(x\;x)\mathit{zero})((\lambda y.\,(\lambda z.\,z))((\lambda x.\,x\;x)(\lambda x.\,x\;x)))\\
&\Rightarrow (((\lambda y.\,(\lambda z.\,z))((\lambda x.\,x\;x)(\lambda x.\,x\;x)))\;((\lambda y.\,(\lambda z.\,z))((\lambda x.\,x\;x)(\lambda x.\,x\;x))))\mathit{zero}\\
&\Rightarrow ((\lambda z.\,z)\;((\lambda y.\,(\lambda z.\,z))((\lambda x.\,x\;x)(\lambda x.\,x\;x))))\mathit{zero}\\
&\Rightarrow ((\lambda y.\,(\lambda z.\,z))((\lambda x.\,x\;x)(\lambda x.\,x\;x)))\mathit{zero}\\
&\Rightarrow (\lambda z.\,z)\mathit{zero}\\
&\Rightarrow \mathit{zero}
\end{aligned}
$$

One way of implementing the leftmost-outermost reduction strategy is to represent the expression to be reduced as a tree. The evaluator does a left-to-right, depth-first traversal of the tree. When a node in the tree is visited, the evaluator determines if the subtree whose root is the visited node is a redex. If it is not, the evaluator visits the next node in its traversal. But if it is, the evaluator removes the tree, does the reduction, and inserts the contractum for the redex. The next node visited is the parent node of the contractum's, for the evaluator must backtrack up the tree to see if the insertion of the contractum created a new outermost redex.

An inefficiency of the tree reduction method lies in its reduction of a redex $(\lambda x.\,M)N$: occurrences of N must be inserted in place of occurrences of x in M in the contractum. A traversal of M's tree is required for the insertions. Then, M is traversed a second time to reduce its redexes. These two traversals can be combined into one: the evaluator can insert an N for an x when it encounters x during its traversal of M for reductions. In the meantime, the binding of x to N can be kept in an environment. An *environment* is a collection of identifier, expression pairs, chained together in the shape of an inverted tree. The environment holds the arguments bound to identifiers as a result of β-reductions. Every node in the expression tree has a pointer into the environment. The pointer points to a linked list (that is, a path in the inverted tree) of the bindings that belong to the node. The inverted tree structure of the environment results because distinct nodes sometimes share bindings in their lists.

When a redex $R = (\lambda x.\,M)N$ reduces to M, the binding (x, N) is chained to the front of the list pointed to by M's environment pointer. M's new pointer points to the binding (x, N) followed by the previous list of bindings. When a free occurrence of x is visited in M, the evaluator follows the environment pointer attached to x to find the first pair (x, N) in the chain of bindings. N (and *its* pointer) replace x in the expression. A clever evaluator evaluates x by leaving N in its place in the environment and simplifying it there. Once N reduces to a proper value, that value is copied over into the expression tree in x's place. Subsequent lookups of x in the environment find the reduced value. This approach is known as *call-by-need* evaluation.

10.3.1 A Stack-Based Evaluator

The tree traversal method is slow and bulky. There is too much copying of contractums in place of redexes into the expression tree, and there is too much backtracking during tree traversal. Further, the representation of the expression as a tree occupies a wasteful amount of space. We can represent the leftmost-outermost reduction of an expression in a more conventional form. We use a stack-based machine as an evaluator; an expression is translated into a sequence of machine instructions that describes a leftmost-outermost reduction of the expression. The traversal and reduction steps can be translated into machine code because function expressions are statically scoped, so environment maintenance is routine, and because the traversal path through the expression can be calculated from the structure of the expression. Figure 10.2 shows the stack machine. We call it the *VEC-machine* because it possesses three components:

1. A temporary value stack, v, which holds subexpressions that have been reduced to proper values and expressions whose evaluation has been postponed.
2. An environment, e, which stacks environment pointers and establishes the scope of the current expression being reduced.
3. A code stack, c, which holds the machine instructions for the reduction. Rather than using an instruction counter, we treat the instructions as a stack. The top instruction on the stack is the one executed, and a stack pop corresponds to an increment of the instruction counter to the next instruction in the code.

We represent a machine configuration as a triple $(v\ e\ c)$. Each of the three components in the configuration is represented in the form $a_1{:}a_2{:} \cdots {:}a_n$, where a_1 is the top value on the component's stack.

Two of the machine's key data structures are the environment pointer and the closure. An *environment pointer* is a pointer value to a linked list of identifier, value bindings. (Read the @ symbol as saying "a pointer to.") All the bindings are kept in the environment tree, which has the structure described in the previous section and is not explicitly depicted in the figure. A *closure* represents an expression that has not been reduced but must be saved for later use. Both the instructions for the expression and its environment pointer must be kept in the closure. A *call* instruction activates the closure's code; that is, it initiates the expression's evaluation.

Figure 10.2

VEC-machine components:

$v \in \textit{Temporary-value-stack} = \textit{Value}^*$

$e \in \textit{Environment} = \textit{Environment-pointer}^*$

$c \in \textit{Code-stack} = \textit{Instruction}^*$

where

$\textit{Value} = \textit{Primitive-value} + \textit{Closure}$

$a \in \textit{Primitive-value} = \textit{Nat} + \textit{Tr} + \cdots$

$(\alpha, p) \in \textit{Closure} = \textit{Instruction}^* \times \textit{Environment-pointer}$

$p \in \textit{Environment-pointer} = @((\textit{Identifier} \times \textit{Value} \times \textit{Environment-pointer}) + \textit{nil})$

$\textit{Instruction} = \textit{pushclosure}(\textit{Instruction}^*) + \textit{pushconst}(\textit{Primitive-value}) +$
$\quad \textit{call} + \textit{return} + \textit{push}(\textit{Identifier}) + \textit{bind}(\textit{Identifier}) + \textit{Primitive-operator}$
$\quad \textit{test}(\textit{Instruction}^* \times \textit{Instruction}^*)$

Instruction interpretation (note: the operator ":" stands for stack *cons*):

(1)	v	$p{:}e$	$\textit{pushclosure}\ \alpha{:}c$	$\Rightarrow$	$(\alpha, p){:}v$	$p{:}e$	c	
(2)	v	e	$\textit{pushconst}\ k{:}c$	$\Rightarrow$	$k{:}v$	e	c	
(3)	$(\alpha, p){:}v$	e	$\textit{call}{:}c$	$\Rightarrow$	v	$p{:}e$	$\alpha{:}c$	
(4)	v	$p{:}e$	$\textit{return}{:}c$	$\Rightarrow$	v	e	c	
(5)	v	e	$\textit{push}\ x{:}c$	$\Rightarrow$	$a{:}v$	e	c	
			where $a \in \textit{Primitive-value}$, $a = \textit{lookup}\ x\ (\textit{hd}\ e)$					
			and $\textit{lookup}\ x\ p = \text{let}\ (i, r, p') = p@\ \text{in}\ \textit{if}\ i{=}x\ \textit{then}\ r\ \textit{else}\ \textit{lookup}\ x\ p'$					
(6)	v	e	$\textit{push}\ x{:}c$	$\Rightarrow$	v	$p{:}e$	$\alpha{:}c$	
			where $(\alpha, p) \in \textit{Closure}$, $(\alpha, p) = \textit{lookup}\ x\ (\textit{hd}\ e)$					
(7)	$r{:}v$	$p{:}e$	$\textit{bind}\ x{:}c$	$\Rightarrow$	v	$p'{:}e$	c	
			where $p' = @(x, r, p)$					
(8)	$a_n : \cdots : a_1{:}v$	e	$f{:}c$	$\Rightarrow$	$a{:}v$	e	c	
			where $(f\ a_1 \cdots a_n) = a$					
(9)	$\textit{true}{:}v$	e	$\textit{test}(\alpha, \beta){:}c$	$\Rightarrow$	v	e	$\alpha{:}c$	
(10)	$\textit{false}{:}v$	e	$\textit{test}(\alpha, \beta){:}c$	$\Rightarrow$	v	e	$\beta{:}c$	

The operation of the machine is expressed with rewriting rules. A rule of the form $v \quad e \quad ins{:}c \quad \Rightarrow v' \quad e' \quad c'$ shows the effect of the instruction *ins* on the machine's three components. Here is a brief explanation of the instructions. The *pushclosure* instruction creates a closure out of its code argument. The current environment pointer establishes the scope of the code, so it is included in the closure (see rule 1). A real implementation would not store the code in the closure but would store a pointer to where the code resides in the program store. A *pushconst* instruction pushes its primitive value argument onto the value stack (see rule 2). The *call* instruction activates the closure that resides at the top of the value stack. The closure's code is loaded onto the code stack, and its environment pointer is pushed onto the environment (see rule 3). A hardware implementation would jump to the first instruction in the closure's code rather than copy the code into a stack. The *return* instruction cleans up after a call by popping the top pointer off the environment stack (see rule 4). A hardware implementation would reset the instruction counter as well. The *push* instruction does an environment lookup to find the value bound to its argument. The lookup is done through the linked list of bindings that the active environment pointer marks. In the case that the argument x is bound to a primitive value (rule 5), the value is placed onto the value stack. If x is bound to a closure (rule 6), the closure is invoked so that the argument can be reduced. The *bind* instruction augments the active environment by binding its argument to the top value on the value stack (see rule 7). A primitive operator f takes its arguments from the value stack and places its result there (see rule 8). The *test* instruction is a conditional branch and operates in the expected way (see rules 9 and 10). A hardware implementation would use branches to jump around the clause not selected.

Figure 10.3 defines the code generation map $\mathbf{T}: \textit{Function-Expr} \rightarrow \textit{Instruction}^*$ for mapping a function expression into a sequence of instructions for doing a

Figure 10.3

$\mathbf{T}[\![(E_1\, E_2)]\!] = \textit{pushclosure}(\mathbf{T}[\![E_2]\!]: \textit{return}): \mathbf{T}[\![E_1]\!]: \textit{call}$

$\mathbf{T}[\![\lambda x.\, E]\!] = \textit{pushclosure}(\textit{bind}\ [\![x]\!]: \mathbf{T}[\![E]\!]: \textit{return})$

$\mathbf{T}[\![\underline{\lambda} x.\, E]\!] = \textit{pushclosure}(\textit{call}: \textit{bind}\ [\![x]\!]: \mathbf{T}[\![E]\!]: \textit{return})$

$\mathbf{T}[\![x]\!] = \textit{push}\ [\![x]\!]$

$\mathbf{T}[\![k]\!] = \textit{pushconst}\ k$

$\mathbf{T}[\![(f\, E_1 \cdots E_n)]\!] = \mathbf{T}[\![E_1]\!]: \cdots : \mathbf{T}[\![E_n]\!]: f$

$\mathbf{T}[\![E_1 \rightarrow E_2\ [\,]\ E_3]\!] = \mathbf{T}[\![E_1]\!]: \textit{test}(\mathbf{T}[\![E_2]\!], \mathbf{T}[\![E_3]\!])$

---

leftmost-outermost reduction. The leftmost-outermost strategy is easy to discern; consider $\mathbf{T}[\![(E_1\ E_2)]\!]$: the generated code says to postpone the traversal of E_2 by creating a closure and placing it on the value stack. The code for E_1, the left component of the combination, is evaluated first. E_1's code will (ultimately) create a closure that represents an abstraction. This closure will also be pushed onto the value stack. The *call* instruction invokes the closure representing the abstraction. Studying the translation of abstractions, we see that the code in an abstraction's closure binds the top value on the value stack to the abstraction's identifier. In the case of a nonstrict abstraction, a closure is bound. In the case of a strict abstraction, the closure on the value stack is first invoked so that a proper value is calculated and placed onto the value stack, and then the argument is bound. The translations of the other constructs are straightforward.

Figure 10.3 omitted the translations of product and sum elements; these are left as an exercise. A translation of an expression is given in Figure 10.4. The code in the figure can be improved fairly easily: let *popbinding* be a machine instruction with the action:

$$v \quad p{:}e \quad popbinding{:}c \;\Rightarrow\; v \quad p'{:}e \quad c, \quad \text{where } p = @(x, r, p')$$

Then a combination's code can be improved to:

$$\mathbf{T}[\![(\lambda x.\,E_1)E_2]\!] = pushclosure(\mathbf{T}[\![E_2]\!]{:}\ return){:}\ bind\ x{:}\ \mathbf{T}[\![E_1]\!]{:}\ popbinding$$
$$\mathbf{T}[\![(\underline{\lambda} x.E_1)E_2]\!] = \mathbf{T}[\![E_2]\!]{:}\ bind\ x{:}\ \mathbf{T}[\![E_1]\!]{:}\ popbinding$$

eliminating many of the *pushclosure*, *call*, and *return* instructions.

We should prove that the translated code for a function expression does indeed express a leftmost-outermost reduction. We will say that the machine is

Figure 10.4

$\mathbf{T}[\![(\lambda y.\ zero)((\lambda x.\ x\ x)(\lambda x.\ x\ x))]\!] =$

let Δ be $\mathbf{T}[\![(\lambda x.\ x\ x)]\!] =$

pushclosure(*bind x*:
pushclosure(*push x*: *return*):
push x: *call*: *return*)

in

pushclosure(
pushclosure(Δ: *return*): Δ: *call*):
pushclosure(*bind y*: *pushconst zero*: *return*): *call*

faithful to the reduction rules if the computation taken by the machine on a program corresponds to a reduction on the original function expression. Indeed, the VEC-machine is faithful to the rules of function notation. The proof is long, but here is an outline of it. First, we define a mapping *Unload* : *VEC-machine* → *Function-Expr* that maps a machine configuation back to a function expression. Then we prove: for all $E \in$ *Function-Expr*, $(nil\ p_0\ \mathbf{T}[\![E]\!]) \Rightarrow^* (v\ e\ c)$ implies $E \Rightarrow^*$ *Unload*$(v\ e\ c)$, where $p_0 = @nil$. The proof is an induction on the number of machine moves. The basis, zero moves, is the proof that *Unload*$(nil\ p_0\ \mathbf{T}[\![E]\!]) = E$; the inductive step follows from the proof that $(v\ e\ c) \Rightarrow (v'\ e'\ c')$ implies *Unload*$(v\ e\ c) \Rightarrow^*$ *Unload*$(v'\ e'\ c')$. *Unload*'s definition and the proof are left as exercises.

Another aspect of the correctness of the VEC-machine is its termination properties: does the machine produce a completely simplified answer exactly when the reduction rules do? Actually, the VEC-machine is conservative. It ceases evaluation on an abstraction when the abstraction has no argument; the abstraction's body is not simplified. Nonetheless, the machine *does* reduce to final answers those terms that reduce to nonabstraction (hereafter called *first-order*) values. The VEC-machine resembles a real-life machine in this regard.

The VEC-machine evaluates function expressions more efficiently than the reduction rules because it uses its stacks to hold intermediate values. Rather than searching through the expression for a redex, the code deterministically traverses through the expression until (the code for) a redex appears on the top of the c stack. Simplified values are moved to the v stack— substitutions into the expression are never made.

Here is the current version of the compile-evaluate method that we have developed. The compile step is:

1. Map a program P to its denotation $\mathbf{P}[\![\mathrm{P}]\!]$.
2. Perform static semantics analysis on $\mathbf{P}[\![\mathrm{P}]\!]$, producing a denotation d.
3. Map d to its machine code $\mathbf{T}[\![d]\!]$.

The evaluate step is: load $\mathbf{T}[\![d]\!]$ into the VEC-machine, creating a configuration $(nil\ @nil\ \mathbf{T}[\![d]\!])$, and run the machine to a final configuration $(r{:}v\ e\ nil)$. The answer is r.

10.3.2 PSP and Appel's System

Paulson's Semantic Processor (PSP) system generates compilers that map programs into stack machine code. The PSP evaluator resembles the stack architecture just developed. In PSP, a language is defined with semantic grammars, a hybrid of denotational semantics and attribute grammars. The semantic grammar for a language is input to the *grammar analyzer*, which produces a language description file containing an LALR(1) parse table and the semantic equations for the language. Figure 10.5 shows the components.

The universal translator uses the language description file to compile a source program. A source program is parsed, mapped to its function expression form, partially evaluated, and mapped to stack machine code.

The static semantics stage in PSP does more than just partial evaluation. It also enforces contextual constraints (such as data type compatibility) that are specified in the semantic grammar. Efficient representations of abstractions and data values (like stores) are created. PSP has been used to generate a compiler for a large subset of Pascal; the generated compiler runs roughly 25 times slower than a handwritten one but is *smaller* than the handwritten compiler.

Appel's compiler-generating system produces compilers that translate source programs to register machine code. Static semantics and code generation are simultaneously performed by a *reducer* module, which completely reduces a denotation down to an empty expression. During the process, certain simplifications cause machine code to be emitted as a side effect. For example, the reducer reduces the expression (*update i n s*) to *s*, emitting the code "*s*[*i*]:=*n*" as a side effect. Appel's system is intended as a tool for generating quality code for conventional machines.

Figure 10.5

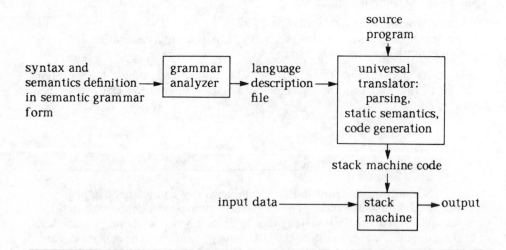

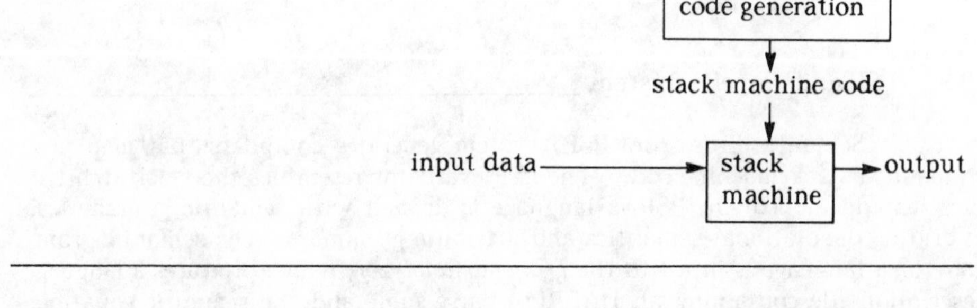

10.4 COMBINATOR-BASED SEMANTIC NOTATIONS

It is difficult to develop an efficient evaluator for function notation because the notation is so general. In particular, the binding of values to identifiers requires costly time- and space-consuming environment maintenance and lookups. A number of researchers have designed notations for specialized classes of languages. These notations make use of *combinators* that have efficient evaluations.

A *combinator* is a function expression that has no free identifiers. A combinator is normally given a name, and the name is used in place of the expression. As an example, let's use the name ; for the expression $(\lambda f_1.\lambda f_2.\underline{\lambda} s. f_2(f_1\, s))$. Hence, $E_1;E_2$ is $(\underline{\lambda} s. E_2(E_1\, s))$. The advantage of using the combinator is that a complicated binding and composition structure is hidden within the combinator. The expression $E_1;E_2$ is easier to read than the function expression form. The (derived) rewriting rule $(E_1;E_2)\, s \Rightarrow E_2(E_1 s)$ expresses the binding of argument to abstraction in a fashion that eliminates the binding identifier. If combinators are used exclusively as the semantic notation, then the binding identifiers (and their maintenance) disappear altogether.

Let's design a combinator set for writing definitions of simple imperative languages. The combinators will manipulate stores and temporary value stacks. Underlying the notation are two semantic algebras: the *Store* algebra and the algebra of lists of expressible values, $EVlist = (Nat + Tr)^*$. An expressible value list, store pair is called a *state*. All expressions written in the combinator notation are mappings from states to states. The combinators are ;, !, *cond*, and *skip*. Here are their rewriting rules:

$(E_1;E_2)(v,s) \Rightarrow E_2(E_1(v,s))$

$f!(v_n: \cdots :v_1:v, s) \Rightarrow (v':v, s)$

where $f: Exprval_1 \times \cdots \times Exprval_n \times Store \rightarrow Exprval$ is $(f\, v_1 \cdots v_n\, s) = v'$

$f!(v_n: \cdots :v_1:v, s) \Rightarrow (v, s')$

where $f: Exprval_1 \times \cdots \times Exprval_n \times Store \rightarrow Store$ is $(f\, v_1 \cdots v_n\, s) = s'$

$cond(E_1, E_2)(true:v, s) \Rightarrow E_1(v, s)$

$cond(E_1, E_2)(false:v, s) \Rightarrow E_2(v, s)$

$skip(v, s) \Rightarrow (v, s)$

The expression $E_1;E_2$ composes the state-altering actions of E_1 with those of E_2. The expression $f!$ is a primitive state-altering action. If f requires n arguments (plus the store), the top n arguments are taken off the expressible value list and are given to f (along with the store). The answer is pushed onto the list. (If f produces a store for an answer, it replaces the existing one.) The expression $cond(E_1, E_2)$ selects one of its two argument values based on the value at the front of the expressible value list; *skip* is the null expression.

The combinators must be assigned denotations. Then they can be used in semantic definitions and their rewriting rules can be proved sound. The denotation of $E_1;E_2$ is $\lambda(v,s)$. let $(v',s') = E_1(v,s)$ in $E_2(v',s')$. The soundness of its rewriting rule easily follows. The denotations and soundness proofs for the other combinators are left as exercises. An important feature of the rewriting rules is that binding identifiers are never used— the state pair (v,s) is passed from combinator to combinator. This suggests that a machine for the combinator language be configured as $(c\ v\ s)$, where c is a combinator expression $c_1; c_2; \cdots ; c_n$. The machine language consists of the *f*!, *cond*, and *skip* operators, and the actions of the machine are defined by the rewriting rules. For example, $(cond(E_1,E_2);c\ true{:}v\ s) \Rightarrow (E_1;c\ v\ s)$. By restricting the semantic notation to simple combinators, we obtain a simple evaluator. An imperative language is defined with the combinators in Figure 10.6.

The example combinator notation is ideally suited to expressing the sequencing and updating concepts in a language, but it is inadequate for expressing many other semantic concepts. There are no combinators for identifier declarations, recursively defined values, and nonstandard control forms. A number of researchers, most notably Mosses, are developing truly general combinator notations.

10.4.1 The Plumb and CERES Systems

Sethi's Plumb and Christiansen and Jones's CERES systems both rely on combinator-based semantic notations. The Plumb system uses a combinator set

Figure 10.6

C: Command $\rightarrow$ *State* $\rightarrow$ *State*$_\perp$
$\mathbf{C}[\![C_1;C_2]\!] = \mathbf{C}[\![C_1]\!]; \mathbf{C}[\![C_2]\!]$
$\mathbf{C}[\![I{:=}E]\!] = \mathbf{E}[\![E]\!]; (update\ [\![I]\!]\ !)$
$\mathbf{C}[\![\text{if } B \text{ then } C_1 \text{ else } C_2]\!] = \mathbf{B}[\![B]\!]; cond(\mathbf{C}[\![C_1]\!], \mathbf{C}[\![C_2]\!])$
$\mathbf{C}[\![\text{while } B \text{ do } C]\!] = wh$
where $wh = \mathbf{B}[\![B]\!]; cond(\mathbf{C}[\![C]\!]; wh, skip)$

E: Expression $\rightarrow$ *State* $\rightarrow$ *State*$_\perp$
$\mathbf{E}[\![E_1{+}E_2]\!] = \mathbf{E}[\![E_1]\!]; \mathbf{E}[\![E_2]\!]; add\ !$
$\mathbf{E}[\![I]\!] = access\ [\![I]\!]\ !$
$\mathbf{E}[\![N]\!] = \mathbf{N}[\![N]\!]\ !$

similar to the one defined in the previous section. Instead of manipulating a store and an expressible value stack, the combinators handle *streams* of values. A typical stream consists of a store as the first value and a sequence of expressible values thereafter, that is, $s, x_1, x_2, \cdots$. The primary combinator | is called a *pipe* and is used in roughly the same way as the ; combinator defined in the previous section. An expression $(E_1 \mid E_2)$ maps a stream of values to a stream of values as follows: if E_1 requires m_1 values to produce its n_1 answers, the first m_1 values are removed from the stream and given to E_1; its answers are placed on the front of the stream that passes to E_2. E_2 takes the m_2 values it needs and places its n_2 answers onto the front of the stream. A variation on the pipe is $E_1 \mid_k E_2$, which skips over the first k values in the stream when supplying the stream to E_2.

The semantics of command composition, assignment, and addition read:

$$\mathbf{C}[\![C_1;C_2]\!] = \mathbf{C}[\![C_1]\!] \mid \mathbf{C}[\![C_2]\!]$$
$$\mathbf{C}[\![I{:=}E]\!] = \mathbf{E}[\![E]\!] \mid \mathit{update}\,[\![I]\!]$$
$$\mathbf{E}[\![E_1{+}E_2]\!] = \mathbf{E}[\![E_1]\!] \mid \mathbf{E}[\![E_2]\!] \mid_1 \mathit{plus}$$

The Plumb system uses the YACC parser generator to configure a compiler. The generated compiler maps a source program to its combinator denotation, which is represented as a graph. Static semantics is performed on the graph. The code generator linearizes the graph into machine code. The system does sophisticated analysis on recursively defined objects like **while**-loops and circular environments, finding their optimal representation in machine code form. Plumb has been used on a number of test languages.

The CERES system is parameterized on whatever combinator set the user desires. A combinator set is made known to the system by a *compiler generator definition*, which is a mapping from the combinator set to code generation instructions. The system composes a language's semantic definition with the compiler generator definition to generate the compiler for the language. CERES is designed to be a development tool for a variety of applications, rather than a compiler generator for a narrow class of languages. It also has been used on test languages.

10.5 TRANSFORMATIONS ON THE SEMANTIC DEFINITION

Yet another approach to implementation is to transform the denotational definition into an easily implementable form. The transformations exploit structural properties in the definitions: domains such as *Environment* and *Store* are made into data structures, store arguments are converted into global variables, command denotations become machine code, and so on. The correctness of the transformations is justified with respect to the rewriting rules of the semantic notation; that is, the transformed definition has a reduction strategy that parallels the one used on the original definition. This section presents several useful transformations.

10.5.1 First-Order Data Objects

Those semantic algebras that define data structures should have nonfunctional domains. Then their values are simpler to represent and their associated operations are easier to optimize. We convert a function domain $D = A \to B$ into a first-order (that is, nonfunctional) domain by representing the members of D by tuples (or lists or arrays). The conversion is called *defunctionalization*. Consider the *Store* algebra presented in Figure 5.1. A store is an abstraction value, and a construction operation such as *update* builds an abstraction from its arguments. The defunctionalized version of the algebra is presented in Figure 10.7.

A defunctionalized store value is a now a tuple, tagged with the name of the operation that built it. When a store tuple is used by the *access* operation, (*eval i s*) simulates function application. The definition of *eval* is built directly

Figure 10.7

IV.′ Store

Domain $s \in Store = New + Upd$

where $New = Unit$

$Upd = Identifier \times Nat \times Store$

Operations

newstore : *Store*

newstore = in*New*()

access : *Identifier* → *Store* → *Nat*

access = $\lambda i.\lambda s.(eval\ i\ s)$

update : *Identifier* → *Nat* → *Store* → *Store*

update = $\lambda i.\lambda n.\lambda s.$ in*Upd*(i,n,s)

where

eval = $\lambda i.\lambda s.$ cases s of

is*New*() → *zero*

[] is*Upd*$(i',n',s') \to ((i\ equalid\ i') \to n'\ [\!]\ (eval\ i\ s'))$

end

from the old definitions of the construction operations *newstore* and *update*.

The defunctionalized *Store* domain is *not* isomorphic to the original one (prove this), but every store that was representable using the former versions of the *Store* operations is representable with the new versions. A proof of correctness of the transformation exploits this fact to verify that any reduction using a higher-order store is successfully simulated by a reduction that uses the corresponding first-order store. Further, any reduction using a first-order store parallels a reduction that uses a higher-order store. The proof is left as an exercise.

Figure 10.8 shows a reduction with first-order stores.

It is usually straightforward to convert a defunctionalized algebra into a more efficient form. For example, store tuples are just lists of identifier, number pairs, and an empty store is an empty list. Once an identifier is updated with a new value, its former value is forever inaccessible. This suggests that a store be modelled as an array; that is, $Store = \prod_{i:Identifier} Nat$; the *access* and *update* operations become array indexing and updating.

The PSP system defunctionalizes data domains. The new values are ordered trees, allowing fast versions of access and update operations.

Figure 10.8

$\mathbf{C}[\![X{:=}Z;\ Y{:=}X{+}X]\!](newstore)$

$= F_2(F_1(newstore)),$

$\quad\quad$ where $F_1 = \underline{\lambda}s.\,update\,[\![X]\!]\,(access\,[\![Z]\!]\,s)\,s$

$\quad\quad\quad\quad F_2 = \underline{\lambda}s.\,update\,[\![Y]\!]\,((access\,[\![X]\!]\,s)\,plus\,(access\,[\![X]\!]\,s))\,s$

$\Rightarrow F_2(F_1\ s_0),$ where $s_0 = \text{in}New()$

$\Rightarrow F_2(update\,[\![X]\!]\,(access\,[\![Z]\!]\,s_0)\,s_0)$

$\Rightarrow F_2(update\,[\![X]\!]\,zero\,s_0)$

$\Rightarrow F_2\ s_1,$ where $s_1 = \text{in}Upd([\![X]\!], zero, s_0)$

$\Rightarrow update\,[\![Y]\!]\,((access\,[\![X]\!]\,s_1)\,plus\,(access\,[\![X]\!]\,s_1))\,s_1$

$\Rightarrow update\,[\![Y]\!]\,((access\,[\![X]\!]\,s_1)\,plus\,zero)\,s_1$

$\Rightarrow update\,[\![Y]\!]\,(zero\,plus\,zero)\,s_1$

$\Rightarrow update\,[\![Y]\!]\,zero\,s_1$

$\Rightarrow s_2,$ where $s_2 = \text{in}Upd([\![Y]\!], zero, s_1)$

10.5.2 Global Variables

Intuition tells us that the store argument in a sequential language's definition should be treated as a global value. To make this point, we replace the *Store* domain by a store *variable*. Then the operations of the *Store* algebra no longer require a store argument, because they use the contents of the store variable. Of course, not all semantic definitions can be altered this way. The semantic equations must handle their store arguments in a "sequential" fashion: a store transformation function receives a single store argument, makes changes to it, and passes it on to the next function. Sequentiality is an operational notion, and we say that an expression is *single-threaded* (in its store argument) if a reduction strategy can be applied to the expression such that, at each stage of the reduction, there is at most one "active" normal form value of store in the stage. (A value is *active* if it does not appear within the body E of an abstraction $(\lambda x.\, E)$.) Raoult and Sethi formalize this concept by using a "pebbling game"; they call single-threading *single pebbling*.

The reduction strategy that works the best to demonstrate the single-threadedness of an expression is a call-by-value one: treat all abstractions in the expression as if they were strict. (This is acceptable if the expression in question contains no abstractions of form $(\lambda x.\, E) : A_{\perp} \rightarrow B$.)

Figure 10.8 shows a call-by-value reduction. The active normal form values of stores are represented by terms s_i. At each stage of the reduction, there is at most one active normal form value of store. For example, the stage *update* [[Y]] ((*access* [[X]] s_1) *plus zero*) s_1 has two occurrences of the one active normal form value s_1. The actions upon the store occur in the same order as they would in a conventional implementation. The multiple copies of the stores could be replaced by a global variable holding a single copy of the store's value. Operations *access* and *update* would use the global variable.

For an expression to be single-threaded, its reduction must never present a stage where a store-updating redex is active at the same time when another active expression is using the current store. This update-access conflict implies that multiple stores are necessary.

Following are syntactic criteria that guarantee that an expression is single-threaded with respect to call-by-value reduction. Say that a *Store*-typed identifier is a *trivial Store*-typed expression; all other *Store*-typed expressions are *nontrivial*. The definition below states that a single-threaded expression is structured so that a store update must not be active in the same subexpression with any other active store expression (the noninterference property), and no store may be bound into an abstraction's body for later use (the immediate evaluation property).

10.1 Definition:

An expression F is single threaded (in its Store argument) if each of its subexpressions E possess the properties:

A (noninterference)

1. *If E is Store-typed, then if E contains multiple, disjoint active occurrences of Store-typed expressions, then they are the same trivial identifier;*
2. *If E is not Store-typed, all occurrences of active Store-typed expressions in E are the same trivial identifier.*

B (immediate evaluation)

1. *If* $E = (\underline{\lambda x}. M)\colon Store \rightarrow D$, *then all free Store-typed identifiers in M are x.*
2. *If* $E = (\underline{\lambda x}. M)\colon C \rightarrow D$, *and C is not Store-typed, then M contains no active Store-typed expressions.*

The noninterference property directly prevents the update-access conflict from arising in active expressions. The immediate evaluation property guarantees that an abstraction will also avoid conflict when it is reduced and its body is made active.

Let's look at some examples; let $\mathbf{C}\colon \text{Command} \rightarrow Store_\bot \rightarrow Store_\bot$ and $\mathbf{E}\colon \text{Expression} \rightarrow Store \rightarrow Expressible\text{-}value$. First, the expression $\mathbf{C}[\![C_2]\!](\mathbf{C}[\![C_1]\!]s)$ is single-threaded. The call-by-value reduction strategy lock-steps the reduction so that $\mathbf{C}[\![C_1]\!]$'s reductions must be performed before $\mathbf{C}[\![C_2]\!]$'s. Another example of compliance is $(\lambda s.\, \mathbf{E}[\![E_1]\!]s\ \mathit{plus}\ \mathbf{E}[\![E_2]\!]s)$, for all the *Store*-typed subterms in it are trivial.

In contrast, $(\mathbf{C}[\![C_1]\!]s\ \mathit{combine}\ \mathbf{C}[\![C_2]\!]s)$ violates clause A1, for $\mathbf{C}[\![C_1]\!]s$ and $\mathbf{C}[\![C_2]\!]s$ are nontrivial and disjoint and active in the same subterm. When the abstraction is given a store, which of the two commands should be reduced first? If a single store variable is used, an incorrect final store will likely result. Next, $\mathbf{E}[\![E]\!](\mathbf{C}[\![C]\!]s)$ violates property A2, because $(\mathbf{C}[\![C]\!]s)$ creates a local side effect that must be forgotten after the reduction of $\mathbf{E}[\![E]\!]$. Apparently $\mathbf{E}[\![E]\!]$ needs its own local copy of the store. The expression $(\underline{\lambda s}.\, \mathbf{C}[\![C]\!]s')$ violates B1, for the store s' is hidden in the abstraction body, and it could be used at some later time in the reduction when a different store is current. Finally, $(\lambda n.\, \mathit{update}\ [\![I]\!]\ n\ s)$ violates B2 and introduces the same problem. All of these constructs would be difficult to implement on a sequential machine.

A denotational definition is single-threaded if all of its semantic equations are. Given a single-threaded denotational definition, we make the *Store* algebra into a *Store* "module" and replace all occurrences of stores in the semantic equations with the value $()\colon Unit$. Figure 10.9 shows the new version of the language in Figure 5.2. (Note: the expressions E_2 and E_3 are treated as *inactive* in $(E_1 \rightarrow E_2 [\!]\, E_3)$.)

The () markers are passed as arguments in place of store values. A () marker is a "pointer" to the store variable, awarding access rights. But, more importantly, () is a *control marker*, for a denotation $(\lambda().\, E)$ can reduce (that is, "get control") only when it receives the (). The transformation has exposed the underlying *store-based control* in the programming language.

A program's denotation is no longer a single function expression E, but a

Figure 10.9

VI. Store module

var $s: Store = New + Upd$, like Figure 10.6

Operations

$newstore : Unit$

$newstore = (s := \text{in}New())$

$access : Identifier \rightarrow Nat \rightarrow Unit \rightarrow Unit$

$access = \lambda i.\lambda n.\lambda().(eval\ i\ s)$

$update : Identifier \rightarrow Nat \rightarrow Unit \rightarrow Unit$

$update = \lambda i.\lambda n.\lambda().\ (s := \text{in}Upd(i, n, s))$

Valuation functions:

C: Command $\rightarrow Unit_\perp \rightarrow Unit_\perp$

$\mathbf{C}[\![C_1;C_2]\!] = \underline{\lambda}().\mathbf{C}[\![C_2]\!](\mathbf{C}[\![C_1]\!]())$

$\mathbf{C}[\![\textbf{if}\ B\ \textbf{then}\ C_1\ \textbf{else}\ C_2]\!] = \underline{\lambda}().\ \mathbf{B}[\![B]\!]() \rightarrow \mathbf{C}[\![C_1]\!]()\ [\!]\ \mathbf{C}[\![C_2]\!]()$

$\mathbf{C}[\![\textbf{while}\ B\ \textbf{do}\ C]\!] = wh$

where $wh = \underline{\lambda}().\ \mathbf{B}[\![B]\!]() \rightarrow wh(\mathbf{C}[\![C]\!]())\ [\!]\ ()$

$\mathbf{C}[\![I{:=}E]\!] = \underline{\lambda}().\ update\ [\![I]\!]\ (\mathbf{E}[\![E]\!]())\ ()$

E: Expression $\rightarrow Unit \rightarrow Nat$

$\mathbf{E}[\![E_1{+}E_2]\!] = \lambda().\ \mathbf{E}[\![E_1]\!]()\ plus\ \mathbf{E}[\![E_2]\!]()$

$\mathbf{E}[\![I]\!] = \lambda().\ access\ [\![I]\!]\ ()$

$\mathbf{E}[\![N]\!] = \lambda().\ \mathbf{N}[\![N]\!]$

---

pair (E, s), where s is the current value of the store variable. Rewrite rules operate on the expression, store pairs; for example, the new version of the β-rule is $(\cdots(\lambda x.M)N\cdots, s) \Rightarrow (\cdots[N/x]M\cdots, s)$. The rewriting rules that manipulate the store are:

$$(\cdots(access\ i\ ())\cdots, s) \Rightarrow (\cdots n \cdots, s) \qquad \text{where } eval\ i\ s = n$$
$$(\cdots(update\ i\ n\ ())\cdots, s) \Rightarrow (\cdots()\cdots, \text{in}Upd(i, n, s))$$

The command in Figure 10.8 is reduced with a store variable in Figure 10.10.

A machine implementation of the transformed denotational definition would treat the store variable as a machine component and *access* and *update* as machine instructions. The VEC-machine in Figure 10.2 becomes the *VECS-*

Figure 10.10

$C[\![X{:=}Z;Y{:=}X{+}X]\!](newstore) = F_2(F_1\ newstore)$,
  where $F_1 = \underline{\lambda}().\ update\,[\![X]\!]\ (access\,[\![Z]\!]())\ ()$
    $F_2 = \underline{\lambda}().\ update\,[\![Y]\!]\ ((access\,[\![X]\!]\ ())\ plus\ (access\,[\![X]\!]\ ())\ ()$
$\Rightarrow F_2(F_1())$, and $s: Store$ has value $in New()$.
$\Rightarrow F_2(update\,[\![X]\!]\ (access\,[\![Z]\!]\ ())\ ())$
$\Rightarrow F_2(update\,[\![X]\!]\ zero\ ())$
$\Rightarrow F_2()$ and $s: Store$ has value $in Upd([\![X]\!], zero, in New())$
$\Rightarrow update\,[\![Y]\!]\ ((access\,[\![X]\!]\ ())\ plus\ (access\,[\![X]\!]\ ()))\ ()$
$\Rightarrow update\,[\![Y]\!]((access\,[\![X]\!]\ ())\ plus\ zero)\ ()$
$\Rightarrow update\,[\![Y]\!]\ (zero\ plus\ zero)\ ()$
$\Rightarrow update\,[\![Y]\!]\ zero\ ()$
$\Rightarrow ()$ and $s: Store$ has value $in Upd([\![Y]\!], zero, in Upd([\![X]\!], zero, in New()))$.

---

machine, and it uses a machine configuration $(v\ e\ c\ s)$. The modification of Figure 10.2 to include the store variable is left as an exercise.

10.5.3 Control Structures

The definition in Figure 10.9 can be improved by writing it in a combinator format. We define the following combinators:

$E_1; E_2 = (\lambda().\ E_2(E_1()))$
$if\ B\ then\ E_1\ else\ E_2 = (\lambda().\ B() \rightarrow E_1()\ []\ E_2())$
$upd\ i\ E_1 = (\lambda().\ update\ i\ E_1()\ ())$
$skip = (\lambda().\ ())$
$E_1{+}E_2 = (\lambda().\ E_1()\ plus\ E_2())$
$n! = (\lambda().\ n)$

Figure 10.11 presents Figure 10.9 in combinator form.

Each of the combinators has a useful rewriting rule. A combinator $M = (\lambda().\ N)$ has the rewriting rule $M() \Rightarrow N$. The rewriting rules eliminate the lambda bindings but still distribute the control markers () throughout the subexpressions of an expression. The combinators are rightly called *control*

Figure 10.11

$\mathbf{C}[\![C_1;C_2]\!] = \mathbf{C}[\![C_1]\!]; \mathbf{C}[\![C_2]\!]$
$\mathbf{C}[\![I{:=}E]\!] = upd\ [\![I]\!]\ \mathbf{E}[\![E]\!]$
$\mathbf{C}[\![\textbf{if}\ B\ \textbf{then}\ C_1\ \textbf{else}\ C_2]\!] = if\ \mathbf{B}[\![B]\!]\ then\ \mathbf{C}[\![C_1]\!]\ else\ \mathbf{C}[\![C_2]\!]$
$\mathbf{C}[\![\textbf{while}\ B\ \textbf{do}\ C]\!] = wh$
  where $wh = if\ \mathbf{B}[\![B]\!]\ then\ \mathbf{C}[\![C]\!]; wh\ else\ skip$
$\mathbf{E}[\![E_1{+}E_2]\!] = \mathbf{E}[\![E_1]\!] + \mathbf{E}[\![E_2]\!]$
$\mathbf{E}[\![I]\!] = access\ [\![I]\!]$
$\mathbf{E}[\![N]\!] = \mathbf{N}[\![N]\!]\,!$

---

structures, for they distribute control to their arguments. For example, the rewriting rule for $E_1;E_2$ makes it clear that E_1 gets control before E_2. The rule for $E_1{+}E_2$ shows that control can be given to the arguments in any order, even in parallel.

A stored program machine can be derived from the rewriting rules. With its instruction counter, the machine mimics the distribution of the () markers. The control markers become redundant— the instruction counter *is* (), and when the counter points to (the code of) an expression E, this represents the combination $E()$. You are given the exercise of defining such a machine for the language in Figure 10.11.

We make one remark regarding the **while**-loop in Figure 10.11. The rewriting rules evaluate a recursively defined object like *wh* by unfolding:

$$wh \Rightarrow if\ \mathbf{B}[\![B]\!]\ then\ \mathbf{C}[\![C]\!]; wh\ else\ skip$$

Unfolding is not an efficient operation on a stored program machine. Steele (1977) points out, however, that certain recursively defined objects *do* have efficient representations: the *tail-recursive* ones. A recursively defined object is tail-recursive if the final value resulting from a reduction sequence of recursive unfoldings is the value produced by the last unfolding in the sequence. (Stated in another way, a return from a recursive call leads immediately to another return; no further computation is done.) An important property of a tail-recursive function is that its code can be abbreviated to a loop. This is justified by applying the ideas in Section 6.6.5; *wh* defines the infinite sequence:

$$if\ \mathbf{B}[\![B]\!]\ \begin{array}{l} then\ \mathbf{C}[\![C]\!];\ if\ \mathbf{B}[\![B]\!]\ \begin{array}{l} then\ \mathbf{C}[\![C]\!];\ if\ \mathbf{B}[\![B]\!]\ \begin{array}{l} \ldots \\ else\ skip \end{array} \\ else\ skip \end{array} \\ else\ skip \end{array}$$

It is easy to see that this sequence has a finite abbreviation, just like the example in Section 6.6.5. Using *label* and *jump* operators, we abbreviate the infinite sequence to:

$$\mathbf{C}[\![\mathbf{while}\ \mathrm{B}\ \mathbf{do}\ \mathrm{C}]\!] = wh$$

$$\text{where } wh = \mathit{label}\ L{:}\ \mathit{if}\ \mathbf{B}[\![\mathrm{B}]\!]\ \mathit{then}\ \mathbf{C}[\![\mathrm{C}]\!];\ \mathit{jump}\ L\ \mathit{else}\ \mathit{skip}$$

The *label* and *jump* instructions are put to good use by the stored program machine. An induction on the number of unfoldings of an evaluation proves that the original and abbreviated definitions of *wh* are operationally equivalent on the stored program machine.

10.6 IMPLEMENTATION OF CONTINUATION-BASED DEFINITIONS

Many workers prefer to implement a language from its continuation semantics definition. An evaluator for a continuation semantics definition is straightforward to derive, because the nesting structure of the continuations suggests a sequential flow of control. The instruction set of the evaluator is just the collection of operations from the continuation algebras, and the evaluator's components are derived from the semantic domains in the semantic definition.

In this section, we develop a compiler and an evaluator for the language in Figure 9.5. To see the evaluator structure suggested by that definition, consider the denotation of [[X:=1; X:=X+2; C]]; it is:

$$(\mathit{return\text{-}value}\ \mathit{one}\ {}^{\text{'}a\text{'}}(\mathit{assign}\ l\ {}^{\text{'}b\text{'}}(\mathit{fetch}\ l\ {}^{\text{'}c\text{'}}(\mathit{save\text{-}arg}\ {}^{\text{'}d\text{'}}(\mathit{return\text{-}value}\ \mathit{two})$$
$$\quad {}^{\text{'}e\text{'}}(\mathit{add}\ {}^{\text{'}f\text{'}}(\mathit{assign}\ l\ {}^{\text{'}g\text{'}}(c_0)))))))$$

The letters in quotes prefix and name the continuations in the expression. For a hypothetical store s_0, a simplification sequence for the denotation is:

$$\begin{aligned}
&(\mathit{return\text{-}value}\ \mathit{one}\ \text{`}a\text{'})\ s_0\\
&= (\mathit{assign}\ l\ \ \text{`}b\text{'})\ \mathit{one}\ s_0\\
&= (\mathit{fetch}\ l\ \ \text{`}c\text{'})\ s_1 \quad \text{where } s_1 = [\,l \mapsto \mathit{one}\,]s_0\\
&= (\mathit{save\text{-}arg}\ \ \text{`}d\text{'}\ \text{`}e\text{'})\ \mathit{one}\ s_1\\
&= (\mathit{return\text{-}value}\ \mathit{two}\ \ (\text{`}e\text{'}\ \mathit{one}))\ s_1 \quad (*)\\
&= (\mathit{add}\ \ \text{`}f\text{'})\ \mathit{one}\ \mathit{two}\ s_1\\
&= (\mathit{assign}\ l\ \ \text{`}g\text{'})\ \mathit{three}\ s_1\\
&= c_0\,[\,l \mapsto \mathit{three}\,]s_1
\end{aligned}$$

At each stage (except the stage labeled (*)) the configuration has the form $(c\ n^*\ s)$; that is, a continuation c followed by zero or more expressible values n^*, followed by the store s. These three components correspond to the control, temporary value stack, and store components, respectively, of the VECS-machine. An environment component is not present, because the continuation operations hide binding identifiers.

The configurations suggest that the evaluator for the language has a configuration $(c\ v\ s)$, where $c \in$ *Control-stack* = *Instruction**, $v \in$ *Value-stack* = *Exprval**, and $s \in$ *Store*. The evaluator's instruction set consists of the operations of the continuation algebras. A nested continuation $c_1(c_2(\cdots c_n \cdots))$ is represented as a control stack $c_1{:}c_2{:} \cdots {:}c_n$.

The denotational definition is not perfectly mated to the machine structure. The problem appears in stage (*): the *save-arg* operation forces its second continuation argument to hold an expressible value that should be left on the value stack. This is not an isolated occurrence; the functionality of expression continuations forces those expression continuations that require multiple expressible values to acquire them one at a time, creating local "pockets" of storage. We would like to eliminate these pockets and remove the *save-arg* operation altogether. One way is to introduce a value stack *Exprval** for the expression continuations' use. We define:

$v \in$ *Value-stack* = *Exprval**
$k \in$ *Exprcont* = *Value-stack* $\rightarrow$ *Cmdcont*

Regardless of how many expressible values an expression continuation requires, its argument is always the value stack. This form of semantics is called a *stack semantics*. It was designed by Milne, who used it in the derivation of a compiler for an ALGOL68 variant. Figure 10.12 shows the stack semantics corresponding to the definition in Figure 9.5.

Now command continuations pass along both the value stack and the store. The **if** and **while** commands use a different version of the *choose* operation; the new version eliminates redundant continuations. The *save-arg* operation disappears from the semantics of addition.

It is nontrivial to prove that the stack semantics denotation of a program is the same as its continuation semantics denotation (see Milne & Strachey 1976). Since we have altered the expression continuation domain, its correspondence to the original domain is difficult to state. A weaker result, but one that suffices for implementation questions, is that the reduction of a stack semantics denotation of a program parallels the reduction of its continuation semantics denotation. We must show: for every syntactic form [[M]]; for environment e and its corresponding environment e' in the stack semantics; for corresponding continuations k and k'; value stack v; store s; and expressible value n:

$$\mathbf{M}[\![\mathrm{m}]\!] e\ k\ s \Rightarrow^* k(n)\ s' \text{ iff } \mathbf{M}'[\![\mathrm{m}]\!] e'\ k'\ v\ s \Rightarrow^* k'(n{:}v)\ s'$$

By "corresponding" continuations k and k', we mean that $(k\ n\ s')$ equals $(k'(n{:}v)\ s')$. Environments e and e' correspond when they map identifiers to corresponding continuations (or the same values, if the identifier's denotable value is not a continuation). Most of the cases in the proof are easy; the proof

Figure 10.12

XII′. Command continuations

Domain $c \in$ *Cmdcont* = *Value-stack* → *Store* → *Answer*

Operations

$finish : Cmdcont$

$finish = \lambda v.\lambda s.\ \text{in}OK(s)$

$err : String \to Cmdcont$

$err = \lambda t.\lambda v.\lambda s.\ \text{in}Err(t)$

$skip : Cmdcont \to Cmdcont$

$skip = \lambda c.\, c$

XIII′. Expression continuations

Domain $k \in$ *Exprcont* = *Value-stack* → *Store* → *Answer*

Operations

$return\text{-}value : Exprval \to Exprcont \to Exprcont$

$return\text{-}value = \lambda n.\lambda k.\lambda v.\ k(n\ cons\ v)$

$add : Exprcont \to Exprcont$

$add = \lambda k.\lambda v.\ k(\ ((hd(tl\ v))\ plus\ (hd\ v))\ cons\ (tl(tl\ v)))$

$fetch : Location \to Exprcont \to Exprcont$

$fetch = \lambda l.\lambda k.\lambda v.\lambda s.\ k((access\ l\ s)\ cons\ v)\ s$

$assign : Location \to Cmdcont \to Exprcont$

$assign = \lambda l.\lambda c.\lambda v.\lambda s.\ c(tl\ v)\ (update\ l\ (hd\ v)\ s)$

$choose : (Cmdcont \to Cmdcont) \to (Cmdcont \to Cmdcont) \to Cmdcont \to Exprcont$

$choose = \lambda f.\lambda g.\lambda c.\lambda v.\ ((hd\ v)\ greaterthan\ zero \to (f\ c)\ [\!]\ (g\ c))\ (tl\ v)$

Valuation functions:

$\mathbf{P}'$: Program → *Location* → *Cmdcont* (like Figure 9.5)

$\mathbf{B}'$: Block → *Environment* → *Cmdcont* → *Cmdcont* (like Figure 9.5)

$\mathbf{D}'$: Declaration → *Environment* → *Environment* (like Figure 9.5)

$\mathbf{C}'$: Command → *Environment* → *Cmdcont* → *Cmdcont* (like Figure 9.5, except for)

$\mathbf{C}'[\![\mathbf{if}\ B\ \mathbf{then}\ C_1\ \mathbf{else}\ C_2]\!] = \lambda e.\ \mathbf{E}'[\![E]\!] \circ (choose\ (\mathbf{C}'[\![C_1]\!]e)\ (\mathbf{C}'[\![C_2]\!]e))$

$\mathbf{C}'[\![\mathbf{while}\ B\ \mathbf{do}\ C]\!] = \lambda e.\ fix(\lambda g.\ \mathbf{E}'[\![E]\!]e \circ (choose\ (\mathbf{C}'[\![C]\!]e \circ g)\ skip))$

$\mathbf{E}'$: Expression → *Environment* → *Exprcont* → *Exprcont* (like Figure 9.5, except for)

$\mathbf{E}'[\![E_1 + E_2]\!] = \lambda e.\ \lambda k.\ \mathbf{E}'[\![E_1]\!]e\ (\mathbf{E}'[\![E_2]\!]e\ (add\ k))$

---

for the **while**-loop is by induction on the number of unfoldings of *fix* in a reduction sequence. The block construct is proved similarly to the loop but we must also show that the respective environments created by the block correspond.

The evaluator for the stack semantics appears in Figure 10.13. The evaluator's rules are just the definitions of the continuation operations. A source program is executed by mapping it to its stack semantics denotation, performing static semantics, and evaluating the resulting continuation on the evaluator.

A similar method for inducing the temporary value stack has been developed by Wand. He does not introduce a value stack domain but inserts "argument steering" combinators into the semantic equations instead. Run-time configurations take the form $(c\ n_1 \cdots n_m\ s)$. The net result is the same, but the proof that the new semantic definition is equal to the original is much simpler than the one needed for our example. Wand's research papers document the method.

Figure 10.13

$c \in Control\text{-}stack = Instruction^*$
$v \in Value\text{-}stack = Exprval^*$
$s \in Store$
where $Instruction = return\text{-}value + add + fetch + assign +$
$choose + skip + finish + err$

Instruction interpretation:

$return\text{-}value\ n{:}c \quad v \quad s \;\Rightarrow\; c \quad n{:}v \quad s$
$add{:}c \quad n_2{:}n_1{:}v \quad s \;\Rightarrow\; c \quad n_3{:}v \quad s$
where n_3 is the sum of n_1 and n_2
$fetch\ l{:}c \quad v \quad s \;\Rightarrow\; c \quad n{:}v \quad s$
where $n = access\ l\ s$
$assign\ l{:}c \quad n{:}v \quad s \;\Rightarrow\; c \quad v \quad s'$
where $s' = update\ l\ n\ s$
$(choose\ f\ g){:}c \quad zero{:}v \quad s \;\Rightarrow\; g{:}c \quad v \quad s$
$(choose\ f\ g){:}c \quad n{:}v \quad s \;\Rightarrow\; f{:}c \quad v \quad s$
where n is greater than $zero$
$finish \quad v \quad s \;\Rightarrow\; \text{in}OK(s)$
$err\ t \quad v \quad s \;\Rightarrow\; \text{in}Err(t)$
$skip{:}c \quad v \quad s \;\Rightarrow\; c \quad v \quad s$

Although the instruction set for the interpreter is in place, *fix* operators still appear in those translated programs containing **while**-loops and labels. The fixed point simplification property $(fix\ F) = F(fix\ F)$ can be used by the interpreter, but we choose to introduce the operation *while f do g*, representing the expression $fix(\lambda c'. f \circ (choose\ (g \circ c')\ skip))$ so that $\mathbf{C}[\![\mathbf{while\ B\ do\ C}]\!] = \lambda e.\ while\ \mathbf{E}[\![\mathrm{E}]\!]e\ do\ \mathbf{C}[\![\mathrm{C}]\!]e$. The evaluation rule is:

$$while\ f\ do\ h{:}c \quad v \quad s \quad \Rightarrow \quad f{:}(choose\ (h{:}while\ f\ do\ h)\ skip){:}c \quad v \quad s$$

The **gotos** present a more serious problem. A block with labels does not have a simple, tail-recursive expansion like the **while**-loop. One solution is to carry over the language's environment argument into the evaluator to hold the continuations associated with the labels. A **goto** causes a lookup into the environment and a reloading of the control stack with the continuation associated with the **goto**.

The problem with the **gotos** is better resolved when an instruction counter is incorporated into the evaluator, *jump* and *jumpfalse* instructions are added, and the code for blocks is generated with jumps in it. A continuation $(ctuple{\downarrow}i)$ is a tail-recursive call to the ith *ctuple* component. If the ith component begins at label L, we generate *jump L*. (Also, the **while**-loop can be compiled to conventional loop code.) The proof of correctness of these transformations is involved and you are referred to Milne & Strachey (1976) and Sethi (1981).

10.6.1 The CGP and VDM Methods

Raskovsky's Code Generator Process (CGP) is a transformation-oriented compiler generation method. It transforms a denotational definition into a BCPL-coded code generator in a series of transformation steps. Each transformation exploits a property of the semantic definition. Defunctionalization, continuation introduction, and global variable introduction for stores and environments are examples of transformations. The generated compiler maps source programs to BCPL code; the evaluator is the BCPL system. The system has been used to develop compilers for nontrivial languages such as GEDANKEN.

Bjørner and Jones advocate a stepwise transformation method that also uses transformations described in this chapter. Their work is part of a software development methodology known as the Vienna Development Method (VDM). VDM system specifications are denotational definitions; the semantic notation is a continuation-style, combinator-based notation called META-IV. Evaluators for VDM specifications are derived using the ideas in the previous section. Compilers, data bases, and other systems software have been specified and implemented using the method. See Bjørner and Jones, 1978 and 1982, for a comprehensive presentation.

10.7 CORRECTNESS OF IMPLEMENTATION AND FULL ABSTRACTION

In previous sections, we stated criteria for correctness of implementation. We now consider the general issue of correctness and provide standards for showing that an operational semantics definition is complementary to a denotational one. The study leads to a famous research problem known as the *full abstraction problem*.

Recall that an operational semantics definition of a language is an intepreter. When the interpreter evaluates a program, it generates a sequence of machine configurations that define the program's operational semantics. We can treat the interpreter as an evaluation relation $\Rightarrow$ that is defined by rewriting rules. A program's operational semantics is just its reduction sequence. For a source language L, we might define an interpreter that reduces L-programs directly. However, we have found it convenient to treat L's semantic function $\mathbf{P}: L \rightarrow D$ as a syntax-directed translation scheme and use it to translate L-programs to function expressions. Then we interpret the function expressions. Let $e \in$ *Function-expr* be a function expression representation of a source program after it has been translated by **P**. Since expressions are treated as syntactic entities by the interpreter for function expressions, we write $e_1 \equiv e_2$ to assert that the denotations of the function expressions e_1 and e_2 are the same value.

Let I be the set of interpreter configurations and let ϕ : *Function-expr* $\rightarrow I$ be a mapping that loads a function expression into an initial interpreter configuration. A configuration is *final* if it cannot be reduced further. The set of final interpreter configurations is called **Fin**. We also make use of an "abstraction" map $\psi : I \rightarrow$ *Function-expr*, which restores the function expression corresponding to an interpreter configuation. The minimum required to claim that an operational semantics definition is complementary to a denotational one is a form of soundness we call *faithfulness*.

10.2 Definition:

An operational semantics $\Rightarrow$ is faithful to the semantics of Function-expr if for all $e \in$ Function-expr and $i \in I$, $\phi(e) \Rightarrow^* i$ implies $e \equiv \psi(i)$.

Faithfulness by itself is not worth much, for the interpreter can have an empty set of evaluation rules and be faithful. Therefore, we define some subset **Ans** of *Function-expr* to be answer forms. For example, the set of constants in *Nat* can be an answer set, as can the set of all normal forms. A guarantee of forward progress to answers is a form of completeness we call *termination*.

10.3 Definition:

An operational semantics $\Rightarrow$ is terminating in relation to the semantics of Function-expr if, for all $e \in$ Function-expr and $a \in$ **Ans**, *if $e \equiv a$, then there exists some $i \in$* **Fin** *such that $\phi(e) \Rightarrow^* i$, $\psi(i) \in$* **Ans**, *and $\psi(i) \equiv a$.*

Termination is the converse of faithfulness, restricted to the i in **Fin**. We use the requirement $\psi(i) \equiv a$ (rather than $\psi(i) = a$) because two elements of **Ans** may share the same value (e.g., normal form answers $(\lambda t.\, t \rightarrow a \,[]\, b)$ and $(\lambda t.\, not(t) \rightarrow b \,[]\, a)$ are distinct answers with the same value). If **Ans** is a set whose elements all have distinct values (e.g., the constants in *Nat*), then $\psi(i)$ must be a. If the operational semantics is faithful, then the requirement that $\psi(i) \equiv a$ is always satisfied.

We apply the faithfulness and termination criteria to the compile-evaluate method described in Sections 10.1 and 10.3. Given a denotational definition $\mathbf{P}: L \rightarrow D$, we treat **P** as a syntax-directed translation scheme to function expressions. For program [[P]], the expression P[[P]] is loaded into the interpreter. In its simplest version, the interpreter requires no extra data structures, hence both ϕ and ψ are identity maps. Recall that the interpreter uses a leftmost-outermost reduction strategy. A final configuration is a normal form. An answer is a (non-$\perp$) normal form expression. By exercise 11 in Chapter 3, the reductions preserve the meaning of the function expression, so the implementation is faithful. In Section 10.3 we remarked that the leftmost-outermost method always locates a normal form for an expression if one exists. Hence the method is terminating.

The definitions of faithfulness and termination are also useful to prove that a low-level operational semantics properly simulates a high-level one: let (the symmetric, transitive closure of) the evaluation relation for the high-level interpreter define $\equiv$ and let the low-level evaluation relation define $\Rightarrow$. **Ans** is the set of final configurations for the high-level interpreter, and **Fin** is the set of final configurations for the low-level one. This method was used in Sections 10.3 and 10.6.

There are other versions of termination properties. We develop these versions using the function expression interpreter. In this case, ϕ and ψ are identity maps, and the **Ans** and **Fin** sets are identical, so we dispense with the two maps and **Fin** and work directly with the function expressions and **Ans**. We define a *context* to be a function expression with zero or more "holes" in it. If we view a context as a derivation tree, we find that zero or more of its leaves are nonterminals. We write a hypothetical context as $C[\ ]$. When we use an expression E to fill the holes in a context $C[\ ]$, giving a well-formed expression, we write $C[E]$. We fill the holes by attaching E's derivation tree to all the nonterminal leaves in $C[\ ]$'s tree. The formalization of contexts is left as an exercise.

A context provides an operating environment for an expression and gives us a criterion for judging information content and behavior. For example, we can use structural induction to prove that for expressions M and N and context $C[\ ]$, $M \sqsubseteq N$ implies that $C[M] \sqsubseteq C[N]$. We write $M \lessapprox N$ if, for all contexts $C[\ ]$ and $a \in$ **Ans**, $C[M] \Rightarrow^* a$ implies that $C[N] \Rightarrow^* a'$ and $a \equiv a'$. We write $M \approx N$ if $M \lessapprox N$ and $N \lessapprox M$ and say that M and N are *operationally equivalent*. The following result is due to Plotkin (1977).

10.4 Proposition:

If $\Rightarrow$ is faithful to the semantics of Function-expr, then $\Rightarrow$ is terminating iff for all $M, N \in$ Function-expr, $M \equiv N$ implies $M \approx N$.

Proof: Left as an exercise. □

This result implies that denotational semantics equality implies operational equivalence under the assumption that the operational semantics is faithful and terminating. Does the converse hold? That is, for a faithful and terminating operational semantics, does operational equivalence imply semantic equality? If it does, we say that the denotational semantics of *Function-expr* is *fully abstract* in relation to its operational semantics.

Plotkin (1977) has shown that the answer to the full abstractness question for *Function-expr* and its usual interpreter is *no*. Let $F_b\colon (Tr_\perp \times Tr_\perp) \to Tr_\perp$ be the function expression:

$$
\begin{aligned}
&\lambda a.\ \text{let } t_1 = a(true, \perp) \text{ in} \\
&\qquad t_1 \to (\text{let } t_2 = a(\perp, true) \text{ in} \\
&\qquad\qquad t_2 \to (\text{let } t_3 = a(false, false) \text{ in} \\
&\qquad\qquad\qquad t_3 \to \perp \,[\!]\, b) \\
&\qquad\qquad [\!]\, \perp) \\
&\qquad [\!]\, \perp
\end{aligned}
$$

We see that $F_{true} \not\sqsubseteq F_{false}$ (and vice versa) by considering the continuous function $v\colon Tr_\perp \times Tr_\perp \to Tr_\perp$ whose graph is $\{ ((\perp, true), true),\ ((true, \perp), true),\ ((true, true), true),\ ((true, false), true),\ ((false, true), true),\ ((false, false), false) \}$ (as usual, pairs $((m, n), \perp)$ are omitted). The function v is the "parallel or" function, and $F_{true}(v) = true$ but $F_{false}(v) = false$. But Plotkin proved, for the language of function expressions and its usual operational semantics, that $F_{true} \approx F_{false}$! The reason that the two expressions are operationally equivalent is that "parallel" functions like v are not representable in the function notation; the notation and its interpreter are inherently "sequential."

There are two possibilities for making the denotational semantics of *Function-expr* fully abstract in relation to its interpreter. One is to extend *Function-expr* so that "parallel" functions are representable. Plotkin did this by restricting the **Ans** set to be the set of constants for *Nat* and *Tr* and introducing a parallel conditional operation *par-cond* : $Tr_\perp \times D_\perp \times D_\perp \to D_\perp$, for $D \in \{ Nat, Tr \}$, with reduction rules:

$$
\begin{aligned}
&\textit{par-cond}(true, d_1, d_2) \Rightarrow d_1 \\
&\textit{par-cond}(false, d_1, d_2) \Rightarrow d_2 \\
&\textit{par-cond}(\perp, d, d) \Rightarrow d
\end{aligned}
$$

Then $v = \lambda(t_1, t_2).\ \textit{par-cond}(t_1, true, t_2)$. Plotkin showed that the extended notation and its denotational semantics are fully abstract in relation to the operational semantics.

Another possibility for creating a fully abstract semantics is to reduce the size of the semantic domains so that the nonrepresentable "parallel" functions are no longer present. A number of researchers have proposed domain constructions that do this. The constructions are nontrivial, and you should research the suggested readings for further information.

SUGGESTED READINGS

General compiler generating systems: Appel 1985; Ganzinger, Ripken & Wilhelm 1977; Jones 1980; Mosses 1975, 1976, 1979; Paulson 1982, 1984; Pleban 1984; Wand 1983

Static semantics processing: Ershov 1978; Jones et al. 1985; Mosses 1975; Paulson 1982;Sethi 1981

Rewriting rules & evaluators for function notation: Berry & Levy 1979; Burge 1975; Hoffman & O'Donnell 1983; Huet & Oppen 1980; Landin 1964; Vegdahl 1984

Combinator systems & evaluators: Christiansen & Jones 1983; Clarke et al. 1980; Curry & Feys 1958; Hudak & Krantz 1984; Hughes 1982; Mosses 1979a, 1980, 1983a, 1984; Raoult & Sethi 1982; Sethi 1983; Turner 1979

Transformation methods: Bjørner & Jones 1978, 1982; Georgeff 1984; Hoare 1972; Raoult & Sethi 1984; Raskovsky & Collier 1980; Raskovsky 1982; Reynolds 1972; Schmidt 1985a, 1985b; Steele 1977; Steele & Sussman 1976a, 1976b

Continuation-based implementation techniques: Clinger 1984; Henson & Turner 1982; Milne & Strachey 1976; Nielson 1979; Polak 1981; Sethi 1981; Wand 1980a, 1982a, 1982b, 1983, 1985b

Full abstraction: Berry, Curien, & Levy 1983; Milner 1977; Mulmuley 1985; Plotkin 1977; Stoughton 1986

EXERCISES

1. a. Using the semantics of Figure 5.2, evaluate the program P⟦Z:=A+1⟧*four* using the compile-evaluate method and using the interpreter method.
   b. Repeat part a for the program P⟦**begin var** A; A:=A+1 **end**⟧ l_0 ($\lambda l.\ zero$) and the language of Figures 7.1 and 7.2.

2. If you have access to a parser generator system such as YACC and a functional language implementation such as Scheme, ML, or LISP, implement an SPS-like compiler generating system for denotational semantics.

3. Using the criteria for determining unfrozen expressions, work in detail the static semantics processing of:
   a. The example in Section 10.2.
   b. The program in part b of Exercise 1 (with the *Store*, *Nat*, and *Tr* algebras frozen).
   c. The program in Figure 7.6 (with the *Function*, *List*, and *Environment* algebras frozen; and again with just the *Function* and *List* algebras frozen).

4. Let the *Store* algebra be unfrozen; redo the static semantics of parts a and b of Exercise 3. Why don't real life compilers perform a similar service? Would this approach work well on programs containing loops?

5. The example of static semantics simplification in Section 10.2 showed combinations of the form $(\underline{\lambda}s.M)s$ simplified to M. Why is this acceptable in the example? When is it not?

6. Recall that the simplification rule for the *fix* operation is $(fix\ F) = F(fix\ F)$. How should this rule be applied during static semantics analysis? Consider in particular the cases of:
   i. Recursively defined environments $e = fix(\lambda e'. \cdots)$.
   ii. Recursively defined commands and procedures $p = fix(\lambda p.\underline{\lambda}s. \cdots)$.

7. A number of researchers have proposed that a language's valuation function be divided into a static semantics valuation function and a dynamic semantics valuation function:

   $\mathbf{C}_S$: Command $\rightarrow$ *Environment* $\rightarrow$ *Tr*

   $\mathbf{C}_D$: Command $\rightarrow$ *Environment'* $\rightarrow$ ((*Store* $\rightarrow$ *Poststore*) + *Err*)

   such that a well typed command $[\![C]\!]$ has denotation $\mathbf{C}_S[\![C]\!] = true$ and a denotation $\mathbf{C}_D[\![C]\!]$ in the summand (*Store* $\rightarrow$ *Poststore*). Similarly, an ill typed program has a denotation of *false* with respect to $\mathbf{C}_S$ and an in*Err*() denotation with respect to $\mathbf{C}_D$.

   a. Formulate these valuation functions for the language in Figures 7.1 and 7.2.
   b. Comment on the advantages of this approach for implementing the language. Are there any disadvantages?

8. a. Perform leftmost-outermost reductions on the following expressions. If the expression does not appear to have a normal form, halt your reduction and justify your decision.

i. $(\lambda x.\ zero)((\lambda x.\ x\,x)(\lambda x.\ x\,x))$
ii. $(\underline{\lambda x}.\ zero)((\lambda x.\ x\,x)(\lambda x.\ x\,x))$
iii. $((\lambda x.\lambda y.\ y(y\,x))(one\ plus\ one))(\lambda z.\ z\ times\ z)$
iv. $((\underline{\lambda x}.\underline{\lambda y}.\ y(y\,x))(one\ plus\ one))(\lambda z.\ z\ times\ z)$
v. $((\underline{\lambda x}.\underline{\lambda y}.\ y(y\,x))(one\ plus\ one))(\underline{\lambda z}.\ z\ times\ z)$

b. Redo part a, representing the expressions as trees. Show the traversal through the trees that a tree evaluator would take.

9. Implement the tree evaluator for function notation. (It is easiest to implement it in a language that supports list processing.) Next, improve the evaluator to use an environment table. Finally, improve the evaluator to use call-by-need evaluation.

10. Evaluate the code segment *pushclosure*(Δ: *return*): Δ: *call* from Figure 10.4 on the VEC-machine.

11. Translate the expressions in exercise 8 into VEC-machine code and evaluate them on the VEC-machine.

12. Improve the code generation map T for the VEC-machine so that it generates assembly code that contains jumps and conditional jumps.

13. Improve the VEC-machine so that *push x* becomes *push* "*offset*," where "*offset*" is the offset into the environment where the value bound to x can be found. Improve the code generation map so it correctly calculates the offsets for binding identifiers.

14. Augment the VEC-machine with instructions for handling pairs and sum values. Write the translations $\mathrm{T}[\![(E_1, E_2)]\!]$ and $\mathrm{T}[\![\text{cases } E_1 \text{ of } G]\!]$, where G ::= in$I_1(I_2) \rightarrow E$ [] G | end.

15. Compile the programs in Exercise 3 to VEC-code after static semantics has been performed. Can you suggest an efficient way to perform static semantics?

16. a. Augment the combinator language definition in Figure 10.7 with combinators for building environments.
b. Rewrite the semantics of the language in Figures 7.1 and 7.2 in combinator form.
c. Propose a method for doing static semantics analysis on the semantics in part b.

17. Convert the *Store* algebra in Figure 10.7 into one that manipulates ordered tree values. Are the new versions of *access* and *update* more efficient than the existing ones?

18. a. Verify that the **C** and **E** valuation functions of the language of Figure 5.2 are single-threaded. Does the **P** function satisfy the criteria of Definition 10.1? Is it single-threaded?
    b. Extend Definition 10.1 so that a judgement can be made about the single-threadedness of the language in Figures 7.1 and 7.2. Is that language single-threaded? Derive control combinators for the language.

19. An alternative method of generating a compiler from a continuation semantics of a language is to replace the command and expression continuation algebras by algebras of machine code. Let *Code* be the domain of machine code programs for a VEC-like stack machine, and use the following two algebras in place of the command and expression continuation algebras in Figure 9.5 (note: the ":" denotes the code concatenation operator):

    XII′. Command code
    Domain $c \in Cmdcont = Code$
    Operations
    $finish = \mathbf{stop}$
    $error = \lambda t.\ \mathbf{pushconst}\ t$

    XIII′. Expression code
    Domain $k \in Exprcont = Code$
    Operations
    $return\text{-}value = \lambda n.\lambda k.\ \mathbf{pushconst}\ n{:}\ k$
    $save\text{-}arg = \lambda f.\lambda g.\ f(g)$
    $add = \lambda k.\ \mathbf{add}{:}\ k$
    $fetch = \lambda l.\lambda k.\ \mathbf{pushvar}\ l{:}\ k$
    $assign = \lambda l.\lambda c.\ \mathbf{storevar}\ l{:}\ c$
    $choose = \lambda c_1.\lambda c_2.\ \mathbf{jumpzero}\ L_1{:}\ c_1{:}\ \mathbf{jump}\ L_2{:}\ \mathbf{label}\ L_1{:}\ c_2{:}\ \mathbf{label}\ L_2$

    a. Generate the denotations of several programs using the new algebras.
    b. Outline a proof that shows the new algebras are faithful to the originals in an operational sense.

20. Revise the stack semantics in Figure 10.13 so that the expressible value stack isn't used by command continuations; that is, the *Cmdcont* domain remains as it is in Figure 9.5, but the stack is still used by the *Exprcont* domain, that is, *Exprcont* is defined as in Figure 10.13. What are the pragmatics of this semantics and its implementation?

21. a. Prove that the evaluator with an environment in Section 10.3 is faithful and terminating in relation to the evaluator in Section 10.1.
    b. Prove that the VEC-machine in Section 10.3.1 is faithful and terminating in relation to the evaluator with environment in Section 10.3 when the answer set is limited to first-order normal forms.
    c. Prove that the defunctionalized version of a semantic algebra is faithful and terminating in relation to the orignal version of the algebra.

22. Prove that the properties of faithfulness and termination compose; that is, for operational semantics A, B, and C, if C is faithful/terminating in relation to B, and B is faithful/terminating in relation to A, then C is faithful/terminating in relation to A.

23. a. Give the graph of the function $\textit{par-cond} : Tr_{\perp} \times D_{\perp} \times D_{\perp} \rightarrow D_{\perp}$ for $D \in \{ \mathit{Nat}, \mathit{Tr} \}$, prove that the function is continuous, and prove that its rewriting rules are sound.
    b. Attempt to define the graph of a continuous function $\textit{par-cond} : Tr_{\perp} \times D \times D \rightarrow D$ for arbitrary D and show that its rewriting rules in Section 10.7 are sound. What goes wrong?

Chapter 11

Domain Theory III: Recursive Domain Specifications

Several times we have made use of recursively defined domains (also called *reflexive domains*) of the form $D = F(D)$. In this chapter, we study recursively defined domains in detail, because:

1. Recursive definitions are natural descriptions for certain data structures. For example, the definition of binary trees, $Bintree = (Data + (Data \times Bintree \times Bintree))_{\perp}$, clearly states that a binary tree is a leaf of data or two trees joined by a root node of data. Another example is the definition of linear lists of A-elements $Alist = (Nil + (A \times Alist))_{\perp}$, where $Nil = Unit$. The definition describes the internal structure of the lists better than the A^* domain does. *Alist*'s definition also clearly shows why the operations *cons*, *hd*, *tl*, and *null* are essential for assembling and disassembling lists.
2. Recursive definitions are absolutely necessary to model certain programming language features. For example, procedures in ALGOL60 may receive procedures as actual parameters. The domain definition must read $Proc = Param \to Store \to Store_{\perp}$, where $Param = Int + Real + \cdots + Proc$, to properly express the range of parameters.

Like the recursively defined functions in Chapter 6, recursively defined domains require special construction. Section 11.1 introduces the construction through an example, Section 11.2 develops the technical machinery, and Section 11.3 presents examples of reflexive domains.

11.1 REFLEXIVE DOMAINS HAVE INFINITE ELEMENTS

We motivated the least fixed point construction in Chapter 6 by treating a recursively defined function f as an operational definition— f's application to an argument a was calculated by recursively unfolding f's definition as needed. If the combination $(f\,a)$ simplified to an answer b in a finite number of unfoldings, the function satisfying the recursive specification mapped a to b as well. We used this idea to develop a sequence of functions that approximated the solution; a sequence member f_i resulted from unfolding f's specification i times. The f_i's formed a chain whose least upper bound was the function satisfying the recursive specification. The key to finding the solution was building the sequence of approximations. A suitable way of combining these approximations was found and the problem was solved.

Similarly, we build a solution to a recursive domain definition by building a sequence of approximating domains. The elements in each approximating domain will be present in the solution domain, and each approximating domain D_i will be a *subdomain* of approximating domain D_{i+1}; that is, the elements and partial ordering structure of D_i are preserved in D_{i+1}. Since semantic domains are nonempty collections, we take domain D_0 to be $\{ \bot \}$. D_0 is a pointed cpo, and in order to preserve the subdomain property, each approximating domain D_i will be a pointed cpo as well. Domain D_{i+1} is built from D_i and the recursive definition.

Let's apply these ideas to $Alist = (Nil + (A \times Alist))_\bot$ as an example. $Nil = Unit$ represents the empty list, and a nonempty list of A-elements has the structure $A \times Alist$. An $Alist$ can also be undefined. Domain $Alist_0 = \{ \bot \}$, and for each $i{>}0$, $Alist_{i+1} = (Nil + (A \times Alist_i))_\bot$. To get started, we draw $Alist_1 = (Nil + (A \times Alist_0))_\bot$ as:

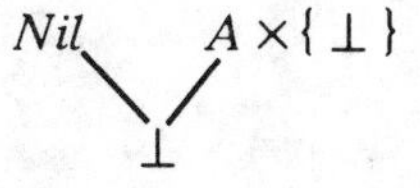

because $A \times Alist_0 = A \times \{ \bot \} = \{ (a, \bot) \mid a \in A \}$. (For readability, from here on we will represent a k-element list as $[a_0, a_1, \cdots, a_k]$, omitting the injection tags. Hence, $Alist_1 = \{ \bot, [nil] \} \cup \{ [a, \bot] \mid a \in A \}$.) $Alist_0$ is a subdomain of $Alist_1$, as $\bot \in Alist_0$ embeds to $\bot \in Alist_1$.

Next, $Alist_2 = (Nil + (A \times Alist_1))_\bot$. The product $A \times Alist_1 = A \times (Nil + (A \times Alist_0))_\bot$ can be visualized as a union of three distinct sets of elements: $\{ [a, \bot] \mid a \in A \}$, the set of *partial* lists of one element; $\{ [a, nil] \mid a \in A \}$, the set of *proper* lists of one element, and $\{ [a_1, a_2, \bot] \mid a_1, a_2 \in A \}$, the set of partial lists of two elements. Drawing $A \times Alist_1$ with these sets, we obtain:

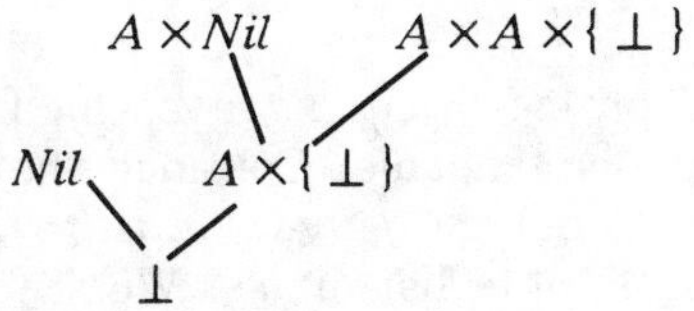

It is easy to see where $Alist_1$ embeds into $Alist_2$— into the lower portion. $Alist_2$ contains elements with more information than those in $Alist_1$.

A pattern is emerging: $Alist_i$ contains $\bot$; nil; proper lists of $(i{-}1)$ or less

A-elements; and partial lists of i A-elements, which are capable of expanding to lists of greater length in the later, larger domains. The element $\bot$ serves double duty: it represents both a nontermination situation and a "don't know yet" situation. That is, a list $[a_0, a_1, \bot]$ may be read as the result of a program that generated two output elements and then "hung up," or it may be read as an approximation of a list of length greater than two, where information as to what follows a_1 is not currently available.

What is the limit of the family of domains $Alist_i$? Using the least fixed point construction as inspiration, we might take $Alist_{fin} = \bigcup_{i=0}^{\infty} Alist_i$, partially ordered to be consistent with the $Alist_i$'s. (That is, $x \sqsubseteq_{Alist_{fin}} x'$ iff there exists some $j \geqslant 0$ such that $x \sqsubseteq_{Alist_j} x'$.) Domain $Alist_{fin}$ contains $\bot$, *nil*, and all proper lists of finite length. But it also contains all the partial lists! To discard the partial lists would be foolhardy, for partial lists have real semantic value. But they present a problem: $Alist_{fin}$ is not a cpo, for the chain $\bot$, $[a_0, \bot]$, $[a_0, a_1, \bot]$, $\cdots$, $[a_0, a_1, \cdots, a_i, \bot]$, $\cdots$ does not have a least upper bound in $Alist_{fin}$.

The obvious remedy to the problem is to add the needed upper bounds to the domain. The lub of the aforementioned chain is the *infinite* list $[a_0, a_1, \cdots, a_i, a_{i+1}, \cdots]$. It is easy to see where the infinite lists would be added to the domain. The result, called $Alist_\infty$, is:

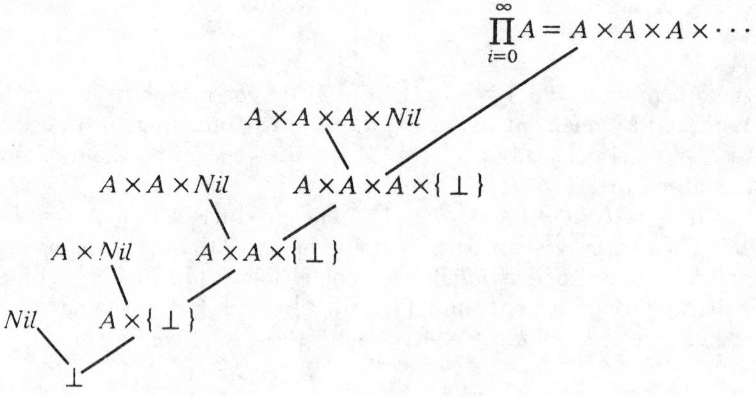

The infinite elements are a boon; realistic computing situations involving infinite data structures are now expressible and understandable. Consider the list l specified by $l = (a\ cons\ l)$, for $a \in A$. The functional $(\lambda l.\ a\ cons\ l)$: $Alist_\infty \rightarrow Alist_\infty$ has as its least fixed point $[a, a, a, \cdots]$, the infinite list of a's. We see that l satisfies the properties $(hd\ l) = a$, $(tl\ l) = l$, and $(null\ l) = false$. The term *lazy list* has been coined for recursively specified lists like l, for when one is used in computation, no attempt is ever made to completely evaluate it to its full length. Instead it is "lazy"— it produces its next element only when asked (by the disassembly operation *hd*).

$Alist_\infty$ appears to be the solution to the recursive specification. But a formal construction is still needed. The first step is formalizing the notion of subdomain. We introduce a family of continuous functions $\phi_i : Alist_i \rightarrow Alist_{i+1}$ for $i \geq 0$. Each ϕ_i embeds $Alist_i$ into $Alist_{i+1}$. By continuity, the partial ordering and lubs in $Alist_i$ are preserved in $Alist_{i+1}$. However, it is easy to find ϕ_i functions that do an "embedding" that is unnatural (e.g., $\phi_i = \lambda x. \perp_{Alist_{i+1}}$). To guarantee that the function properly embeds $Alist_i$ into $Alist_{i+1}$, we also define a family of continuous functions $\psi_i : Alist_{i+1} \rightarrow Alist_i$ that map the elements in $Alist_{i+1}$ to those in $Alist_i$ that best approximate them. $Alist_i$ is a subdomain of $Alist_{i+1}$ when $\psi_i \circ \phi_i = id_{Alist_i}$ holds; that is, every element in $Alist_i$ can be embedded by ϕ_i and recovered by ψ_i. To force the embedding of $Alist_i$ into the "lower portion" of $Alist_{i+1}$, we also require that $\phi_i \circ \psi_i \sqsubseteq id_{Alist_{i+1}}$. This makes it clear that the new elements in $Alist_{i+1}$ not in $Alist_i$ "grow out of" of $Alist_i$.

The function pairs (ϕ_i, ψ_i), $i \geq 0$, are generated from the recursive specification. To get started, we define $\phi_0 : Alist_0 \rightarrow Alist_1$ as $(\lambda x. \perp_{Alist_1})$ and $\psi_0 : Alist_1 \rightarrow Alist_0$ as $(\lambda x. \perp_{Alist_0})$. It is easy to show that the (ϕ_0, ψ_0) pair satisfies that two properties mentioned above. For every $i > 0$:

$$
\begin{aligned}
\phi_i : Alist_i \rightarrow Alist_{i+1} = \underline{\lambda} x.\ & \text{cases } x \text{ of} \\
& \text{is}Nil() \rightarrow \text{in}Nil() \\
& [\,]\ \text{is}A \times Alist_{i-1}(a, l) \rightarrow \text{in}A \times Alist_i(a, \phi_{i-1}(l)) \text{ end}
\end{aligned}
$$

The embedding is based on the structure of the argument from $Alist_i$. The structures of undefined and empty lists are preserved, and a list with head element $a \in A$ and tail $l \in Alist_{i-1}$ is mapped into a pair $(a, \phi_{i-1}(l)) \in A \times Alist_i$, courtesy of $\phi_{i-1} : Alist_{i-1} \rightarrow Alist_i$. Similarly:

$$
\begin{aligned}
\psi_i : Alist_{i+1} \rightarrow Alist_i = \underline{\lambda} x.\ & \text{cases } x \text{ of} \\
& \text{is}Nil() \rightarrow \text{in}Nil() \\
& [\,]\ \text{is}A \times Alist_i(a, l) \rightarrow \text{in}A \times Alist_{i-1}(a, \psi_{i-1}(l)) \text{ end}
\end{aligned}
$$

The function converts its argument to its best approximation in $Alist_i$ by analyzing its structure and using ψ_{i-1} where needed. A mathematical induction proof shows that each pair (ϕ_i, ψ_i) satisifies the required properties.

A chain-like sequence has been created:

$$
Alist_0 \underset{\phi_0}{\overset{\psi_0}{\rightleftarrows}} Alist_1 \underset{\phi_1}{\overset{\psi_1}{\rightleftarrows}} Alist_2 \quad \cdots \quad Alist_i \underset{\phi_i}{\overset{\psi_i}{\rightleftarrows}} Alist_{i+1} \quad \cdots
$$

What is the "lub" of this chain? (It will be $Alist_\infty$.) To give us some intuition about the lub, we represent the elements of an $Alist_i$ domain as tuples. An element $x \in Alist_i$ appears as an $(i+1)$-tuple of the form $(x_0, x_1, \cdots, x_{i-1}, x_i)$, where $x_i = x$, $x_{i-1} = \psi_{i-1}(x_i)$, $\cdots$, $x_1 = \psi_1(x_2)$, and $x_0 = \psi_0(x_1)$. For example, $[a_0, a_1, nil] \in Alist_3$ has tuple form $(\perp, [a_0, \perp], [a_0, a_1, \perp], [a_0, a_1, nil])$; $[a_0, a_1, a_2, \perp] \in Alist_3$ has form $(\perp, [a_0, \perp], [a_0, a_1, \perp], [a_0, a_1, a_2, \perp])$; $[a_0, nil] \in Alist_3$ has form $(\perp, [a_0, \perp], [a_0, nil], [a_0, nil])$; and $\perp \in Alist_3$ has form $(\perp, \perp, \perp, \perp)$. The tuples trace the incrementation of information in an element until the information is complete. They suggest that the limit domain of the chain, $Alist_\infty$, has elements whose tuple representations have *infinite* length. A finite list x with i A-elements belongs to $Alist_\infty$ and has tuple representation $(x_0, x_1, \cdots, x_{i-1}, x, x, \cdots)$— it stabilizes. The infinite lists have tuple representations that never stabilize: for example, an infinite list of a's has the representation $(\perp, [a, \perp], [a, a, \perp], [a, a, a, \perp], \cdots, [a, a, a, \cdots, a, \perp], \cdots)$. The tuple shows that the infinite list has information content that sums all the finite partial lists that approximate it.

Since there is no real difference between an element and its tuple representation (like functions and their graphs), we take the definition of the limit domain $Alist_\infty$ to be the set of infinite tuples induced from the $Alist_i$'s and the ψ_i's:

$$Alist_\infty = \{\, (x_0, x_1, \cdots, x_i, \cdots) \mid \textit{for all } n \geq 0,\ x_n \in Alist_n \text{ and } x_n = \psi_n(x_{n+1}) \,\}$$

partially ordered by, for all $x, y \in Alist_\infty$, $x \sqsubseteq y$ iff for all $n \geq 0$, $x{\downarrow}n \sqsubseteq_{Alist_n} y{\downarrow}n$. $Alist_\infty$ contains only those tuples with information consistent with the $Alist_i$'s. The partial ordering is the natural one for a subdomain of a product domain.

Now we must show that $Alist_\infty$ satisfies the recursive specification; that is, $Alist_\infty = (Nil + (A \times Alist_\infty))_\perp$. Unfortunately this equality doesn't hold! The problem is that the domain on the right-hand side uses the one on the left-hand side as a component— the left-hand side domain is a set of tuples but the right-hand side one is a lifted disjoint union. The situation isn't hopeless, however, as the two domains have the same size (cardinality) and possess the same partial ordering structure. The two domains are *order isomorphic*. The isomorphism is proved by functions $\Phi: Alist_\infty \rightarrow (Nil + (A \times Alist_\infty))_\perp$ and $\Psi: (Nil + (A \times Alist_\infty))_\perp \rightarrow Alist_\infty$ such that $\Psi \circ \Phi = id_{Alist_\infty}$ and $\Phi \circ \Psi = id_{Nil + (A \times Alist_\infty))_\perp}$. The Φ function exposes the list structure inherent in an $Alist_\infty$ element, and the Ψ map gives the tuple representation of list structured objects.

The isomorphism property is strong enough that $Alist_\infty$ may be considered a solution of the specification. The Φ and Ψ maps are used in the definitions of operations on the domain. For example, $head : Alist_\infty \rightarrow A_\perp$ is defined as:

$$head = \underline{\lambda} x.\ \text{cases}\ \Phi(x)\ \text{of is}Nil() \rightarrow \perp\ []\ \text{is}A{\times}Alist_\infty(a, l) \rightarrow a\ \text{end}$$

tail : $Alist_\infty \to Alist_\infty$ is similar. The map *construct*: $A \times Alist_\infty \to Alist_\infty$ is $construct(a, x) = \Psi(\mathrm{in}A{\times}Alist_\infty(a, x))$. These conversions of structure from $Alist_\infty$ to list form and back are straightforward and weren't mentioned in the examples in the previous chapters. The isomorphism maps can always be inserted when needed.

The Φ and Ψ maps are built from the (ϕ_i, ψ_i) pairs. A complete description is presented in the next section.

11.2 THE INVERSE LIMIT CONSTRUCTION

The method just described is the *inverse limit construction.* It was developed by Scott as a justification of Strachey's original development of denotational semantics. The formal details of the construction are presented in this section. The main result is that, for any recursive domain specification of form $D = F(D)$ (where F is an expression built with the constructors of Chapter 3 such that $F(E)$ is a pointed cpo when E is), there is a domain D_∞ that is isomorphic to $F(D_\infty)$. D_∞ is the *least* such pointed cpo that satisfies the specification. If you take faith in the above claims, you may wish to skim this section and proceed to the examples in Section 11.3.

Our presentation of the inverse limit construction is based on an account by Reynolds (1972) of Scott's results. We begin by formalizing the relationship between the ϕ_i and ψ_i maps.

11.1 Definition:

For pointed cpos D and D', a pair of continuous functions $(f\colon D \to D', g : D' \to D)$ is a retraction pair iff:

1. $g \circ f = id_D$
2. $f \circ g \sqsubseteq id_{D'}$

f is called an embedding *and g is called a* projection.

11.2 Proposition:

The composition $(f_2 \circ f_1, g_1 \circ g_2)$ of retraction pairs $(f_1\colon D \to D', g_1\colon D' \to D)$ and $(f_2\colon D' \to D'', g_2\colon D'' \to D')$ is itself a retraction pair.

Proof: $(g_1 \circ g_2) \circ (f_2 \circ f_1) = g_1 \circ (g_2 \circ f_2) \circ f_1) = g_1 \circ id_{D'} \circ f_1 = g_1 \circ f_1 = id_D$. The proof that $(f_2 \circ f_1) \circ (g_1 \circ g_2) \sqsubseteq id_{D''}$ is similar. □

11.3 Proposition:

An embedding (projection) has a unique corresponding projection (embedding).

Proof: Let (f, g_1) and (f, g_2) both be retraction pairs. We must show that $g_1 = g_2$. First, $f \circ g_1 \sqsubseteq id_{D'}$ which implies $g_2 \circ f \circ g_1 \sqsubseteq g_2 \circ id_{D'}$ by the monotonicity of g_2. But $g_2 \circ f \circ g_1 = (g_2 \circ f) \circ g_1 = id_D \circ g_1 = g_1$, implying $g_1 \sqsubseteq g_2$. Repeating the above derivation with g_1 and g_2 swapped gives $g_1 \sqsubseteq g_2$, implying that $g_1 = g_2$. The uniqueness of an embedding f to a projection g is left as an exercise. □

11.4 Proposition:

The components of a retraction pair are strict functions.

Proof: Left as an exercise. □

Retraction pairs are special cases of function pairs $(f: D \to D', g: D' \to D)$ for cpos D and D'. Since we will have use for function pairs that may not be retraction pairs on pointed cpos, we assign the name *r-pair* to a function pair like the one just seen.

11.5 Definition:

For cpos D and D', a continuous pair of functions $(f: D \to D', g: D' \to D)$ is called an r-pair *and is written $(f,g): D \leftrightarrow D'$. The operations on r-pairs are:*

1. *Composition: for $(f_1, g_1): D \leftrightarrow D'$ and $(f_2, g_2): D' \leftrightarrow D''$, $(f_2, g_2) \circ (f_1, g_1): D \leftrightarrow D''$ is defined as $(f_2 \circ f_1, g_1 \circ g_2)$.*
2. *Reversal: for $(f,g): D \leftrightarrow D'$, $(f,g)^R: D' \leftrightarrow D$ is defined as (g,f).*

The reversal of a retraction pair might not be a retraction pair. The identity r-pair for the domain $D \leftrightarrow D$ is $id_{D \leftrightarrow D} = (id_D, id_D)$. It is easy to show that the composition and reversal operations upon r-pairs are continuous. We use the letters $r, s, t, \cdots$ to denote r-pairs.

11.6 Proposition:

For r-pairs $r: D \leftrightarrow D'$ and $s: D' \leftrightarrow D''$:

1. $(r \circ s)^R = s^R \circ r^R$
2. $(r^R)^R = r$.

Proof: Left as an exercise. □

When we build a solution to $D = F(D)$, we build the approximating domains $\{ D_i \mid i \geqslant 0 \}$ from an initial domain D_0 by systematically applying the domain construction F. We use a similar procedure to generate the r-pairs $(\phi_i, \psi_i) : D_i \leftrightarrow D_{i+1}$ from a starting pair (ϕ_0, ψ_0). First, the domain builders defined in Chapter 3 are extended to build r-pairs.

11.7 Definition:

For r-pairs $r = (f, g) : C \leftrightarrow E$ and $s = (f', g') : C' \leftrightarrow E'$, let:

1. *$r \times s$ denote:*
   $((\lambda(x,y).\,(f(x), f'(y))),\ (\lambda(x,y).\,(g(x), g'(y)))) : C \times C' \leftrightarrow E \times E'$
2. *$r + s$ denote:*
   $((\lambda x.$ cases x of is$C(c) \rightarrow$ in$E(f(c))$ [] is$C'(c) \rightarrow$ in$E'(f'(c))$ end,
   $(\lambda x.$ cases y of is$E(e) \rightarrow$ in$C(g(e))$ [] is$E'(e) \rightarrow$ in$C'(g'(e))$ end$))$
   $: C{+}C' \leftrightarrow E{+}E'$
3. *$r \rightarrow s$ denote: $((\lambda x.\, f' \circ x \circ g),\ (\lambda y.\, g' \circ y \circ f)) : (C \rightarrow C') \leftrightarrow (E \rightarrow E')$*
4. *$(r)_\perp$ denote: $((\underline{\lambda} x.\, f\, x),\ (\underline{\lambda} y.\, g\, y)) : C_\perp \leftrightarrow E_\perp$*

For $D = F(D)$, the domain expression F determines a construction for building a new domain $F(A)$ from argument domain A and a construction for building a new r-pair $F(r)$ from an argument r-pair r. For example, the recursive specification $Nlist = (Nil + (Nat \times Nlist))_\perp$ gives a construction $F(D) = ((Nil + (Nat \times D))_\perp$ such that, for any cpo A, $(Nil + (Nat \times A))_\perp$ is also a cpo, and for any r-pair r, $(Nil + (Nat \times r))_\perp$ is an r-pair. The r-pair is constructed using Definition 11.7; the r-pairs corresponding to Nil and Nat in the example are the identity r-pairs (id_{Nil}, id_{Nil}) and (id_{Nat}, id_{Nat}), respectively. You are left with the exercise of formalizing what a "domain expression" is. Once you have done so, produce a structural induction proof of the following important lemma.

11.8 Lemma:

For any domain expression F and r-pairs $r : D \leftrightarrow D'$ and $s : D' \leftrightarrow D''$:

1. $F(id_{E \leftrightarrow E}) = id_{F(E) \leftrightarrow F(E)}$
2. $F(s) \circ F(r) = F(s \circ r)$
3. $(F(r))^R = F(r^R)$
4. *if r is a retraction pair, then so is $F(r)$*

The lemma holds for the domain expressions built with the domain calculus of Chapter 3.

Now that r-pairs and their fundamental properties have been stated, we formulate the inverse limit domain.

11.9 Definition:

A retraction sequence *is a pair* $(\{ D_i \mid i \geq 0 \}, \{ r_i: D_i \leftrightarrow D_{i+1} \mid i \geq 0 \})$ *such that for all* $i \geq 0$, D_i *is a pointed cpo, and each r-pair* r_i *is a retraction pair.*

We often compose retraction pairs from a retraction sequence. Let $t_{mn}: D_m \leftrightarrow D_n$ be defined as:

$$t_{mn} = \begin{cases} r_{n-1} \circ \cdots \circ r_m & \text{if } m < n \\ id_{D_m \leftrightarrow D_m} & \text{if } m = n \\ r_n^R \circ \cdots \circ r_{m-1}^R & \text{if } m > n \end{cases}$$

To make this clear, let each r_i be the r-pair $(\phi_i: D_i \to D_{i+1}, \psi_i: D_{i+1} \to D_i)$ and each t_{mn} be the r-pair $(\theta_{mn} : D_m \to D_n, \theta_{nm} : D_n \to D_m)$. Then for $m<n$, $t_{mn} = (\theta_{mn}, \theta_{nm}) = (\phi_{n-1}, \psi_{n-1}) \circ \cdots \circ (\phi_{m+1}, \psi_{m+1}) \circ (\phi_m, \psi_m) = (\phi_{n-1} \circ \cdots \circ \phi_{m+1} \circ \phi_m, \psi_m \circ \psi_{m+1} \circ \cdots \circ \psi_{n-1})$, which is drawn as:

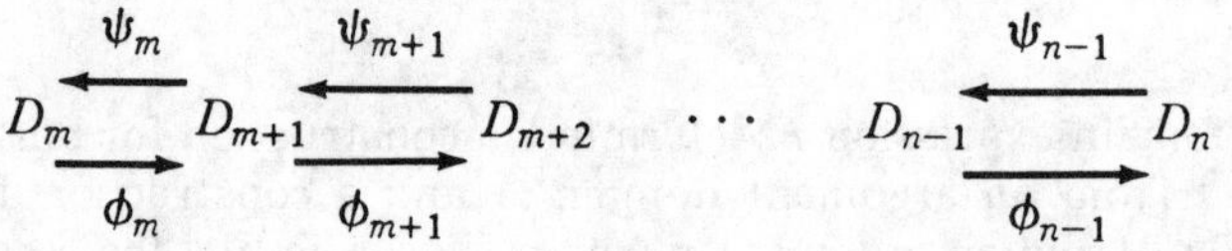

Drawing a similar diagram for the case when $m>n$ makes it clear that $t_{mn} = (\theta_{mn}, \theta_{nm}) = (\theta_{nm}, \theta_{mn})^R = t_{nm}^R$, so the use of the θ_{mn}'s is consistent.

11.10 Proposition:

For any retraction sequence and $m,n,k \geq 0$:

1. $t_{mn} \circ t_{km} \sqsubseteq t_{kn}$
2. $t_{mn} \circ t_{km} = t_{kn}$, *when* $m \geq k$ *or* $m \geq n$
3. t_{mn} *is a retraction pair when* $m \leq n$

Proof: Left as an exercise. □

As the example in Section 11.1 pointed out, the limit of a retraction sequence is built from the members of the D_i domains and the ψ_i embeddings.

11.11 Definition:

The inverse limit of a retraction sequence:

$$(\{ D_i \mid i \geq 0 \}, \{ (\phi_i, \psi_i): D_i \leftrightarrow D_{i+1} \mid i \geq 0 \})$$

is the set:

$D_\infty = \{ (x_0, x_1, \cdots, x_i, \cdots) \mid$ *for all* $n > 0$, $x_n \in D_n$ *and* $x_n = \psi_n(x_{n+1}) \}$

partially ordered by the relation: for all $x,y \in D_\infty$, $x \sqsubseteq y$ *iff for all* $n \geqslant 0$, $x{\downarrow}n \sqsubseteq_{D_n} y{\downarrow}n$.

11.12 Theorem:

D_∞ *is a pointed cpo.*

Proof: Recall that each D_i in the retraction sequence is a pointed cpo. First, $\bot_{D_\infty} = (\bot_{D_0}, \bot_{D_1}, \cdots, \bot_{D_i}, \cdots) \in D_\infty$, since every $\psi_i(\bot_{D_{i+1}}) = \bot_{D_i}$, by Proposition 11.4. Second, for any chain $C = \{ c_i \mid i \in I \}$ in D_∞, the definition of the partial ordering on D_∞ makes $C_n = \{ c_i{\downarrow}n \mid i \in I \}$ a chain in D_n with a lub of $\bigsqcup C_n$, $n \geqslant 0$. Now $\psi_n(\bigsqcup C_{n+1}) = \bigsqcup \{ \psi_n(c_i{\downarrow}(n+1)) \mid i \in I \} = \bigsqcup \{ c_i{\downarrow}n \mid i \in I \} = \bigsqcup C_n$. Hence $(\bigsqcup C_0, \bigsqcup C_1, \cdots, \bigsqcup C_i, \cdots)$ belongs to D_∞. It is clearly the lub of C. □

Next, we show how a domain expression generates a retraction sequence.

11.13 Proposition:

If domain expression F maps a pointed cpo E to a pointed cpo F(E), then the pair:

$$(\{ D_i \mid D_0 = \{ \bot \}, D_{i+1} = F(D_i), \textit{for } i \geqslant 0 \},$$
$$\{ (\phi_i, \psi_i) : D_i \leftrightarrow D_{i+1} \mid \phi_0 = (\lambda x.\ \bot_{D_1}), \psi_0 = (\lambda x.\ \bot_{D_0}),$$
$$(\phi_{i+1}, \psi_{i+1}) = F(\phi_i, \psi_i), \textit{for } i \geqslant 0) \}$$

is a retraction sequence.

Proof: From Lemma 11.8, part 4, and mathematical induction. □

Thus, the inverse limit D_∞ exists for the retraction sequence generated by F. The final task is to show that D_∞ is isomorphic to $F(D_\infty)$ by defining functions $\Phi: D_\infty \to F(D_\infty)$ and $\Psi: F(D_\infty) \to D_\infty$ such that $\Psi \circ \Phi = id_{D_\infty}$ and $\Phi \circ \Psi = id_{F(D_\infty)}$. Just as the elements of D_∞ were built from elements of the D_i's, the maps Φ and Ψ are built from the retraction pairs (ϕ_i, ψ_i). For $m \geqslant 0$:

$t_{m\infty}: D_m \leftrightarrow D_\infty$ is:

$$(\theta_{m\infty}, \theta_{\infty m}) = ((\lambda x. (\theta_{m0}(x), \theta_{m1}(x), \cdots, \theta_{mi}(x), \cdots)), (\lambda x.\ x{\downarrow}n))$$

$t_{\infty m}: D_\infty \leftrightarrow D_m$ is: $(\theta_{\infty m}, \theta_{m\infty}) = t^R_{m\infty}$

$t_{\infty\infty}: D_\infty \leftrightarrow D_\infty$ is: $(\theta_{\infty\infty}, \theta_{\infty\infty}) = (id_{D_\infty}, id_{D_\infty})$

You are given the exercises of showing that $\theta_{m\infty}: D_m \to D_\infty$ is well defined and proving the following proposition.

11.14 Proposition:

Proposition 11.10 holds when ∞ subscripts are used in place of m and n in the t_{mn} pairs.

Since each $t_{m\infty}$ is a retraction pair, the value $\theta_{m\infty}(\theta_{\infty m}(x))$ is less defined than $x \in D_\infty$. As m increases, the approximations to x become better. A pleasing and important result is that as m tends toward ∞, the approximations approach identity.

11.15 Lemma:

$id_{D_\infty} = \bigsqcup_{m=0}^{\infty} \theta_{m\infty} \circ \theta_{\infty m}$.

Proof: For every $m \geq 0$, $t_{m\infty}$ is a retraction pair, so $\theta_{m\infty} \circ \theta_{\infty m} \sqsubseteq id_{D_\infty}$. Because $\{\, \theta_{m\infty} \circ \theta_{\infty m} \mid m \geq 0 \,\}$ is a chain in $D_\infty \rightarrow D_\infty$, $\bigsqcup_{m=0}^{\infty} \theta_{m\infty} \circ \theta_{\infty m} \sqsubseteq id_{D_\infty}$ holds. Next, for any $x = (x_0, x_1, \cdots, x_i, \cdots) \in D_\infty$ and any $i \geq 0$, $\theta_{i\infty} \circ \theta_{\infty i}(x) = \theta_{i\infty}(\theta_{\infty i}(x)) = (\theta_{i0}(x{\downarrow}i), \theta_{i1}(x{\downarrow}i), \ldots, \theta_{ii}(x{\downarrow}i), \cdots)$. Since $\theta_{ii}(x{\downarrow}i) = (x{\downarrow}i) = x_i$, each mth component of tuple x will appear as the mth component in $\theta_{m\infty}(\theta_{\infty m}(x))$, for all $m \geq 0$. So $x \sqsubseteq \bigsqcup_{m=0}^{\infty} (\theta_{m\infty} \circ \theta_{\infty m})(x) = (\bigsqcup_{m=0}^{\infty} \theta_{m\infty} \circ \theta_{\infty m})(x)$. By extensionality, $id_{D_\infty} \sqsubseteq \bigsqcup_{m=0}^{\infty} \theta_{m\infty} \circ \theta_{\infty m}$, which implies the result. □

11.16 Corollary:

$id_{D_\infty \leftrightarrow D_\infty} = \bigsqcup_{m=0}^{\infty} t_{m\infty} \circ t_{\infty m}$

11.17 Corollary:

$id_{F(D_\infty) \leftrightarrow F(D_\infty)} = \bigsqcup_{m=0}^{\infty} F(t_{m\infty}) \circ F(t_{\infty m})$

Proof: $id_{F(D_\infty) \leftrightarrow F(D_\infty)} = F(id_{D_\infty \leftrightarrow D_\infty})$, by Lemma 11.8, part 1

$= F(\bigsqcup_{m=0}^{\infty} t_{m\infty} \circ t_{\infty m})$, by Corollary 11.16

$= \bigsqcup_{m=0}^{\infty} F(t_{m\infty} \circ t_{\infty m})$, by continuity

$= \bigsqcup_{m=0}^{\infty} F(t_{m\infty}) \circ F(t_{\infty m})$, by Lemma 11.8, part 2 □

The isomorphism maps are defined as a retraction pair (Φ, Ψ) in a fashion similar to the r-pairs in Corollaries 11.16 and 11.17. The strategy is to combine the two r-pairs into one on $D_\infty \leftrightarrow F(D_\infty)$:

$$(\Phi, \Psi) : D_\infty \leftrightarrow F(D_\infty) = \bigsqcup_{m=0}^{\infty} F(t_{m\infty}) \circ t_{\infty(m+1)}$$

The r-pair structure motivates us to write the isomorphism requirements in the form $(\Phi, \Psi)^R \circ (\Phi, \Psi) = id_{D_\infty \leftrightarrow D_\infty}$ and $(\Phi, \Psi) \circ (\Phi, \Psi)^R = id_{F(D_\infty) \leftrightarrow F(D_\infty)}$. The proofs require the following technical lemmas.

11.18 Lemma:

For any $m \geqslant 0$, $F(t_{\infty m}) \circ (\Phi, \Psi) = t_{\infty(m+1)}$

Proof: $F(t_{\infty m}) \circ (\Phi, \Psi)$

$= F(t_{\infty m}) \circ \bigsqcup_{n=0}^{\infty} F(t_{n\infty}) \circ t_{\infty(n+1)}$

$= \bigsqcup_{n=0}^{\infty} F(t_{\infty m}) \circ F(t_{n\infty}) \circ t_{\infty(n+1)}$, by continuity

$= \bigsqcup_{n=0}^{\infty} F(t_{\infty m} \circ t_{n\infty}) \circ t_{\infty(n+1)}$, by Lemma 11.8, part 2

$= \bigsqcup_{n=0}^{\infty} F(t_{nm}) \circ t_{\infty(n+1)}$, by Proposition 11.14

$= \bigsqcup_{n=0}^{\infty} t_{(n+1)(m+1)} \circ t_{\infty(n+1)}$

By Proposition 11.14, $t_{(n+1)(m+1)} \circ t_{\infty(n+1)} = t_{\infty(m+1)}$, for $n \geqslant m$. Thus, the least upper bound of the chain is $t_{\infty(m+1)}$. □

11.19 Lemma:

For any $m \geqslant 0$, $(\Phi, \Psi) \circ t_{(m+1)\infty} = F(t_{m\infty})$

Proof: Similar to the proof of Lemma 11.18 and left as an exercise. □

11.20 Theorem:

$(\Phi, \Psi)^R \circ (\Phi, \Psi) = id_{D_\infty \leftrightarrow D_\infty}$

Proof: $(\Phi, \Psi)^R \circ (\Phi, \Psi) = (\bigsqcup_{m=0}^{\infty} F(t_{m\infty}) \circ t_{\infty(m+1)})^R \circ (\Phi, \Psi)$

$= (\bigsqcup_{m=0}^{\infty} (F(t_{m\infty}) \circ t_{\infty(m+1)})^R) \circ (\Phi, \Psi)$, by continuity of R

$= (\bigsqcup_{m=0}^{\infty} t^R_{\infty(m+1)} \circ F(t_{m\infty})^R) \circ (\Phi, \Psi)$, by Proposition 11.6

$= (\bigsqcup_{m=0}^{\infty} t_{(m+1)\infty} \circ F(t_{\infty m})) \circ (\Phi, \Psi)$, by Lemma 11.8, part 3

$= \bigsqcup_{m=0}^{\infty} t_{(m+1)\infty} \circ F(t_{\infty m}) \circ (\Phi, \Psi)$, by continuity

$$= \bigsqcup_{m=0}^{\infty} t_{(m+1)\infty} \circ t_{\infty(m+1)}, \text{ by Lemma 11.18}$$
$$= \bigsqcup_{m=0}^{\infty} t_{m\infty} \circ t_{\infty m}, \text{ as } t_{0\infty} \circ t_{\infty 0} \sqsubseteq t_{1\infty} \circ t_{\infty 1}$$
$$= id_{D_\infty \leftrightarrow D_\infty}, \text{ by Corollary 11.16 } \Box$$

11.21 Theorem:
$(\Phi, \Psi) \circ (\Phi, \Psi)^R = id_{F(D_\infty) \leftrightarrow F(D_\infty)}$

Proof: Similar to the proof of Theorem 11.20 and left as an exercise. □

Analogies of the inverse limit method to the least fixed point construction are strong. So far, we have shown that D_∞ is a "fixed point" of the "chain" generated by a "functional" F. To complete the list of parallels, we can show that D_∞ is the "least upper bound" of the retraction sequence. For the retraction sequence $(\{ D_i \mid i \geq 0 \}, \{ (\phi_i, \psi_i) \mid i \geq 0 \})$ generated by F, assume that there exists a pointed cpo D' and retraction pair $(\Phi', \Psi'): D' \leftrightarrow F(D')$ such that (Φ', Ψ') proves that D' is isomorphic to $F(D')$. Then define the following r-pairs:

$t'_{0\infty}: D_0 \leftrightarrow D'$ as $((\lambda x. \bot_{D'}), (\lambda x. \bot_{D_0}))$
$t'_{(m+1)\infty}: D_{m+1} \leftrightarrow D'$ as $(\Psi', \Phi') \circ F(t'_{m\infty})$

Each $t'_{m\infty}$ is a retraction pair, and $\{ t'_{m\infty} \circ t_{\infty m} \mid m \geq 0 \}$ is a chain in $D_\infty \leftrightarrow D'$. Next, define $(\alpha, \beta): D_\infty \leftrightarrow D'$ to be $\bigsqcup_{m=0}^{\infty} t'_{m\infty} \circ t_{\infty m}$. We can show that (α, β) is a retraction pair; that is, D_∞ embeds into D'. Since D' is arbitrary, D_∞ must be the least pointed cpo solution to the retraction sequence.

We gain insight into the structure of the isomorphism maps Φ and Ψ by slightly abusing our notation. Recall that a domain expression F is interpreted as a map on r-pairs. F is required to work upon r-pairs because it must "invert" a function's domain and codomain to construct a map upon function spaces (see Definition 11.7, part 3). The inversion is done with the function's r-pair mate. But for retraction components, the choice of mate is unique (by Proposition 11.3). So, if r-pair $r = (f, g)$ is a retraction pair, let $F(f, g)$ be alternatively written as (Ff, Fg), with the understanding that any "inversions" of f or g are fulfilled by the function's retraction mate. Now the definition of (Φ, Ψ), a retraction pair, can be made much clearer:

$$(\Phi, \Psi) = \bigsqcup_{m=0}^{\infty} F(t_{m\infty}) \circ t_{\infty(m+1)}$$
$$= \bigsqcup_{m=0}^{\infty} F(\theta_{m\infty}, \theta_{\infty m}) \circ (\theta_{\infty(m+1)}, \theta_{(m+1)\infty})$$

$$= \bigsqcup_{m=0}^{\infty} (F\theta_{m\infty}, F\theta_{\infty m}) \circ (\theta_{\infty(m+1)}, \theta_{(m+1)\infty})$$
$$= \bigsqcup_{m=0}^{\infty} (F\theta_{m\infty} \circ \theta_{\infty(m+1)}, \theta_{(m+1)\infty} \circ F\theta_{\infty m})$$
$$= (\bigsqcup_{m=0}^{\infty} F\theta_{m\infty} \circ \theta_{\infty(m+1)}, \bigsqcup_{m=0}^{\infty} \theta_{(m+1)\infty} \circ F\theta_{\infty m})$$

We see that $\Phi: D_\infty \to F(D_\infty)$ maps an $x \in D_\infty$ to an element $x_{(m+1)} \in D_{m+1}$ and then maps x_{m+1} to an F-structured element whose components come from D_∞. The steps are performed for each $m>0$, and the results are joined. The actions of $\Psi: F(D_\infty) \to D_\infty$ are similarly interpreted. This roundabout method of getting from D_∞ to $F(D_\infty)$ and back has the advantage of being entirely representable in terms of the elements of the retraction sequence. We exploit this transparency in the examples in the next section.

11.3 APPLICATIONS

We now examine three recursive domain specifications and their inverse limit solutions. The tuple structure of the elements of the limit domain and the isomorphism maps give us deep insights into the nature and uses of recursively defined domains.

11.3.1 Linear Lists

This was the example in Section 11.1. For the recursive definition $Alist = (Nil + (A \times Alist))_\bot$, the retraction sequence is $(\{ D_n \mid n \geqslant 0 \}, \{ (\phi_n, \psi_n) \mid n \geqslant 0 \})$, where:

$$D_0 = \{ \bot \}$$
$$D_{i+1} = (Nil + (A \times D_i))_\bot$$

and

$$\phi_0 : D_0 \to D_1 = (\lambda x. \bot_{D_1})$$
$$\psi_0 : D_1 \to D_0 = (\lambda x. \bot_{D_0})$$
$$\phi_i : D_i \to D_{i+1} = (id_{Nil} + (id_A \times \phi_{i-1}))_\bot$$
$$= \underline{\lambda} x.\ \text{cases } x \text{ of}$$
$$\text{is}Nil() \to \text{in}Nil()$$
$$[]\ \text{is}A{\times}D_{i+1}(a,d) \to \text{in}A{\times}D_i(a, \phi_{i-1}(d))\ \text{end}$$

$$\psi_i : D_{i+1} \rightarrow D_i = (id_{Nil} + (id_A \times \psi_{i-1}))_\perp$$
$$= \underline{\lambda} x.\ \text{cases } x \text{ of}$$
$$\text{is}Nil() \rightarrow \text{in}Nil()$$
$$[]\ \text{is}A{\times}D_i(a,d) \rightarrow \text{in}A{\times}D_{i-1}(a, \psi_{i-1}(d))\ \text{end}$$

An element in D_n is a list with n or less A-elements. The map $\theta_{mn} : D_m \rightarrow D_n$ converts a list of m (or less) A-elements to one of n (or less) A-elements. If $m > n$, the last $m-n$ elements are truncated and replaced by $\perp$. If $m \leqslant n$, the list is embedded intact into D_n. An $Alist_\infty$ element is a tuple $x = (x_0, x_1, \cdots, x_i, \cdots)$, where each x_i is a list from D_i and x_i and x_{i+1} agree on their first i A-elements, because $x_i = \psi_i(x_{i+1})$. The map $\theta_{\infty m}$: $Alist_\infty \rightarrow D_m$ projects an infinite tuple into a list of m elements $\theta_{\infty m}(x) = x_i$, and $\theta_{m\infty}$: $D_m \rightarrow Alist_\infty$ creates the tuple corresponding to an m-element list $\theta_{m\infty}(l) = (\theta_{m0}(l), \theta_{m1}(l), \cdots, \theta_{mm}(l), \theta_{m(m+1)}, \cdots)$, where $\theta_{mk}(l) = l$ for $k \geqslant m$. It is easy to see that any finite list has a unique representation in $Alist_\infty$, and Lemma 11.15 clearly holds. But why can we treat $Alist_\infty$ as if it were a domain of lists? And where are the infinite lists? The answers to both these questions lie with Φ: $Alist_\infty \rightarrow F(Alist_\infty)$. It is defined as:

$$\Phi = \bigsqcup_{m=0}^{\infty} (id_{Nil} + (id_A \times \theta_{m\infty}))_\perp \circ \theta_{\infty(m+1)}$$
$$= \bigsqcup_{m=0}^{\infty} (\underline{\lambda} x.\ \text{cases } x \text{ of}$$
$$\text{is}Nil() \rightarrow \text{in}Nil()$$
$$[]\ \text{is}A{\times}D_m(a,d) \rightarrow \text{in}A{\times}Alist_\infty(a, \theta_{m\infty}(d))$$
$$\text{end}) \circ \theta_{\infty(m+1)}$$

Φ reveals the list structure in an $Alist_\infty$ tuple. A tuple $x \in Alist_\infty$ represents:

1. The undefined list when $\Phi(x) = \perp$ (then x is $(\perp, \perp, \perp, \cdots)$).
2. The *nil* list when $\Phi(x) = \text{in}Nil()$ (then x is $(\perp, [nil], [nil], \cdots)$).
3. A list whose head element is a and tail component is d when $\Phi(x) = \text{in}A{\times}Alist_\infty(a, d)$ (then x is $(\perp, [a,\theta_{\infty 0}(d)], [a,\theta_{\infty 1}(d)], \cdots, [a,\theta_{\infty(i-1)}(d)], \cdots)$). $\Phi(d)$ shows the list structure in the tail.

As described in Section 11.1, an infinite list is represented by a tuple x such that for all $i \geqslant 0$ $x_i \neq x_{i+1}$. Each $x_i \in D_i$ is a list with i (or less) A-elements; hence the kth element of the infinite list that x represents is embedded in those x_j such that $j \geqslant k$. Φ finds the kth element: it is a_k, where $\Phi(x) = \text{in}A{\times}Alist_\infty(a_1, d^2)$, and $\Phi(d^i) = \text{in}A{\times}Alist_\infty(a_i, d^{i+1})$, for $i > 1$.

The inverse map to Φ is Ψ: $F(Alist_\infty) \rightarrow Alist_\infty$. It embeds a list into $Alist_\infty$ so that operations like *cons*: $A{\times}Alist_\infty \rightarrow Alist_\infty$ have well-formed definitions. For $a \in A$ and $x \in Alist_\infty$, $\Psi(a, d) = (\perp, [a,\theta_{\infty 0}(x)], [a,\theta_{\infty 1}(x)], \cdots, [a,\theta_{\infty(i-1)}(x)], \cdots)$. The isomorphism properties of Φ and Ψ assure us that this method of unpacking and packing tuples is sound and useful.

11.3.2 Self-Applicative Procedures

Procedures in ALGOL60 can take other procedures as arguments, even to the point of self-application. A simplified version of this situation is $Proc = Proc \rightarrow A_\perp$. The family of pointed cpos that results begins with:

$$D_0 = \{ \perp \}$$
$$D_1 = D_0 \rightarrow A_\perp$$

The argument domain to D_1-level procedures is just the one-element domain, and the members of D_1 are those functions with graphs of form $\{ (\perp, a) \}$, for $a \in A_\perp$.

$$D_2 = D_1 \rightarrow A_\perp$$

A D_2-level procedure accepts D_1-level procedures as arguments.

$$D_{i+1} = D_i \rightarrow A_\perp$$

In general, a D_{i+1}-level procedure accepts D_i-level arguments. (Note that D_{i-1}, D_{i-2}, $\cdots$ are all embedded in D_i.) If we sum the domains, the result, $\sum_{i=0}^{\infty} D_i$, resembles a Pascal-like hierarchy of procedures. But we want a procedure to accept arguments from a level equal to or greater than the procedure's own. The inverse limit's elements do just that.

Consider an element $(p_0, p_1, \cdots, p_i, \cdots) \in Proc_\infty$. It has the capability of handling a procedure argument at any level. For example, an argument $q_k : D_k$ is properly handled by p_{k+1}, and the result is $p_{k+1}(q_k)$. But the tuple is intended to operate upon arguments in $Proc_\infty$, and these elements no longer have "levels." The solution is simple: take the argument $q \in Proc_\infty$ and map it down to level D_0 (that is, $\theta_{\infty 0}(q)$) and apply p_1 to it; map it down to level D_1 (that is, $\theta_{\infty 1}(q)$) and apply p_2 to it; . . .; map it down to level D_i (that is, $\theta_{\infty i}(q)$) and apply p_{i+1} to it; . . . ; and lub the results! This is *precisely* what $\Phi : Proc_\infty \rightarrow F(Proc_\infty)$ does:

$$\Phi = \bigsqcup_{m=0}^{\infty} (\theta_{m\infty} \rightarrow id_{A_\perp}) \circ \theta_{\infty(m+1)}$$
$$= \bigsqcup_{m=0}^{\infty} (\lambda x.\, id_{A_\perp} \circ x \circ \theta_{\infty m}) \circ \theta_{\infty(m+1)}$$

The application $p(q)$ is actually $(\Phi(p))(q)$. Consider $\Phi(p)$; it has value:

$$\Phi(p) = \bigsqcup_{m=0}^{\infty} (\lambda x.\, id_{A_\perp} \circ x \circ \theta_{\infty m})(\theta_{\infty(m+1)}(p))$$
$$= \bigsqcup_{m=0}^{\infty} (\theta_{\infty(m+1)}(p)) \circ \theta_{\infty m}$$
$$= \bigsqcup_{m=0}^{\infty} (p \downarrow (m+1)) \circ \theta_{\infty m}$$
$$= \bigsqcup_{m=0}^{\infty} p_{m+1} \circ \theta_{\infty m}$$

Thus:

$$(\Phi(p))(q) = (\bigsqcup_{m=0}^{\infty} p_{m+1} \circ \theta_{\infty m})(q)$$
$$= \bigsqcup_{m=0}^{\infty} p_{m+1}(\theta_{\infty m}(q))$$
$$= \bigsqcup_{m=0}^{\infty} p_{m+1}(q{\downarrow}m)$$
$$= \bigsqcup_{m=0}^{\infty} p_{m+1}(q_m)$$

The scheme is general enough that even self-application is understandable.

11.3.3 Recursive Record Structures

Recall that the most general form of record structure used in Chapter 7 was:

$$Record = Id \rightarrow Denotable\text{-}value$$
$$Denotable\text{-}value = (Record + Nat + \cdots)_\bot$$

Mutually defined sets of equations like the one above can also be handled by the inverse limit technique. We introduce m-tuples of domain equations, approximation domains, and r-pairs. The inverse limit is an m-tuple of domains. In this example, m=2, so a pair of retraction sequences are generated. We have:

$$R_0 = Unit$$
$$D_0 = Unit$$
$$R_{i+1} = Id \rightarrow D_i$$
$$D_{i+1} = (R_i + Nat + \cdots)_\bot, \text{ for } i \geqslant 0$$

and

$$R\phi_0 : R_0 \rightarrow R_1 = (\lambda x. \bot_{R_1})$$
$$R\psi_0 : R_1 \rightarrow R_0 = (\lambda x. \bot_{R_0})$$
$$D\phi_0 : D_0 \rightarrow D_1 = (\lambda x. \bot_{D_1})$$
$$D\psi_0 : D_1 \rightarrow D_0 = (\lambda x. \bot_{D_0})$$
$$R\phi_i : R_i \rightarrow R_{i+1} = (\lambda x. D\phi_{i-1} \circ x \circ id_{Id})$$
$$R\psi_i : R_{i+1} \rightarrow R_i = (\lambda x. D\psi_{i-1} \circ x \circ id_{Id})$$
$$D\phi_i : D_i \rightarrow D_{i+1} = (R\phi_{i-1} + id_{Nat} + \cdots)_\bot$$
$$D\psi_i : D_{i+1} \rightarrow D_i = (R\psi_{i-1} + id_{Nat} + \cdots)_\bot, \text{ for } i > 0$$

The inverse limits are $Record_\infty$ and $Denotable\text{-}value_\infty$. Two pairs of isomorphism maps result: $(R\Phi, R\Psi)$ and $(D\Phi, D\Psi)$. Elements of $Record_\infty$ represent record structures that map identifiers to values in $Denotable\text{-}value_\infty$. $Denotable\text{-}value_\infty$

contains $Record_\infty$ as a component, hence any $r \in Record_\infty$ exists as the denotable value in$Record_\infty(r)$. Actually, the previous sentence is a bit imprecise—$(Record_\infty + Nat + \cdots)_\perp$ contains $Record_\infty$ as a component, and an $r \in Record_\infty$ is embedded in $Denotable\text{-}value_\infty$ by writing $D\Psi(\text{in}Record_\infty(r))$. Like all the other inverse limit domains, $Denotable\text{-}value_\infty$ and $Record_\infty$ are domains of infinite tuples, and the isomorphism maps are necessary for unpacking and packing the denotable values and records.

Consider the recursively defined record:

$$r = [\,[\![A]\!] \mapsto \text{in}Nat(zero)\,][\,[\![B]\!] \mapsto \text{in}Record_\infty(r)\,](\lambda i.\, \perp)$$

Record r contains an infinite number of copies of itself. Any indexing sequence $(r\,[\![B]\!]\,[\![B]\!] \cdots [\![B]\!])$ produces r again. Since $Record_\infty$ is a pointed cpo, the recursive definition of r has a least fixed point solution, which is a tuple in $Record_\infty$. You should consider how the least fixed point solution is calculated in $Record_\infty$ and why the structure of r is more complex than that of a recursively defined record from a nonrecursive domain.

SUGGESTED READINGS

Inverse limit construction: Plotkin 1982; Reynolds 1972; Scott 1970, 1971, 1972; Scott & Strachey 1971

Generalizations & alternative approaches: Adamek & Koubek 1979; Barendregt 1977, 1981; Gunter 1985a, 1985b, 1985c; Kamimura & Tang 1984a; Kanda 1979; Lehman & Smyth 1981; Milner 1977; Scott 1976, 1983; Smyth & Plotkin 1982; Stoy 1977; Wand 1979

EXERCISES

1. Construct the approximating domains $D_0, D_1, D_2, \ldots, D_{i+1}$ for each of the following:

   a. $N = (Unit + N)_\perp$
   b. $Nlist = \mathbb{N}_\perp \times Nlist$
   c. $Mlist = (\mathbb{N} \times Mlist)_\perp$
   d. $P = P \to \mathbb{B}_\perp$
   e. $Q = (Q \to \mathbb{B})_\perp$

   Describe the structure of D_∞ for each of the above.

2. Define the domain $D = D \to (D + Unit)_\perp$. What D_∞ element is the denotation of each of the following?

a. $(\lambda d. \bot)$
b. $(\lambda d. \text{in}D(d))$
c. $f = (\lambda d. \text{in}D(f))$

3. Let $Nlist = (Nat^*)_\bot$ and $Natlist = (Unit + (Nat \times Natlist))_\bot$.
   a. What lists does *Natlist* have that *Nlist* does not?
   b. Define $cons: Nat \times Nlist \to Nlist$ for *Nlist*. Is your version strict in its second argument? Is it possible to define a version of *cons* that is nonstrict in its second argument? Define a *cons* operation for *Natlist* that is nonstrict in its second argument.
   c. Determine the denotation of $l \in Nlist$ in $l = zero\ cons\ l$ and of $l \in Natlist$ in $l = zero\ cons\ l$.
   d. A *lazy list* is an element of *Natlist* that is built with the nonstrict version of *cons*. Consider the list processing language in Figure 7.5. Make the *Atom* domain be *Nat*, and make the *List* domain be a domain of lazy lists of denotable values. Redefine the semantics. Write an expression in the language whose denotation is the list of all the positive odd numbers.

4. One useful application of the domain $Natlist = (Unit + (Nat \times Natlist))_\bot$ is to the semantics of programs that produce infinite streams of output.
   a. Consider the language of Figure 9.5. Let its domain *Answer* be *Natlist*. Redefine the command continuations $finish: Cmdcont$ to be $finish = (\lambda s. \text{in}Unit())$ and $error: String \to Cmdcont$ to be $error = (\lambda t. \lambda s. \bot)$. Add this command to the language:

$$\mathbf{C}[\![\mathbf{print}\ \mathrm{E}]\!] = \lambda e.\lambda c.\, \mathbf{E}[\![\mathrm{E}]\!](\lambda n.\lambda s.\ \text{in}Nat{\times}Natlist(n, (c\ s)))$$

   Prove for $e \in Environment$, $c \in Cmdcont$, and $s \in Store$ that $\mathbf{C}[\![\mathbf{while}\ 1\ \mathbf{do}\ \mathbf{print}\ 0]\!]e\ c\ s$ is an infinite list of *zero*s.
   b. Construct a programming language with a direct semantics that can also generate streams. The primary valuation functions are $\mathbf{P}_D$: Program $\to Store \to Natlist$ and $\mathbf{C}_D$: Command $\to Environment \to Store \to Poststore$, where $Poststore = Natlist \times Store_\bot$. (Hint: make use of an operation $strict: (A \to B) \to (A_\bot \to B)$, where B is a pointed cpo, such that:

$$strict(f)(\bot) = \bot_B, \quad \text{that is, the least element in } B$$
$$strict(f)(a) = f(a), \quad \text{for a proper value } a \in A$$

   Then define the composition of command denotations $f, g \in Store \to Poststore$ as:

$$g{*}f = \lambda s. (\lambda(l, p). (\lambda(l', p'). (l\ append\ l', p'))(strict(g)(p)))(f\ s)$$

   where $append: Natlist \times Natlist \to Natlist$ is the list concatenation operation and is nonstrict in its second argument.) Prove that

$\mathbf{C}_D$[[**while** 1 **do print** 0]]$e\ s$ is an infinite list of *zeros*.

c. Define a programming language whose programs map an infinite stream of values and a store to an infinite stream of values. Define the language using both direct and continuation styles. Attempt to show a congruence between the two definitions.

5. a. The specification of record r in Section 11.3 is incomplete because the isomorphism maps are omitted. Insert them in their proper places.

b. How can recursively defined records be used in a programming language? What pragmatic disadvantages result?

6. a. Why does the inverse limit method require that a domain expression f in $D = F(D)$ map pointed cpos to pointed cpos?

b. Why must we work with r-pairs when an inverse limit domain is always built from a sequence of retraction pairs?

c. Can a retraction sequence have a domain D_0 that is not $\{\bot\}$? Say that a retraction sequence had $D_0 = Unit_\bot$. Does an inverse limit still result? State the conditions under which $\mathbb{B}_\bot$ could be used as D_0 in a retraction sequence generated from a domain expression F in $D = F(D)$. Does the inverse limit satisfy the isomorphism? Is it the least such domain that does so?

7. a. Show the approximating domains $D_0, D_1, \ldots, D_i$ for each of the following:

i. $D = D \to D$
ii. $D = D_\bot \to D_\bot$
iii. $D = (D \to D)_\bot$

b. Recall the lambda calculus system that was introduced in exercise 11 of Chapter 3. Once again, its syntax is:

$$\mathrm{E} ::= (E_1\ E_2) \mid (\lambda I.\,E) \mid I$$

Say that the meaning of a lambda-expression $(\lambda I.E)$ is a function. Making use of the domain $Environment = Identifier \to D$ with the usual operations, define a valuation function $\mathbf{E}$: Lambda-expression $\to Environment \to D$ for each of the three versions of D defined in part a. Which of the three semantics that you defined is extensional; that is, in which of the three does the property "(for all $[\![E]\!]$, $\mathbf{E}[\![(E_1\ E)]\!] = \mathbf{E}[\![(E_2\ E)]\!]$) implies $\mathbf{E}[\![E_1]\!] = \mathbf{E}[\![E_2]\!]$" hold? (Warning: this is a nontrivial problem.)

c. For each of the three versions of $\mathbf{E}$ that you defined in part b, prove that the β-rule is sound, that is, prove:

$$\mathbf{E}[\![(\lambda I.\,E_1)E_2]\!] = \mathbf{E}[\![[E_2/I]E_1]\!]$$

d. Augment the syntax of the lambda-calculus with the abstraction form (λ**val** $I.E$). Add the following reduction rule:

β**val**-rule: (λ**val** $I.E_1)E_2 \Rightarrow [E_2/I]E_1$
where E_2 is not a combination $(E_1{}'E_2{}')$

Define a semantics for the new version of abstraction for each of the three versions of valuation function in part b and show that the βval-rule is sound with respect to each.

8. For the definition $D = D \rightarrow D$, show that an inverse limit can be generated starting from $D_0 = Unit_\perp$ and that D_∞ is a nontrivial domain. Prove that this inverse limit is the smallest nontrivial domain that satisfies the definition.

9. Scott proposed the following domain for modelling flowcharts:

$C = (Skip + Assign + Comp + Cond)_\perp$
where $Skip = Unit$ represents the **skip** command
Assign is a set of primitive assigment commands
$Comp = C \times C$ represents command composition
$Cond = Bool \times C \times C$ represents conditional
Bool is a set of primitive Boolean expressions

a. What relationship does domain C have to the set of derivation trees of a simple imperative language? What "trees" are lacking? Are there any extra ones?
b. Let $wh(b,c)$ be the C-value $wh(b,c)$ = in$Cond(b,$ in$Comp(c, wh(b,c))$, in$Skip())$, for $c \in C$ and $b \in Bool$. Using the methods outlined in Section 6.6.5, draw a tree-like picture of the denotation of $wh(b_0, c_0)$. Next, write the tuple representation of the value as it appears in C_∞.
c. Define a function $sem : C \rightarrow Store_\perp \rightarrow Store_\perp$ that maps a member of C to a store transformation function. Define a congruence between the domains *Bool* and Boolean-expr and between *Assign* and the collection of trees of the form [[I:=E]]. Prove for all $b \in Bool$ and its corresponding [[B]] and for $c \in C$ and its corresponding [[C]] that $sem(wh(b,c))$ = **C**[[**while** B **do** C]].

10. The domain $I = (Dec \times I)_\perp$, where $Dec = \{0, 1, \cdots, 9\}$, defines a domain that contains infinite lists of decimal digits. Consider the interval [0,1], that is, all the real numbers between 0 and 1 inclusive.

a. Show that every value in [0,1] has a representation in I. (Hint: consider the decimal representation of a value in the interval.) Are the representations unique? What do the partial lists in I represent?

b. Recall that a number in [0,1] is *rational* if it is represented by a value m/n, for $m,n \in \mathbb{N}$. Say that an I-value is *recursive* if it is representable by a (possibly recursive) function expression $f = \alpha$. Is every rational number recursive? Is every recursive value rational? Are there any non-recursive values in I?

c. Call a domain value *transcendental* if it does not have a function expression representation. State whether or not there are any trancendental values in the following domains. ($\mathbb{N}$ has none.)

   i. $\mathbb{N} \times \mathbb{N}$
   ii. $\mathbb{N} \to \mathbb{N}$
   iii. $Nlist = (\mathbb{N} \times Nlist)_\perp$
   iv. $N = (Unit + N)_\perp$

11. Just as the inverse limit D_∞ is determined by its approximating domains D_i, a function $g: D_\infty \to C$ is determined by a family of approximating functions. Let $G = \{ g_i : D_i \to C \mid i \geqslant 0 \}$ be a family of functions such that, for all $i \geqslant 0$, $g_{i+1} \circ \phi_i = g_i$. (That is, the maps always agree on elements in common.)

a. Prove that for all $i \geqslant 0$, $g_i \circ \psi_i \sqsubseteq g_{i+1}$.

b. Prove that there exists a unique $g: D_\infty \to C$ such that for all $i \geqslant 0$, $g \circ \theta_{i\infty} = g_i$. Call g the *mediating morphism for* G, and write $g = med\,G$.

c. For a continuous function $h: D_\infty \to C$, define the family of functions $H = \{ h_i : D_i \to C \mid i \geqslant 0, h_i = h \circ \theta_{i\infty} \}$.

   i. Show that $h_{i+1} \circ \phi_i = h_i$ for each $i \geqslant 0$.
   ii. Prove that $h = med\,H$ and that $H = \{ (med\,H) \circ \theta_{i\infty} \mid i \geqslant 0 \}$.

   Thus, the approximating function families are in 1-1, onto correspondence with the continuous functions in $D_\infty \to C$.

d. Define the approximating function family for the map $hd: Alist \to A_\perp$, $Alist = (Unit + (A \times Alist))_\perp$, $hd = \lambda l.$ cases $\Phi(l)$ of is$Unit() \to \perp$ [] is$A{\times}Alist(a, l) \to a$ end. Describe the graph of each hd_i.

e. Let $p_i : D_i \to \mathbb{B}$ be a family of continuous predicates. Prove that for all $i \geqslant 0$, p_i holds for $d_i \in D_i$, (that is, $p_i(d_i) = true$) iff $med\{ p_i \mid i \geqslant 0 \}(d) = true$, where $d = (d_0, d_1, \cdots, d_i, \cdots): D_\infty$. Conversely, let $P: D_\infty \to \mathbb{B}$ be a continuous predicate. Prove that P holds for a $d \in D_\infty$ (that is, $P(d) = true$) iff for all $i \geqslant 0$, $P \circ \theta_{i\infty}(d_i) = true$.

f. Results similar to those in parts a through c hold for function families $\{ f_i : C \to D_i \mid i \geqslant 0 \}$ such that for all $i \geqslant 0$, $f_i = \psi_i \circ f_{i+1}$. Prove that there exists a unique $f: C \to D_\infty$ such that for all $i \geqslant 0$, $f_i = \theta_{\infty i} \circ f$.

Chapter 12

Nondeterminism and Concurrency

A program is *deterministic* if its evaluations on the same input always produce the same output. The evaluation strategy for a deterministic program might not be unique. For example, side effect-free arithmetic addition can be implemented in more than one fashion:

1. Evaluate the left operand; evaluate the right operand; add.
2. Evaluate the right operand; evaluate the left operand; add.
3. Evaluate the two operands in parallel; add.

A program is *nondeterministic* if it has more than one allowable evaluation strategy and different evaluation strategies lead to different outputs. One example of a nondeterministic construct is addition *with* side effects, using the three evaluation strategies listed above. If an operand contains a side effect, then the order of evaluation of the operands can affect the final result. This situation is considered a result of bad language design, because elementary arithmetic is better behaved. It is somewhat surprising that the situation is typically resolved by outlawing all but one of the allowable evaluation strategies and embracing hidden side effects!

There are situations where nondeterminism is acceptable. Consider an error-handling routine that contains a number of commands, each indexed by a specific error condition. If a run-time error occurs, the handler is invoked to diagnose the problem and to compensate for it. Perhaps the diagnosis yields multiple candidate error conditions. Only one correction command is executed within the handler, so the choice of which one to use may be made nondeterministically.

A concept related to nondeterminism is *parallel evaluation*. Some language constructs can be naturally evaluated in parallel fashion, such as side effect-free addition using the third strategy noted above. This "nice" form of parallelism, where the simultaneous evaluation of subparts of the construct do not interact, is called *noninterfering parallelism*. In *interfering parallelism*, there is interaction, and the relative speeds of the evaluations of the subparts do affect the final result. We call a *concurrent language* one that uses interfering parallelism in its evaluation of programs. The classic example of a concurrent language is an imperative language that evaluates in parallel commands that share access and update rights to a common variable.

We require new tools to specify the semantics of nondeterministic and concurrent languages. A program's answer denotation is no longer a single value d from a domain D, but a set of values $\{ d_0, d_1, \cdots, d_i, \cdots \}$ describing all the results possible from the different evaluations. The set of values is an element from the *powerdomain* $\mathbb{P}(D)$. The powerdomain corresponds to the powerset in Chapter 2, but the underlying mathematics of the domain-based version is more involved. The members of $\mathbb{P}(D)$ must be related in terms of both subset properties and the partial ordering properties of D. Unfortunately, there is no best powerdomain construction, and a number of serious questions remain regarding the theory.

Section 12.1 describes the properties of the powerdomain construction, and Section 12.2 uses it to model a nondeterministic language. Section 12.3 presents one approach to modelling interfering parallelism. Section 12.4 presents an alternative approach to nondeterministic and parallel evaluation, and Section 12.5 gives an overview to the mathematics underlying powerdomain construction.

12.1 POWERDOMAINS

The *powerdomain* construction builds a domain of sets of elements. For domain A, the powerdomain builder $\mathbb{P}(\_)$ creates the domain $\mathbb{P}(A)$, a collection whose members are sets $X \subseteq A$. The associated assembly operations are:

$\emptyset : \mathbb{P}(A)$, a constant that denotes the smallest element in $\mathbb{P}(A)$.

$\{ \_ \} : A \rightarrow \mathbb{P}(A)$, which maps its argument $a \in A$ to the *singleton set* $\{ a \}$.

$\_ \cup \_ : \mathbb{P}(A) \times \mathbb{P}(A) \rightarrow \mathbb{P}(A)$, the *binary union* operation, which combines its two arguments $M = \{ a_0, a_1, \cdots \}$ and $N = \{ b_0, b_1, \cdots \}$ into the set $M \cup N = \{ a_0, a_1, \cdots, b_0, b_1, \cdots \}$.

The disassembly operation builder for powerdomains converts an operation on A-elements into one on $\mathbb{P}(A)$-elements.

For $f : A \rightarrow \mathbb{P}(B)$, there exists a unique operation $f^+ : \mathbb{P}(A) \rightarrow \mathbb{P}(B)$ such that for any $M \in \mathbb{P}(A)$, $f^+(M) = \bigcup \{ f(m) \mid m \in M \}$.

The operation builder can be applied to operations $g : A \rightarrow B$ to produce a function in the domain $\mathbb{P}(A) \rightarrow \mathbb{P}(B)$: use $(\lambda a. \{ g(a) \})^+$.

12.2 THE GUARDED COMMAND LANGUAGE

A well-defined programming language depends on explicit evaluation strategies as little as possible. Imperative languages require sequencing at the command level to clarify the order of updates to the store argument. The sequencing is critical to understanding command composition, but it need not be imposed on the other command builders. As an example, a useful generalization of the conditional command **if** B **then** C_1 **else** C_2 is the multichoice **cases** command:

cases
    $B_1 : C_1$;
    $B_2 : C_2$;
    . . .
    $B_n : C_n$
end

A command C_i is executed when test B_i evaluates to *true*. A problem is that more than one B_i may hold. Normally, we want only one command in the **cases** construct to be evaluated, so we must make a choice. The traditional choice is to execute the "first" C_i, reading from "top to bottom," whose test B_i holds, but this choice adds little to the language. A better solution is to nondeterministically choose any one of the candidate commands whose test holds. In Dijkstra (1976), this form of conditional naturally meshes with the development of programs from formal specifications. As an exercise, we define a denotational semantics of the imperative language proposed by Dijkstra.

Dijkstra's language, called the *guarded command language*, is an assignment language augmented by the nondeterministic conditional command and a nondeterministic multitest loop, which iterates as long as one of its tests is true. The language is presented in Figure 12.1.

The domain of possible answers of a nondeterministic computation is a powerdomain of post-store elements. The operation of primary interest is *then*, which sequences two nondeterministic commands. The semantics of an expression $(f_1\ then\ f_2)(s)$ says that f_1 operates on s, producing a set of post-stores. Each post-store is passed through f_2 to produce an answer set. The answer sets are unioned.

The functionality of the **C** valuation function points out that a command represents a nondeterministic computation. The semantic equations for the conditional and loop commands both use an auxiliary valuation function **T** to determine if at least one of the tests (*guards*) of the construct holds. In the case of the conditional, failure of all guards causes an abortion; failure of all the guards of the loop construct causes exit of the loop. The **G** function defines the meaning of a conditional/loop body. The updates of all the guarded commands whose tests hold are joined together, and a set of stores result.

Figure 12.1

C∈ Command
G∈ Guarded-command
E∈ Expression
B∈ Boolean-expression
I ∈ Identifier

C ::= C_1;C_2 | I:=E | **if** G **fi** | **do** G **od**
G ::= G_1 [] G_2 | B→C

Semantic algebras:

I.-IV. Truth values, identifiers, natural numbers, and stores
(the usual definitions)

V. Results of nondeterministic computations

Domains $p \in Poststore = (Store + Errvalue)$
where $Errvalue = Unit$
$a \in Answer = \mathbb{P}(Poststore_{\perp})$

Operations

$no\text{-}answer : Answer$
$no\text{-}answer = \emptyset$

$return : Store \to Answer$
$return = \lambda s. \{ \text{in}Store(s) \}$

$abort : Store \to Answer$
$abort = \lambda s. \{ \text{in}Errvalue() \}$

$join : Answer \times Answer \to Answer$
$a_1 \; join \; a_2 = a_1 \cup a_2$

$then : (Store \to Answer) \times (Store \to Answer) \to (Store \to Answer)$
$f_1 \; then \; f_2 = (\underline{\lambda}p. \text{ cases } p \text{ of}$
$\text{is}Store(s) \to f_2(s)$
$[] \; \text{is}Errvalue() \to \{ \text{in}Errvalue() \}$
$\text{end})^{+} \circ f_1$

Valuation functions:

C: Command → *Store* → *Answer*

$\mathbf{C}[\![C_1;C_2]\!] = \mathbf{C}[\![C_1]\!] \; then \; \mathbf{C}[\![C_2]\!]$
$\mathbf{C}[\![I:=E]\!] = \lambda s. \, return \, (update \, [\![I]\!] \, (\mathbf{E}[\![E]\!]s) \, s)$
$\mathbf{C}[\![\textbf{if } G \textbf{ fi}]\!] = \lambda s. \, \mathbf{T}[\![G]\!]s \to \mathbf{G}[\![G]\!]s \; [] \; abort \; s$
$\mathbf{C}[\![\textbf{do } G \textbf{ od}]\!] = fix(\lambda f.\lambda s. \, \mathbf{T}[\![G]\!]s \to (\mathbf{G}[\![G]\!] \; then \; f)(s) \; [] \; return \; s)$

Figure 12.1 (continued)

T: Guarded-command → *Store* → *Tr*
  $\mathbf{T}[\![G_1 \,[\!]\, G_2]\!] = \lambda s.\,(\mathbf{T}[\![G_1]\!]s)\; or\; (\mathbf{T}[\![G_2]\!]s)$
  $\mathbf{T}[\![B \to C]\!] = \mathbf{B}[\![B]\!]$

G: Guarded-command → *Store* → *Answer*
  $\mathbf{G}[\![G_1 \,[\!]\, G_2]\!] = \lambda s.\,(\mathbf{G}[\![G_1]\!]s)\; join\; (\mathbf{G}[\![G_2]\!]s)$
  $\mathbf{G}[\![B \to C]\!] = \lambda s.\, \mathbf{B}[\![B]\!]s \to \mathbf{C}[\![C]\!]s \,[\!]\, no\text{-}answer$

E:Expression → *Store* → *Nat* (usual)

B: Boolean-expr → *Store* → *Tr* (usual)

Here is a small example. For:

$C_0 = G_1 \,[\!]\, G_2$
$G_1 = X \geqslant 0 \to Y{:=}1$
$G_2 = X{=}\,0 \to Y{:=}0$

we derive:

$\mathbf{C}[\![C_0]\!] = \mathbf{C}[\![G_1 \,[\!]\, G_2]\!]$
$= \lambda s.\; \mathbf{T}[\![G_1 \,[\!]\, G_2]\!]s \to \mathbf{G}[\![G_1 \,[\!]\, G_2]\!]s \,[\!]\, abort\ s$
$= \lambda s.\,(\mathbf{B}[\![X \geqslant 0]\!]s)\; or\; (\mathbf{B}[\![X{=}\,0]\!]s) \to \mathbf{G}[\![G_1 \,[\!]\, G_2]\!]s \,[\!]\, abort\ s$

$(\mathbf{B}[\![X \geqslant 0]\!]s)\; or\; (\mathbf{B}[\![X{=}\,0]\!]s)$ must be *true*, so we simplify to:

$$\lambda s.\, \mathbf{G}[\![G_1 \,[\!]\, G_2]\!]s = \lambda s.\,(\mathbf{B}[\![X \geqslant 0]\!]s \to \mathbf{C}[\![Y{:=}1]\!]s \,[\!]\, noanswer)$$
$$join\; (\mathbf{B}[\![X{=}\,0]\!]s \to \mathbf{C}[\![Y{:=}0]\!]s \,[\!]\, noanswer)$$

Consider a store s_0 such that $(access\,[\![X]\!]\, s_0)$ is greater than *zero*. Then the above expression simplifies to:

$(\mathbf{C}[\![Y{:=}1]\!]s_0)\; join\; noanswer$
$= return\,(s_1) \cup \varnothing$, where $s_1 = (update\,[\![Y]\!]\, one\ s_0)$
$= \{\, inStore(s_1) \,\} \cup \varnothing$

Similarly, for a store s'_0 such that $(access\,[\![X]\!]\, s'_0)$ is *zero*, we see that the expression simplifies to:

$(\mathbf{C}[\![Y{:=}1]\!]s'_0)\; join\; (\mathbf{C}[\![Y{:=}0]\!]s'_0)$
$= return(s'_1)\; join\; return(s'_2)$
  where $s'_1 = (update\,[\![Y]\!]\, one\ s'_0)$ and $s'_2 = (update\,[\![Y]\!]\, zero\ s'_0)$
$= \{\, inStore(s'_1) \,\} \cup \{\, inStore(s'_2) \,\}$

$= \{ \text{in}Store(s'_1), \text{in}Store(s'_2) \}$

You may have noticed that the phrase $\{ \text{in}Store(s_1) \} \cup \emptyset$ was not simplified to $\{ \text{in}Store(s_1) \}$ in the first simplification. This step was omitted, for the property $a \cup \emptyset = a$, for $a \in \mathbb{P}(A)$, does *not* hold for all of the versions of powerdomains! This discouraging result is discussed in Section 12.5.

12.3 CONCURRENCY AND RESUMPTION SEMANTICS

As mentioned in the introduction, there are two kinds of parallelism: noninterfering and interfering. The modelling of noninterfering parallelism requires no new concepts, but modelling interfering parallelism does. When assignments evaluate concurrently on the same store, the result is a set of possible result stores, and the powerdomain construction is needed. Further, we require a technique for representing the operational aspects of concurrency in the semantics. We follow Plotkin's method, which depicts the concurrent evaluation of commands C_1 and C_2 by interleaving the evaluation steps of C_1 with those of C_2. This leads to a form of denotational definition called *resumption semantics*.

Figure 12.2 shows a simple imperative language augmented by a parallel evaluation operator $||$. The language's assignment statement is *noninterruptable* and has exclusive rights to the store. We treat a noninterruptable action as the "evaluation step" mentioned above. The evaluation of $C_1 || C_2$ interleaves the assignments of C_1 with those of C_2. A semantics of $C_1 || C_2$ generates the set of results of all possible interleavings. Here are some example program fragments and an informal description of their actions.

Figure 12.2

Abstract syntax:

P ∈ Program
C ∈ Command
E ∈ Expression
B ∈ Boolean-expr
I ∈ Identifier

P ::= C.

C ::= I:=E | C_1;C_2 | $C_1 || C_2$ | **if** B **then** C_1 **else** C_2 | **while** B **do** C

12.1 Example:

[[X:=X+1]] is an ordinary assignment. Given a store argument, the command updates [[X]]'s cell. No other command may access or alter the store while the assignment is performed.

12.2 Example:

[[X:=X+2; X:=X−1]] is a compound command. Although each of the two assignments receives exclusive rights to the store when executing, another command operating in parallel may interrupt the composition after the evaluation of the first assignment and before the evaluation of the second. Thus, the composition is *not* semantically equivalent to [[X:=X+1]]. Consider [[(X:=X+2; X:=X−1) || (X:=3)]]. The possible interleavings of this concurrent command are:

X:=X+2; X:=X-1; X:=3
X:=X+2; X:=3; X:=X-1
X:=3; X:=X+2; X:=X-1

Each of the interleavings yields a different output store. Command composition must have a denotational semantics that is different from the ones used in previous chapters.

12.3 Example:

[[(**if** X=0 **then** Y:=1 **else** Y:=2) || (X:=X+1)]]. The evaluation of the test of a conditional is noninterruptable. The possible evaluation sequences are:

for X having an initial value of *zero*:
test X=0; Y:=1; X:=X+1
test X=0; X:=X+1; Y:=1
X:=X+1; test X=0; Y:=2

for X having an initial positive value:
test X=0; Y:=2; X:=X+1
test X=0; X:=X+1; Y:=2
X:=X+1; test X=0; Y:=2

12.4 Example:

[[(X:=1; **while** X>0 **do** Y:=Y+1) || (X:=0)]]. Like Example 12.3, a command executing concurrently with a **while**-loop may be interleaved with the loop's evaluation sequence. When [[X]] is zero, the loop terminates, so the interleaving of [[X:=0]] into the loop's evaluation becomes critical to the result of the program. The possible evaluation sequences are:

X:=0; X:=1; test X>0; Y:=Y+1; test X>0; Y:=Y+1; · · ·
X:=1; X:=0; test X>0
X:=1; test X>0; X:=0; Y:=Y+1; test X>0
X:=1; test X>0; Y:=Y+1; X:=0; test X>0
X:=1; test X>0; Y:=Y+1; test X>0; X:=0; Y:=Y+1; test X>0
X:=1; test X>0; Y:=Y+1; test X>0; Y:=Y+1; X:=0; test X>0
· · ·

These evaluation sequences are called *fair* because the assignment [[X:=0]] eventually appears in the evaluation sequence. A fair evaluation of $C_1 || C_2$ eventually evaluates both C_1 and C_2. An unfair sequence would evaluate the loop all its nonterminating way and *then* "perform" [[X:=0]]. The resumption semantics assigned to this example will include the fair sequences plus the unfair sequence just mentioned.

As we saw in Example 12.2, even apparently sequential constructs are impacted by possible outside interference. The denotation of a command can no longer be a map from an input to an output store but must become a new entity, a *resumption*. Figure 12.3 presents the semantic algebra of resumptions.

A resumption can be thought of as a set of interruptable evaluation sequences. Let r be a resumption and s be a store. If r consists of just a single step, as in Example 12.1, $r(s)$ is (a set containing) a new store, that is, $\{$ in*Store*$(s')\}$. If r is a single sequence of steps, as in Example 12.2, $r(s)$ is not the application of all the steps to s, but the application of just the first of the steps, producing (a set containing) a new store plus the remaining steps that need to be done, that is, $\{$ in*Store*×*Res*$(s', r')\}$, where s' is the store resulting from the first step and r' is the remainder of the steps. This structure is necessary so that the interleaving of other evaluation sequences, that is, other resumptions, can be handled if necessary. When resumption r depicts a parallel evaluation, as in Examples 12.3 and 12.4, r contains a number of evaluation sequences, and $r(s)$ is a nonsingleton set of partial computations.

The operations upon resumptions show how resumptions are defined from atomic actions, paused to allow interleavings, sequentially composed, interleaved, and evaluated to an answer set. The first of these constructions is *step*, which builds a single step evaluation sequence that immediately and noninterruptedly performs its actions upon a store. A sequence r that can be interrupted before it performs any action at all is defined by (*pause* r), which holds its store argument without applying any of r to it. The expression $r_1 * r_2$ is the composition of the evaluation steps of resumption r_1 with the steps of r_2. The interleaving of resumptions is defined by *par*. A resumption is converted into a set of

Figure 12.3

IV. Resumptions

Domains $p \in Pgm\text{-}state = (Store + (Store \times Res))$

$r \in Res = Store \rightarrow \mathbb{P}(Pgm\text{-}state_\perp)$

Operations

$step : (Store \rightarrow Store) \rightarrow Res$

$step = \lambda f.\lambda s.\{\, \text{in}Store(f\, s)\,\}$

$pause : Res \rightarrow Res$

$pause = \lambda r.\lambda s.\{\, \text{in}Store{\times}Res(s, r)\,\}$

$\_*\_ : Res \times Res \rightarrow Res$

$$
\begin{aligned}
r_1 * r_2 = (\underline{\lambda} p.\ &\text{cases } p \text{ of}\\
&\text{is}Store(s') \rightarrow \{\, \text{in}Store{\times}Res(s', r_2)\,\}\\
&[\!]\ \text{is}Store{\times}Res(s', r') \rightarrow \{\, \text{in}Store{\times}Res(s', r' * r_2)\,\}\\
&\text{end})^+ \circ r_1
\end{aligned}
$$

$par : Res \times Res \rightarrow Res$

$r_1\ par\ r_2 = \lambda s.(r_1\ then\ r_2)(s) \cup (r_2\ then\ r_1)(s)$

where $then : Res \times Res \rightarrow Res$ is

$$
\begin{aligned}
r_1\ then\ r_2 = (\underline{\lambda} p.\ &\text{cases } p \text{ of}\\
&\text{is}Store(s') \rightarrow \{\, \text{in}Store{\times}Res(s', r_2)\,\}\\
&[\!]\ \text{is}Store{\times}Res(s', r') \rightarrow \{\, \text{in}Store{\times}Res(s', r'\ then\ r_2)\,\}\\
&\qquad\qquad\qquad\qquad \cup \{\, \text{in}Store{\times}Res(s', r_2\ then\ r')\,\}\\
&\text{end})^+ \circ r_1
\end{aligned}
$$

$flatten : Res \rightarrow Store \rightarrow \mathbb{P}(Store_\perp)$

$$
\begin{aligned}
flatten = \lambda r.(\underline{\lambda} p.\ &\text{cases } p \text{ of}\\
&\text{is}Store(s') \rightarrow \{\, s'\,\}\\
&[\!]\ \text{is}Store{\times}Res(s', r') \rightarrow (flatten\ r')(s')\\
&\text{end})^+ \circ r
\end{aligned}
$$

---

noninterruptable evaluation sequences by *flatten*. The expression $(flatten\ r)(s)$ evaluates each of the sequences in r with s to an output store. The result is a set of stores.

The valuation functions are specified in Figure 12.4.

The denotation of a command in the language is a resumption because the command might be embedded in a parallel evaluation. If so, the command's evaluation sequence would have to be interleaved with the other parts of the parallel construction. Once the command is completely built into a program,

Figure 12.4

P: Program $\rightarrow$ *Store* $\rightarrow \mathbb{P}(Store_\perp)$
P[[C.]] = *flatten*(C[[C]])

C: Command $\rightarrow$ *Res*
C[[I:=E]] = *step* ($\lambda s.$ *update* [[I]] (E[[E]]s) s)
C[[C_1;C_2]] = C[[C_1]] * C[[C_2]]
C[[C_1 || C_2]] = C[[C_1]] *par* C[[C_2]]
C[[**if** B **then** C_1 **else** C_2]] = $\lambda s.$B[[B]]$s \rightarrow$ (*pause* (C[[C_1]]) s) [] (*pause* (C[[C_2]]) s)
C[[**while** B **do** C]] = *fix*($\lambda f.\lambda s.$ B[[B]]$s \rightarrow$ (*pause* (C[[C]] * f) s) [] (*step* ($\lambda s.\ s$) s))

E: Expression $\rightarrow$ *Store* $\rightarrow$ *Nat* (like Figure 5.2)

B: Boolean-expr $\rightarrow$ *Store* $\rightarrow$ *Tr* (like Figure 5.2)

---

the resumption is flattened into the family of possible evaluation sequences that it represents. Since a conditional can be interrupted after its test and before its clauses are evaluated, the *pause* operation must be inserted to create an explicit interrupt point. The loop is handled similarly.

The **E** and **B** functions are not written in the resumption style. As we saw in Chapter 9, the sequencing aspects of a language may be specified at certain levels and ignored at others. The language in Figure 12.4 interleaves evaluation steps only at the command level. Nonetheless, expression resumptions can be introduced, just as expression continuations were introduced to augment command continuations in Chapter 9. This is left as an exercise.

You should determine the denotations of the commands in Examples 12.1 through 12.4.

12.4 AN ALTERNATIVE SEMANTICS FOR CONCURRENCY

Although we have given a denotational semantics to a concurrent language, the definitions of the resumption operations are far too complex. The problem is that our function notation is ill-suited for representing multivalued objects; at most, one function can "own" an argument. In a description of a concurrent language, more than one function competes for the same argument— in Figure 12.4, it was the computer store. We seek a natural way of describing this competition.

Consider a generalization of function notation such that more than one function can be applied to, or choose to communicate with, an argument. Further, the argument may choose which function it wishes to interact with. This recalls Hewitt's actor theory (Hewitt & Baker 1978).

We must make some notational changes. First, the application of a function to an argument is no longer written as $f(a)$, as we will have situations in which both f_1 and f_2 desire the same a. We "specialize" the λ in $f = \lambda x.M$ to name a *port* or argument path by using Greek letters $\alpha, \beta, \gamma, \cdots$ in place of the λ. The argument is marked with the same Greek letter with a bar over it. Thus, the application $(\lambda x.M)(a)$ becomes $(\alpha x.M) \mid (\overline{\alpha} a)$, and, in the general case, $(\alpha x_1.M_1) \mid \cdots \mid (\alpha x_n.M_n) \mid (\overline{\alpha} a)$ describes the situation where all of the functions $(\lambda x_1.M_1), \cdots, (\lambda x_n.M_n)$ wish to use a, but only one of them will receive it.

The notation that we are developing is called a *Calculus for Communicating Systems* (CCS), and it was defined by Milner. Lack of space prevents us from giving a complete presentation of CCS, so you should read Milner's book (Milner 1980). We will study the basic features of CCS and see how the parallel language of the previous section can be described with it.

The syntax of CCS *behavior expressions* is given in Figure 12.5.

Consider the BNF rule for behavior expressions. The first two forms in the rule are the generalized versions of function abstraction and argument application that we were considering. Note that the argument construct $\overline{P}E.B$ is generalized to have an argument E and a body B, just like an abstraction has. Once the argument part E binds to some abstraction, the body B evaluates. Abstractions and arguments are symmetrical and autonomous objects in CCS. The third form, $B_1 \mid B_2$, is parallel composition; behavior expressions B_1 and B_2 may evaluate in parallel and pass values back and forth. The behavior expression $B_1 + B_2$ represents nondeterministic choice: either B_1 or B_2 may evaluate, but not

Figure 12.5

B∈ Behavior-expression
E∈ Function-expression
P∈ Port
I ∈ Identifier

$$B ::= PI.B \mid \overline{P}E.B \mid B_1 | B_2 \mid B_1 + B_2 \mid B_1 * B_2$$
$$\mid \textit{if } E \textit{ then } B_1 \textit{ else } B_2 \mid B \S P \mid B[P_1/P_2] \mid \textit{nil}$$

$E ::=$ (defined in Chapter 3)

---

both. $B_1 * B_2$ represents sequential evaluation; at the end of B_1's evaluation, B_2 may proceed. The *if* construct is the usual conditional. The behavior expression $B\S P$ hides the port P in B from outside communication; $B\S P$ cannot send or receive values along port P, so any use of P must be totally within B. $B[P_1/P_2]$ renames all nonhidden occurrences of port P_2 to P_1. Finally, *nil* is the inactive behavior expression.

What is the meaning of a behavior expression? We could provide a resumption semantics, but since we wish to forgo resumptions, we follow Milner's lead: he suggests that the meaning of a behavior expression is a tree showing all the possible evaluation paths that the expression might take. The arcs of such a *communication tree* are labeled with the values that can be sent or received by the behavior expression. Some examples are seen in Figure 12.6. Nondeterministic and parallel composition cause branches in a communication tree. An internal communication of a value within a behavior expression produces an arc labeled by a τ symbol. Actually, the trees in Figure 12.6 are overly simplistic because they use identifiers on the arcs instead of values. A completely expanded rendition of expression 2 in that figure is:

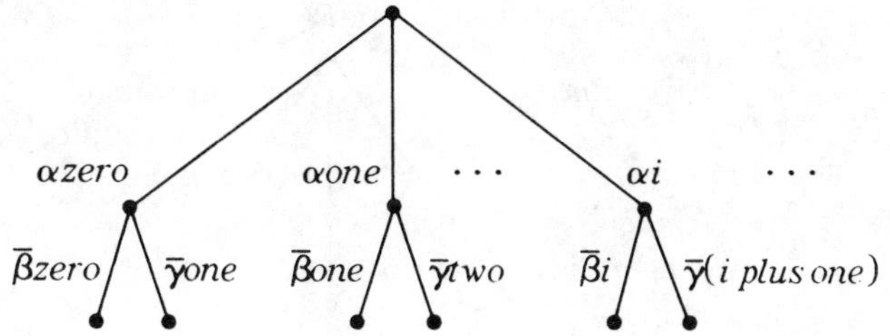

because the behavior expression is a function of $n \in Nat$. The communication tree represents the "graph" of the behavior expression.

Like function graphs, communication trees are somewhat awkward to use. Just as we use simplification rules on function expressions to determine the unique meaning of an expression, we use inference rules on behavior expressions to determine an evaluation path in a behavior expression's communication tree. Inference rules for CCS and some useful equivalences for behavior expressions are given in Figure 12.7. An axiom $B \xrightarrow{\mu v} B'$ says that on reception of a v value along port μ, behavior expression B progresses to B'. An inference rule:

$$\frac{B'_1 \xrightarrow{\mu v} B'_1}{B_2 \xrightarrow{\mu v} B'_2}$$

says that if behavior expression B_1 can progress to B'_1 via communication μv, then expression B_2 can progress to B'_2 with the same communication. An equivalence $B \equiv B'$ says that behavior expression B may be rewritten to B'

Figure 12.6

Behavior expression | Communication tree

(1) *nil*

(2) $\alpha n. ((\bar{\beta} n. nil) + (\bar{\gamma}(x \text{ plus one}). nil))$

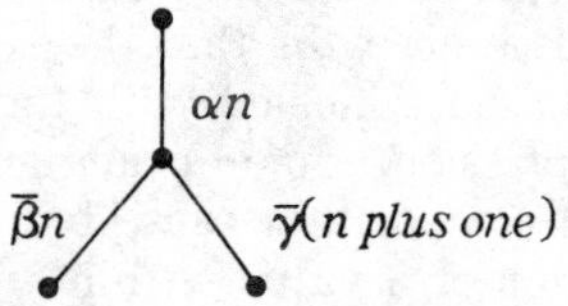

(3) $(\alpha n. nil) \mid (\beta m. \bar{\alpha}(m \text{ plus one}). nil)$

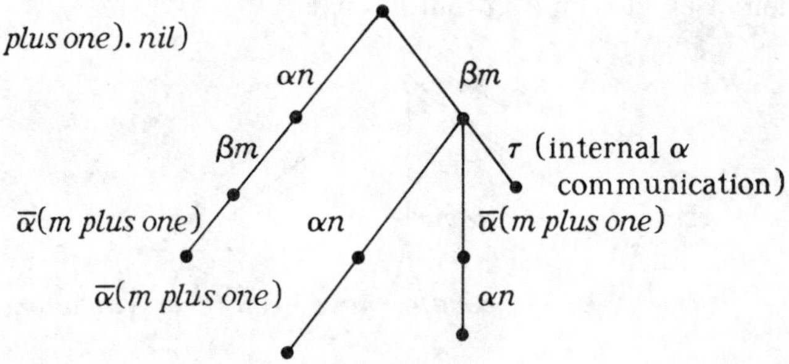

(4) $((\alpha n. nil) \mid (\beta m. \bar{\alpha}(m \text{ plus one}). nil))\S\alpha$

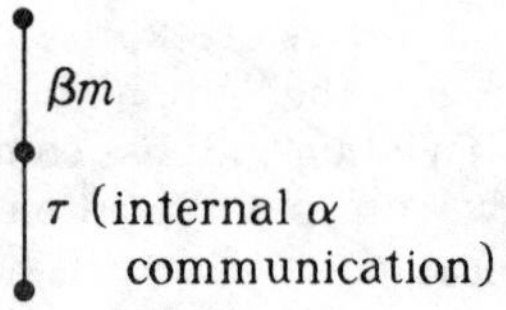

(5) $((\bar{\alpha} two. nil) * (\alpha x. \bar{\beta} x. nil))[\gamma/\beta]$

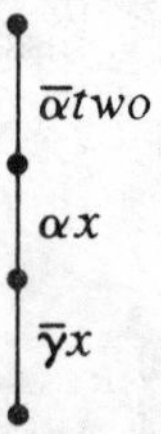

Figure 12.7

Inference rules:

Act→ (1) $\alpha x.B \xrightarrow{\alpha v} [v/x]B$

(2) $\overline{\alpha}v.B \xrightarrow{\overline{\alpha}v} B$

Com→ (1) $\dfrac{B_1 \xrightarrow{\mu v} B'_1}{B_1 \mid B_2 \xrightarrow{\mu v} B'_1 \mid B_2}$ where μ may be either α or $\overline{\alpha}$, $\alpha \in P$

(2) $\dfrac{B_2 \xrightarrow{\mu v} B'_2}{B_1 \mid B_2 \xrightarrow{\mu v} B_1 \mid B'_2}$ (3) $\dfrac{B_1 \xrightarrow{\alpha v} B'_1 \quad B_2 \xrightarrow{\overline{\alpha}v} B'_2}{B_1 \mid B_2 \xrightarrow{\tau} B'_1 \mid B'_2}$

Sum→ (1) $\dfrac{B_1 \xrightarrow{\mu v} B'_1}{B_1 + B_2 \xrightarrow{\mu v} B'_1}$ (2) $\dfrac{B_2 \xrightarrow{\mu v} B'_2}{B_1 + B_2 \xrightarrow{\mu v} B'_2}$

Seq→ $\dfrac{B_1 \xrightarrow{\mu v} B'_1}{B_1 * B_2 \xrightarrow{\mu v} B'_1 * B_2}$

Con→ (1) $\dfrac{B_1 \xrightarrow{\mu v} B'_1}{\textit{if true then } B_1 \textit{ else } B_2 \xrightarrow{\mu v} B'_1}$ (2) $\dfrac{B_2 \xrightarrow{\mu v} B'_2}{\textit{if false then } B_1 \textit{ else } B_2 \xrightarrow{\mu v} B'_2}$

Res→ $\dfrac{B \xrightarrow{\mu v} B'}{B\S\alpha \xrightarrow{\mu v} B'\S\alpha}$ where μ is not in $\{\alpha, \overline{\alpha}\}$

Rel→ $\dfrac{B \xrightarrow{\mu v} B'}{B[\gamma/\mu] \xrightarrow{\gamma v} B'[\gamma/\mu]}$

Equivalences:

$B_1 \mid B_2 \equiv B_2 \mid B_1$

$(B_1 \mid B_2) \mid B_3 \equiv B_1 \mid (B_2 \mid B_3)$

$nil \mid B \equiv B$

$B_1 + B_2 \equiv B_2 + B_1$

$(B_1 + B_2) + B_3 \equiv B_1 + (B_2 + B_3)$

$nil + B \equiv B$

$nil * B \equiv B$

$(B_1 * B_2) * B_3 \equiv B_1 * (B_2 * B_3)$

(without any communication) since both expressions represent equivalent communication trees. The descriptions of the rules and trees are necessarily brief, and you are referred to Milner's book.

We can put the inference rules to good use. Here is a derivation of a path in the communication tree for expression 3 in Figure 12.6:

$(\alpha n.\, nil) \mid (\beta m.\, \overline{\alpha}(m\ plus\ one).\, nil)$
$\xrightarrow{\beta two}$ $(\alpha n.\, nil) \mid (\overline{\alpha}(two\ plus\ one).\, nil)$, by Com→(1), Act→(1)
$\equiv (\alpha n.\, nil) \mid (\overline{\alpha}(three).\, nil)$
$\xrightarrow{\tau}$ $nil \mid nil$, by Com→(3), Act→(3)
$\equiv nil$

and the path is $\beta two, \tau$. The path shows a result of supplying the argument *two* on the β port to the behavior expression. From here on, we will only be interested in deriving paths that contain no instances of external input or output; all value communication will be internal. These "closed derivations" correspond to the simplification sequences built for function expressions. The behavior expression just given does not have a closed derivation to *nil*, for some value must be given to the β port. The following expression does have a closed derivation to *nil:*

$(\alpha n.\, nil) \mid (\beta m.\, \overline{\alpha}(m\ plus\ one).\, nil) \mid (\overline{\beta} two.\, nil)$
$\xrightarrow{\tau} (\alpha n.\, nil) \mid (\overline{\alpha}.(two\ plus\ one).\, nil) \mid nil$
$\equiv (\alpha n.\, nil) \mid (\overline{\alpha}(three).\, nil) \mid nil$
$\xrightarrow{\tau} nil \mid nil \mid nil$
$\equiv nil$

We will also allow named behavior expressions, and the namings may be recursive. For example:

$binary\text{-}semaphore = \overline{\alpha}().\, \beta().\, binary\text{-}semaphore$

describes a simple binary semaphore. The argument values transmitted along the α- and β-ports are from the *Unit* domain. Named behavior expressions can be abstracted on function expression values. For example:

$counting\text{-}sem(n) = if\ n\ equals\ zero$
$\qquad then\ \beta().\, counting\text{-}sem(one)$
$\qquad else\ ((\overline{\alpha}().\, counting\text{-}sem(n\ minus\ one)))$
$\qquad\quad + (\beta().\, counting\text{-}sem(n\ plus\ one))$

is a definition of a counting semaphore. The rewriting rule for recursively named behavior expressions is the usual unfolding rule for recursively defined expressions.

The CCS-based semantics of the language in Figure 12.4 is given in Figure 12.8. The store is managed by a semaphore-like behavior expression, which transmits and receives the store from communicating commands. The new semantics is faithful to the one in Figure 12.4 because it treats assignments as noninterruptable primitive commands, allows interleaving of commands in parallel evaluation, and admits interleaving into a conditional command between the test and the selected clause. A derivation of a program denotation is seen in Figure 12.9.

Figure 12.8

Abstract syntax:

P∈ Program
C∈ Command
E∈ Expression
B∈ Boolean-expr

P ::= C.
C ::= C_1;C_2 | C_1 || C_2 | I:=E | **if** B **then** C_1 **else** C_2 | **while** B **do** C

Semantic algebras: (usual)

Store manager behavior expression:

$sem(s) = \overline{\alpha}s.\ \mu s'.\ sem(s')$

Valuation functions:

P: Program → *Behavior-expression*

$\mathbf{P}[\![C.]\!] = \lambda s.\ \mathbf{C}[\![C]\!] \mid sem(s)$

C: Command → *Behavior-expression*

$\mathbf{C}[\![C_1;C_2]\!] = \mathbf{C}[\![C_1]\!] * \mathbf{C}[\![C_2]\!]$

$\mathbf{C}[\![C_1 \,||\, C_2]\!] = \mathbf{C}[\![C_1]\!] \mid \mathbf{C}[\![C_2]\!]$

$\mathbf{C}[\![I{:=}E]\!] = \alpha s.\ \overline{\mu}(update\,[\![I]\!]\,(\mathbf{E}[\![E]\!]s)\ s).\ nil$

$\mathbf{C}[\![\textbf{if } B \textbf{ then } C_1 \textbf{ else } C_2]\!] = \alpha s.\ if\ \mathbf{B}[\![B]\!]s\ then\ \overline{\mu}s.\ \mathbf{C}[\![C_1]\!]\ else\ \overline{\mu}s.\ \mathbf{C}[\![C_2]\!]$

$\mathbf{C}[\![\textbf{while } B \textbf{ do } C]\!] = f$

where $f = \alpha s.\ if\ \mathbf{B}[\![B]\!]s\ then\ \overline{\mu}s.\ (\mathbf{C}[\![C_1]\!] * f)\ else\ \overline{\mu}s.\ nil$

Figure 12.9

Let

B_{IN} stand for $\alpha s.\ \bar{\mu}(update\ [\![I]\!]\ N[\![N]\!]\ s).\ nil$

in

$P[\![X{:=}0 \mid\mid X{:=}1;\ \textbf{if}\ X{=}0\ \textbf{then}\ Y{:=}0\ \textbf{else}\ Y{:=}1]\!] =$

$\lambda s.\ B_{X0} \mid B_{X1} * B_{if} \mid sem(s)$

where $B_{if} = \alpha s.\ if\ (access\ [\![X]\!]\ s)\ then\ \bar{\mu}s.\ B_{Y0}\ else\ \bar{\mu}s.B_{Y1}$

A derivation is:

$(\lambda s.\ B_{X0} \mid B_{X1} * B_{if} \mid sem(s))(s_0)$

$\equiv B_{X0} \mid B_{X1} * B_{if} \mid sem(s_0)$

$\equiv B_{X0} \mid B_{X1} * B_{if} \mid \bar{\alpha}s_0.\ \mu s'.\ sem(s')$

$\xrightarrow{\tau} B_{X0} \mid \bar{\mu}(s_1).\ nil * B_{if} \mid \mu s'.\ sem(s')$ where $s_1 = (update\ [\![X]\!]\ one\ s_0)$

$\xrightarrow{\tau} B_{X0} \mid nil * B_{if} \mid sem(s_1)$

$\equiv B_{X0} \mid \alpha s.\ if\ (access\ [\![X]\!]\ s)\ equals\ zero\ then \cdots \mid \bar{\alpha}s_1.\ \mu s'.\ sem(s')$

$\xrightarrow{\tau} B_{X0} \mid if\ (access\ [\![X]\!]\ s_1)\ equals\ zero\ then \cdots \mid \mu s'.\ sem(s')$

$\equiv B_{X0} \mid if\ false\ then\ \bar{\mu}s_1.\ B_{Y0}\ else\ \bar{\mu}s_1.\ B_{Y1} \mid \mu s'.\ sem(s')$

$\xrightarrow{\tau} B_{X0} \mid B_{Y1} \mid sem(s_1)$

$\equiv \alpha s.\ \bar{\mu}(update\ [\![X]\!]\ zero\ s).\ nil \mid B_{Y1} \mid \bar{\alpha}s_1.\mu s'.\ sem(s')$

$\xrightarrow{\tau} \bar{\mu}(s_2).\ nil \mid B_{Y1} \mid \mu s'.\ sem(s')$ where $s_2 = (update\ [\![X]\!]\ zero\ s_1)$

$\xrightarrow{\tau} nil \mid B_{Y1} \mid sem(s_2)$

$\equiv \alpha s.\ \bar{\mu}(update\ [\![Y]\!]\ one\ s).\ nil \mid \bar{\alpha}s_2.\mu s'.\ sem(s')$

$\xrightarrow{\tau} \bar{\mu}(s_3).\ nil \mid \mu s'.\ sem(s')$ where $s_3 = (update\ [\![Y]\!]\ one\ s_2)$

$\xrightarrow{\tau} nil \mid sem(s_3)$

$\equiv sem(s_3).$

The CCS-based denotation makes the competition for the store easier to see and the possible outcomes easier to determine. Although the resumption semantics provides a precise function meaning for a parallel program, the CCS version provides a depiction that is easier to read, contains many operational analogies, and has a precise meaning in communication tree form.

12.5 THE POWERDOMAIN STRUCTURE

We conclude this chapter by studying the mathematics of powerdomain construction. As mentioned in the introduction, there is no "best" version of a powerdomain. This is because the clash between the subset properties of the powerdomain and the partial ordering properties of its component domain can be resolved in several ways. We present the methods in two stages: we first construct powerdomains from domains that have trivial partial order structure, and then we generalize to arbitrary domains. The first stage is straightforward, but the second is somewhat involved and only an overview is given. Plotkin's and Smyth's original articles give a complete presentation.

12.5.1 Discrete Powerdomains

A domain A with a trivial partial ordering (that is, for all $a,b \in A$, $a \sqsubseteq b$ iff $a=b$ or $a=\bot$) is called a *flat domain*. Powerdomains built from flat domains are called *discrete powerdomains*. Examples of flat domains are $\mathbb{N}$, $\mathbb{N}_\bot$, $\mathbb{N}\times\mathbb{N}$, *Identifier*, *Identifier* $\rightarrow\mathbb{N}$, and $(\textit{Identifier}\rightarrow\mathbb{N})_\bot$, but *not* *Identifier* $\rightarrow\mathbb{N}_\bot$ or $\mathbb{N}_\bot\times\mathbb{N}$. A flat domain has almost no internal structure.

The first method builds the set-of-all-sets construction from a flat domain.

12.5 Definition:

For a flat domain D, the discrete relational powerdomain of D, written $\mathbb{P}_R(D)$, is the collection of all subsets of proper (that is, non-$\bot$) elements of D, partially ordered by the subset relation $\subseteq$.

Let $\sqsubseteq_R$ stand for the partial ordering relation $\subseteq$ on $\mathbb{P}_R(D)$. In preparation for the construction of relational powerdomains from nonflat domains, we note that for all $A,B \in \mathbb{P}_R(D)$:

$$A \sqsubseteq_R B \text{ iff for every } a \in A \text{ there exists some } b \in B \text{ such that } a \sqsubseteq_D b$$

This property ties together the structural and subset properties of elements in the powerdomains. The only element in the flat domain that might have caused structural problems, $\bot \in D$, is handled by making it "disappear" from the construction of $\mathbb{P}_R(D)$. Thus, the domain $\mathbb{P}_R(\mathbb{N})$ is identical to $\mathbb{P}_R(\mathbb{N}_\bot)$: both are just the powerset of $\mathbb{N}$, partially ordered by $\subseteq$.

In the relational powerdomain, the constant $\varnothing$ does indeed stand for the empty set in the domain. As an exercise, you are asked to show that the associated assembly and disassembly operations are continuous.

The relational powerdomain construction is a natural one for a cpo lacking $\bot$. When used with a pointed cpo, it ignores the possibility of nontermination as a viable answer. For this reason, the relational powerdomain is useful in those cases where only partial correctness issues are of primary concern. The domain works well with the semantics in Figure 12.1, because the property $\emptyset \cup d = d$ is necessary to supply the expected semantics for conditional and loop commands.

The relational powerdomain is inadequate for modelling operational concerns. If the $\bot$ element of a flat domain is introduced into the elements of the powerdomain, the result is an Egli-Milner powerdomain.

12.6 Definition:

For a pointed cpo D, the discrete Egli-Milner powerdomain of D, written $\mathbb{P}_{EM}(D)$, *is the collection of nonempty subsets of D which are either finite or contain* $\bot$, *partially ordered as follows: for all* $A,B \in \mathbb{P}_{EM}(D)$, $A \sqsubseteq_{EM} B$ *iff:*

1. *For every* $a \in A$, *there exists some* $b \in B$ *such that* $a \sqsubseteq_D b$.
2. *For every* $b \in B$, *there exists some* $a \in A$ *such that* $a \sqsubseteq_D b$.

The construction only operates upon pointed cpos. All sets in the powerdomain are nonempty, because an element denotes a set of possible results of a computation, and the empty set has no significance, for it contains no results, not even $\bot$. The infinite elements of the powerdomain contain $\bot$ to show that, if a computation has an infinite set of possible results, it will have to run forever to cover all the possibilities, hence nontermination is also a viable result.

A partial drawing of $\mathbb{P}_{EM}(\mathbb{N}_\bot)$ is:

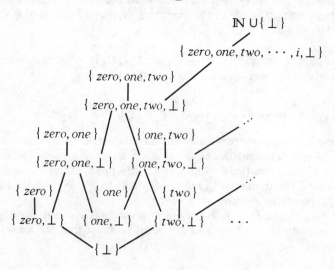

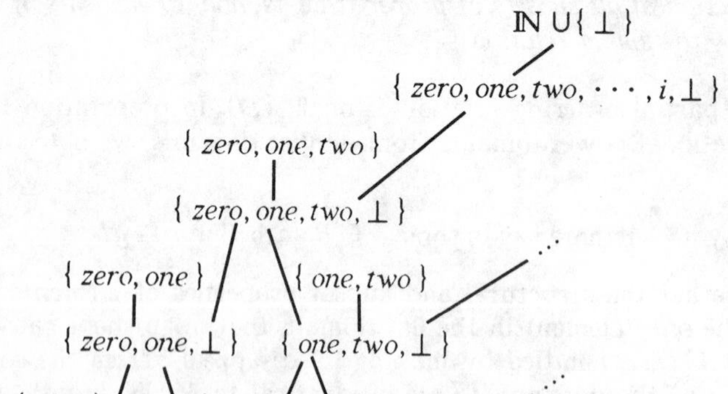

The subset ordering is restricted to those relations that are computationally feasible. We read an element $\{ m_1, m_2, \cdots, m_n \}$ not containing $\perp$ as the final result of a computation. An element $\{ m_1, m_2, \cdots, m_n, \perp \}$ may be read as either a partial result of a computation, where $\perp$ denotes a lack of knowledge about the remaining output values, or as the final result of a computation that might not terminate. Thus, $\{ one, \perp \} \sqsubseteq \{ one, two, three \}$, as $\perp$ is "completed" to $\{ two, three \}$, but $\{ one \} \not\sqsubseteq \{ one, two \}$, as the output information in the set $\{ one \}$ is complete. Also, the least upper bound of the chain $\{ \perp \}$, $\{ zero, \perp \}$, $\{ zero, one, \perp \}$, $\cdots$, must be $\mathbb{N} \cup \{ \perp \}$, rather than $\mathbb{N}$ (if $\mathbb{N}$ were indeed in $\mathbb{P}_{EM}(\mathbb{N}_\perp)$), for $(\mathbb{N} \cup \{ \perp \}) \sqsubseteq_{EM} \mathbb{N}$, and since all elements of the chain possess the property of "noncompletion of output," so must the least upper bound.

In the Egli-Milner powerdomain, the constant $\emptyset$ represents the set $\{ \perp \}$. A consequence is that $\emptyset \cup d$ does *not* equal d. You should show that the singleton and union operations are continuous and that the operation f^+ is continuous when f is continuous and strict.

The Egli-Milner powerdomain is useful for analyzing the operational properties of a language. For this reason, it is the choice for supplying the semantics of the concurrent language in Section 12.3.

The final example of discrete powerdomain uses the third variant of partial ordering on set elements.

12.7 Definition:

For a flat domain D, the discrete Smyth powerdomain of D, written $\mathbb{P}_S(D)$, is the collection of finite, nonempty sets of proper elements of D along with D itself, partially ordered as follows: for all $A,B \in \mathbb{P}_S(D)$, $A \sqsubseteq_S B$ iff for every $b \in B$ there exists some $a \in A$ such that $a \sqsubseteq_D b$

Since $\sqsubseteq_S$ is the inverse of $\sqsubseteq_R$, $A \sqsubseteq_S B$ iff $B \subseteq A$. The reverse subset ordering suggests that a set B is better defined than A when B's information is more specific than A's. Computation upon a Smyth powerdomain can be viewed as the process of determining what *cannot* be an answer. A nonterminating computation rules out nothing; that is, virtually anything might result. Thus, D is the least defined element in $\mathbb{P}_S(D)$. A partial drawing of $\mathbb{P}_S(\mathbb{N}_\perp)$ is:

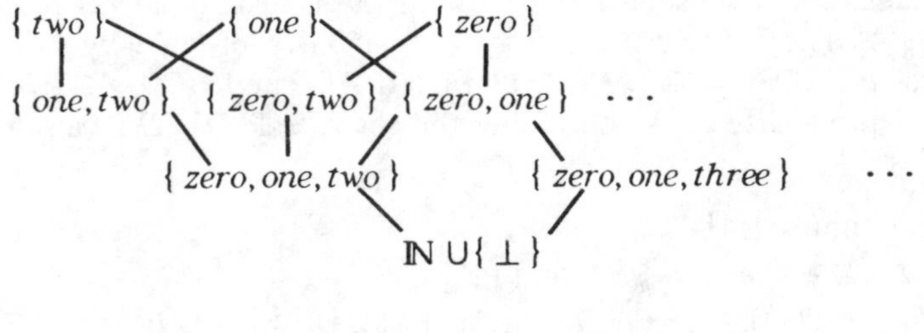

As with the Egli-Milner powerdomain, the value of $\emptyset \cup d$ is not d— it is $\emptyset$! This is because $\emptyset$ represents the set D. The Smyth powerdomain is appropriate for total correctness studies, that is, results that are valid only if the program examined always terminates. The guarded command language of Section 12.2 was designed by Dijkstra to be understood in terms of total correctness. He introduced an assertion language and described the actions of commands in terms of their assertion transformation properties. The semantics of the language in Figure 12.1 is *not* faithful to Dijkstra's ideas when the Smyth powerdomain is used. You are given the exercise of rewriting the semantics of the language to match Dijkstra's intentions.

12.5.2 General Powerdomains

We now generalize the discrete powerdomain constructions to handle nonflat domains. The problems inherent in handling nonflat domains are examined first, and the general versions of the three powerdomains are presented.

Let us begin with the generalization of the relational powerdomain. We would like to define the relational powerdomain of an arbitrary domain D in a fashion similar to the discrete version: the elements of $\mathbb{P}_R(D)$ should be the subsets of proper elements of D, ordered by the relation formulated earlier: $A \sqsubseteq_R B$ iff for all $a \in A$ there exists some $b \in B$ such that $a \sqsubseteq_D b$. Unfortunately, this ordering leads to:

12.8 Problem:

$\sqsubseteq_R$ is not a partial ordering. As an example, for proper elements $d_1, d_2 \in D$ such that $d_1 \sqsubseteq_D d_2$, both $\{ d_2 \} \sqsubseteq_R \{ d_1, d_2 \}$ and $\{ d_1, d_2 \} \sqsubseteq_R \{ d_2 \}$. The reason for this equivalence is that the total information contents of the two sets are identical. This example shows the clash of the structure of D with the subset properties of the powerset.

We might attempt a solution by grouping together those sets that are equivalent with respect to the ordering $\sqsubseteq_R$. Let $\mathbb{P}(D)/\sqsubseteq_R$, the *quotient of* $\mathbb{P}(D)$ *with respect to* $\sqsubseteq_R$, be the sets of proper elements of D grouped into collections called *equivalence classes*. Two sets A and B are in the same equivalence class iff $A \sqsubseteq_R B$ and $B \sqsubseteq_R A$. The equivalence classes are partially ordered by $\sqsubseteq_R$: for equivalence classes $P, Q \in \mathbb{P}(D)/\sqsubseteq_R$, $P \sqsubseteq Q$ iff for all $A \in P$ and $B \in Q$, $A \sqsubseteq_R B$. Let $[A]$ represent the equivalence class containing the set $A \in \mathbb{P}(D)$. We can define the operations:

$\emptyset : \mathbb{P}(D)/\sqsubseteq_R$ denotes $[\{\}]$
$\{\_\} : D \rightarrow \mathbb{P}(D)/\sqsubseteq_R$ maps $d \in D$ to $[\{d\}]$
$\_\cup\_ : \mathbb{P}(D)/\sqsubseteq_R \times \mathbb{P}(D)/\sqsubseteq_R \rightarrow \mathbb{P}(D)/\sqsubseteq_R$ is $[A] \cup [B] = [A \cup B]$

Least upper bounds in the domain are determined by set union: for a chain $C = \{ [A_i] \mid i \in I \}$, $\bigsqcup C$ is $[\bigcup \{ A_i \mid i \in I \}]$; the proof is left as an exercise. Unfortunately, this quotient domain isn't good enough.

12.9 Problem:

The singleton operation is not continuous. For example, if $c \in D$ is the least upper bound of the chain $\{ d_i \mid i \in I \}$ in D, then $\bigsqcup \{ [\{ d_i \}] \mid i \in I \}$ $= [\bigcup \{ \{ d_i \} \mid i \in I \}] = [\{ d_i \mid i \in I \}]$, but this *not* the same equivalence class as $[\{ c \}]$. We can also show that the usual definition of f^+ for continuous f is also discontinuous. The quotient relation is inadequate; a set such as $\{ c \}$ must belong to the same equivalence class as $\{ d_i \mid i \in I \}$, because both have the same information content.

We must define a quotient relation that better describes the total information content of sets of elements. The best measure of information content was introduced in exercise 17 of Chapter 6: it is the topological open set. Recall that the *Scott-topology* upon a domain D is a collection of subsets of D known as *open sets*. A set $U \subseteq D$ is open in the Scott-topology on D iff:

1. U is closed upwards, that is, for every $d_2 \in D$, if there exists some $d_1 \in U$ such that $d_1 \sqsubseteq_D d_2$, then $d_2 \in U$.
2. If $d \in U$ is the least upper bound of a chain C in D, then some $c \in C$ is in U.

An open set represents a property or an information level. Clause 1 says that if $d_1 \in U$ has enough information to fulfill property U, then so must any d_2 such that $d_1 \sqsubseteq_D d_2$. Clause 2 says that if $\bigsqcup C \in U$ satisifes a property, it is only because it contains some piece of information $c \in C$ that makes it so, and c must satisfy the property, too. These intuitions are justified by exercise 20 of Chapter 6, which shows that a function $f\colon D \rightarrow E$ is partial order continuous iff f is topologically continuous on the Scott-topologies for D and E.

Here is a domain with its open set structure "drawn in":

Simp =

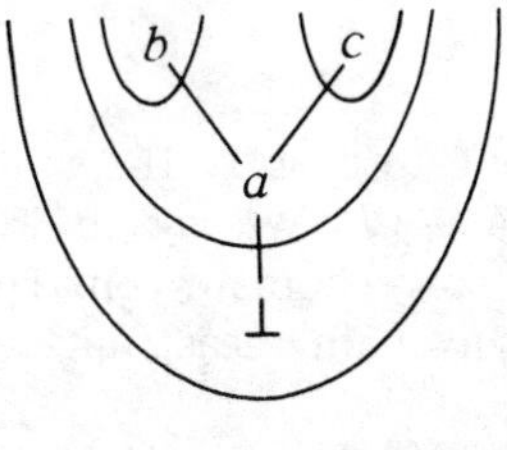

Each semicircular region represents an open set. The open sets of *Simp* are $\{ b \}$, $\{ c \}$, $\{ a, b, c \}$, $\{ \bot, a, b, c \}$, $\{ b, c \}$ (why?), and $\varnothing$ (why?).

A more interesting example is:

Ord =

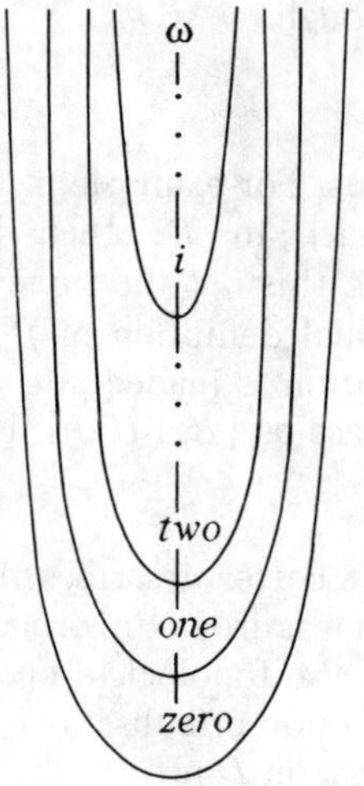

Note that { ω } is *not* an open set, for it is the least upper bound of the chain { *zero*, *one*, *two*, · · · }, and whenever ω belongs to an open set, so must one of the members of the chain. An open set in *Ord* is either empty or has the structure { *j*, (*j plus one*), (*j plus two*), · · · , ω }.

The open sets of a domain *D* define all the properties on *D*. The total information content of a set of elements from *D* can be precisely stated by listing all the open sets to which the elements of the set belong. For sets $A,B \subseteq D$, say that:

$A \underset{\sim}{\sqsubset}_R B$ iff for every $a \in A$ and open set $U \subseteq D$, if $a \in U$, then there exists a $b \in B$ such that $b \in U$ as well

Further, say that:

$A \approx_R B$ iff $A \underset{\sim}{\sqsubset}_R B$ and $B \underset{\sim}{\sqsubset}_R A$

That is, the elements of *A* and *B* belong to exactly the same collection of open sets in *D*. Note that $A \sqsubseteq_R B$ implies $A \underset{\sim}{\sqsubset}_R B$. We use the relation $\approx_R$ to define the equivalence classes in the general powerdomain construction. The relation equates a chain with a set containing the chain's least upper bound. This solves Problem 12.9.

An alternative presentation of $\underset{\sim}{\sqsubset}_R$ is done without topological concepts; for $A,B \subseteq D$:

$A \underset{\sim}{\sqsubset}_R B$ iff for all continuous functions $f: D \rightarrow Unit_\perp$, $f(A) \sqsubseteq_R f(B)$

The definition is equivalent to the topological one, for the open sets of a domain D are in one-to-one correspondence with the continuous functions in $D \rightarrow Unit_{\perp}$.

12.10 Definition:

For domain D, the (general) relational powerdomain of D, written $\mathbb{P}_R(D)$, is the collection of the subsets of the proper elements of D, quotiented by the relation $\approx_R$, partially ordered by $\sqsubseteq_R$. The associated operations are defined as:

$\varnothing : \mathbb{P}_R(D)$ *denotes* $[\{\}]$
$\{\_\} : D \rightarrow \mathbb{P}_R(D)$ *maps* $d \in D$ *to* $[\{d\}]$
$\_\cup\_ : \mathbb{P}_R(D) \times \mathbb{P}_R(D) \rightarrow \mathbb{P}_R(D)$ *is* $[A] \cup [B] = [A \cup B]$
for $f: D \rightarrow \mathbb{P}_R(E)$, $f^+ : \mathbb{P}_R(D) \rightarrow \mathbb{P}_R(E)$ *is* $f^+[A] = [\bigcup\{f(a) \mid a \in A\}]$

The operations are well defined and continuous, and least upper bound corresponds to set union: $\bigsqcup\{[A_i] \mid i \in I\} = [\bigcup\{A_i \mid i \in I\}]$. Examples of relational powerdomains are:

$\mathbb{P}_R(Simp) =$

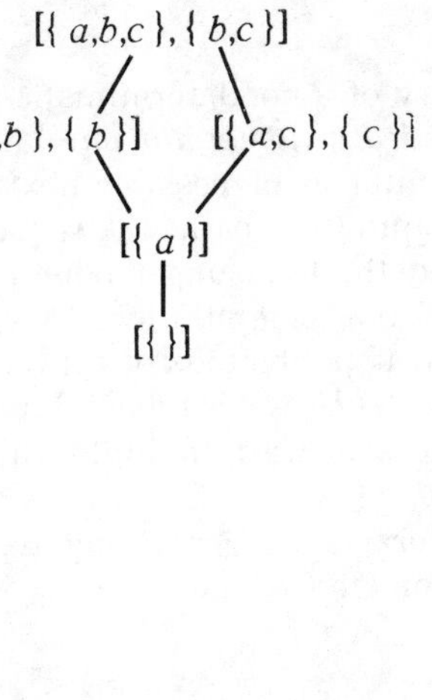

$\mathbb{P}_R(Ord) =$

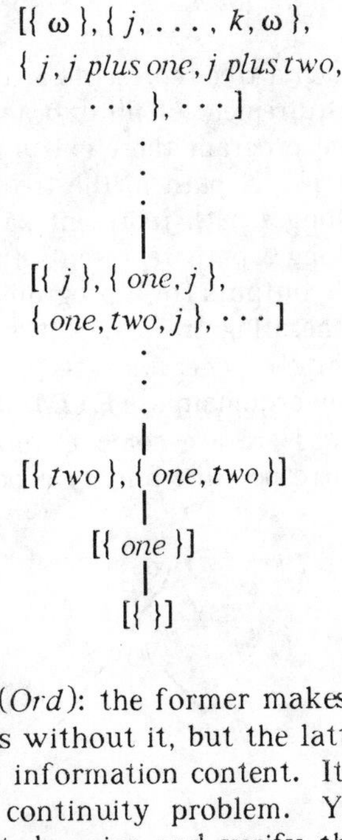

Note the difference between $\mathbb{P}(Ord)/\equiv_R$ and $\mathbb{P}_R(Ord)$: the former makes a distinction between sets containing ω and infinite sets without it, but the latter does not, since both kinds of sets have the same total information content. It is exactly this identification of sets that solves the continuity problem. You should construct $\mathbb{P}_R(D)$ for various examples of flat domains and verify that the domains are identical to the ones built in Section 12.4.

In summary, we can think of the powerdomain $\mathbb{P}_R(D)$ as the set of all subsets of D but must also remember that some sets are equivalent to others in terms of total information content. This equivalence becomes important when the assembly and disassembly operations associated with the powerdomain are defined, for they must be consistent in their mapping of equivalent sets to equivalent answers.

The general Egli-Milner powerdomain, also called the Plotkin powerdomain, is constructed along the same lines as the general relational powerdomain. Differences exist in the sets of elements included and in the quotient relation applied. Since the powerdomain is operationally oriented, sets of elements are chosen that are computationally feasible. Recall that not all subsets of D-elements were used in the discrete Egli-Milner powerdomain: infinite sets included $\perp$. A general definition of acceptable set starts from the notion of a finitely branching generating tree:

12.11 Definition:

A finitely branching generating tree for domain D is a finitely branching, possibly infinite tree whose nodes are labeled with elements of D such that for all nodes m and n in the tree, if m is an ancestor to n, them m's label is $\sqsubseteq_D$ *n's label.*

Such a tree represents a computation history of a nondeterministic program. The requirement of finite branching forces *bounded nondeterminism*— at any point in the program there exists at most a finite number of possible next computation steps. A path in the tree is a possible computation path; the sequence of labels along a path represent partial outputs; and the least upper bound of the labels along a path represents the final output of that computation. The set of possible outputs for a program is the set of least upper bounds of all the paths of the generating tree. Call this set a *finitely generable set*, and let $\mathbf{F}_g(D)$ be all the finitely generable sets of domain D. The sets used to build the Egli-Milner powerdomain are $\mathbf{F}_g(D)$.

Here are some examples of finitely branching generating trees and their corresponding finitely generable sets. For domain *Ord* and trees:

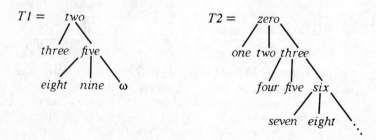

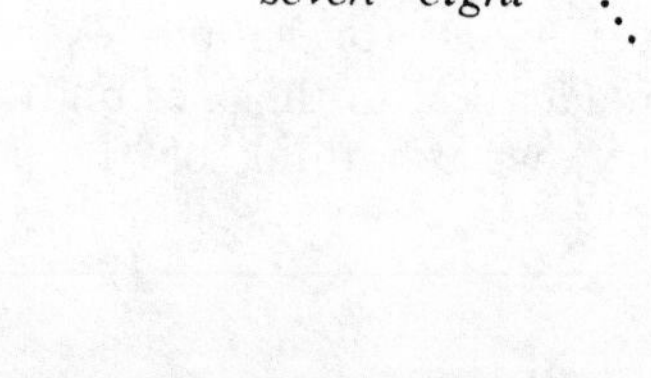

The paths generated from *T1* are *two, three*; *two, five, eight*; *two, five, nine*; and *two, five,* ω. The finitely generable set is $\{$ *three, eight, nine,* $\omega \}$. For *T2*, the finitely generable set is $\{ n \mid (n \bmod three) \neq zero \} \cup \{ \omega \}$. The ω element is the least upper bound of the infinite path *zero, three, six, nine,* $\cdots$. For domain $\mathbb{N}_\perp$ and tree:

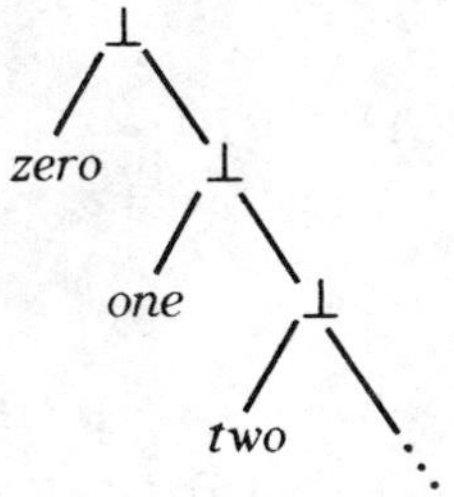

the finitely generable set is $\{$ *zero, one, two,* $\cdots, \perp \}$. We can prove that any finitely generable infinite set for domain $\mathbb{N}_\perp$ must contain $\perp$: if the set is infinite, its generating tree has an infinite number of nodes; by Konig's lemma, the tree must have an infinite path. The proof that this path must be $\perp, \perp, \perp, \cdots$ is left as an exercise.

Problems 12.8 and 12.9 also arise if the elements $\mathbf{F}_g(D)$ are ordered by $\sqsubseteq_{EM}$. The topology of domain D again comes to the rescue: for $A,B \subseteq D$, $A \lessapprox_{EM} B$ iff:

1. For every $a \in A$ and open set $U \subseteq D$, if $a \in U$, then there exists some $b \in B$ such that $b \in U$ as well.
2. For every $b \in B$ and open set $U \subseteq D$, if b is in U's complement $\overline{U}$, then there exists some $a \in A$ such that $a \in \overline{U}$ as well.

Condition 1 was seen in the previous section. Condition 2 states that if B is inadequate in information content with respect to one of its elements, A is inadequate in a similar way. Thus, A can reach an answer in "no better way" than B can. The two conditions are embodied in the claim:

$A \lessapprox_{EM} B$ iff for all continuous functions f: $D \rightarrow Unit_\perp$, $f(A) \sqsubseteq_{EM} f(B)$

We say that $A \approx_{EM} B$ iff $A \lessapprox_{EM} B$ and $B \lessapprox_{EM} A$.

12.12 Definition:

For a pointed cpo D, the general Egli-Milner powerdomain of D, written $\mathbb{P}_{EM}(D)$, *is the collection* $\mathbf{F}_g(D)$ *quotiented by the relation* $\approx_{EM}$, *partially ordered by* $\lessapprox_{EM}$.

The definitions of the associated operations are left as exercises.

The general version of the Smyth construction follows the lines of the Egli-Milner construction. The sets used to build the domain are again $\mathbf{F}_g(D)$. For all $A,B \subseteq D$, say that:

$A \sqsubseteq_S B$ iff for every $b \in B$ and open set $U \subseteq D$, if $b \in \bar{U}$, then there exists some $a \in A$ such that $a \in \bar{U}$ as well

This is clause 2 of the $\sqsubseteq_{EM}$ definition, so:

$A \sqsubseteq_S B$ iff for all continuous function $f\colon D \to Unit_\perp$, $f(A) \sqsubseteq_S f(B)$

Let $A \approx_S B$ iff $A \sqsubseteq_S B$ and $B \sqsubseteq_S A$.

12.13 Definition:

For pointed cpo D, the general Smyth powerdomain of D, written $\mathbb{P}_S(D)$, *is the collection* $\mathbf{F}_g(D)$ *quotiented by the relation* $\approx_S$, *partially ordered by* $\sqsubseteq_S$.

The operations upon $\mathbb{P}_S(D)$ are the expected ones.

SUGGESTED READINGS

Nondeterminism & parallelism: Apt & Olderog 1984; Apt & Plotkin 1981; Dijkstra 1976; Hennessy & Plotkin 1979; Hewitt & Baker 1978; Main & Benson 1984; Park 1981

CCS: Milner 1980, 1983, 1985

Powerdomains: Abramsky 1983; Nielsen, Plotkin, & Winskel 1981; Plotkin 1976, 1982a, 1982b; Smyth 1978, 1983

EXERCISES

1. a. Draw $\mathbb{P}_R(D)$, $\mathbb{P}_{EM}(D)$, and $\mathbb{P}_S(D)$ for each of the following D:

   i. $\mathbb{N}$
   ii. $\mathbb{N}_\perp$
   iii. $\mathbb{B}_\perp \times \mathbb{B}_\perp$
   iv. $\mathbb{B} \to \mathbb{B}$
   v. $\mathbb{B} \to Unit_\perp$

   b. Draw:

   i. $\mathbb{P}_R(\mathbb{P}_R(\mathbb{B}_\perp))$
   ii. $\mathbb{P}_{EM}(\mathbb{P}_{EM}(\mathbb{B}_\perp))$
   iii. $\mathbb{P}_S(\mathbb{P}_S(\mathbb{B}_\perp))$

2. For a flat domain D, model a set $A \in \mathbb{P}(D)$ as a function $A : D \rightarrow Unit_{\bot}$ such that $d \in D$ belongs to A iff $A(d) = ()$.

   a. Define the appropriate functions for $\emptyset$, $\{\_\}$, $\_\cup\_$. To which version of discrete powerdomain is $D \rightarrow Unit_{\bot}$ isomorphic?
   b. What goes wrong when using $A : D \rightarrow \mathbb{B}$ and saying that $d \in A$ iff $A(d) = true$? What goes wrong when the definition in part a is applied to nonflat domains?

3. Revise the semantics of the guarded command language of Figure 12.1 so that $Answer = \mathbb{P}_S(Poststore)$. Rewrite the valuation functions so that a command [[C]] that always terminates with a store s_0 has denotation $\mathbf{C}[\![\mathrm{C}]\!]s_0 \neq \emptyset$.

4. Redefine the semantics of the **if** statement in Figure 12.4 so that interruption and interleaving may not occur between evaluation of the test and the first step of evaluation of the chosen clause. Do the same with the semantics of **if** in Figure 12.8.

5. (Plotkin) Extend the syntax of the language of Figure 12.2 to include [[**critical** C]], a critical region construct. Define the resumption and CCS semantics for the construct so that [[C]] evaluates to completion without interruption.

6. a. Let $\mathbf{C}[\![\mathbf{skip}]\!] = step(\lambda s. s)$ be added to the language in Figure 12.4. Show that $\mathbf{C}[\![\mathbf{skip;skip}]\!] \neq \mathbf{C}[\![\mathbf{skip}]\!]$, but that $\mathbf{P}[\![\mathbf{skip;skip}]\!] = \mathbf{P}[\![\mathbf{skip}]\!]$.
   b. Let the CCS semantics of the construct be $\mathbf{C}[\![\mathbf{skip}]\!] = nil$; show that $\mathbf{C}[\![\mathbf{skip;skip}]\!] = \mathbf{C}[\![\mathbf{skip}]\!]$.

7. Give two commands in the language of Figure 12.8:

   a. That have the same semantics for the relational powerdomain but different semantics for the Egli-Milner and Smyth powerdomains.
   b. That have the same semantics for the Smyth powerdomain but different semantics for the Egli-Milner and relational powerdomains.

8. Consider the domain of expression resumptions:

$$Expr\text{-}res = Store \rightarrow \mathbb{P}((Expressible\text{-}value \times Store) + (Store \times Expr\text{-}res))$$

   a. Use *Expr-res* to define the semantics of interleaved evaluation of expressions E ::= $\mathrm{E}_1 + \mathrm{E}_2$ | N | I .
   b. Integrate the semantics you defined in part a with the language in Figure 12.4.
   c. Repeat parts a and b using CCS semantics and the semantics in Figure 12.8.

9. a. Show (or describe) all the closed derivations of the program in Figure 12.9. Draw the corresponding behavior tree, showing just the closed derivations.
   b. Using the semantics in Figure 12.8, draw the behavior tree denotations for $\mathbf{C}[\![X{:=}0]\!]$ and $\mathbf{C}[\![\text{if } X{:=}0 \text{ then } Y{:=}0 \text{ else } Y{:=}1]\!]$.

10. Rewrite the semantics of the guarded command language using CCS.

11. Use resumption semantics to redefine the semantics of the PROLOG-like language of Figure 9.3 so that the denotation of a program is a set of all the possible successful evaluation strategies that a program can take. Repeat the exercise for CCS semantics.

12. Give a resumption semantics to the CCS notation. Prove the soundness of the derivation rules in Figure 12.7.

13. a. What similarities exist between the resumption semantics method of Section 12.3 and the behavior trees model of Section 12.4? What are the primary differences?
    b. What similarities exist between behavior trees and finite generating trees? What are the primary differences?

14. Prove that the $\{\_\}$, $\_\cup\_$ and f^+ operations are well defined in Definition 12.10; that is, show that the choice of representatives A and B in $[A]\cup[B]$ and $f^+[A]$ do not affect the result.

15. Attempt to solve Problem 12.9 by defining $A \sqsubseteq_R B$ iff $\bigsqcup\{\, a \mid a \in A \,\} \sqsubseteq \bigsqcup\{\, b \mid b \in B \,\}$. What goes wrong?

16. A set $U \subseteq A$ is (Scott-) *closed* if $A - U$ is open in the Scott-topology on A.

    a. Prove that $U \subseteq A$ is closed iff:

       i. For all $d, e \in A$, if $d \in U$ and $e \sqsubseteq d$ then $e \in U$.
       ii. For all directed $D \subseteq A$, $D \subseteq U$ implies $\bigsqcup D \in U$.

    b. Prove that if cpo A is pointed, the relational powerdomain $\mathbb{P}_R(A)$ is isomorphic to the collection of all the nonempty closed subsets of A partially ordered by subset inclusion.

17. a. Why must $f: D \to \mathbb{P}(E)$ be strict to build $f^+ : \mathbb{P}(D) \to \mathbb{P}(E)$ in the case of the Egli-Milner and Smyth powerdomains?
    b. What problems arise in building and using the Egli-Milner and Smyth powerdomains when D is not pointed?

18. For $x, y \in \mathbb{P}(D)$, for which versions of the powerdomains do the following hold?

    a. $x \sqsubseteq x \cup y$
    b. $x \cup y \sqsubseteq x$
    c. $x = \{x\} \cup \emptyset$
    c. $\emptyset = x \cup \emptyset$
    d. $x \cup x = x$

19. a. Consider $\mathbb{P}_R'(D)$, a variant of the relational powerdomain such that the elements consist of all subsets of a cpo D, quotiented by $\approx_R$, partially ordered by $\sqsubseteq_R$. What is unsatisfactory about $\mathbb{P}_R'(D)$?
    b. In a similar fashion, comment on the suitability of $\mathbb{P}_{EM}'(D)$, built from all subsets of D, quotiented by $\approx_{EM}$, partially ordered by $\sqsubseteq_{EM}$.
    c. In a similar fashion, comment on the suitability of $\mathbb{P}_S'(D)$, built from all the subsets of D, quotiented by $\approx_S$, partially ordered by $\sqsubseteq_S$.

20. a. For each of the powerdomain constructions, attempt to define a continuous function $\_\mathbf{in}\_ : D \times \mathbb{P}(D) \rightarrow \mathbb{B}$ such that for all $d \in D$, $U \subseteq D$, d **in** $[U] = true$ iff $d \in U$. (Hint: first attempt to define **in** for the discrete powerdomains and then generalize.)
    b. For each of the powerdomain constructions upon which you succeeded in defining **in**, for all $d \in D$, $U, V \subseteq D$:

       i. Attempt to show d **in** $([U] \cup [V]) = true$ iff d **in** $[U] = true$ or d **in** $[V] = true$.
       ii. Attempt to define a continuous function $\cap : \mathbb{P}(D) \times \mathbb{P}(D) \rightarrow \mathbb{P}(D)$ such that d **in** $([U] \cap [V]) = true$ iff d **in** $[U] = true$ and d **in** $[V] = true$.

Bibliography

Abdali, S. K., "A lambda-calculus model of programming languages— jumps and functions," *J. of Computer Languages*, vol. 1, pp. 303-320, 1975.

Abelson, H. and G. Sussman, *Structure and Interpretation of Computer Programs*, MIT Press/McGraw-Hill, New York, 1984.

Abramsky, S., "On semantic foundations for applicative multiprogramming," in *LNCS 154: Proc. 10th ICALP*, pp. 1-14, Springer, Berlin, 1982.

Abramsky, S., "Experiments, powerdomains, and fully abstract models for applicative multiprogramming," in *LNCS 158: Foundations of Computation Theory*, pp. 1-13, Springer, Berlin, 1983.

Adamek, J. and V. Koubek, "Least fixed point of a functor," *Journal of Computer and System Sciences*, vol. 19, pp. 163-178, 1979.

Aho, A. and J. D. Ullman, *Principles of Compiler Design*, Addison-Wesley, Reading, Mass., 1977.

Anderson, E. R. and F. C. Belz, "Issues in the formal specification of programming languages," in *Formal Description of Programming Concepts*, ed. E. J. Neuhold, North-Holland, Amsterdam, 1978.

Anderson, E. R., F. C. Belz, and E. K. Blum, "SEMANOL (73): A metalanguage for programming the semantics of programming languages," *Acta Informatica*, vol. 6, pp. 109-132, 1976.

Andrews, D. and W. Henhapl, "Pascal," in *Formal Specification and Software Development*, ed. D. Bjørner and C. Jones, pp. 175-252, Prentice-Hall, Englewood Cliffs, N.J., 1982.

Appel, A., "Semantics-directed code generation," in *Proc. 12th ACM Symp. on Prin. of Prog. Lang.*, pp. 315-324, New Orleans, 1985.

Apt, K. R., "Equivalence of operational and denotational semantics for a fragment of Pascal," in *Formal Descriptions of Programming Concepts*, ed. E. J. Neuhold, pp. 141-163, North-Holland, Amsterdam, 1978.

Apt, K. R., "Ten years of Hoare's logic: a survey— part I," *ACM Trans. on Prog. Lang. and Systems*, vol. 3, pp. 431-483, 1981.

Apt, K. R., "Ten years of Hoare's logic: a survey— part II: nondeterminism," *Theoretical Computer Science*, vol. 28, pp. 83-110, 1984.

Apt, K. R. and A. Olderog, "Proof rules and transformations dealing with fairness," *Science of Comp. Programming*, vol. 3, pp. 65-100, 1983.

Apt, K. and G. D. Plotkin, "A Cook's tour of countable nondeterminism," in *LNCS 115: Proc. 9th ICALP*, pp. 479-494, Springer, Berlin, 1981.

Arbib, M. A. and E. G. Manes, "The pattern-of-calls expansion is the canonical fixpoint for recursive definitions," *Journal of the ACM*, vol. 29, pp. 577-602, 1982.

Artesiano, E. and G. Costa, "Languages with reducing reflexive types," in *LNCS 85: Proc. 7th ICALP*, Springer, Berlin, 1980.

Ashcroft, E. A. and W. W. Wadge, "Lucid, a nonprocedural language with iteration," *Comm. of the ACM*, vol. 20, pp. 519-526, 1977.

Ashcroft, E. A. and W. W. Wadge, "Prescription for semantics," *ACM Trans. on Prog. Lang. and Sys.*, vol. 4, pp. 283-194, 1982.

Augustsson, L., "A compiler for lazy ML," in *Proc. ACM Conf. on LISP and Functional Programming*, pp. 218-227, Austin, Texas, 1984.

Backus, J., "Can programming be liberated from the von Neumann style? A functional style and its algebra of programs," *Comm. of the ACM*, vol. 21, pp. 613-641, 1978.

deBakker, J. W., "Recursive programs as predicate transformers," in *Formal Descriptions of Programming Concepts*, ed. E.J. Neuhold, pp. 165-181, North-Holland, Amsterdam, 1978.

deBakker, J. W., *Mathematical Theory of Program Correctness*, Prentice-Hall, Englewood Cliffs, N.J., 1980.

Barendregt, H., "The type free lambda calculus," in *Handbook of Mathematical Logic*, ed. J. Barwise, pp. 1091-1132, North-Holland, Amsterdam, 1977.

Barendregt, H., *The Lambda Calculus— Its Syntax and Semantics*, North-Holland, Amsterdam, 1981.

Barendregt, H., "Introduction to lambda calculus," *Niew Archief Voor Wiskunde*, vol. 4, pp. 337-372, 1984.

Barrett, W. A. and J. D. Couch, *Compiler Construction: Theory and Practice*, S.R.A., Chicago, 1979.

Barron, D. W., *An Introduction to the Study of Programming Languages*, Cambridge University Press, Cambridge, 1977.

Bauer, F. L. and H. Wossner, *Algorithmic Language and Program Development*, Springer, Berlin, 1982.

Berry, D. M., "Remarks on R. D. Tennent's language design methods based on semantic principles," *Acta Informatica*, vol. 15, pp. 83-98, 1981.

Berry, D. M., "A denotational semantics for shared memory parallelism and nondeterminism," *Acta Informatica*, vol. 21, pp. 599-628, 1985.

Berry, G., "Some syntactic and categorical constructions of lambda calculus models," *Report 80*, INRIA, Sophia Antipolis, 1981.

Berry, G. and J.-J. Levy, "A survey of some syntactic results of the lambda calculus," in *LNCS 74: Proc. 8th Symp. Math. Foundations of Computer Science*, pp. 552-566, Springer, Berlin, 1979.

Berry, G. and P.-L. Curien, "Sequential algorithms on concrete data structures," *Theoretical Computer Science*, vol. 20, pp. 265-322, 1982.

Berry, G., P.-L. Curien, and J.-J. Levy, "Full abstraction for sequential languages: the state of the art," in *Proc. French-American Seminar on Semantics*, Fontainebleau, France, 1982.

Bird, R. S., *Programs and Machines*, Wiley, New York, 1976.

Birkhoff, G., *Lattice Theory, 3rd Edition*, American Mathematical Society, Providence, R.I., 1967.

Bjørner, D., "The Vienna development method," in *LNCS 75: Mathematical studies of information processing*, pp. 326-359, Springer, Berlin, 1978.

Bjørner, D., ed., *LNCS 86: Abstract Software Specifications*, Springer, Berlin, 1980.

D., Bjørner, ed., *Formal Description of Programming Concepts II*, North-Holland, Amsterdam, 1983.

Bjørner, D. and C. B. Jones, eds., *LNCS 61: The Vienna Development Method: the Metalanguage*, Springer, Berlin, 1978.

Bjørner, D. and C. B. Jones, *Formal Specification and Software Development*, Prentice-Hall, Englewood Cliffs, N.J., 1982.

Bjørner, D. and O. N. Oest, *LNCS 98: Towards a formal description of Ada*, Springer, Berlin, 1980.

Blikle, A. and A. Tarlecki, "Naive denotational semantics," in *Proc. IFIP Congress 83*, pp. 345-356, North-Holland, Amsterdam, 1983.

Bodwin, J., L. Bradley, J. Kanda, D. Little, and U. Pleban, "Experience with an experimental compiler-compiler based on denotational semantics," in *Proc. SIGPLAN 82 Symp. on Compiler Construction*, *SIGPLAN Notices*, vol. 17, pp. 216-229, 1982.

Bohm, C., ed., *LNCS 37: Lambda-calculus and Computer Science Theory*, Springer, Berlin, 1975.

Branquart, P., G. Louis, and P. Wodon, *LNCS 128: An Analytical Description of CHILL, the CCITT High Level Language*, Springer, Berlin, 1982.

Brookes, S. D., "A fully abstract semantics and a proof system for an ALGOL-like language with sharing," in *LNCS: Proc. Workshop on Foundations of Programming Semantics*, Springer, Berlin, 1985a.

Brookes, S. D., A. W. Roscoe, and G. Winskel, eds., *LNCS 197: Seminar on Concurrency*, Springer, Berlin, 1985.

Burge, W. H., *Recursive Programming Techniques*, Addison-Wesley, Reading, Mass., 1975.

Burstall, R., "Proving properties of programs by structural induction," *Computer Journal*, vol. 12, pp. 41-48, 1969.

Burstall, R. and J. Darlington, "A transformation system for developing recursive programs," *Journal of the ACM*, vol. 24, pp. 44-67, 1977.

Burstall, R. and J. Goguen, "Putting theories together to make specifications," in *Proc. 5th Int. Joint Conf. on Artificial Intelligence*, pp. 1045-1058, Cambridge, Mass., 1977.

Burstall, R. and J. Goguen, "Algebras, theories, and freeness: an introduction for computer scientists," in *Proc. Marktoberdorf Summer School on Theoretical Foundations of Programming Methodology*, August 1981.

Burstall, R. M., D. B. MacQueen, and D. T. Sannella, "HOPE: an experimental applicative language," CSR-62-80, Computer Science Dept., Edinburgh University, Edinburgh, Scotland, 1981.

Christiansen, H. and N. D. Jones, "Control flow treatment in a simple semantics-directed compiler," in *Formal Descriptions of Programming Concepts II*, ed. D. Bjørner, pp. 73-97, North-Holland, Amsterdam, 1983.

Church, A., *The Calculi of Lambda Conversion*, Princeton Univ. Press, Princeton, N.J., 1951.

Clarke, T. J., P. J. Gladstone, C. D. MacClean, and A. C. Norman, "SKIM— the S, K, I reduction machine," in *Proc. ACM LISP conference*, pp. 128-135, 1980.

Cleaveland, J. C., "Mathematical specifications," *ACM SIGPLAN Notices*, vol. 15-12, pp. 31-42, 1980.

Cleaveland, J. C. and R. C. Uzgalis, *Grammars for Programming Languages*, Elsevier, New York, 1977.

Clinger, W., "Foundations of actor semantics," Ph.D. thesis, AI lab report AI-TR-633, MIT, 1981.

Clinger, W., "Summary of the Scheme 311 compiler: an exercise in denotational semantics," in *Proc. ACM Symp. on LISP and Functional Programming*, pp. 356-364, Austin, Texas, August, 1984.

Cohn, A. J., "The equivalence of two semantic definitions: a case study in LCF," *SIAM J. of Computing*, vol. 12, pp. 267-285, 1983.

Cohn, P. M., *Universal Algebra (rev. ed.)*, D. Reidel Pub., Boston, 1981.

Courcelle, B. and I. Guessarian, "On some classes of interpretations," *J. of Computer and System Sciences*, vol. 17, pp. 388-413, 1978.

Cousot, P. and R. Cousot, "Abstract interpretation: a unified lattice model for static analysis of programs," in *Poc. 4th ACM Symp. on Prin. of Prog. Lang.*, pp. 238-252, Los Angeles, 1977.

Cousot, P. and R. Cousot, "Systematic design of program analysis frameworks," in *Proc. 6th ACM Symp. on Prin. of Prog. Lang.*, pp. 269-282, San Antonio, Texas, 1979.

Curien, P.-L., "Categorical combinatory logic," in *LNCS 194: Proc. 12th ICALP*, pp. 130-139, Springer, Berlin, 1985.

Curry, H. B. and R. Feys, *Combinatory Logic, Vol. 1*, North-Holland, Amsterdam, 1958.

Darlington, J., P. Henderson, and D. Turner, eds., *Functional Programming and its Applications*, Cambridge Univ. Press, Cambridge, 1982.

Demers, A., J. Donohue, and G. Skinner, "Data types as values: polymorphism, type-checking, and encapsulation," in *Proc. 5th ACM Symp. on Prin. of Prog. Lang.*, pp. 23-30, Tucson, Arizona, 1978.

Devlin, K. J., *Fundamentals of Contemporary Set Theory*, Springer, Berlin, 1979.

Dijkstra, E. W., *A Discipline of Programming*, Prentice-Hall, Englewood Cliffs, N.J., 1976.

Donahue, J., *LNCS 42: Complementary Definitions of Programming Language Semantics*, Springer, Berlin, 1976.

Donahue, J., "Locations considered unnecessary," *Acta Informatica*, vol. 8, pp. 221-242, 1977.

Donohue, J., "On the semantics of 'data type'," *SIAM J. of Computing*, vol. 8, pp. 546-560, 1979.

Donzeau-Gouge, V., "On the formal description of Ada," in *LNCS 94: Semantics-Directed Compiler Generation*, ed. N.D. Jones, Springer, Berlin, 1980.

Donzeau-Gouge, V., "Denotational definition of properties of program computations," in *Program Flow Analysis: Theory and Applications*, ed. S.S. Muchnick and N. D. Jones, pp. 343-379, Prentice-Hall, Englewood Cliffs, N.J., 1982.

Dybjer, P., "Using domain algebras to prove the correctness of a compiler," in *LNCS 182: Proc. 2nd Symp. on Theoretical Aspects of Comp. Sci.*, pp. 98-108, Springer, Berlin, 1985.

Enderton, H., *A Mathematical Introduction to Logic*, Academic Press, New York, 1974.

Enderton, H., *Elements of Set Theory*, Academic Press, New York, 1977.

Ershov, E. P., "On the essence of compilation," in *Formal Description of Programming Concepts*, ed. E.J. Neuhold, North-Holland, Amsterdam, 1978.

Ershov, E. P., "Mixed computation: potential applications and problems for study," *Theoretical Computer Science*, vol. 18, pp. 41-68, 1982.

Fairbairn, J., "PONDER and its type system," Tech. rpt. 31, Computer Laboratory, University of Cambridge, 1982.

Filman, R. E. and D. E. Friedman, *Coordinated Computing*, McGraw-Hill, New York, 1984.

Friedman, D. and D. S. Wise, "CONS should not evaluate its arguments," in *Proc. 3rd ICALP*, ed. S. Michaelson and R. Milner, pp. 257-284, Edinburgh, 1976.

Friedman, D., M. Wand, C. Haynes, E. Kohlbecker, and W. Clinger, "Programming Languages: A Hitchhiker's Guide to the Meta-Universe," Course notes, Computer Science Dept., Indiana Univ., 1984.

Ganzinger, H., K. Ripken, and R. Wilhelm, "Automatic generation of optimizing multipass compilers," in *Proc. IFIP Congress 77*, pp. 535-540, North-Holland, Amsterdam, 1977.

Ganzinger, H., "Transforming denotational semantics into practical attribute grammars," in *LNCS 94: Semantics-Directed Compiler Generation*, ed. N.D. Jones, pp. 1-69, Springer, Berlin, 1980.

Ganzinger, H., "Denotational semantics for languages with modules," in *Formal Description of Programming Concepts II*, ed. D. Bjørner, pp. 3-23, North-Holland, Amsterdam, 1983.

Ganzinger, H., R. Giegerich, U. Moncke, and R. Wilhelm, "A truly generative semantics-directed compiler generator," *ACM SIGPLAN Notices 17-6*, pp. 172-184, Boston, 1982.

Gaudel, M.-C., "Specification of compilers as abstract data type representations," in *LNCS 94: Semantics-directed compiler generation*, pp. 140-164, Springer, Berlin, 1980.

Gaudel, M.-C., "Compiler definitions from formal definitions of programming languages: a survey," in *LNCS 107: Formalization of Programming Concepts*, pp. 96-114, Springer, Berlin, 1981.

Georgeff, M., "Transformations and reduction strategies for typed lambda expressions," *ACM Trans. on Prog. Lang. and Sys.*, vol. 6, pp. 603-631, 1984.

Gierz, G., K. H. Hoffmann, K. Keimel, J. D. Lawson, M. Mislove, and D. S. Scott, *A Compendium of Continuous Lattices*, Springer, Berlin, 1980.

Glaser, H., C. Hankin, and D. Till, *Principles of Functional Programming*, Prentice-Hall, Englewood Cliffs, N.J., 1985.

Goguen, J. A., "Some design principles and theory for OBJ-0," in *LNCS 75: Mathematical Studies of Information Processing*, ed. E. Blum, M. Paul, and S. Takasu, pp. 425-471, Springer, Berlin, 1979.

Goguen, J. A. and K. Parsaye-Ghomi, "Algebraic denotational semantics using parameterized abstract modules," in *LNCS 107: Formalization of Programming Concepts*, ed. I. Ramos, pp. 292-309, Springer, Berlin, 1981.

Goguen, G., J. W. Thatcher, E. G. Wagner, and J. B. Wright, "Initial algebra semantics and continuous algebras," *Journal of the ACM*, vol. 24, pp. 68-95, 1977.

Gordon, M. J. C., "Models of Pure LISP," Experimental Programming Reports 31, Machine Intelligence Dept., Edinburgh Univ., Scotland, 1973.

Gordon, M. J. C., "Towards a semantic theory of dynamic binding," STAN-CS-75-507, Computer Science Dept., Stanford Univ., 1975.

Gordon, M. J. C., "Operational reasoning and denotational semantics," in *Proc. Int. Symp. on Proving and Improving Programs*, pp. 83-98, Arc-et-Senans, France, 1978.

Gordon, M. J. C., *The Denotational Description of Programming Languages*, Springer, Berlin, 1979.

Gordon, M. J. C., R. Milner, and C. Wadsworth, *LNCS 78: Edinburgh LCF*, Springer, Berlin, 1979.

Gratzer, G., *Universal Algebra, 2nd Edition*, Springer, Berlin, 1979.

Grief, I. and A. Meyer, "Specifying the semantics of while-programs: a tutorial and critique of a paper by Hoare and Lauer," *ACM Trans. of Prog. Lang. and Sys.*, vol. 3, pp. 484-507, 1981.

Guessarian, I., *LNCS 99: Algebraic Semantics*, Springer, Berlin, 1981.

Gunter, C., "Profinite domains for recursive domain equations," Tech. rpt. CMU-CS-85-107, Computer Science Dept., Carnegie-Mellon Univ., Pittsburgh, 1985a.

Gunter, C., "Comparing categories of domains," in *LNCS: Proc. Workshop on Mathematical Foundations of Programming Semantics*, Springer, Berlin, 1985b.

Gunter, C., "A universal domain technique for profinite posets," in *LNCS 194: Proc. 12th ICALP*, pp. 232-243, Springer, Berlin, 1985c.

Halmos, P., *Naive Set Theory*, Van Nostrand, Princeton, 1960.

Halpern, J., J. Williams, E. Wimmers, and T. Winkler, "Denotational semantics and rewrite rules for FP," in *Proc. 12th ACM Symp. on Princ. of Prog. Lang.*, pp. 108-120, New Orleans, 1986.

Henderson, P., *Functional Programming*, Prentice-Hall, Englewood Cliffs, N.J., 1980.

Henderson, P. and L. Morris, "A lazy evaluator," in *3rd ACM Symp. on Prin. of Prog. Lang.*, pp. 95-103, 1976.

Henhapl, W. and C. Jones, "ALGOL 60," in *Formal Specification and Software Development*, ed. D. Bjørner and C. Jones, pp. 141-174, Prentice-Hall, Englewood Cliffs, N.J., 1982.

Hennessy, M. and G. D. Plotkin, "Full abstraction for a simple parallel programming language," in *LNCS 74: Proc. Math. Foundations of Comp. Sci.*, Springer, Berlin, 1979.

Henson, M. C. and R. Turner, "Completion semantics and interpreter generation," in *Proc. 9th ACM Symp. on Prin. of Prog. Lang.*, pp. 242-254, Albuquerque, N.M., 1982.

Herrlich, H. and G. E. Strecker, *Category Theory*, Allyn and Bacon, Boston, 1973.

Hewitt, C. and H. Baker, "Actors and continuous functionals," in *Formal Description of Programming Concepts*, ed. E. J. Neuhold, pp. 367-390, North-Holland, Amsterdam, 1978.

Hoare, C. A. R., "An axiomatic basis for computer programming," *Comm. of the ACM*, vol. 12, pp. 576-580, 1969.

Hoare, C. A. R., "Proof of correctness of data representations," *Acta Informatica*, vol. 1, pp. 271-281, 1972.

Hoare, C. A. R., "Recursive data structures," *Int. J. of Computer and Info. Sciences*, vol. 4, pp. 105-132, 1975.

Hoare, C. A. R. and P. E. Lauer, "Consistent and complementary formal theories of the semantics of programming languages," *Acta Informatica*, vol. 3, pp. 135-153, 1974.

Hoare, C. A. R. and N. Wirth, "An axiomatic definition of the programming language Pascal," *Acta Informatica*, vol. 2, pp. 335-355, 1973.

Hoffman, C. M. and M. J. O'Donnell, "Programming with equations," *ACM Trans. Prog. Lang. and Systems*, vol. 4, pp. 83-112, 1983.

Hopcroft, J. and J. Ullman, *Introduction to Automata Theory, Languages, and Computation*, Addison-Wesley, Reading, Mass., 1979.

Hudak, P. and D. Krantz, "A combinator-based compiler for a functional language," in *Proc. 11th ACM Symp. on Prin. of Prog. Lang.*, pp. 122-132, Salt Lake City, Utah, 1984.

Huet, G. and D. C. Oppen, "Equations and rewrite rules: a survey," in *Formal Language Theory*, ed. R. Book, Academic Press, New York, 1980.

Hughes, R. J., "Super combinators: a new implementation method for applicative languages," in *Proc. ACM Symp. on LISP and Functional Programming*, pp. 1-10, 1982.

Jensen, K., "Connection between Dijkstra's predicate transformers and denotational continuation semantics," Report DAIMI PB-86, Computer Science Dept., Aarhus Univ., Denmark, 1978.

Johnsson, T., "Efficient compilation of lazy evaluation," *ACM SIGPLAN Notices*, vol. 19-6, pp. 58-69, 1984.

Johnston, J. B., "The contour model of block structured processes," *ACM SIGPLAN Notices* , vol. 6, pp. 55-82, 1971.

Jones, C., "Modelling concepts of programming languages," in *Formal Specification and Software Development*, ed. D. Bjørner and C. Jones, pp. 85-124, Prentice-Hall, Englewood Cliffs, N.J., 1982a.

Jones, C., "More on exception mechanisms," in *Formal Specification and Software Development*, ed. D. Bjørner and C. Jones, pp. 125-140, Prentice-Hall, Englewood Cliffs, N.J., 1982b.

Jones, N. D., ed., *LNCS 94: Semantics-Directed Compiler Generation*, Springer, Berlin, 1980a.

Jones, N. D., "Flow analysis of lambda expressions," in *LNCS 85: Proc. 7th ICALP*, Springer, Berlin, 1980b.

Jones, N. D. and S. S. Muchnick, *LNCS 66: TEMPO: A Unified Treatment of Binding Time and Parameter Passing Concepts in Programming Languages*, Springer, Berlin, 1978.

Jones, N. D. and S. S. Muchnick, "A fixed-program machine for combinator expression evaluation," in *Proc. ACM Conf. on LISP and Functional Programming*, 1982.

Jones, N. D. and D. A. Schmidt, "Compiler generation from denotational semantics," in *LNCS 94: Semantics-Directed Compiler Generation*, pp. 70-93, Springer, Berlin, 1980.

Jones, N. D., P. Sestoft, and H. Sondergaard, "An experiment in partial evaluation: the generation of a compiler generator," *ACM SIGPLAN Notices*, vol. 20-8, pp. 82-87, 1985.

Kahn, G., D. B. MacQueen, and G. D. Plotkin, eds., *LNCS 173: Semantics of Data Types*, Springer, Berlin, 1984.

Kamimura, T. and A. Tang, "Algebraic relations and presentations," *Theoretical Comp. Science*, vol. 27, pp. 39-60, 1983.

Kamimura, T. and A. Tang, "Effectively given spaces," *Theoretical Comp. Science*, vol. 29, pp. 155-166, 1984a.

Kamimura, T. and A. Tang, "Total objects of domains," *Theoretical Comp. Science*, 1984b.

Kanda, A., "Data types as initial algebras," in *19th Symp. on Foundations of Comp. Science*, 1978.

Kanda, A., "Effective solutions of recursive domain equations," Ph.D. thesis, University of Warwick, 1979.

Karlsson, K. and K. Petersson, "Notes from the Aspenas symposium on functional languages and computer architectures," *ACM SIGPLAN Notices*, vol. 17-11, pp. 14-23, 1982.

Kini, V., D. Martin, and A. Stoughton, "Testing the INRIA Ada formal definition: the USC-ISI formal semantics project," in *Proc. ADATec Meeting*, 1982.

Kleene, S. C., *Introduction to Metamathematics*, Van Nostrand, Princeton, N.J., 1952.

Knuth, D., "The semantics of context free languages," *Math. Systems Theory*, vol. 2, pp. 127-145, 1968. (Corrigenda, vol. 5, p. 95, 1971)

Lambek, J., "From lambda-calculus to cartesian closed categories," in *To H.B. Curry: Essays on Combinatory Logic, Lambda Calculus and Formalism*, ed. J. P. Seldin and J. R. Hindley, pp. 375-402, Academic Press, New York, 1980.

Landin, P., "The mechanical evaluation of expressions," *Computer Journal*, vol. 6, pp. 308-320, 1964.

Landin, P., "A correspondence between ALGOL60 and Church's lambda notation," *Comm. of the ACM*, vol. 8, pp. 89-101, 158-165, 1965.

Landin, P. and R. Burstall, "Programs and their proofs: an algebraic approach," in *Machine Intelligence 4*, ed. D. Michie, pp. 17-44, Edinburgh Univ. Press, 1969.

Ledgard, H., "Ten mini-languages: a study of topical issues in programming languages," *ACM Computing Surveys*, vol. 3, pp. 115-146, 1971.

Lee, J. A. N., *Computer Semantics*, Van Nostrand-Reinhold, New York, 1972.

Lehmann, D. J. and M. B. Smyth, "Algebraic specification of data types: a synthetic approach," *Math. Systems Theory*, vol. 14, pp. 97-139, 1981.

Lemmon, E. J., *Beginning Logic*, Thomas Nelson and Sons, Pub., London, 1965.

Lemmon, E. J., *Introduction to Axiomatic Set Theory*, Routledge and Kegan Paul, Ltd., London, 1968.

Levy, J.-J., "An algebraic interpretation of the lambda-beta-kappa-calculus and an application of a labelled lambda calculus," *Theoretical Computer Science*, vol. 2, pp. 97-114, 1976.

Ligler, G. T., "A mathematical approach to language design," in *Proc. 2nd ACM Symp. on Prin. of Prog. Lang.*, Palo Alto, Cal., 1975.

Ligler, G. T., "Surface properties of programming language constructs," *Theoretical Comp. Science* , vol. 2, 1976.

Lucas, P., "Main approaches to formal semantics," in *Formal Specification and Software Development*, ed. D. Bjørner and C. Jones, pp. 3-24, Prentice-Hall, Englewood Cliffs, N.J., 1982.

Lucas, P. and K. Walk, "On the formal definition of PL/1," *Annual Review in Automatic Programming*, vol. 6, pp. 105-152, Pergammon Press, London, 1963.

McCarthy, J., "Towards a mathematical science of computation," in *Proc. IFIP Congress 63*, pp. 21-28, North-Holland, Amsterdam, 1963.

McCarthy, J. and J. Painter, "The correctness of a compiler for arithmetic expressions," in *Mathematical Aspects of Computer Science, Proc. Symp. Applied Math. 19*, pp. 33-41, American Math. Society, 1967.

McCracken, N., "The typechecking of programs with implicit type structure," in *LNCS 173: Semantics of Data Types*, pp. 301-316, Springer, Berlin, 1984.

McGraw, J. R., "The Val language: description and analysis," *ACM Trans. on Prog. Lang. and Systems*, vol. 4, pp. 44-82, 1982.

MacQueen, D. B. and R. Sethi, "A semantic model of types for applicative languages," in *Proc. ACM Conf. on LISP and Functional Programming*, pp. 243-252, Pittsburgh, 1982.

MacQueen, D. B., G. Plotkin, and R. Sethi, "An ideal model for recursive polymorphic types," in *Proc. 11th ACM Symp. on Princ. of Prog. Lang.*, pp. 165-174, Salt Lake City, Utah, 1984.

Main, M. and D. Benson, "Functional behavior of nondeterministic and concurrent programs," *Information and Control*, vol. 62, pp. 144-189, 1984.

Manes, E. G., ed., *LNCS 25: Category Theory Applied to Computation and Control*, Springer, Berlin, 1975.

Manna, Z., *Mathematical Theory of Computation*, McGraw-Hill, New York, 1974.

Manna, Z. and J. Vuillemin, "Fixpoint approach to the theory of computation," *Comm. of the ACM*, vol. 15, pp. 528-536, 1972.

Manna, Z., S. Ness, and J. Vuillemin, "Inductive methods for proving properties of programs," *ACM SIGPLAN Notices*, vol. 7-1, pp. 27-50, 1972.

Manna, Z. and R. Waldinger, *The Logical Basis for Computer Programming, Vol. 1*, Addison Wesley, Reading, Mass., 1985.

Marcotty, M., H. F. Ledgaard, and G. V. Bochmann, "A sampler of formal definitions," *ACM Computing Surveys*, vol. 8, pp. 191-276, 1976.

Markowski, G., "A motivation and generalization of Scott's notion of a continuous lattice," in *LNM 871: Continuous Lattices*, pp. 298-307, Springer, Berlin, 1981.

Markowski, G. and B. K. Rosen, "Bases for chain-complete posets," *IBM J. or Research and Development*, vol. 20, pp. 138-147, 1976.

Mauny, M., P. L. Curien, and G. Cousineau, "The categorical abstract machine," in *Proc. IFIP Conf. on Functional Programming Languages and Computer Architecture*, Nancy, France, Sept. 1985.

Mayoh, B. H., "Attribute grammars and mathematical semantics," *SIAM Journal of Computing*, vol. 10, pp. 503-518, 1981.

Melton, A. C. and D. A. Schmidt, "A topological framework for cpos lacking bottom elements," in *LNCS: Mathematical Foundations of Programming Semantics*, Springer, Berlin, 1986.

Mazurkiewicz, A., "Proving algorithms by tail functions," *Information and Control*, vol. 18, pp. 220-226, 1970.

Meyer, A. R., "What is a model of the lambda calculus?," *Information and Control*, vol. 52, pp. 87-122, 1982.

Meyer, A. R., "Understanding ALGOL: a view of a recent convert to denotational semantics," in *Proc. IFIP Congress 1983*, pp. 951-962, North-Holland, Amsterdam, 1983.

Meyer, A. and M. Wand, "Continuation semantics in the typed lambda-calculus," in *LNCS 193: Proc. Logics of Programs*, pp. 219-224, Springer, Berlin, 1985.

Milne, R., "Transforming predicate transformers," in *Formal Description of Programming Concepts*, ed. E.J. Neuhold, North-Holland, Amsterdam, 1978.

Milne, R. and C. Strachey, *A Theory of Programming Language Semantics*, Chapman and Hall, London, 1976.

Milner, R., "Models of LCF," in *Mathematical Centre Tracts 82: Foundations of Computer Science II, part 2*, ed. K. Apt, pp. 49-63, Mathematisch Centrum, Amsterdam, 1976a.

Milner, R., "Program semantics and mechanized proof," in *Mathematical Centre Tracts 82: Foundations of Computer Science II, part 2*, ed. K. Apt, pp. 3-44, Mathematisch Centrum, Amsterdam, 1976b.

Milner, R., "Fully abstract models of typed lambda-calculi," *Theoretical Computer Science*, vol. 4, pp. 1-22, 1977.

Milner, R., "A theory of type polymorphism in programming," *J. of Computer and System Sciences*, vol. 17, pp. 348-375, 1978.

Milner, R., *LNCS 92: A Calculus of Communicating Systems*, Springer, Berlin, 1980.

Milner, R., "Calculi for synchrony and asynchrony," *Theoretical Comp. Sci.*, vol. 25, pp. 267-310, 1983.

Milner, R., "Lectures on a Calculus for Communicating Systems," in *LNCS 197: Seminar on Concurrency*, pp. 197-220, Springer, Berlin, 1985.

Milos, D., U. Pleban, and G. Loegel, "Direct implementation of compiler specifications or the Pascal P-code compiler revisited," in *Proc. 11th ACM Symp. on Princ. of Prog. Lang.*, pp. 196-207, Salt Lake City, Utah, 1984.

Mitchell, J., "Coercion and type inference," in *Proc. 11th ACM Symp. on Pric. of Prog. Lang.*, pp. 175-185, Salt Lake City, Utah, 1984.

Morris, F. L., "Advice on structuring compilers and proving them correct," in *Proc. 1st ACM Symp. on Prin. of Prog. Lang.*, pp. 144-152, Boston, 1973.

Morris, J. H., "Lambda-calculus models of programming languages," Ph.D. thesis, Project MAC report TR-57, MIT, Cambridge, Mass., 1968.

Morris, J. H. and B. Wegbreit, "Subgoal induction," *Comm. of the ACM*, vol. 20, pp. 209-222, 1977.

Mosses, P. D., "The mathematical semantics of Algol60," Tech. monograph PRG12, Programming Research Group, Oxford Univ., Oxford, 1974.

Mosses, P. D., "Mathematical semantics and compiler generation," Ph.D. Thesis, Oxford University, 1975.

Mosses, P. D., "Compiler generation using denotational semantics," in *LNCS 45: Proc. Math. Foundations of Comp. Science*, pp. 436-441, Springer, Berlin, 1976.

Mosses, P. D., "Making denotational semantics less concrete," in *Workshop on semantics of programming languages*, Bad Honnef, Germany, 1977. Univ. of Dortmund, FRG, tech. rpt. 41.

Mosses, P. D., "Modular denotational semantics," draft 1979-3-17, Computer science dept., Aarhus Univ., Aarhus, Denmark, 1979a.

Mosses, P. D., "SIS— semantics implementation system: reference manual and user guide," Report DAIMI MD-30, Computer Science Dept., Aarhus University, 1979b.

Mosses, P. D., "SIS— semantics implementation system: tested examples," Report DAIMI MD-33, Computer Science Dept., Aarhus University, 1979c.

Mosses, P. D., "A constructive approach to compiler correctness," in *LNCS 85: 7th ICALP*, Springer, Berlin, 1980.

Mosses, P. D., "Abstract semantic algebras!," in *Formal Description of Programming Concepts II*, ed. D. Bjørner, pp. 45-72, North-Holland, Amsterdam, 1983a.

Mosses, P. D., "A short course on denotational semantics," Course notes, Facultad de Informatica, Universidad del Pais Vasco, San Sebastian, Spain, 1983b.

Mosses, P. D., "A basic abstract semantic algebra," in *LNCS 173: Semantics of data types*, pp. 87-108, Springer, Berlin, 1984.

Muchnick, S. S. and U. Pleban, "A semantic comparison of LISP and Scheme," in *Proc. ACM Conf. on LISP and Functional Programming*, pp. 56-64, 1982.

Mulmuley, K., "Full abstraction and semantic equivalence," Ph.D. thesis, Computer Science Dept., Carnegie-Mellon University, Pittsburgh, PA, 1985.

Mycroft, A., "Abstract interpretation and optimizing transformations for applicative programs," Ph.D. thesis, Computer Science Dept., University of Edinburgh, Scotland, 1981.

Naur, P., et al., "Revised report on the algorithmic language ALGOL60," *Comm. of the ACM*, vol. 6, pp. 1-17, 1963.

Nielsen, M., G. D. Plotkin, and G. Winskel, "Petri nets, event structures, and domains," *Theoretical Comp. Science*, vol. 13, pp. 85-108, 1981.

Nielson, F., "Compiler writing using denotational semantics," Report DAIMI TR-10, Computer science dept., Aarhus Univ., Denmark, 1979.

Nielson, F., "A denotational framework for data flow analysis," *Acta Informatica*, vol. 18, pp. 265-288, 1983.

Nielson, F., "Program transformations in a denotational setting," *ACM Trans. on Prog. Lang. and Sys.*, vol. 7, pp. 359-379, 1985.

Nivat, M., "On the interpretation of recursive polyadic program schemes," *Symp. Mathematica*, vol. 15, pp. 255-281, 1975.

Nordstrom, B. and K. Petersson, "Types and specifications," in *Proc. IFIP Congress 83*, pp. 915-920, North-Holland, Amsterdam, 1983.

Oles, F., "Type algebras, functor categories, and block structure," in *Algebraic Methods in Semantics*, ed. M. Nivat and J. Reynolds, Cambridge Univ. Press, Cambridge, in press.

Ollengren, A., *Definition of Programming Languages by Interpreting Automata*, Academic Press, New York, 1974.

Pagan, F. G., *Semantics of Programming Languages: A Panoramic Primer*, Prentice-Hall, Englewood Cliffs, N.J., 1981.

Paulson, L., "A semantics-directed compiler generator," in *Proc. 9th ACM Symp. on Prin. of Prog. Lang.*, pp. 224-233, 1982.

Paulson, L., "Compiler generation from denotational semantics," in *Methods and Tools for Compiler Construction*, ed. B. Lorho, pp. 219-250, 1984.

Park, D., "Fixpoint induction and proofs of program properties," in *Machine Intelligence*, ed. D. Michie, vol. 5, pp. 59-78, Edinburgh Univ. Press, Edinburgh, 1969.

Park, D., "A predicate transformer for weak fair iteration," in *Proc., 6th IBM Symp. on Math. Foundations of Computer Science*, Hakene, Japan, 1981.

Pleban, U., "Compiler prototyping using formal semantics," *SIGPLAN Notices 19-6*, pp. 94-105, Montreal, June, 1984.

Plotkin, G. D., "Call-by-name, call-by-value and the lambda calculus," *Theoretical Computer Science*, vol. 1, pp. 125-159, 1975.

Plotkin, G. D., "A powerdomain construction," *SIAM J. of Computing*, vol. 5, pp. 452-487, 1976.

Plotkin, G. D., "LCF considered as a programming language," *Theoretical Comp. Science*, vol. 5, pp. 223-255, 1977.

Plotkin, G. D., "A structural approach to operational semantics," Report DAIMI FN-19, Computer Science Dept., Aarhus Univ., 1981.

Plotkin, G. D., "Dijkstra's predicate transformers and Smyth's powerdomains," in *LNCS 86: Abstract Software Specifications*, pp. 527-553, Springer, Berlin, 1982a.

Plotkin, G. D., "A powerdomain for countable nondeterminism," in *LNCS 140: Proc. 9th ICALP*, pp. 412-428, Springer, 1982b.

Plotkin, G. D., "The category of complete partial orders: a tool for making meanings," Postgraduate lecture notes, Computer Science Dept., Univ. of Edinburgh, Edinburgh, 1982c.

Polak, W., "Program verification based on denotational semantics," in *Proc. 8th ACM Symp. on Prin. of Prog. Lang.*, 1981a.

Polak, W., *LNCS 124: Compiler Specification and Verification*, Springer, Berlin, 1981b.

Raskovsky, M. R., "A correspondence between denotational semantics and code generation," Ph.D. thesis, Univ. of Essex, 1982a.

Raskovsky, M. R., "Denotational semantics as a specification of code generators," *ACM SIGPLAN Notices 17-6*, pp. 230-244, Boston, 1982b.

Raskovsky, M. R. and P. Collier, "From standard to implementation denotational semantics," in *LNCS 94: Semantics-Directed Compiler Generation*, ed. N.D. Jones, pp. 94-139, Springer, Berlin, 1980.

Raoult, J.-C. and R. Sethi, "Properties of a notation for combining functions," in *LNCS 140: Proc. 9th ICALP*, pp. 429-441, Springer, Berlin, 1982.

Raoult, J.-C. and R. Sethi, "The global storage needs of a subcomputation," in *Proc. ACM Symp. on Prin. of Prog. Lang.*, pp. 148-157, Salt Lake City, Utah, 1984.

Reynolds, J. C., "GEDANKEN— a simple typeless language based on the principle of completeness and the reference concept," *Comm. of the ACM*, vol. 13, pp. 308-319, 1970.

Reynolds, J. C., "Definitional interpreters for higher order programming languages," in *Proc. ACM Annual Conf.*, pp. 717-740, 1972a.

Reynolds, J. C., "Notes on a lattice-theoretic approach to the theory of computation," Report, Systems and Info. Sciences Dept., Syracuse Univ., Syracuse, N.Y., 1972b.

Reynolds, J. C., "Towards a theory of type structure," in *LNCS 19: Proc. Paris Programming Symp.*, pp. 408-425, Springer, Berlin, 1974a.

Reynolds, J. C., "On the relation between direct and continuation semantics," in *LNCS 14: Proc. 2nd ICALP*, pp. 157-168, Springer, Berlin, 1974b.

Reynolds, J. C., "Semantics of the domain of flow diagrams," *J. of the ACM*, vol. 24, pp. 484-503, 1977.

Reynolds, J. C., "The essence of Algol," in *Int. Symp. on Algorithmic Languages*, ed. van Vliet, pp. 345-372, North-Holland, Amsterdam, 1981.

Reynolds, J. C., "Types, abstraction, and parametric polymorphism," in *Proc. IFIP Congress*, ed. R.E.A. Mason, pp. 513-524, North-Holland, Amsterdam, 1983.

Reynolds, J. C., "Three approaches to type structure," in *LNCS 185: Mathematical Foundations of Software Development*, pp. 97-138, Springer, Berlin, 1985.

Richards, H., "An applicative programming bibliography," Report, Burroughs Corp., Austin Research Center, Austin, Texas, 1985.

Rogers, H. R., *Theory of Recursive Functions and Effective Computability*, McGraw-Hill, New York, 1967.

Royer, V., "Deriving stack semantics congruent to standard denotational semantics," in *LNCS 182: Proc. 2nd Symp. on Theoretical Aspects of Comp. Sci.*, pp. 299-309, Springer, Berlin, 1985.

Rustin, R. ed., *Formal Semantics of Programming Languages*, Prentice-Hall, Englewood Cliffs, N.J., 1972.

Sanchis, L. E., "Data types as lattices: retractions, closures, and projections," *RAIRO Informatique theorique*, vol. 11, pp. 329-344, 1977.

Schmidt, D. A., "State transition machines for lambda-calculus expressions," in *LNCS 94: Semantics-Directed Compiler Generation*, pp. 415-440, Springer, Berlin, 1980.

Schmidt, D. A., "Detecting global variables in denotational specifications," *ACM Trans. on Prog. Lang. and Sys.*, vol. 7, pp. 299-310, 1985a.

Schmidt, D. A., "An implementation from a direct semantics definition," in *LNCS: Proc. Workshop on Programs as Data Objects*, Springer, Berlin, 1985b.

Scott, D. S., "The lattice of flow diagrams," in *LNM 188: Semantics of Algorithmic Languages*, ed. E. Engeler, pp. 311-366, Springer, Berlin, 1970.

Scott, D. S., "Outline of a mathematical theory of computation," Tech. monograph PRG-2, Programming Research Group, Univ. of Oxford, 1971.

Scott, D. S., "Continuous lattices," in *LNM 274: Proc. Dahlhousie Conf.*, pp. 97-136, Springer, Berlin, 1972.

Scott, D. S., "Data types as lattices," *SIAM J. of Computing*, vol. 5, pp. 522-587, 1976.

Scott, D. S., "Lectures on a mathematical theory of computation," Report PRG-19, Programming Research Group, Univ. of Oxford, 1980a.

Scott, D. S., "Relating theories of the lambda calculus," in *To H. B. Curry: Essays on Combinatory Logic, Lambda Calculus and Formalism*, ed. J. R. Hindley, pp. 403-450, Academic Press, New York, 1980b.

Scott, D. S., "Domains for denotational semantics," in *LNCS 140: Proc. 9th ICALP*, pp. 577-613, Springer, Berlin, 1982a.

Scott, D. S., "Some ordered sets in computer science," in *Ordered Sets*, ed. I. Rival, pp. 677-718, D. Reidel Pub., 1982b.

Scott, D. S. and C. Strachey, "Towards a mathematical semantics for computer languages," Tech. monograph PRG-6, Programming Research Group, Univ. of Oxford, 1971.

Sethi, R., "Control flow aspects of semantics-directed compiling," *ACM Trans. on Prog. Lang. and Systems*, vol. 5, pp. 554-596, 1983.

Sethi, R., "Circular expressions: elimination of static environments," in *LNCS 115: Proc. 8th ICALP*, pp. 378-392, Springer, Berlin, 1981.

Sethi, R. and A. Tang, "Transforming direct into continuation semantics for a simple imperative language," Unpublished manuscript, 1978.

Sethi, R. and A. Tang, "Constructing call-by-value continuation semantics," *J. of the ACM*, vol. 27, pp. 580-597, 1980.

Smyth, M. B., "Effectively given domains," *Theoretical Comp. Science*, vol. 5, pp. 257-274, 1977.

Smyth, M. B., "Powerdomains," *J. of Computer and System Sciences*, pp. 23-36, 1978.

Smyth, M. B., "Power domains and predicate transformers: a topological view," in *LNCS 154: Proc. 10th ICALP*, pp. 662-675, Springer, Berlin, 1982.

Smyth, M. B., "The largest cartesian closed category of domains," *Theoretical Computer Science*, vol. 27, pp. 109-120, 1983.

Smyth, M. B. and G. D. Plotkin, "The category-theoretic solution of recursive domain equations," *SIAM J. of Computing*, vol. 11, pp. 761-783, 1982.

Steele, G. L., "Debunking the 'expensive procedure call' myth," in *Proc. ACM Annual Conf.*, pp. 153-162, 1977.

Steele, G. L. and G. J. Sussman, "LAMBDA: the ultimate imperative," AI memo 353, AI Lab., MIT, 1976a.

Steele, G. L. and G. J. Sussman, "LAMBDA: the ultimate declarative," AI Memo 379, AI Lab., MIT, 1976b.

Steele, G. L. and G. J. Sussman, "The revised report on SCHEME," AI Memo 452, MIT, Cambridge, Mass., 1978.

Stoughton, A., Ph.D. thesis, Computer Science Dept., University of Edinburgh, Edinburgh, Scotland, 1986.

Stoy, J. E., *Denotational Semantics: The Scott-Strachey Approach to Programming Language Theory*, MIT Press, Cambridge, Mass., 1977.

Stoy, J. E., "The congruence of two programming language definitions," *Theoretical Comp. Science*, vol. 13, pp. 151-174, 1981.

Stoy, J. E., "Some mathematical aspects of functional programming," in *Functional Programming and its Applications*, ed. J. Darlington, et. al., pp. 217-252, Cambridge Univ. Press, Cambridge, 1982.

Strachey, C., "Towards a formal semantics," in *Formal Language Description Languages*, ed. T.B. Steele, pp. 198-220, North-Holland, Amsterdam, 1966.

Strachey, C., "Fundamental concepts in programming languages," Unpublished manuscript, Programming Research Group, Univ. of Oxford, 1968.

Strachey, C., "The varieties of programming language," Tech. monograph PRG-10, Programming Research Group, Univ. of Oxford, 1973.

Strachey, C. and C. P. Wadsworth, "Continuations: a mathematical semantics for handling full jumps," Tech. monograph PRG-11, Programming Research Group, Univ. of Oxford, 1974.

Tennent, R. D., "Mathematical semantics of SNOBOL4," in *Proc. 1st ACM Symp. on Prin. of Prog. Lang.*, pp. 95-107, Boston, 1973.

Tennent, R. D., "The denotational semantics of programming languages," *Comm. of the ACM*, vol. 19, pp. 437-452, 1976.

Tennent, R. D., "A denotational definition of the programming language Pascal," Tech. report 77-47, Department of Computing and Information Sciences, Queen's Univ., Kingston, Ontario, 1977a.

Tennent, R. D., "Language design methods based on semantic principles," *Acta Informatica*, vol. 8, pp. 97-112, 1977b.

Tennent, R. D., "On a new approach to representation-independent data classes," *Acta Informatica*, vol. 8, pp. 315-324, 1977c.

Tennent, R. D., *Principles of Programming Languages*, Prentice-Hall, Englewood Cliffs, N.J., 1981.

Tennent, R. D., "Semantics of inference control," in *LNCS 140: Proc. 9th ICALP*, pp. 532-545, Springer, Berlin, 1982.

Thatcher, J., E. Wagner, and J. Wright, "More on advice on structuring compilers and proving them correct," in *LNCS 71: Proc. 6th ICALP*, pp. 596-615, Springer, Berlin, 1979.

Turner, D., "A new implementation technique for applicative languages," *Software Practice and Experience*, vol. 9, pp. 31-49, 1979.

Vegdahl, S. R., "A survey of proposed architectures for the execution of functional languages," *IEEE Trans. on Computers*, vol. c-33, 1984.

Vickers, T., "Quokka: a translator generator using denotational semantics," Report, Computer Science Dept., University of New South Wales, Kensington, Australia, 1985.

Vuillemin, J., "Correct and optimal implementations of recursion in a simple programming language," *J. of Computer and System Sciences*, vol. 9, pp. 1050-1071, 1974.

Wadsworth, C. P., "The relation between computational and denotational properties for Scott's D∞-models of the lambda-calculus," *SIAM J. of Computing*, vol. 5, pp. 488-521, 1976.

Wadsworth, C. P., "Approximate reductions and lambda calculus models," *SIAM J. of Computing*, vol. 7, pp. 337-356, 1978.

Wadsworth, C. P., Postgraduate lecture notes on domain theory, Computer science dept., Univ. of Edinburgh, 1978.

Wand, M., "Fixed point constructions in order-enriched categories," *Theoretical Computer Science*, vol. 8, pp. 13-30, 1979.

Wand, M., "Continuation-based program transformation strategies," *J. of the ACM*, vol. 27, pp. 164-180, 1980a.

Wand, M., *Induction, Recursion, and Programming*, Elsevier North Holland, New York, 1980b.

Wand, M., "Semantics-directed machine architecture," in *ACM Symp. on Prin. of Prog. Lang.*, pp. 234-241, 1982a.

Wand, M., "Deriving target code as a representation of continuation semantics," *ACM Trans. on Prog. Lang. and Systems*, vol. 4, pp. 496-517, 1982b.

Wand, M., *Different advice on structuring compilers and proving them correct*, Computer Science Dept., Indiana University, Bloomington, 1982c.

Wand, M., "Loops in combinator-based compilers," *Information and Control*, vol. 57, pp. 148-164, 1983.

Wand, M., "A types-as-sets semantics for Milner-style polymorphism," in *Proc. ACM Conf. on Princ. of Prog. Lang.*, pp. 158-164, Salt Lake City, Utah, 1984a.

Wand, M., "A semantic prototyping system," in *Proc. SIGPLAN '84 Symp. on Compiler Construction*, pp. 213-221, Montreal, 1984b.

Wand, M., "Embedding type structure in semantics," in *Proc. 12th ACM Symp. on Princ. of Prog. Lang.*, pp. 1-6, New Orleans, 1985a.

Wand, M., "From interpreter to compiler: a representational derivation," in *LNCS: Proc. Workshop on Programs as Data Objects*, Springer, Berlin, 1985b.

Ward, S., "Functional domains of applicative languages," Project MAC Report TR-136, MIT, Cambridge, Mass., 1974.

Wegner, P., "The Vienna Definition language," *ACM Computing Surveys*, vol. 4, pp. 5-63, 1972a.

Wegner, P., "Programming language semantics," in *Formal Semantics of Programming Languages*, ed. R. Rustin, pp. 149-248, Prentice-Hall, Englewood Cliffs, N.J., 1972b.

vanWijngaarden, A., et al., "Report on the algorithmic language ALGOL68," *Numer. Math.*, vol. 14, pp. 79-218, 1969.

Winskel, G., "Events in computation," Ph.D. thesis, Univ. of Edinburgh, Scotland, 1980.

Index